John W. Barry

The Coalier's Actuary

John W. Barry

The Coalier's Actuary

ISBN/EAN: 9783337064136

Printed in Europe, USA, Canada, Australia, Japan

Cover: Foto ©Andreas Hilbeck / pixelio.de

More available books at **www.hansebooks.com**

COALIER'S ACTUARY

Showing at a Glance the Amount of Any Quantity of
Coal from 5 Pounds to 1100 Tons, at Prices
from 25 Cents to $15.00 a Ton.

By JOHN W. BARRY,

AUSTIN, ILLINOIS.
(CHICAGO SUBURB WEST SIDE.)

LINCOLN, NEB.:
STATE JOURNAL COMPANY, PRINTERS.
1899.

CONTENTS.

In computing by the bushel (of 80 lbs.) or by the 100 pounds, turn to the equivalent rate per ton. The rate by the 100 lbs. is useful in figuring the freight.

Bushel.	100 lbs.	Equivalent per ton.	Bushel.	100 lbs.	Equivalent per ton.	Bushel.	100 lbs.	Equivalent per ton.
.01	.01¼	.25	.21	.26¼	5.25	.41	.51¼	10.25
.02	.02½	.50	.22	.27½	5.50	.42	.52½	10.50
.03	.03¾	.75	.23	.28¾	5.75	.43	.53¾	10.75
.04	.05	1.00	.24	.30	6.00	.44	.55	11.00
.05	.06¼	1.25	.25	.31¼	6.25	.45	.56¼	11.25
.06	.07½	1.50	.26	.32½	6.50	.46	.57½	11.50
.07	.08¾	1.75	.27	.33¾	6.75	.47	.58¾	11.75
.08	.10	2.00	.28	.35	7.00	.48	.60	12.00
.09	.11¼	2.25	.29	.36¼	7.25	.49	.61¼	12.25
.10	.12½	2.50	.30	.37½	7.50	.50	.62½	12.50
.11	.13¾	2.75	.31	.38¾	7.75	.51	.63¾	12.75
.12	.15	3.00	.32	.40	8.00	.52	.65	13.00
.13	.16¼	3.25	.33	.41¼	8.25	.53	.66¼	13.25
.14	.17½	3.50	.34	.42½	8.50	.54	.67½	13.50
.15	.18¾	3.75	.35	.43¾	8.75	.55	.68¾	13.75
.16	.20	4.00	.36	.45	9.00	.56	.70	14.00
.17	.21¼	4.25	.37	.46¼	9.25	.57	.71¼	14.25
.18	.22½	4.50	.38	.47½	9.50	.58	.72½	14.50
.19	.23¾	4.75	.39	.48¾	9.75	.59	.73¾	14.75
.20	.25	5.00	.40	.50	10.00	.60	.75	15.00

MISCELLANEOUS.

Long and Short Tons.

Bushel Tables.

Down the center are the prices per ton, and to the right and left the equivalent prices per bushel of 75, 70, 56, 60, 32, and 48 pounds respectively. For example, a load of ear corn weighs net 1980 pounds. What is its value at 28 cents a bushel of 70 pounds? The equivalent of 28 cents for 70 pounds is $8 a ton, to which page turn and read the correct amount, $7.92, without even reducing to bushels.

Equivalent rate per bushel			RATE PER TON.	Equivalent rate per bushel		
of 75 lbs.	of 70 lbs.	of 56 lbs.		of 60 lbs.	of 32 lbs.	of 48 lbs.
.05⅝	.05¼	. . . .	$1.50	.04½	. . . .	. . . .
.07½	.07	. . . .	2.00	.06	. . . .	. . . .
.09⅜	.08¾	.07	2.50	.07½	.04	.06
.11¼	.10½	. . . .	3.00	.09	. . . .	. . . .
.13⅛	·.12¼	. . . .	3.50	.10½	. . . .	. . . .
. . . .	. . . .	.10½	3.75	. . . . . .	.06	.09
.15	.14	. . . .	4.00	.12	. . . .	. . . .
.16⅞	.15¾	. . . .	4.50	.13½	. . . .	. . . .
.18¾	.17½	.14	5.00	.15	.08	.12
.20⅝	.19¼	. . . .	5.50	.16½	. . . .	. . . .
.22½	.21	. . . .	6.00	.18	. . . .	. . . .
. . . .	. . . .	.17½	6.25	. . . .	.10	.15
.24⅜	.22¾	. . . .	6.50	.19½	. . . .	. . . .
.26¼	.24½	. . . .	7.00	.21	. . . .	. . . .
.28⅛	.26¼	.21	7.50	.22½	.12	.18
.30	.28	. . . .	8.00	.24	. . . .	. . . .
.31⅞	.29¾	. . . .	8.50	.25½	. . . .	. . . .
. . . .	. . . .	.24½	8.75	. . . .	.14	.21
.33¾	.31½	. . . .	9.00	.27	. . . .	. . . .
.35⅝	.33¼	. . . .	9.50	.28½	. . . .	. . . .
.37½	.35	.28	10.00	.30	.16	.24
.39⅜	.36¾	. . . .	10.50	.31½	. . . .	. . . .
.41¼	.38½	. . . .	11.00	.33	. . . .	. . . .
. . . .	. . . .	.31½	11.25	. . . .	.18	.27
.43⅛	.40¼	. . . .	11.50	.34½	. . . .	. . . .
.45	.42	. . . .	12.00	.36	. . . .	. . . .
.46⅞	.43¾	.35	12.50	.37½	.20	.30
.48¾	.45½	. . . .	13.00	.39	. . . .	. . . .
.50⅝	.47¼	. . . .	13.50	.40½	. . . .	. . . .
. . . .	. . . .	.38½	13.75	. . . .	.22	.33
.52½	.49	. . . .	14.00	.42	. . . .	. . . .
.54⅜	.50¾	. . . .	14.50	.43½	. . . .	. . . .
.56¼	.52½	.42	15.00	.45	.24	.36

POUNDS

Under 100	100	200	300	400		500	600	700	800	900
	AMOUNT							AMOUNT		
	.01	.03	.04	.05		.06	.08	.09	.10	.11
	.01	.03	.04	.05	5	.06	.08	.09	.10	.11
	.01	.03	.04	.05	10	.06	.08	.09	.10	.11
	.01	.03	.04	.05	15	.06	.08	.09	.10	.11
	.02	.03	.04	.05	20	.07	.08	.09	.10	.12
	.02	.03	.04	.05	25	.07	.08	.09	.10	.12
	.02	.03	.04	.05	30	.07	.08	.09	.10	.12
	.02	.03	.04	.05	35	.07	.08	.09	.10	.12
.01	.02	.03	.04	.06	40	.07	.08	.09	.11	.12
.01	.02	.03	.04	.06	45	.07	.08	.09	.11	.12
.01	.02	.03	.04	.06	50	.07	.08	.09	.11	.12
.01	.02	.03	.04	.06	55	.07	.08	.09	.11	.12
.01	.02	.03	.05	.06	60	.07	.08	.10	.11	.12
.01	.02	.03	.05	.06	65	.07	.08	.10	.11	.12
.01	.02	.03	.05	.06	70	.07	.08	.10	.11	.12
.01	.02	.03	.05	.06	75	.07	.08	.10	.11	.12
.01	.02	.04	.05	.06	80	.07	.09	.10	.11	.12
.01	.02	.04	.05	.06	85	.07	.09	.10	.11	.12
.01	.02	.04	.05	.06	90	.07	.09	.10	.11	.12
.01	.02	.04	.05	.06	95	.07	.09	.10	.11	.12

POUNDS

1000	1100	1200	1300	1400		1500	1600	1700	1800	1900
	AMOUNT							AMOUNT		
.13	.14	.15	.16	.18		.19	.20	.21	.23	.24
.13	.14	.15	.16	.18	5	.19	.20	.21	.23	.24
.13	.14	.15	.16	.18	10	.19	.20	.21	.23	.24
.13	.14	.15	.16	.18	15	.19	.20	.21	.23	.24
.13	.14	.15	.17	.18	20	.19	.20	.22	.23	.24
.13	.14	.15	.17	.18	25	.19	.20	.22	.23	.24
.13	.14	.15	.17	.18	30	.19	.20	.22	.23	.24
.13	.14	.15	.17	.18	35	.19	.20	.22	.23	.24
.13	.14	.16	.17	.18	40	.19	.21	.22	.23	.24
.13	.14	.16	.17	.18	45	.19	.21	.22	.23	.24
.13	.14	.16	.17	.18	50	.19	.21	.22	.23	.24
.13	.14	.16	.17	.18	55	.19	.21	.22	.23	.24
.13	.15	.16	.17	.18	60	.20	.21	.22	.23	.25
.13	.15	.16	.17	.18	65	.20	.21	.22	.23	.25
.13	.15	.16	.17	.18	70	.20	.21	.22	.23	.25
.13	.15	.16	.17	.18	75	.20	.21	.22	.23	.25
.14	.15	.16	.17	.19	80	.20	.21	.22	.24	.25
.14	.15	.16	.17	.19	85	.20	.21	.22	.24	.25
.14	.15	.16	.17	.19	90	.20	.21	.22	.24	.25
.14	.15	.16	.17	.19	95	.20	.21	.22	.24	.25

Even tons, 1 to 50 inclusive.

1-10		11-20		21-30		31-40		41-50	
T	Am't	T	Am't	T	Am't	T	Am't	T	Am't
1	.25	11	2.75	21	5.25	31	7.75	41	10.25
2	.50	12	3.00	22	5.50	32	8.00	42	10.50
3	.75	13	3.25	23	5.75	33	8.25	43	10.75
4	1.00	14	3.50	24	6.00	34	8.50	44	11.00
5	1.25	15	3.75	25	6.25	35	8.75	45	11.25
6	1.50	16	4.00	26	6.50	36	9.00	46	11.50
7	1.75	17	4.25	27	6.75	37	9.25	47	11.75
8	2.00	18	4.50	28	7.00	38	9.50	48	12.00
9	2.25	19	4.75	29	7.25	39	9.75	49	12.25
10	2.50	20	5.00	30	7.50	40	10.00	50	12.50

200	50	300	75	400	100	500	125	600	150

POUNDS

2000	2100	2200	2300	2400	POUNDS	2500	2600	2700	2800	2900
.25	.26	.28	.29	.30		.31	.33	.34	.35	.36
.25	.26	.28	.29	.30	5	.31	.33	.34	.35	.36
.25	.26	.28	.29	.30	10	.31	.33	.34	.35	.36
.25	.26	.28	.29	.30	15	.31	.33	.34	.35	.36
.25	.27	.28	.29	.30	20	.32	.33	.34	.35	.37
.25	.27	.28	.29	.30	25	.32	.33	.34	.35	.37
.25	.27	.28	.29	.30	30	.32	.33	.34	.35	.37
.25	.27	.28	.29	.30	35	.32	.33	.34	.35	.37
.26	.27	.28	.29	.31	40	.32	.33	.34	.36	.37
.26	.27	.28	.29	.31	45	.32	.33	.34	.36	.37
.26	.27	.28	.29	.31	50	.32	.33	.34	.36	.37
.26	.27	.28	.29	.31	55	.32	.33	.34	.36	.37
.26	.27	.28	.30	.31	60	.32	.33	.35	.36	.37
.26	.27	.28	.30	.31	65	.32	.33	.35	.36	.37
.26	.27	.28	.30	.31	70	.32	.33	.35	.36	.37
.26	.27	.28	.30	.31	75	.32	.33	.35	.36	.37
.26	.27	.29	.30	.31	80	.32	.34	.35	.36	.37
.26	.27	.29	.30	.31	85	32	.34	.35	.36	.37
.26	.27	.29	.30	.31	90	.32	.34	.35	.36	.37
.26	.27	.29	.30	.31	95	.32	.34	.35	.36	.37

POUNDS

3000	3100	3200	3300	3400	POUNDS	3500	3600	3700	3800	3900
.38	.39	.40	.41	.43		.44	.45	.46	.48	.49
.38	.39	.40	.41	.43	5	.44	.45	.46	.48	.49
.38	.39	.40	.41	.43	10	.44	.45	.46	.48	.49
.38	.39	.40	.41	.43	15	.44	.45	.46	.48	.49
.38	.39	.40	.42	.43	20	.44	.45	.47	.48	.49
.38	.39	.40	.42	.43	25	.44	.45	.47	.48	.49
.38	.39	.40	.42	.43	30	.44	.45	.47	.48	.49
.38	.39	.40	.42	.43	35	.44	.45	.47	.48	.49
.38	.39	.41	.42	.43	40	.44	.46	.47	.48	.49
.38	.39	.41	.42	.43	45	.44	.46	.47	.48	.49
.38	.39	.41	.42	.43	50	.44	.46	.47	.48	.49
.38	.39	.41	.42	.43	55	.44	.46	.47	.48	.49
.38	.40	.41	.42	.43	60	.45	.46	.47	.48	.50
.38	.40	.41	.42	.43	65	.45	.46	.47	.48	.50
.38	.40	.41	.42	.43	70	.45	.46	.47	.48	.50
.38	.40	.41	.42	.43	75	.45	.46	.47	.48	.50
.39	.40	.41	.42	.44	80	.45	.46	.47	.49	.50
.39	.40	.41	.42	.44	85	.45	.46	.47	.49	.50
.39	.40	.41	.42	.44	90	.45	.46	.47	.49	.50
.39	.40	.41	.42	.44	95	.45	.46	.47	.49	.50

Even tons, 51 to 100 inclusive.

51-60		61-70		71-80		81-90		91-100	
T	Am't	T	Am't	T	Am't	T	Am't	T	Am't
51	12.75	61	15.25	71	17.75	81	20.25	91	22.75
52	13.00	62	15.50	72	18.00	82	20.50	92	23.00
53	13.25	63	15.75	73	18.25	83	20.75	93	23.25
54	13.50	64	16.00	74	18.50	84	21.00	94	23.50
55	13.75	65	16.25	75	18.75	85	21.25	95	23.75
56	14.00	66	16.50	76	19.00	86	21.50	96	24.00
57	14.25	67	16.75	77	19.25	87	21.75	97	24.25
58	14.50	68	17.00	78	19.50	88	22.00	98	24.50
59	14.75	69	17.25	79	19.75	89	22.25	99	24.75
60	15.00	70	17.50	80	20.00	90	22.50	100	25.00
700	175	800	200	900	225	1000	250	1100	275

POUNDS

Under 100	100	200	300	400		500	600	700	800	900
		AMOUNT						AMOUNT		
	.03	.05	.08	.10		.13	.15	.18	.20	.23
	.03	.05	.08	.10	5	.13	.15	.18	.20	.23
	.03	.05	.08	.10	10	.13	.15	.18	.20	.23
	.03	.05	.08	.10	15	.13	.15	.18	.20	.23
.01	.03	.06	.08	.11	20	.13	.16	.18	.21	.23
.01	.03	.06	.08	.11	25	.13	.16	.18	.21	.23
.01	.03	.06	.08	.11	30	.13	.16	.18	.21	.23
.01	.03	.06	.08	.11	35	.13	.16	.18	.21	.23
.01	.04	.06	.09	.11	40	.14	.16	.19	.21	.24
.01	.04	.06	.09	.11	45	.14	.16	.19	.21	.24
.01	.04	.06	.09	.11	50	.14	.16	.19	.21	.24
.01	.04	.06	.09	.11	55	.14	.16	.19	.21	.24
.02	.04	.07	.09	.12	60	.14	.17	.19	.22	.24
.02	.04	.07	.09	.12	65	.14	.17	.19	.22	.24
.02	.04	.07	.09	.12	70	.14	.17	.19	.22	.24
.02	.04	.07	.09	.12	75	.14	.17	.19	.22	.24
.02	.05	.07	.10	.12	80	.15	.17	.20	.22	.25
.02	.05	.07	.10	.12	85	.15	.17	.20	.22	.25
.02	.05	.07	.10	.12	90	.15	.17	.20	.22	.25
.02	.05	.07	.10	.12	95	.15	.17	.20	.22	.25

POUNDS

1000	1100	1200	1300	1400		1500	1600	1700	1800	1900
		AMOUNT						AMOUNT		
.25	.28	.30	.33	.35		.38	.40	.43	.45	.48
.25	.28	.30	.33	.35	5	.38	.40	.43	.45	.48
.25	.28	.30	.33	.35	10	.38	.40	.43	.45	.48
.25	.28	.30	.33	.35	15	.38	.40	.43	.45	.48
.26	.28	.31	.33	.36	20	.38	.41	.43	.46	.48
.26	.28	.31	.33	.36	25	.38	.41	.43	.46	.48
.26	.28	.31	.33	.36	30	.38	.41	.43	.46	.48
.26	.28	.31	.33	.36	35	.38	.41	.43	.46	.48
.26	.29	.31	.34	.36	40	.39	.41	.44	·46	.49
.26	.29	.31	.34	.36	45	.39	.41	.44	.46	.49
.26	.29	.31	.34	.36	50	.39	.41	.44	.46	.49
.26	.29	.31	.34	.36	55	.39	.41	.44	.46	.49
.27	.29	.32	.34	.37	60	.39	.42	.44	.47	.49
.27	.29	.32	.34	.37	65	.39	.42	.44	.47	.49
.27	.29	.32	.34	.37	70	.39	.42	.44	.47	.49
.27	.29	.32	.34	.37	75	.39	.42	.44	.47	.49
.27	.30	.32	.35	.37	80	.40	.42	.45	.47	.50
.27	.30	.32	.35	.37	85	.40	.42	.45	.47	.50
.27	.30	.32	.35	.37	90	.40	.42	.45	.47	.50
.27	.30	.32	.35	.37	95	.40	.42	.45	.47	.50

Even tons, 1 to 50 inclusive.

1-10		11-20		21-30		31-40		41-50	
T	Am't	T	Am't	T	Am't	T	Am't	T	Am't
1	.50	11	5.50	21	10.50	31	15.50	41	20.50
2	1.00	12	6.00	22	11.00	32	16.00	42	21.00
3	1.50	13	6.50	23	11.50	33	16.50	43	21.50
4	2.00	14	7.00	24	12.00	34	17.00	44	22.00
5	2.50	15	7.50	25	12.50	35	17.50	45	22.50
6	3.00	16	8.00	26	13.00	36	18.00	46	23.00
7	3.50	17	8.50	27	13.50	37	18.50	47	23.50
8	4.00	18	9.00	28	14.00	38	19.00	48	24.00
9	4.50	19	9.50	29	14.50	39	19.50	49	24.50
10	5.00	20	10.00	30	15.00	40	20.00	50	25.00
200	100	300	150	400	200	500	250	600	300

POUNDS

2000	2100	2200	2300	2400		2500	2600	2700	2800	2900
		AMOUNT						AMOUNT		
.50	.53	.55	.58	.60		.63	.65	.68	.70	73
.50	.53	.55	.58	.60	5	.63	.65	.68	.70	73
.50	.53	.55	.58	.60	10	.63	.65	.68	.70	.73
.50	.53	.55	.58	.60	15	.63	.65	.68	.70	.73
.51	.53	.56	.58	.61	20	.63	.66	.68	.71	.73
.51	.53	.56	.58	.61	25	.63	.66	.68	.71	.73
.51	.53	.56	.58	.61	30	.63	.66	.68	.71	.73
.51	.53	.56	.58	.61	35	.63	.66	.68	.71	.73
.51	.54	.56	.59	.61	40	.64	.66	.69	.71	.74
.51	.54	.56	.59	.61	45	.64	.66	.69	.71	.74
.51	.54	.56	.59	.61	50	.64	.66	.69	.71	.74
.51	.54	.56	.59	.61	55	.64	.66	.69	.71	.74
.52	.54	.57	.59	.62	60	.64	.67	.69	.72	.74
.52	.54	.57	.59	.62	65	.64	.67	.69	.72	.74
.52	.54	.57	.59	.62	70	.64	.67	.69	.72	.74
.52	.54	.57	.59	.62	75	.64	.67	.69	.72	.74
.52	.55	.57	.60	.62	80	.65	.67	.70	.72	.75
.52	.55	.57	.60	.62	85	.65	.67	.70	.72	.75
.52	.55	.57	.60	.62	90	.65	.67	.70	.72	.75
.52	.55	.57	.60	.62	95	.65	.67	.70	.72	.75

POUNDS

3000	3100	3200	3300	3400		3500	3600	3700	3800	3900
		AMOUNT						AMOUNT		
.75	.78	.80	.83	.85		.88	.90	.93	.95	.98
.75	.78	.80	.83	.85	5	.88	.90	.93	.95	.98
.75	.78	.80	.83	.85	10	.88	.90	.93	.95	.98
.75	.78	.80	.83	.85	15	.88	.90	.93	.95	.98
.76	.78	.81	.83	.86	20	.88	.91	.93	.96	.98
.76	.78	.81	.83	.86	25	.88	.91	.93	.96	.98
.76	.78	.81	.83	.86	30	.88	.91	.93	.96	.98
.76	.78	.81	.83	.86	35	.88	.91	.93	.96´	.98
.76	.79	.81	.84	.86	40	.89	.91	.94	.96	.99
.76	.79	.81	.84	.86	45	.89	.91	.94	.96	.99
.76	.79	.81	.84	.86	50	.89	.91	.94	.96	.99
.76	.79	.81	.84	.86	55	.89	.91	.94	.96	.99
.77	.79	.82	.84	.87	60	.89	.92	.94	.97	.99
.77	.79	.82	.84	.87	65	.89	.92	.94	.97	.99
.77	.79	.82	.84	.87	70	.89	.92	.94	.97	.99
.77	.79	.82	.84	.87	75	.89	.92	.94	.97	.99
.77	.80	.82	.85	.87	80	.90	.92	.95	.97	1.00
.77	.80	.82	.85	.87	85	.90	.92	.95	.97	1.00
.77	.80	.82	.85	.87	90	.90	.92	.95	.97	1.00
.77	.80	.82	.85	.87	95	.90	.92	.95	.97	1 00

Even tons, 51 to 100 inclusive.

51-60		61-70		71-80		81-99		91-100	
T	Am't	T	Am't	T	Am't	T	Am't	T	Am't
51	25.50	61	30.50	71	35.50	81	40.50	91	45.50
52	26.00	62	31.00	72	36.00	82	41.00	92	46.00
53	26.50	63	31.50	73	36.50	83	41.50	93	46.50
54	27.00	64	32.00	74	37.00	84	42.00	94	47.00
55	27.50	65	32.50	75	37.50	85	42.50	95	47.50
56	28.00	66	33.00	76	38.00	86	43.00	96	48.00
57	28.50	67	33.50	77	38.50	87	43.50	97	48.50
58	29.00	68	34.00	78	39.00	88	44.00	98	49.00
59	29.50	69	34.50	79	39.50	89	44.50	99	49.50
60	30.00	70	35 00	80	40.00	90	45.00	100	50.00

700	350	800	400	900	450	1000	500	1100	550

POUNDS

Under 100	100	200	300	400		500	600	700	800	900
			AMOUNT					AMOUNT		
	.04	.08	.11	.15		.19	.23	.26	.30	.34
	.04	.08	.11	.15	5	.19	.23	.26	.30	.34
	.04	.08	.12	.15	10	.19	.23	.27	.30	.34
.01	.04	.08	.12	.16	15	.19	.23	.27	.31	.34
.01	.05	.08	.12	.16	20	.20	.23	.27	.31	.35
.01	.05	.08	.12	.16	25	.20	.23	.27	.31	.35
.01	.05	.09	.12	.16	30	.20	.24	.27	.31	.35
.01	.05	.09	.13	.16	35	.20	.24	.28	.31	.35
.02	.05	.09	.13	.17	40	.20	.24	.28	.32	.35
.02	.05	.09	.13	.17	45	.20	.24	.28	.32	.35
.02	.06	.09	.13	.17	50	.21	.24	.28	.32	.36
.02	.06	.10	.13	.17	55	.21	.25	.28	.32	.36
.02	.06	.10	.14	.17	60	.21	.25	.29	.32	.36
.02	.06	.10	.14	.17	65	.21	.25	.29	.32	.36
.03	.06	.10	.14	.18	70	.21	.25	.29	.33	.36
.03	.07	.10	.14	.18	75	.22	.25	.29	.33	.37
.03	.07	.11	.14	.18	80	.22	.26	.29	.33	.37
.03	.07	.11	.14	.18	85	.22	.26	.29	.33	.37
.03	.07	.11	.15	.18	90	.22	.26	.30	.33	.37
.04	.07	.11	.15	.19	95	.22	.26	.30	.34	.37

POUNDS

1000	1100	1200	1300	1400		1500	1600	1700	1800	1900
		AMOUNT						AMOUNT		
.38	.41	.45	.49	.53		.56	.60	.64	.68	.71
.38	·41	.45	.49	.53	5	.56	.60	.64	.68	.71
.38	.42	.45	.49	.53	10	.57	.60	.64	.68	.72
.38	.42	.46	.49	.53	15	.57	.61	.64	.68	.72
.38	.42	.46	.50	.53	20	.57	.61	.65	.68	.72
.38	.42	.46	.50	.53	25	.57	.61	.65	.68	.72
.39	.42	.46	.50	.54	30	.57	.61	.65	.69	.72
.39	.43	.46	.50	.54	35	.58	.61	.65	.69	.73
.39	.43	.47	.50	.54	40	.58	.62	.65	.69	.73
.39	.43	.47	.50	.54	45	.58	.62	.65	.69	.73
.39	.43	.47	.51	.54	50	.58	.62	.66	.69	.73
.40	.43	.47	.51	.55	55	.58	.62	.66	.70	.73
.40	.44	.47	.51	.55	60	.59	.62	.66	.70	.74
.40	.44	.47	.51	.55	65	.59	.62	.66	.70	.74
.40	.44	.48	.51	.55	70	.59	.63	.66	.70	.74
.40	.44	.48	.52	.55	75	.59	.63	.67	.70	.74
.41	.44	.48	.52	.56	80	.59	.63	.67	.71	.74
.41	.44	.48	.52	.56	85	.59	.63	.67	.71	.74
.41	.45	.48	.52	.56	90	.60	.63	.67	.71	.75
.41	.45	.49	.52	.56	95	.60	.64	.67	.71	.75

Even tons, 1 to 50 inclusive.

1-10		11-20		21-30		31-40		41-50	
T	Am't	T	Am't	T	Am't	T	Am't	T	Am't
1	.75	11	8.25	21	15.75	31	23.25	41	30.75
2	1.50	12	9.00	22	16.50	32	24.00	42	31.50
3	2.25	13	9.75	23	17.25	33	24.75	43	32.25
4	3.00	14	10.50	24	18.00	34	25.50	44	33.00
5	3.75	15	11.25	25	18.75	35	26.25	45	33.75
6	4.50	16	12.00	26	19.50	36	27.00	46	34.50
7	5.25	17	12.75	27	20.25	37	27.75	47	35.25
8	6.00	18	13.50	28	21.00	38	28.50	48	36.00
9	6.75	19	14.25	29	21.75	39	29.25	49	36.75
10	7.50	20	15.00	30	22.50	40	30.00	50	37.50
200	150	300	225	400	300	500	375	600	450

2000	2100	2200	2300	2400		2500	2600	2700	2800	2900
		AMOUNT						AMOUNT		
.75	.79	.83	.86	.90		.94	.98	1.01	1.05	1.09
.75	.79	.83	.86	.90	5	.94	.98	1.01	1.05	1.09
.75	.79	.83	.87	.90	10	.94	.98	1.02	1.05	1.09
.76	.79	.83	.87	.91	15	.94	.98	1.02	1.06	1.09
.76	.80	.83	.87	.91	20	.95	.98	1.02	1.06	1.10
.76	.80	.83	.87	.91	25	.95	.98	1.02	1.06	1.10
.76	.80	.84	.87	.91	30	.95	.99	1.02	1.06	1.10
.76	.80	.84	.88	.91	35	.95	.99	1.03	1.06	1.10
.77	.80	.84	.88	.92	40	.95	.99	1.03	1.07	1.10
.77	.80	.84	.88	.92	45	.95	.99	1.03	1.07	1.10
.77	.81	.84	.88	.92	50	.96	.99	1.03	1.07	1.11
.77	.81	.85	.88	.92	55	.96	1.00	1.03	1.07	1.11
.77	.81	.85	.89	.92	60	.96	1.00	1.04	1.07	1.11
.77	.81	.85	.89	.92	65	.96	1.00	1.04	1.07	1.11
.78	.81	.85	.89	.93	70	.96	1.00	1.04	1.08	1.11
.78	.82	.85	.89	.93	75	.97	1.00	1.04	1.08	1.12
.78	.82	.86	.89	.93	80	.97	1.01	1.04	1.08	1.12
.78	.82	.86	.89	.93	85	.97	1.01	1.04	1.08	1.12
.78	.82	.86	.90	.93	90	.97	1.01	1.05	1.08	1.12
.79	.82	.86	.90	.94	95	.97	1.01	1.05	1.09	1.12

POUNDS

3000	3100	3200	3300	3400		3500	3600	3700	3800	3900
		AMOUNT						AMOUNT		
1.13	1.16	1.20	1.24	1.28		1.31	1.35	1.39	1.43	1.46
1.13	1.16	1.20	1.24	1.28	5	1.31	1.35	1.39	1.43	1.46
1.13	1.17	1.20	1.24	1.28	10	1.32	1.35	1.39	1.43	1.47
1.13	1.17	1.21	1.24	1.28	15	1.32	1.36	1.39	1.43	1.47
1.13	1.17	1.21	1.25	1.28	20	1.32	1.36	1.40	1.43	1.47
1.13	1.17	1.21	1.25	1.28	25	1.32	1.36	1.40	1.43	1.47
1.14	1.17	1.21	1.25	1.29	30	1.32	1.36	1.40	1.44	1.47
1.14	1.18	1.21	1.25	1.29	35	1.33	1.36	1.40	1.44	1.48
1.14	1.18	1.22	1.25	1.29	40	1.33	1.37	1.40	1.44	1.48
1.14	1.18	1.22	1.25	1.29	45	1.33	1.37	1.40	1.44	1.48
1.14	1.18	1.22	1.26	1.29	50	1.33	1.37	1.41	1.44	1.48
1.15	1.18	1.22	1.26	1.30	55	1.33	1.37	1.41	1.45	1.48
1.15	1.19	1.22	1.26	1.30	60	1.34	1.37	1.41	1.45	1.49
1.15	1.19	1.22	1.26	1.30	65	1.34	1.37	1.41	1.45	1.49
1.15	1.19	1.23	1.26	1.30	70	1.34	1.38	1.41	1.45	1.49
1.15	1.19	1.23	1.27	1.30	75	1.34	1.38	1.42	1.45	1.49
1.16	1.19	1.23	1.27	1.31	80	1.34	1.38	1.42	1.46	1.49
1.16	1.19	1.23	1.27	1.31	85	1.34	1.38	1.42	1.46	1.49
1.16	1.20	1.23	1.27	1.31	90	1.35	1.38	1.42	1.46	1.50
1.16	1.20	1.24	1.27	1.31	95	1.35	1.39	1.42	1.46	1.50

Even tons, 51 to 100 inclusive.

51-60		61-70		71-80		81-90		91-100	
T	Am't	T	Am't	T	Am't	T	Am't	T	Am't
51	38.25	61	45.75	71	53.25	81	60.75	91	68.25
52	39.00	62	46.50	72	54.00	82	61.50	92	69.00
53	39.75	63	47.25	73	54.75	83	62.25	93	69.75
54	40.50	64	48.00	74	55.50	84	63.00	94	70.50
55	41.25	65	48.75	75	56.25	85	63.75	95	71.25
56	42.00	66	49.50	76	57.00	86	64.50	96	72.00
57	42.75	67	50.25	77	57.75	87	65.25	97	72.75
58	43.50	68	51.00	78	58.50	88	66.00	98	73.50
59	44.25	69	51.75	79	59.25	89	66.75	99	74.25
60	45.00	70	52.50	80	60.00	90	67.50	100	75.00

700	525	800	600	900	675	1000	750	1100	825

4c a bu. $1.00 a T. 5c a 100 lbs.

—POUNDS—

Under 100	100	200	300	400		500	600	700	800	900
	—AMOUNT—						—AMOUNT—			
	.05	.10	.15	.20		.25	.30	.35	.40	.45
	.05	.10	.15	.20	5	.25	.30	.35	.40	.45
.01	.06	.11	.16	.21	10	.26	.31	.36	.41	.46
.01	.06	.11	.16	.21	15	.26	.31	.36	.41	.46
.01	.06	.11	.16	.21	20	.26	.31	.36	.41	.46
.01	.06	.11	.16	.21	25	.26	.31	.36	.41	.46
.02	.07	.12	.17	.22	30	.27	.32	.37	.42	.47
.02	.07	.12	.17	.22	35	.27	.32	.37	.42	.47
.02	.07	.12	.17	.22	40	.27	.32	.37	.42	.47
.02	.07	.12	.17	.22	45	.27	.32	.37	.42	.47
.03	.08	.13	.18	.23	50	.28	.33	.38	.43	.48
.03	.08	.13	.18	.23	55	.28	.33	.38	.43	.48
.03	.08	.13	.18	.23	60	.28	.33	.38	.43	.48
.03	.08	.13	.18	.23	65	.28	.33	.38	.43	.48
.04	.09	.14	.19	.24	70	.29	.34	.39	.44	.49
.04	.09	.14	.19	.24	75	.29	.34	.39	.44	.49
.04	.09	.14	.19	.24	80	.29	.34	.39	.44	.49
.04	.09	.14	.19	.24	85	.29	.34	.39	.44	.49
·05	.10	.15	.20	.25	90	.30	.35	.40	.45	.50
.05	.10	.15	.20	.25	95	.30	.35	.40	.45	.50

—POUNDS—

1000	1100	1200	1300	1400		1500	1600	1700	1800	1900
—AMOUNT—							—AMOUNT—			
.50	.55	.60	.65	.70		.75	.80	.85	.90	.95
.50	.55	.60	.65	.70	5	.75	.80	.85	.90	.95
.51	.56	.61	.66	.71	10	.76	.81	.86	.91	.96
.51	.56	.61	.66	.71	15	.76	.81	.86	.91	.96
.51	.56	.61	.66	.71	20	.76	.81	.86	.91	.96
.51	.56	.61	.66	.71	25	.76	.81	.86	.91	.96
.52	.57	.62	.67	.72	30	.77	.82	.87	.92	.97
.52	.57	.62	.67	.72	35	.77	.82	.87	.92	.97
.52	.57	.62	.67	.72	40	.77	.82	.87	.92	.97
.52	.57	.62	.67	.72	45	.77	.82	.87	.92	.97
.53	.58	.63	.68	.73	50	.78	.83	.88	.93	.98
.53	.58	.63	.68	.73	55	.78	.83	.88	.93	.98
.53	.58	.63	.68	.73	60	.78	.83	.88	.93	.98
.53	.58	.63	.68	.73	65	.78	.83	.88	.93	.98
.54	.59	.64	.69	.74	70	.79	.84	.89	.94	.99
.54	.59	.64	.69	.74	75	.79	.84	.89	.94	.99
.54	.59	.64	.69	.74	80	.79	.84	.89	.94	.99
.54	.59	.64	.69	.74	85	.79	.84	.89	.94	.99
.55	.60	.65	.70	.75	90	.80	.85	.90	.95	1.00
.55	.60	.65	.70	.75	95	.80	.85	.90	.95	1.00

Even tons, 1 to 50 inclusive.

1-10		11-20		21-30		31-40		41-50	
T	Am't	T	Am't	T	Am't	T	Am't	T	Am't
1	1.00	11	11.00	21	21.00	31	31.00	41	41.00
2	2.00	12	12.00	22	22.00	32	32.00	42	42.00
3	3.00	13	13.00	23	23.00	33	33.00	43	43.00
4	4.00	14	14.00	24	24.00	34	34.00	44	44.00
5	5.00	15	15.00	25	25.00	35	35.00	45	45.00
6	6.00	16	16.00	26	26.00	36	36.0u	46	46.00
7	7.00	17	17.00	27	27.00	37	37.00	47	47.00
8	8.00	18	18.00	28	28.00	38	38.00	48	48.00
9	9.00	19	19.00	29	29.00	39	39.00	49	49.00
10	10.00	20	20.00	30	30.00	40	40.00	50	50.00
200	200	300	300	400	400	500	500	600	600

——Pounds——

2000	2100	2200	2300	2400		2500	2600	2700	2800	2900
		—Amount—						-Amount-		
1.00	1.05	1.10	1.15	1.20		1.25	1.30	1.35	1.40	1.45
1.00	1.05	1.10	1.15	1.20	5	1.25	1.30	1.35	1.40	1.45
1.01	1.06	1.11	1.16	1.21	10	1.26	1.31	1.36	1.41	1.46
1.01	1.06	1.11	1.16	1.21	15	1.26	1.31	1.36	1.41	1.46
1.01	1.06	1.11	1.16	1.21	20	1.26	1.31	1.36	1 41	1.46
1.01	1.06	1.11	1.16	1.21	25	1.26	1.31	1.36	1.41	1.46
1.02	1.07	1.12	1.17	1.22	30	1.27	1.32	1.37	1.42	1.47
1.02	1.07	1.12	1.17	1.22	35	1.27	1.32	1.37	1.42	1.47
1.02	1.07	1.12	1.17	1.22	40	1.27	1.32	1.37	1.42	1.47
1.02	1.07	1.12	1.17	1.22	45	1.27	1.32	1.37	1.42	1.47
1.03	1.08	1.13	1.18	1.23	50	1.28	1.33	1.38	1.43	1.48
1.03	1.08	1.13	1.18	1.23	55	1.28	1.33	1.38	1.43	1.48
1.03	1.08	1.13	1.18	1.23	60	1.28	1.33	1.38	1.43	1.48
1.03	1.08	1.13	1.18	1.23	65	1.28	1.33	1.38	1.43	1.48
1.04	1.09	1.14	1.19	1.24	70	1.29	1.34	1.39	1.44	1.49
1.04	1.09	1.14	1.19	1.24	75	1.29	1.34	1.39	1.44	1.49
1.04	1.09	1.14	1.19	1.24	80	1.29	1.34	1.39	1.44	1.49
1.04	1.09	1.14	1.19	1.24	85	1.29	1.34	1.39	1.44	1.49
1.05	1.10	1.15	1.20	1.25	90	1.30	1.35	1.40	1.45	1.50
1.05	1.10	1.15	1.20	1.25	95	1.30	1.35	1.40	1.45	1.50

——Pounds——

3000	3100	3200	3300	3400		3500	3600	3700	3800	3900
		—Amount—						-Amount-		
1.50	1.55	1.60	1.65	1.70		1.75	1.80	1.85	1.90	1.95
1.50	1.55	1.60	1.65	1.70	5	1.75	1.80	1.85	1.90	1.95
1.51	1.56	1.61	1.66	1.71	10	1.76	1.81	1.86	1.91	1.96
1.51	1.56	1.61	1.66	1.71	15	1.76	1.81	1.86	1.91	1.96
1.51	1.56	1.61	1.66	1.71	20	1.76	1.81	1.86	1.91	1.96
1.51	1.56	1.61	1.66	1.71	25	1.76	1.81	1.86	1.91	1.96
1.52	1.57	1.62	1.67	1.72	30	1.77	1.82	1.87	1.92	1.97
1.52	1.57	1.62	1.67	1.72	35	1.77	1.82	1.87	1.92	1.97
1.52	1.57	1.62	1.67	1.72	40	1.77	1.82	1.87	1.92	1.97
1.52	1.57	1.62	1.67	1.72	45	1.77	1.82	1.87	1.92	1.97
1.53	1.58	1.63	1.68	1.73	50	1.78	1.83	1.88	1.93	1.98
1.53	1.58	1.63	1.68	1.73	55	1.78	1.83	1.88	1.93	1.98
1.53	1.58	1.63	1.68	1.73	60	1.78	1.83	1.88	1.93	1.98
1.53	1.58	1.63	1.68	1.73	65	1.78	1.83	1.88	1.93	1.98
1.54	1.59	1.64	1.69	1.74	70	1.79	1.84	1.89	1.94	1.99
1.54	1.59	1.64	1.69	1.74	75	1.79	1.84	1.89	1.94	1.99
1.54	1.59	1.64	1.69	1.74	80	1.79	1.84	1.89	1.94	1.99
1.54	1.59	1.64	1.69	1.74	85	1.79	1.84	1.89	1.94	1.99
1.55	1.60	1.65	1.70	1.75	90	1.80	1.85	1.90	1.95	2.00
1.55	1.60	1.65	1.70	1.75	95	1.80	1.85	1.90	1.95	2.00

Even tons, 51 to 100 inclusive.

51-60		61-70		71-80		81-90		91-100	
T	Am't	T	Am't	T	Am't	T	Am't	T	Am't
51	51.00	61	61.00	71	71.00	81	81.00	91	91.00
52	52.00	62	62.00	72	72.00	82	82.00	92	92.00
53	53.00	63	63.00	73	73.00	83	83.00	93	93.00
54	54.00	64	64.00	74	74.00	84	84.00	94	94.00
55	55.00	65	65.00	75	75.00	85	85.00	95	95.00
56	56.00	66	66.00	76	76.00	86	86.00	96	96.00
57	57.00	67	67.00	77	77.00	87	87.00	97	97.00
58	58.00	68	68.00	78	78.00	88	88.00	98	98.00
59	59.00	69	69.00	79	79.00	89	89.00	99	99.00
60	60.00	70	70.00	80	80.00	90	90.00	100	100.00

700	700	800	800	900	900	1000	1000	1100	1100

POUNDS

Under 100	100	200	300	400		500	600	700	800	900
		AMOUNT						AMOUNT		
	.06	.13	.19	.25		.31	.38	.44	.50	.56
	.07	.13	.19	.25	5	.32	.38	.44	.50	.57
.01	.07	.13	.19	.26	10	.32	.38	.44	.51	.57
.01	.07	.13	.20	.26	15	.32	.38	.45	.51	.57
.01	.08	.14	.20	.26	20	.33	.39	.45	.51	.58
.02	.08	.14	.20	.27	25	.33	.39	.45	.52	.58
.02	.08	.14	.21	.27	30	.33	.39	.46	.52	.58
.02	.08	.15	.21	.27	35	.33	.40	.46	.52	.58
.03	.09	.15	.21	.28	40	.34	.40	.46	.53	.59
.03	.09	.15	.22	.28	45	.34	.40	.47	.53	.59
.03	.09	.16	.22	.28	50	.34	.41	.47	.53	.59
.03	.10	.16	.22	.28	55	.35	.41	.47	.53	.60
.04	.10	.16	.23	.29	60	.35	.41	.48	.54	.60
.04	.10	.17	.23	.29	65	.35	.42	.48	.54	.60
.04	.11	.17	.23	.29	70	.36	.42	.48	.54	.61
.05	.11	.17	.23	.30	75	.36	.42	.48	.55	.61
.05	.11	.18	.24	.30	80	.36	.43	.49	.55	.61
.05	.12	.18	.24	.30	85	.37	.43	.49	.55	.62
.06	.12	.18	.24	.31	90	.37	.43	.49	.56	.62
.06	.12	.18	.25	.31	95	.37	.43	.50	.56	.62

POUNDS

1000	1100	1200	1300	1400		1500	1600	1700	1800	1900
		AMOUNT						AMOUNT		
.63	.69	.75	.81	.88		.94	1.00	1.06	1.13	1.19
.63	.69	.75	.82	.88	5	.94	1.00	1.07	1.13	1.19
.63	.69	.76	.82	.88	10	.94	1.01	1.07	1.13	1.19
.63	.70	.76	.82	.88	15	.95	1.01	1.07	1.13	1.20
.64	.70	.76	.83	.89	20	.95	1.01	1.08	1.14	1.20
.64	.70	.77	.83	.89	25	.95	1.02	1.08	1.14	1.20
.64	.71	.77	.83	.89	30	.96	1.02	1.08	1.14	1.21
.65	.71	.77	.83	.90	35	.96	1.02	1.08	1.15	1.21
.65	.71	.78	.84	.90	40	.96	1.03	1.09	1.15	1.21
.65	.72	.78	.84	.90	45	.97	1.03	1.09	1.15	1.22
.66	.72	.78	.84	.91	50	.97	1.03	1.09	1.16	1.22
.66	.72	.78	.85	.91	55	.97	1.03	1.10	1.16	1.22
.66	.73	.79	.85	.91	60	.97	1.04	1.10	1.16	1.23
.67	.73	.79	.85	.92	65	.98	1.04	1.10	1.17	1.23
.67	.73	.79	.86	.92	70	.98	1.04	1.11	1.17	1.23
.67	.73	.80	.86	.92	75	.98	1.05	1.11	1.17	1.23
.68	.74	.80	.86	.93	80	.99	1.05	1.11	1.18	1.24
.68	.74	.80	.87	.93	85	.99	1.05	1.12	1.18	1.24
.68	.74	.81	.87	.93	90	.99	1.06	1.12	1.18	1.24
.68	.75	.81	.87	.93	95	1.00	1.06	1.12	1.18	1.25

Even tons, 1 to 50 inc'usive.

1-10		11-20		21-30		31-40		41-50	
T	Am't	T	Am't	T	Am't	T	Am't	T	Am't
1	1.25	11	13.75	21	26.25	31	38.75	41	51.25
2	2.50	12	15.00	22	27.50	32	40.00	42	52.50
3	3.75	13	16.25	23	28.75	33	41.25	43	53.75
4	5.00	14	17.50	24	30.00	34	42.50	44	55.00
5	6.25	15	18.75	25	31.25	35	43.75	45	56.25
6	7.50	16	20.00	26	32.50	36	45.00	46	57.50
7	8.75	17	21.25	27	33.75	37	46.25	47	58.75
8	10.00	18	22.50	28	35.00	38	47.50	48	60.00
9	11.25	19	23.75	29	36.25	39	48.75	49	61.25
10	12.50	20	25.00	30	37.50	40	50.00	50	62.50
200	250	300	375	400	500	500	625	600	750

—POUNDS—

2000	2100	2200	2300	2400		2500	2600	2700	2800	2900
		AMOUNT						AMOUNT		
1.25	1.31	1.38	1.44	1.50		1.56	1.63	1.69	1.75	1.81
1.25	1.32	1.38	1.44	1.50	5	1.57	1.63	1.69	1.75	1.82
1.26	1.32	1.38	1.44	1.51	10	1.57	1.63	1.69	1.76	1.82
1.26	1.32	1.38	1.45	1.51	15	1.57	1.63	1.70	1.76	1.82
1.26	1.33	1.39	1.45	1.51	20	1.58	1.64	1.70	1.76	1.83
1.27	1.33	1.39	1.45	1.52	25	1.58	1.64	1.70	1.77	1.83
1.27	1.33	1.39	1.46	1.52	30	1.58	1.64	1.71	1.77	1.83
1.27	1.33	1.40	1.46	1.52	35	1.58	1.65	1.71	1.77	1.83
1.28	1.34	1.40	1.46	1.53	40	1.59	1.65	1.71	1.78	1.84
1.28	1.34	1.40	1.47	1.53	45	1.59	1.65	1.72	1.78	1.84
1.28	1.34	1.41	1.47	1.53	50	1.59	1.66	1.72	1.78	1.84
1.28	1.35	1.41	1.47	1.53	55	1.60	1.66	1.72	1.78	1.85
1.29	1.35	1.41	1.48	1.54	60	1.60	1.66	1.73	1.79	1.85
1.29	1.35	1.42	1.48	1.54	65	1.60	1.67	1.73	1.79	1.85
1.29	1.36	1.42	1.48	1.54	70	1.61	1.67	1.73	1.79	1.86
1.30	1.36	1.42	1.48	1.55	75	1.61	1.67	1.73	1.80	1.86
1.30	1.36	1.43	1.49	1.55	80	1.61	1.68	1.74	1.80	1.86
1.30	1.37	1.43	1.49	1.55	85	1.62	1.68	1.74	1.80	1.87
1.31	1.37	1.43	1.49	1.56	90	1.62	1.68	1.74	1.81	1.87
1.31	1.37	1.43	1.50	1.56	95	1.62	1.68	1.75	1.81	1.87

—POUNDS—

3000	3100	3200	3300	3400		3500	3600	3700	3800	3900
		AMOUNT						AMOUNT		
1.88	1.94	2.00	2.06	2.13		2.19	2.25	2.31	2.38	2.44
1.88	1.94	2.00	2.07	2.13	5	2.19	2.25	2.32	2.38	2.44
1.88	1.94	2.01	2.07	2.13	10	2.19	2.26	2.32	2.38	2.44
1.88	1.95	2.01	2.07	2.13	15	2.20	2.26	2.32	2.38	2.45
1.89	1.95	2.01	2.08	2.14	20	2.20	2.26	2.33	2.39	2.45
1.89	1.95	2.02	2.08	2.14	25	2.20	2.27	2.33	2.39	2.45
1.89	1.96	2.02	2.08	2.14	30	2.21	2.27	2.33	2.39	2.46
1.90	1.96	2.02	2.08	2.15	35	2.21	2.27	2.33	2.40	2.46
1.90	1.96	2.03	2.09	2.15	40	2.21	2.28	2.34	2.40	2.46
1.90	1.97	2.03	2.09	2.15	45	2.22	2.28	2.34	2.40	2.47
1.91	1.97	2.03	2.09	2.16	50	2.22	2.28	2.34	2.41	2.47
1.91	1.97	2.03	2.10	2.16	55	2.22	2.28	2.35	2.41	2.47
1.91	1.98	2.04	2.10	2.16	60	2.23	2.29	2.35	2.41	2.48
1.92	1.98	2.04	2.10	2.17	65	2.23	2.29	2.35	2.42	2.48
1.92	1.98	2.04	2.11	2.17	70	2.23	2.29	2.36	2.42	2.48
1.92	1.98	2.05	2.11	2.17	75	2.23	2.30	2.36	2.42	2.48
1.93	1.99	2.05	2.11	2.18	80	2.24	2.30	2.36	2.43	2.49
1.93	1.99	2.05	2.12	2.18	85	2.24	2.30	2.37	2.43	2.49
1.93	1.99	2.05	2.12	2.18	90	2.24	2.31	2.37	2.43	2.49
1.93	2.00	2.06	2.12	2.18	95	2.25	2.31	2.37	2.43	2.50

Even tons, 51 to 100 inclusive.

51-60		61-70		71-80		81-90		91-100	
T	Am't	T	Am't	T	Am't	T	Am't	T	Am't
51	63.75	61	76.25	71	88.75	81	101.25	91	113.75
52	65.00	62	77.50	72	90.00	82	102.50	92	115.00
53	66.25	63	78.75	73	91.25	83	103.75	93	116.25
54	67.50	64	80.00	74	92.50	84	105.00	94	117.50
55	68.75	65	81.25	75	93.75	85	106.25	95	118.75
56	70.00	66	82.50	76	95.00	86	107.50	96	120.00
57	71.25	67	83.75	77	96.25	87	108.75	97	121.25
58	72.50	68	85.00	78	97.50	88	110.00	98	122.50
59	73.75	69	86.25	79	98.75	89	111.25	99	123.75
60	75.00	70	87.50	80	100.00	90	112.50	100	125.00
700	875	800	1000	900	1125	1000	1250	1100	1375

2   (13)

POUNDS

Under 100	100	200	300	400		500	600	700	800	900
			AMOUNT					AMOUNT		
	.08	.15	.23	.30		.38	.45	.53	.60	.68
	.08	.15	.23	.30	5	.38	.45	.53	.60	.68
.01	.08	.16	.23	.31	10	.38	.46	.53	.61	.68
.01	.09	.16	.24	.31	15	.39	.46	.54	.61	.69
.02	.09	.17	.24	.32	20	.39	.47	.54	.62	.69
.02	.09	.17	.24	.32	25	.39	.47	.54	.62	.69
.02	.10	.17	.25	.32	30	.40	.47	.55	.62	.70
.03	.10	.18	.25	.33	35	.40	.48	.55	.63	.70
.03	.11	.18	.26	.33	40	.41	.48	.56	.63	.71
.03	.11	.18	.26	.33	45	.41	.48	.56	.63	.71
.04	.11	.19	.26	.34	50	.41	.49	.56	.64	.71
.04	.12	.19	.27	.34	55	.42	.49	.57	.64	.72
.05	.12	.20	.27	.35	60	.42	.50	.57	.65	.72
.05	.12	.20	.27	.35	65	.42	.50	.57	.65	.72
.05	.13	.20	.28	.35	70	.43	.50	.58	.65	.73
.06	.13	.21	.28	.36	75	.43	.51	.58	.66	.73
.06	.14	.21	.29	.36	80	.44	.51	.59	.66	.74
.06	.14	.21	.29	.36	85	.44	.51	.59	.66	.74
.07	.14	.22	.29	.37	90	.44	.52	.59	.67	.74
.07	.15	.22	.30	.37	95	.45	.52	.60	.67	.75

POUNDS

1000	1100	1200	1300	1400		1500	1600	1700	1800	1900
		AMOUNT						AMOUNT		
.75	.83	.90	.98	1.05		1.13	1.20	1.28	1.35	1.43
.75	.83	.90	.98	1.05	5	1.13	1.20	1.28	1.35	1.43
.76	.83	.91	.98	1.06	10	1.13	1.21	1.28	1.36	1.43
.76	.84	.91	.99	1.06	15	1.14	1.21	1.29	1.36	1.44
.77	.84	.92	.99	1.07	20	1.14	1.22	1.29	1.37	1.44
.77	.84	.92	.99	1.07	25	1.14	1.22	1.29	1.37	1.44
.77	.85	.92	1.00	1.07	30	1.15	1.22	1.30	1.37	1.45
.78	.85	.93	1.00	1.08	35	1.15	1.23	1.30	1.38	1.45
.78	.86	.93	1.01	1.08	40	1.16	1.23	1.31	1.38	1.46
.78	.86	.93	1.01	1.08	45	1.16	1.23	1.31	1.38	1.46
.79	.86	.94	1.01	1.09	50	1.16	1.24	1.31	1.39	1.46
.79	.87	.94	1.02	1.09	55	1.17	1.24	1.32	1.39	1.47
.80	.87	.95	1.02	1.10	60	1.17	1.25	1.32	1.40	1.47
.80	.87	.95	1.02	1.10	65	1.17	1.25	1.32	1.40	1.47
.80	.88	.95	1.03	1.10	70	1.18	1.25	1.33	1.40	1.48
.81	.88	.96	1.03	1.11	75	1.18	1.26	1.33	1.41	1.48
.81	.89	.96	1.04	1.11	80	1.19	1.26	1.34	1.41	1.49
.81	.89	.96	1.04	1.11	85	1.19	1.26	1.34	1.41	1.49
.82	.89	.97	1.04	1.12	90	1.19	1.27	1.34	1.42	1.49
.82	.90	.97	1.05	1.12	95	1.20	1.27	1.35	1.42	1.50

Even tons, 1 to 50 inclusive.

1-10		11-20		21-30		31-40		41-50	
T	Am't	T	Am't	T	Am't	T	Am't	T	Am't
1	1.50	11	16.50	21	31.50	31	46.50	41	61.50
2	3.00	12	18.00	22	33.00	32	48.00	42	63.00
3	4.50	13	19.50	23	34.50	33	49.50	43	64.50
4	6.00	14	21.00	24	36.00	34	51.00	44	66.00
5	7.50	15	22.50	25	37.50	35	52.50	45	67.50
6	9.00	16	24.00	26	39.00	36	54.00	46	69.00
7	10.50	17	25.50	27	40.50	37	55.50	47	70.50
8	12.00	18	27.00	28	42.00	38	57.00	48	72.00
9	13.50	19	28.50	29	43.50	39	58.50	49	73.50
10	15.00	20	30.00	30	45.00	40	60.00	50	75.00
200	300	300	450	400	600	500	750	600	900

POUNDS

2300	2400		2500	2600	2700	2800	2900
					AMOUNT		
1.73	1.80		1.88	1.95	2.03	2.10	2.18
1.73	1.80	5	1.88	1.95	2.03	2.10	2.18
1.73	1.81	10	1.88	1.96	2.03	2.11	2.18
1.74	1.81	15	1.89	1.96	2.04	2.11	2.19
1.74	1.82	20	1.89	1.97	2.04	2.12	2.19
1.74	1.82	25	1.89	1.97	2.04	2.12	2.19
1.75	1.82	30	1.90	1.97	2.05	2.12	2.20
1.75	1.83	35	1.90	1.98	2.05	2.13	2.20
1.76	1.83	40	1.91	1.98	2.06	2.13	2.21
1.76	1.83	45	1.91	1.98	2.06	2.13	2.21
1.76	1.84	50	1.91	1.99	2.06	2.14	2.21
1.77	1.84	55	1.92	1.99	2.07	2.14	2.22
1.77	1.85	60	1.92	2.00	2.07	2.15	2.22
1.77	1.85	65	1.92	2.00	2.07	2.15	2.22
1.78	1.85	70	1.93	2.00	2.08	2.15	2.23
1.78	1.86	75	1.93	2.01	2.08	2.16	2.23
1.79	1.86	80	1.94	2.01	2.09	2.16	2.24
1.79	1.86	85	1.94	2.01	2.09	2.16	2.24
1.79	1.87	90	1.94	2.02	2.09	2.17	2.24
1.80	1.87	95	1.95	2.02	2.10	2.17	2.25

POUNDS

3300	3400		3500	3600	3700	3800	3900
					AMOUNT		
2.48	2.55		2.63	2.70	2.78	2.85	2.93
2.48	2.55	5	2.63	2.70	2.78	2.85	2.93
2.48	2.56	10	2.63	2.71	2.78	2.86	2.93
2.49	2.56	15	2.64	2.71	2.79	2.86	2.94
2.49	2.57	20	2.64	2.72	2.79	2.87	2.94
2.49	2.57	25	2.64	2.72	2.79	2.87	2.94
2.50	2.57	30	2.65	2.72	2.80	2.87	2.95
2.50	2.58	35	2.65	2.73	2.80	2.88	2.95
2.51	2.58	40	2.66	2.73	2.81	2.88	2.96
2.51	2.58	45	2 66	2.73	2.81	2 88	2.96
2.51	2.59	50	2.66	2.74	2.81	2.89	2.96
2.52	2.59	55	2.67	2.74	2.82	2.89	2.97
2.52	2.60	60	2.67	2.75	2.82	2.90	2.97
2.52	2.60	65	2.67	2.75	2.82	2.90	2.97
2.53	2.60	70	2.68	2.75	2.83	2.90	2.98
2.53	2.61	75	2.68	2.76	2.83	2.91	2.98
2.54	2.61	80	2.69	2.76	2.84	2.91	2.99
2.54	2.61	85	2.69	2.76	2.84	2.91	2.99
2.54	2.62	90	2.69	2.77	2.84	2.92	2.99
2.55	2.62	95	2.70	2.77	2.85	2.92	3.00

n tons, 51 to 100 inclusive.

.70		71-80		81-90		91-100	
Am't	T	Am't	T	Am't	T		Am't
91.50	71	106.50	81	121.50	91		136.50
93.00	72	108.00	82	123.00	92		138.00
94.50	73	109.50	83	124.50	93		139.50
96.00	74	111.00	84	126.00	94		141.00
97.50	75	112.50	85	127.50	95		142.50
99.00	76	114.00	86	129.00	96		144.00
100.50	77	115.50	87	130.50	97		145.50
102.00	78	117.00	88	132.00	98		147.00
103.50	79	118.50	89	133.50	99		148.50
105.00	80	120.00	90	135.00	100		150.00
1200	900	1350	1000	1500	1100		1650

POUNDS

Under 100	100	200	300	400		500	600	700	800	900
	.09	.18	.26	.35		.44	.53	.61	.70	.79
⁹	.09	.18	.27	.35	5	.44	.53	.62	.70	.79
.01	.10	.18	.27	.36	10	.45	.53	.62	.71	.80
.01	.10	.19	.28	.36	15	.45	.54	.63	.71	.80
.02	.11	.19	.28	.37	20	.46	.54	.63	.72	.81
.02	.11	.20	.28	.37	25	.46	.55	.63	.72	.81
.03	.11	.20	.29	.38	30	.46	.55	.64	.73	.81
.03	.12	.21	.29	.38	35	.47	.56	.64	.73	.82
.04	.12	.21	.30	.39	40	.47	.56	.65	.74	.82
.04	.13	.21	.30	.39	45	.48	.56	.65	.74	.83
.04	.13	.22	.31	.39	50	.48	.57	.66	.74	.83
.05	.14	.22	.31	.40	55	.49	.57	.66	.75	.84
.05	.14	.23	.32	.40	60	.49	.58	.67	.75	.84
.06	.14	.23	.32	.41	65	.49	.58	.67	.76	.84
.06	.15	.24	.32	.41	70	.50	.59	.67	.76	.85
.07	.15	.24	.33	.42	75	.50	.59	.68	.77	.85
.07	.16	.25	.33	.42	80	.51	.60	.68	.77	.86
.07	.16	.25	.34	.42	85	.51	.60	.69	.77	.86
.08	.17	.25	.34	.43	90	.52	.60	.69	.78	.87
.08	.17	.26	.35	.43	95	.52	.61	.70	.78	.87

POUNDS

1000	1100	1200	1300	1400		1500	1600	1700	1800	1900
.88	.96	1.05	1.14	1.23		1.31	1.40	1.49	1.58	1.66
.88	.97	1.05	1.14	1.23	5	1.32	1.40	1.49	1.58	1.67
.88	.97	1.06	1.15	1.23	10	1.32	1.41	1.50	1.58	1.67
.89	.98	1.06	1.15	1.24	15	1.33	1.41	1.50	1.59	1.68
.89	.98	1.07	1.16	1.24	20	1.33	1.42	1.51	1.59	1.68
.90	.98	1.07	1.16	1.25	25	1.33	1.42	1.51	1.60	1.68
.90	.99	1.08	1.16	1.25	30	1.34	1.43	1.51	1.60	1.69
.91	.99	1.08	1.17	1.26	35	1.34	1.43	1.52	1.61	1.69
.91	1.00	1.09	1.17	1.26	40	1.35	1.44	1.52	1.61	1.70
.91	1.00	1.09	1.18	1.26	45	1.35	1.44	1.53	1.61	1.70
.92	1.01	1.09	1.18	1.27	50	1.36	1.44	1.53	1.62	1.71
.92	1.01	1.10	1.19	1.27	55	1.36	1.45	1.54	1.62	1.71
.93	1.02	1.10	1.19	1.28	60	1.37	1.45	1.54	1.63	1.72
.93	1.02	1.11	1.19	1.28	65	1.37	1.46	1.54	1.63	1.72
.94	1.02	1.11	1.20	1.29	70	1.37	1.46	1.55	1.64	1.72
.94	1.03	1.12	1.20	1.29	75	1.38	1.47	1.55	1.64	1.73
.95	1.03	1.12	1.21	1.30	80	1.38	1.47	1.56	1.65	1.73
.95	1.04	1.12	1.21	1.30	85	1.39	1.47	1.56	1.65	1.74
.95	1.04	1.13	1.22	1.30	90	1.39	1.48	1.57	1.65	1.74
.96	1.05	1.13	1.22	1.31	95	1.40	1.48	1.57	1.66	1.75

Even tons, 1 to 50 inclusive.

1-10		11-20		21-30		31-40		41-50	
T	Am't	T	Am't	T	Am't	T	Am't	T	Am't
1	1.75	11	19.25	21	36.75	31	51.25	41	71.75
2	3.50	12	21.00	22	38.50	32	56.00	42	73.50
3	5.25	13	22.75	23	40.25	33	57.75	43	75.25
4	7.00	14	24.50	24	42.00	34	59.50	44	77.00
5	8.75	15	26.25	25	43.75	35	61.25	45	78.75
6	10.50	16	28.00	26	45.50	36	63.00	46	80.50
7	12.25	17	29.75	27	47.25	37	64.75	47	82.25
8	14.00	18	31.50	28	49.00	38	66.50	48	84.00
9	15.75	19	33.25	29	50.75	39	68.50	49	85.75
10	17.50	20	35.00	30	52.50	40	70.00	50	87.50
200	350	300	525	400	700	500	875	600	1050

POUNDS

2000	2100	2200	2300	2400		2500	2600	2700	2800	2900
		AMOUNT						AMOUNT		
1.75	1.84	1.93	2.01	2.10		2.19	2.28	2.36	2.45	2.54
1.75	1.84	1.93	2.02	2.10	5	2.19	2.28	2.37	2.45	2.54
1.76	1.85	1.93	2.02	2.11	10	2.20	2.28	2.37	2.46	2.55
1.76	1.85	1.94	2.03	2.11	15	2.20	2.29	2.38	2.46	2.55
1.77	1.86	1.94	2.03	2.12	20	2.21	2.29	2.38	2.47	2.56
1.77	1.86	1.95	2.03	2.12	25	2.21	2.30	2.38	2.47	2.56
1.78	1.86	1.95	2.04	2.13	30	2.21	2.30	2.39	2.48	2.56
1.78	1.87	1.96	2.04	2.13	35	2.22	2.31	2.39	2.48	2.57
1.79	1.87	1.96	2.05	2.14	40	2.22	2.31	2.40	2.49	2.57
1.79	1.88	1.96	2.05	2.14	45	2.23	2.31	2.40	2.49	2.58
1.79	1.88	1.97	2.06	2.14	50	2.23	2.32	2.41	2.49	2.58
1.80	1.89	1.97	2.06	2.15	55	2.24	2.32	2.41	2.50	2.59
1.80	1.89	1.98	2.07	2.15	60	2.24	2.33	2.42	2.50	2.59
1.81	1.89	1.98	2.07	2.16	65	2.24	2.33	2.42	2.51	2.59
1.81	1.90	1.99	2.07	2.16	70	2.25	2.34	2.42	2.51	2.60
1.82	1.90	1.99	2.08	2.17	75	2.25	2.34	2.43	2.52	2.60
1.82	1.91	2.00	2.08	2.17	80	2.26	2.35	2.43	2.52	2.61
1.82	1.91	2.00	2.09	2.17	85	2.26	2.35	2.44	2.52	2.61
1.83	1.92	2.00	2.09	2.18	90	2.27	2.35	2.44	2.53	2.62
1.83	1.92	2.01	2.10	2.18	95	2.27	2.36	2.45	2.53	2.62

POUNDS

3000	3100	3200	3300	3400		3500	3600	3700	3800	3900
		AMOUNT						AMOUNT		
2.63	2.71	2.80	2.89	2.98		3.06	3.15	3.24	3.33	3.41
2.63	2.72	2.80	2.89	2.98	5	3.07	3.15	3.24	3.33	3.42
2.63	2.72	2.81	2.90	2.98	10	3.07	3.16	3.25	3.33	3.42
2.64	2.73	2.81	2.90	2.99	15	3.08	3.16	3.25	3.34	3.43
2.64	2.73	2.82	2.91	2.99	20	3.08	3.17	3.26	3.34	3.43
2.65	2.73	2.82	2.91	3.00	25	3.08	3.17	3.26	3.35	3.43
2.65	2.74	2.83	2.91	3.00	30	3.09	3.18	3.26	3.35	3.44
2.66	2.74	2.83	2.92	3.01	35	3.09	3.18	3.27	3.36	3.44
2.66	2.75	2.84	2.92	3.01	40	3.10	3.19	3.27	3.36	3.45
2.66	2 75	2.84	2.93	3.01	45	3.10	3.19	3.28	3.36	3.45
2.67	2.76	2.84	2.93	3.02	50	3.11	3.19	3.28	3.37	3.46
2.67	2.76	2.85	2.94	3.02	55	3.11	3.20	3.29	3.37	3.46
2.68	2.77	2.85	2.94	3.03	60	3.12	3.20	3.29	3.38	3.47
2.68	2.77	2.86	2.94	3.03	65	3.12	3.21	3.29	3.38	3.47
2 69	2.77	2.86	2.95	3.04	70	3 12	3.21	3.30	3.39	3.47
2.69	2.78	2.87	2.95	3.04	75	3.13	3.22	3.30	3.39	3.48
2.70	2.78	2.87	2.96	3.05	80	3.13	3.22	3.31	3.40	3.48
2.70	2.79	2.87	2.96	3.05	85	3.14	3.22	3.31	3.40	3.49
2.70	2.79	2.88	2.97	3.05	90	3.14	3.23	3.32	3.40	3.49
2.71	2.80	2.88	2.97	3.06	95	3.15	3.23	3.32	3.41	3.50

Even tons, 51 to 100 inclusive.

51-60		61-70		71-80		81-90		91-100	
T	Am't	T	Am't	T	Am't	T	Am't	T	Am't
51	89.25	61	106.75	71	124.25	81	141.75	91	159.25
52	91.00	62	108.50	72	126.00	82	143.50	92	161.00
53	92.75	63	110.25	73	127.75	83	145.25	93	162.75
54	94.50	64	112.00	74	129.50	84	147.00	94	164.50
55	96.25	65	113.75	75	131.25	85	148.75	95	166.25
56	98.00	66	115.50	76	133.00	86	150.50	96	168.00
57	99.75	67	117.25	77	134.75	87	152.25	97	169.75
58	101.50	68	119.00	78	136.50	88	154.00	98	171.50
59	103.25	69	120.75	79	138.25	89	155.75	99	173.25
60	105.00	70	122.50	80	140.00	90	157.50	100	175.00

700	1225	800	1400	900	1575	1000	1750	1100	1925

POUNDS

Under 100	100	200	300	400		500	600	700	800	900
	AMOUNT							AMOUNT		
	.10	.20	.30	.40		.50	.60	.70	.80	.90
.01	.11	.21	.31	.41	5	.51	.61	.71	.81	.91
.01	.11	.21	.31	.41	10	.51	.61	.71	.81	.91
.02	.12	.22	.32	.42	15	.52	.62	.72	.82	.92
.02	.12	.22	.32	.42	20	.52	.62	.72	.82	.92
.03	.13	.23	.33	.43	25	.53	.63	.73	.83	.93
.03	.13	.23	.33	.43	30	.53	.63	.73	.83	.93
.04	.14	.24	.34	.44	35	.54	.64	.74	.84	.94
.04	.14	.24	.34	.44	40	.54	.64	.74	.84	.94
.05	.15	.25	.35	.45	45	.55	.65	.75	.85	.95
.05	.15	.25	.35	.45	50	.55	.65	.75	.85	.95
.06	.16	.26	.36	.46	55	.56	.66	.76	.86	.96
.06	.16	.26	.36	.46	60	.56	.66	.76	.86	.96
.07	.17	.27	.37	.47	65	.57	.67	.77	.87	.97
.07	.17	.27	.37	.47	70	.57	.67	.77	.87	.97
.08	.18	.28	.38	.48	75	.58	.68	.78	.88	.98
.08	.18	.28	.38	.48	80	.58	.68	.78	.88	.98
.09	.19	.29	.39	.49	85	.59	.69	.79	.89	.99
.09	.19	.29	.39	.49	90	.59	.69	.79	.89	.99
.10	.20	.30	.40	.50	95	.60	.70	.80	.90	1.00

POUNDS

1000	1100	1200	1300	1400		1500	1600	1700	1800	1900
	AMOUNT							AMOUNT		
1.00	1.10	1.20	1.30	1.40		1.50	1.60	1.70	1.80	1.90
1.01	1.11	1.21	1.31	1.41	5	1.51	1.61	1.71	1.81	1.91
1.01	1.11	1.21	1.31	1.41	10	1.51	1.61	1.71	1.81	1.91
1.02	1.12	1.22	1.32	1.42	15	1.52	1.62	1.72	1.82	1.92
1.02	1.12	1.22	1.32	1.42	20	1.52	1.62	1.72	1.82	1.92
1.03	1.13	1.23	1.33	1.43	25	1.53	1.63	1.73	1.83	1.93
1.03	1.13	1.23	1.33	1.43	30	1.53	1.63	1.73	1.83	1.93
1.04	1.14	1.24	1.34	1.44	35	1.54	1.64	1.74	1.84	1.94
1.04	1.14	1.24	1.34	1.44	40	1.54	1.64	1.74	1.84	1.94
1.05	1.15	1.25	1.35	1.45	45	1.55	1.65	1.75	1.85	1.95
1.05	1.15	1.25	1.35	1.45	50	1.55	1.65	1.75	1.85	1.95
1.06	1.16	1.26	1.36	1.46	55	1.56	1.66	1.76	1.86	1.96
1.06	1.16	1.26	1.36	1.46	60	1.56	1.66	1.76	1.86	1.96
1.07	1.17	1.27	1.37	1.47	65	1.57	1.67	1.77	1.87	1.97
1.07	1.17	1.27	1.37	1.47	70	1.57	1.67	1.77	1.87	1.97
1.08	1.18	1.28	1.38	1.48	75	1.58	1.68	1.78	1.88	1.98
1.08	1.18	1.28	1.38	1.48	80	1.58	1.68	1.78	1.88	1.98
1.09	1.19	1.29	1.39	1.49	85	1.59	1.69	1.79	1.89	1.99
1.09	1.19	1.29	1.39	1.49	90	1.59	1.69	1.79	1.89	1.99
1.10	1.20	1.30	1.40	1.50	95	1.60	1.70	1.80	1.90	2.00

Even tons, 1 to 50 inclusive.

1-10		11-20		21-30		31-40		41-50	
T	Am't	T	Am't	T	Am't	T	Am't	T	Am't
1	2.00	11	22.00	21	42.00	31	62.00	41	82.00
2	4.00	12	24.00	22	44.00	32	64.00	42	84.00
3	6.00	13	26.00	23	46.00	33	66.00	43	86.00
4	8.00	14	28.00	24	48.00	34	68.00	44	88.00
5	10.00	15	30.00	25	50.00	35	70.00	45	90.00
6	12.00	16	32.00	26	52.00	36	72.00	46	92.00
7	14.00	17	34.00	27	54.00	37	74.00	47	94.00
8	16.00	18	36.00	28	56.00	38	76.00	48	96.00
9	18.00	19	38.00	29	58.00	39	78.00	49	98.00
10	20.00	20	40.00	30	60.00	40	80.00	50	100.00

200	400	300	600	400	800	500	1000	600	1200

— POUNDS —

2000	2100	2200	2300	2400	lbs	2500	2600	2700	2800	2900
		AMOUNT						AMOUNT		
2.00	2.10	2.20	2.30	2.40		2.50	2.60	2.70	2.80	2.90
2.01	2.11	2.21	2.31	2.41	5	2.51	2.61	2.71	2.81	2.91
2.01	2.11	2.21	2.31	2.41	10	2.51	2.61	2.71	2.81	2.91
2.02	2.12	2.22	2.32	2.42	15	2.52	2.62	2.72	2.82	2.92
2.02	2.12	2.22	2.32	2.42	20	2.52	2.62	2.72	2.82	2.92
2.03	2.13	2.23	2.33	2.43	25	2.53	2.63	2.73	2.83	2.93
2.03	2.13	2.23	2.33	2.43	30	2.53	2.63	2.73	2.83	2.93
2.04	2.14	2.24	2.34	2.44	35	2.54	2.64	2.74	2.84	2.94
2.04	2.14	2.24	2.34	2.44	40	2.54	2.64	2.74	2.84	2.94
2.05	2.15	2.25	2.35	2.45	45	2.55	2.65	2.75	2.85	2.95
2.05	2.15	2.25	2.35	2.45	50	2.55	2.65	2.75	2.85	2.95
2.06	2.16	2.26	2.36	2.46	55	2.56	2.66	2.76	2.86	2.96
2.06	2.16	2.26	2.36	2.46	60	2.56	2.66	2.76	2.86	2.96
2.07	2.17	2.27	2.37	2.47	65	2.57	2.67	2.77	2.87	2.97
2.07	2.17	2.27	2.37	2.47	70	2.57	2.67	2.77	2.87	2.97
2.08	2.18	2.28	2.38	2.48	75	2.58	2.68	2.78	2.88	2.98
2.08	2.18	2.28	2.38	2.48	80	2.58	2.68	2.78	2.88	2.98
2.09	2.19	2.29	2.39	2.49	85	2.59	2.69	2.79	2.89	2.99
2.09	2.19	2.29	2.39	2.49	90	2.59	2.69	2.79	2.89	2.99
2.10	2.20	2.30	2.40	2.50	95	2.60	2.70	2.80	2.90	3.00

— POUNDS —

3000	3100	3200	3300	3400	lbs	3500	3600	3700	3800	3900
		AMOUNT						AMOUNT		
3.00	3.10	3.20	3.30	3.40		3.50	3.60	3.70	3.80	3.90
3.01	3.11	3.21	3.31	3.41	5	3.51	3.61	3.71	3.81	3.91
3.01	3.11	3.21	3.31	3.41	10	3.51	3.61	3.71	3.81	3.91
3.02	3.12	3.22	3.32	3.42	15	3.52	3.62	3.72	3.82	3.92
3.02	3.12	3.22	3.32	3.42	20	3.52	5.62	3.72	3.82	3.92
3.03	3.13	3.23	3.33	3.43	25	3.53	3.63	3.73	3.83	3.93
3.03	3.13	3.23	3.33	3.43	30	3.53	3.63	3.73	3.83	8.93
3.04	3.14	3.24	3.34	3.44	35	3.54	3.64	3.74	3.84	3.94
3.04	3.14	3.24	3.34	3.44	40	3.54	3.64	3.74	3.84	3.94
3.05	3.15	3.25	3.35	3.45	45	3.55	3.65	3.75	3.85	3.95
3.05	3.15	3.25	3.35	3.45	50	3.55	3.65	3.75	3.85	3.95
3.06	3.16	3.26	3.36	3.46	55	3.56	3.66	3.76	3.86	3.96
3.06	3.16	3.26	3.36	3.46	60	3.56	3.66	3.76	3.86	3.96
3.07	3.17	3.27	3.37	3.47	65	3.57	3.67	3.77	3.87	3.97
3.07	3.17	3.27	3.37	3.47	70	3.57	3.67	3.77	3.87	3.97
3.08	3.18	3.28	3.38	3.48	75	3.58	3.68	3.78	3.88	3.98
3.08	3.18	3.28	3.38	3.48	80	3.58	3.68	3.78	3.88	3.98
3.09	3.19	3.29	3.39	3.49	85	3.59	3.69	3.79	3.89	3.99
3.09	3.19	3.29	3.39	3.49	90	3.59	3.69	3.79	3.89	3.99
3.10	3.20	3.30	3.40	3.50	95	3.60	3.70	3.80	3.90	4.00

Even tons, 51 to 100 inclusive.

51-60		61-70		71-80		81-90		91-100	
T	Am't	T	Am't	T	Am't	T	Am't	T	Am't
51	102.00	61	122.00	71	142.00	81	162.00	91	182.00
52	104.00	62	124.00	72	144.00	82	164.00	92	184.00
53	106.00	63	126.00	73	146.00	83	166.00	93	186.00
54	108.00	64	128.00	74	148.00	84	168.00	94	188.00
55	110.00	65	130.00	75	150.00	85	170.00	95	190.00
56	112.00	66	132.00	76	152.00	86	172.00	96	192.00
57	114.00	67	134.00	77	154.00	87	174.00	97	194.00
58	116.00	68	136.00	78	156.00	88	176.00	98	196.00
59	118.00	69	138.00	79	158.00	89	178.00	99	198.00
60	120.00	70	140.00	80	160.00	90	180.00	100	200.00

700	1400	800	1600	900	1800	1000	2000	1100	2200

— POUNDS —

Under 100	100	200	300	400		500	600	700	800	900
	.11	.23	.34	.45		.56	.68	.79	.90	1.01
.01	.12	.23	.34	.46	5	.57	.68	.79	.91	1.02
.01	.12	.24	.35	.46	10	.57	.69	.80	.91	1.02
.02	.13	.24	.35	.47	15	.58	.69	.80	.92	1.03
.02	.14	.25	.36	.47	20	.59	.70	.81	.92	1.04
.03	.14	.25	.37	.48	25	.59	.70	.82	.93	1.04
.03	.15	.26	.37	.48	30	.60	.71	.82	.93	1.05
.04	.15	.26	.38	.49	35	.60	.71	.83	.94	1.05
.05	.16	.27	.38	.50	40	.61	.72	.83	.95	1.06
.05	.16	.28	.39	.50	45	.61	.73	.84	.95	1.06
.06	.17	.28	.39	.51	50	.62	.73	.84	.96	1.07
.06	.17	.29	.40	.51	55	.62	.74	.85	.96	1.07
.07	.18	.29	.41	.52	60	.63	.74	.86	.97	1.08
.07	.19	.30	.41	.52	65	.64	.75	.86	.97	1.09
.08	.19	.30	.42	.53	70	.64	.75	.87	.98	1.09
.08	.20	.31	.42	.53	75	.65	.76	.87	.98	1.10
.09	.20	.32	.43	.54	80	.65	.77	.88	.99	1.10
.10	.21	.32	.43	.55	85	.66	.77	.88	1.00	1.11
.10	.21	.33	.44	.55	90	.66	.78	.89	1.00	1.11
.11	.22	.33	.44	.56	95	.67	.78	.89	1.01	1.12

— POUNDS —

1000	1100	1200	1300	1400		1500	1600	1700	1800	1900
1.13	1.24	1.35	1.46	1.58		1.69	1.80	1.91	2.03	2.14
1.13	1.24	1.36	1.47	1.58	5	1.69	1.81	1.92	2.03	2.14
1.14	1.25	1.36	1.47	1.59	10	1.70	1.81	1.92	2.04	2.15
1.14	1.25	1.37	1.48	1.59	15	1.70	1.82	1.93	2.04	2.15
1.15	1.26	1.37	1.49	1.60	20	1.71	1.82	1.94	2.05	2.16
1.15	1.27	1.38	1.49	1.60	25	1.72	1.83	1.94	2.05	2.17
1.16	1.27	1.38	1.50	1.61	30	1.72	1.83	1.95	2.06	2.17
1.16	1.28	1.39	1.50	1.61	35	1.73	1.84	1.95	2.06	2.18
1.17	1.28	1.40	1.51	1.62	40	1.73	1.85	1.96	2.07	2.18
1.18	1.29	1.40	1.51	1.63	45	1.74	1.85	1.96	2.08	2.19
1.18	1.29	1.41	1.52	1.63	50	1.74	1.86	1.97	2.08	2.19
1.19	1.30	1.41	1.52	1.64	55	1.75	1.86	1.97	2.09	2.20
1.19	1.31	1.42	1.53	1.64	60	1.76	1.87	1.98	2.09	2.21
1.20	1.31	1.42	1.54	1.65	65	1.76	1.87	1.99	2.10	2.21
1.20	1.32	1.43	1.54	1.65	70	1.77	1.88	1.99	2.10	2.22
1.21	1.32	1.43	1.55	1.66	75	1.77	1.88	2.00	2.11	2.22
1.22	1.33	1.44	1.55	1.67	80	1.78	1.89	2.00	2.12	2.23
1.22	1.33	1.45	1.56	1.67	85	1.78	1.90	2.01	2.12	2.23
1.23	1.34	1.45	1.56	1.68	90	1.79	1.90	2.01	2.13	2.24
1.23	1.34	1.46	1.57	1.68	95	1 79	1.91	2.02	2.13	2.24

Even tons, 1 to 50 inclusive.

T	Am't	T	Am't	T	Am't	T	Am't	T	Am't
1	2.25	11	24.75	21	47.25	31	69.75	41	92.25
2	4.50	12	27.00	22	49.50	32	72.00	42	94.50
3	6.75	13	29.25	23	51.75	33	74.25	43	96.75
4	9.00	14	31.50	24	54.00	34	76.50	44	99.00
5	11.25	15	33.75	25	56.25	35	78.75	45	101.25
6	13.50	16	36.00	26	58.50	36	81.00	46	103.50
7	15.75	17	38.25	27	60.75	37	83.25	47	105.75
8	18.00	18	40.50	28	63.00	38	85.50	48	108.00
9	20.25	19	42.75	29	65.25	39	87.75	49	110.25
10	22.50	20	45.00	30	67.50	40	90.00	50	112.50
200	450	300	675	400	900	500	1125	600	1350

POUNDS

2000	2100	2200	2300	2400		2500	2600	2700	2800	2900
		AMOUNT						AMOUNT		
2.25	2.36	2.48	2.59	2.70		2.81	2.93	3.04	3.15	3.26
2.26	2.37	2.48	2.59	2.71	5	2.82	2.93	3.04	3.16	3.27
2.26	2.37	2.49	2.60	2.71	10	2.82	2.94	3.05	3.16	3.27
2.27	2.38	2.49	2.60	2.72	15	2.83	2.94	3.05	3.17	3.28
2.27	2.39	2.50	2.61	2.72	20	2.84	2.95	3.06	3.17	3.29
2.28	2.39	2.50	2.62	2.73	25	2.84	2.95	3.07	3.18	3.29
2.28	2.40	2.51	2.62	2.73	30	2.85	2.96	3.07	3.18	3.30
2.29	2.40	2.51	2.63	2.74	35	2.85	2.96	3.08	3.19	3.30
2.30	2.41	2.52	2.63	2.75	40	2.86	2.97	3.08	3.20	3.31
2.30	2.41	2.53	2.64	2.75	45	2.86	2.98	3.09	3.20	3.31
2.31	2.42	2.53	2.64	2.76	50	2.87	2.98	3.09	3.21	3.32
2.31	2.42	2.54	2.65	2.76	55	2.87	2.99	3.10	3.21	3.32
2.32	2.43	2.54	2.66	2.77	60	2.88	2.99	3.11	3.22	3.33
2.32	2.44	2.55	2.66	2.77	65	2.89	3.00	3.11	3.22	3.34
2.33	2.44	2.55	2.67	2.78	70	2.89	3.00	3.12	3.23	3.34
2.33	2.45	2.56	2.67	2.78	75	2.90	3.01	3.12	3.23	3.35
2.34	2.45	2.57	2.68	2.79	80	2.90	3.02	3.13	3.24	3.35
2.35	2.46	2.57	2.68	2.80	85	2.91	3.02	3.13	3.25	3.36
2.35	2.46	2.58	2.69	2.80	90	2.91	3.03	3.14	3.25	3.36
2.36	2.47	2.58	2.69	2.81	95	2.92	3.03	3.14	3.26	3.37

POUNDS

3000	3100	3200	3300	3400		3500	3600	3700	3800	3900
		AMOUNT						AMOUNT		
3.38	3.49	3.60	3.71	3.83		3.94	4.05	4.16	4.28	4.39
3.38	3.49	3.61	3.72	3.83	5	3.94	4.06	4.17	4.28	4.39
3.39	3.50	3.61	3.72	3.84	10	3.95	4.06	4.17	4.29	4.40
3.39	3.50	3.62	3.73	3.84	15	3.95	4.07	4.18	4.29	4.40
3.40	3.51	3.62	3.74	3.85	20	3.96	4.07	4.19	4.30	4.41
3.40	3.52	3.63	3.74	3.85	25	3.97	4.08	4.19	4.30	4.42
3.41	3.52	3.63	3.75	3.86	30	3.97	4.08	4.20	4.31	4.42
3.41	3.53	3.64	3.75	3.86	35	3.98	4.09	4.20	4.31	4.43
3.42	3.53	3.65	3.76	3.87	40	3.98	4.10	4.21	4.32	4.43
3.43	3.54	3.65	3.76	3.88	45	3.99	4.10	4.21	4.33	4.44
3.43	3.54	3.66	3.77	3.88	50	3.99	4.11	4.22	4.33	4.44
3.44	3.55	3.66	3.77	3.89	55	4.00	4.11	4.22	4.34	4.45
3.44	3.56	3.67	3.78	3.89	60	4.01	4.12	4.23	4.34	4.46
3.45	3.56	3.67	3.79	3.90	65	4.01	4.12	4.24	4.35	4.46
3.45	3.57	3.68	3.79	3.90	70	4.02	4.13	4.24	4.35	4.47
3.46	3.57	3.68	3.80	3.91	75	4.02	4.13	4.25	4.36	4.47
3.47	3.58	3.69	3.80	3.92	80	4.03	4.14	4.25	4.37	4.48
3.47	3.58	3.70	3.81	3.92	85	4.03	4.15	4.26	4.37	4.48
3.48	3.59	3.70	3.81	3.93	90	4.04	4.15	4.26	4.38	4.49
3.48	3.59	3.71	3.82	3.93	95	4.04	4.16	4.27	4.38	4.49

Even tons, 51 to 100 inclusive.

51-60		61-70		71-80		81-90		91-100	
T	Am't	T	Am't	T	Am't	T	Am't	T	Am't
51	114.75	61	137.25	71	159.75	81	182.25	91	204.75
52	117.00	62	139.50	72	162.00	82	184.50	92	207.00
53	119.25	63	141.75	73	164.25	83	186.75	93	209.25
54	121.50	64	144.00	74	166.50	84	189.00	94	211.50
55	123.75	65	146.25	75	168.75	85	191.25	95	213.75
56	126.00	66	148.50	76	171.00	86	193.50	96	216.00
57	128.25	67	150.75	77	173.25	87	195.75	97	218.25
58	130.50	68	153.00	78	175.50	88	198.00	98	220.50
59	132.75	69	155.25	79	177.75	89	200.25	99	222.75
60	135.00	70	157.50	80	180.00	90	202.50	100	225.00

700	1575	800	1800	900	2025	1000	2250	1100	2475

POUNDS

Under 100	100	200	300	400		500	600	700	800	900
		AMOUNT						AMOUNT		
	.13	.25	.38	.50		.63	.75	.88	1.00	1.13
.01	).13	.26	.38	.51	5	.63	.76	.88	1.01	1.13
.01	.14	.26	.39	.51	10	.64	.76	.89	1.01	1.14
.02	.14	.27	.39	.52	15	.64	.77	.89	1.02	1.14
.03	.15	.28	.40	.53	20	.65	.78	.90	1.03	1.15
.03	.16	.28	.41	.53	25	.66	.78	.91	1.03	1.16
.04	.16	.29	.41	.54	30	.66	.79	.91	1.04	1.16
.04	.17	.29	.42	.54	35	.67	..79	.92	1.04	1.17
.05	.18	.30	.43	.55	40	.68	.80	.93	1.05	1.18
.06	.18	.31	.43	.56	45	.68	.81	.93	1.06	1.18
.06	.19	.31	.44	.56	50	.69	.81	.94	1.06	1.19
.07	.19	.32	.44	.57	55	.69	.82	.94	1.07	1.19
.08	.20	.33	.45	.58	60	.70	.83	.95	1.08	1.20
.08	.21	.33	.46	.58	65	.71	.83	.96	1.08	1.21
.09	.21	.34	.46	.59	70	.71	.84	.96	1.09	1.21
.09	.22	.34	.47	.59	75	.72	.84	.97	1.09	1.22
.10	.23	.35	.48	.60	80	.73	.85	.98	1.10	1.23
.11	.23	.36	.48	.61	85	.73	.86	.98	1.11	1.23
.11	.24	.36	.49	.61	90	.74	.86	.99	1.11	1.24
.12	.24	.37	.49	.62	95	.74	.87	.99	1.12	1.24

POUNDS

1000	1100	1200	1300	1400		1500	1600	1700	1800	1900
		AMOUNT						AMOUNT		
1.25	1.38	1.50	1.63	1.75		1.88	2.00	2.13	2.25	2.38
1.26	1.38	1.51	1.63	1.76	5	1.88	2.01	2.13	2.26	2.38
1.26	1.39	1.51	1.64	1.76	10	1.89	2.01	2.14	2.26	2.39
1.27	1.39	1.52	1.64	1.77	15	1.89	2.02	2.14	2.27	2.39
1.28	1.40	1.53	1.65	1.78	20	1.90	2.03	2.15	2.28	2.40
1.28	1.41	1.53	1.66	1.78	25	1.91	2.03	2.16	2.28	2.41
1.29	1.41	1.54	1.66	1.79	30	1.91	2.04	2.16	2.29	2.41
1.29	1.42	1.54	1.67	1.79	35	1.92	2.04	2.17	2.29	2.42
1.30	1.43	1.55	1.68	1.80	40	1.93	2.05	2.18	2.30	2.43
1.31	1.43	1.56	1.68	1.81	45	1.93	2.06	2.18	2.31	2.43
1.31	1.44	1.56	1.69	1.81	50	1.94	2.06	2.19	2.31	2.44
1.32	1.44	1.57	1.69	1.82	55	1.94	2.07	2.19	2.32	2.44
1.33	1.45	1.58	1.70	1.83	60	1.95	2.08	2.20	2.33	2.45
1.33	1.46	1.58	1.71	1.83	65	1.96	2.08	2.21	2.33	2.46
1.34	1.46	1.59	1.71	1.84	70	1.96	2.09	2.21	2.34	2.46
1.34	1.47	1.59	1.72	1.84	75	1.97	2.09	2.22	2.34	2.47
1.35	1.48	1.60	1.73	1.85	80	1.98	2.10	2.23	2.35	2.48
1.36	1.48	1.61	1.73	1.86	85	1.98	2.11	2.23	2.36	2.48
1.36	1.49	1.61	1.74	1.86	90	1.99	2.11	2.24	2.36	2.49
1.37	1.49	1.62	1.74	1.87	95	1.99	2.12	2.24	2.37	2.49

Even tons, 1 to 50 inclusive.

1-10		11-20		21-30		31-40		41-50	
T	Am't	T	Am't	T	Am't	T	Am't	T	Am't
1	2.50	11	27.50	21	52.50	31	77.50	41	102.50
2	5.00	12	30.00	22	55.00	32	80.00	42	105.00
3	7.50	13	32.50	23	57.50	33	82.50	43	107.50
4	10.00	14	35.00	24	60.00	34	85.00	44	110.00
5	12.50	15	37.50	25	62.50	35	87.50	45	112.50
6	15.00	16	40 00	26	65.00	36	90.00	46	115.00
7	17.50	17	42.50	27	67.50	37	92.50	47	117.50
8	20.00	18	45.00	28	70.00	38	95.00	48	120.00
9	22.50	19	47.50	29	72.50	39	97.50	49	122.50
10	25.00	20	50.00	30	75.00	40	100.00	50	125.00

200	500	300	750	400	1000	500	1250	600	1500

—————POUNDS—————

2000	2100	2200	2300	2400		2500	2600	2700	2800	2900
		—AMOUNT—						—AMOUNT—		
2.50	2.63	2.75	2.88	3.00		3.13	3.25	3.38	3.50	3.63
2.51	2.63	2.76	2.88	3.01	5	3.13	3.26	3.38	3.51	3.63
2.51	2.64	2.76	2.89	3.01	10	3.14	3.26	3.39	3.51	3.64
2.52	2.64	2.77	2.89	3.02	15	3.14	3.27	3.39	3.52	3.64
2.53	2.65	2.78	2.90	3.03	20	3.15	3.28	3.40	3.53	3.65
2.53	2.66	2.78	2.91	3.03	25	3.16	3.28	3.41	3.53	3.66
2.54	2.66	2.79	2.91	3.04	30	3.16	3.29	3.41	3.54	3.66
2.54	2.67	2.79	2.92	3.04	35	3.17	3.29	3.42	3.54	3.67
2.55	2.68	2.80	2.93	3.05	40	3.18	3.30	3.43	3.55	3.68
2.56	2.68	2.81	2.93	3.06	45	3.18	3.31	3.43	3.56	3.68
2.56	2.69	2.81	2.94	3.06	50	3.19	3.31	3.44	3.56	3.69
2.57	2.69	2.82	2.94	3.07	55	3.19	3.32	3.44	3.57	3.69
2.58	2.70	2.83	2.95	3.08	60	3.20	3.33	3.45	3.58	3.70
2.58	2.71	2.83	2.96	3.08	65	3.21	3.33	3.46	3.58	3.71
2.59	2.71	2.84	2.96	3.09	70	3.21	3.34	3.46	3.59	3.71
2.59	2.72	2.84	2.97	3.09	75	3.22	3.34	3.47	3.59	3.72
2.60	2.73	2.85	2.98	3.10	80	3.23	3.35	3.48	3.60	3.73
2.61	2.73	2.86	2.98	3.11	85	3.23	3.36	3.48	3.61	3.73
2.61	2.74	2.86	2.99	3.11	90	3.24	3.36	3.49	3.61	3.74
2.62	2.74	2.87	2.99	3.12	95	3.24	3.37	3.49	3.62	3.74

—————POUNDS—————

3000	3100	3200	3300	3400		3500	3600	3700	3800	3900
		—AMOUNT—						—AMOUNT—		
3.75	3.88	4.00	4.13	4.25		4.38	4.50	4.63	4.75	4.88
3.76	3.88	4.01	4.13	4.26	5	4.38	4.51	4.63	4.76	4.88
3.76	3.89	4.01	4.14	4.26	10	4.39	4.51	4.64	4.76	4.89
3.77	3.89	4.02	4.14	4.27	15	4.39	4.52	4.64	4.77	4.89
3.78	3.90	4.03	4.15	4.28	20	4.40	4.53	4.65	4.78	4.90
3.78	3.91	4.03	4.16	4.28	25	4.41	4.53	4.66	4.78	4.91
3.79	3.91	4.04	4.16	4.29	30	4.41	4.54	4.66	4.79	4.91
3.79	3.92	4.04	4.17	4.29	35	4.42	4.54	4.67	4.79	4.92
3.80	3.93	4.05	4.18	4.30	40	4.43	4.55	4.68	4.80	4.93
3.81	3.93	4.06	4.18	4.31	45	4.43	4.56	4.68	4.81	4.93
3.81	3.94	4.06	4.19	4.31	50	4.44	4.56	4.69	4.81	4.94
3.82	3.94	4.07	4.19	4.32	55	4.44	4.57	4.69	4.82	4.94
3.83	3.95	4.08	4.20	4.33	60	4.45	4.58	4.70	4.83	4.95
3.83	3.96	4.08	4.21	4.33	65	4.46	4.58	4.71	4.83	4.96
3.84	3.96	4.09	4.21	4.34	70	4.46	4.59	4.71	4.84	4.96
3.84	3.97	4.09	4.22	4.34	75	4.47	4.59	4.72	4.84	4.97
3.85	3.98	4.10	4.23	4.35	80	4.48	4.60	4.73	4.85	4.98
3.86	3.98	4.11	4.23	4.36	85	4.48	4.61	4.73	4.86	4.98
3.86	3.99	4.11	4.24	4.36	90	4.49	4.61	4.74	4.86	4.99
3.87	3.99	4.12	4.24	4.37	95	4.49	4.62	4.74	4.87	4.99

Even tons, 51 to 100 inclusive.

51-60		61-70		71-80		81-90		91-100	
T	Am't	T	Am't	T	Am't	T	Am't	T	Am't
51	127.50	61	152.50	71	177.50	81	202.50	91	227.50
52	130.00	62	155.00	72	180.00	82	205.00	92	230.00
53	132.50	63	157.50	73	182.50	83	207.50	93	232.50
54	135.00	64	160.00	74	185.00	84	210.00	94	235.00
55	137.50	65	162.50	75	187.50	85	212.50	95	237.50
56	140.00	66	165.00	76	190.00	86	215.00	96	240.00
57	142.50	67	167.50	77	192.50	87	217.50	97	242.50
58	145.00	68	170.00	78	195.00	88	220.00	98	245.00
59	147.50	69	172.50	79	197.50	89	222.50	99	247.50
60	150.00	70	175.00	80	200.00	90	225.00	100	250.00

700	1750	800	2000	900	2250	1000	2500	1100	2750

POUNDS

Under 100	100	200	300	400		500	600	700	800	900
	AMOUNT						AMOUNT			
	.14	.28	.41	.55		.69	.83	.93	1.10	1.24
.01	.14	.28	.42	.56	5	.69	.83	.97	1.11	1.24
.01	.15	.29	.43	.56	10	.70	.84	.98	1.11	1.25
.02	.16	.30	.43	.57	15	.71	.85	.98	1.12	1.26
.03	.17	.30	.44	.58	20	.72	.85	.99	1.13	1.27
.03	.17	.31	.45	.58	25	.72	.86	1.00	1.13	1.27
.04	.18	.32	.45	.59	30	.73	.87	1.00	1.14	1.28
.05	.19	.32	.46	.60	35	.74	.87	1.01	1.15	1.29
.06	.19	.33	.47	.61	40	.74	.88	1.02	1.16	1.29
.06	.20	.34	.47	.61	45	.75	.89	1.02	1.16	1.30
.07	.21	.34	.48	.62	50	.76	.89	1.03	1.17	1.31
.08	.21	.35	.49	.63	55	.76	.90	1.04	1.18	1.31
.08	.22	.36	.50	.63	60	.77	.91	1.05	1.18	1.32
.09	.23	.36	.50	.64	65	.78	.91	1.05	1.19	1.33
.10	.23	.37	.51	.65	70	.78	.92	1.06	1.20	1.33
.10	.24	.38	.52	.65	75	.79	.93	1.07	1.20	1.34
.11	.25	.39	.52	.66	80	.80	.94	1.07	1.21	1.35
.12	.25	.39	.53	.67	85	.80	.94	1.08	1.22	1.35
.12	.26	.40	.54	.67	90	.81	.95	1.09	1.22	1.36
.13	.27	.41	.54	.68	95	.82	.96	1.09	1.23	1.37

POUNDS

1000	1100	1200	1300	1400		1500	1600	1700	1800	1900
	AMOUNT						AMOUNT			
1.38	1.51	1.65	1.79	1.93		2.06	2.20	2.34	2.48	2.61
1.38	1.52	1.66	1.79	1.93	5	2.07	2.21	2.34	2.48	2.62
1.39	1.53	1.66	1.80	1.94	10	2.08	2.21	2.35	2.49	2.63
1.40	1.53	1.67	1.81	1.95	15	2.08	2.22	2.36	2.50	2.63
1.40	1.54	1.68	1.82	1.95	20	2.09	2.23	2.37	2.50	2.64
1.41	1.55	1.68	1.82	1.96	25	2.10	2.23	2.37	2.51	2.65
1.42	1.55	1.69	1.83	1.97	30	2.10	2.24	2.38	2.52	2.65
1.42	1.56	1.70	1.84	1.97	35	2.11	2.25	2.39	2.52	2.66
1.43	1.57	1.71	1.84	1.98	40	2.12	2.26	2.39	2.53	2.67
1.44	1.57	1.71	1.85	1.99	45	2.12	2.26	2.40	2.54	2.67
1.44	1.58	1.72	1.86	1.99	50	2.13	2.27	2.41	2.54	2.68
1.45	1.59	1.73	1.86	2.00	55	2.14	2.28	2.41	2.55	2.69
1.46	1.60	1.73	1.87	2.01	60	2.15	2.28	2.42	2.56	2.70
1.46	1.60	1.74	1.88	2.01	65	2.15	2.29	2.43	2.56	2.70
1.47	1.61	1.75	1.88	2.02	70	2.16	2.30	2.43	2.57	2.71
1.48	1.62	1.75	1.89	2.03	75	2.17	2.30	2.44	2.58	2.72
1.49	1.62	1.76	1.90	2.04	80	2.17	2.31	2.45	2.59	2.72
1.49	1.63	1.77	1.90	2.04	85	2.18	2.32	2.45	2.59	2.73
1.50	1.64	1.77	1.91	2.05	90	2.19	2.32	2.46	2.60	2.74
1.51	1.64	1.78	1.92	2.06	95	2.19	2.33	2.47	2.61	2.74

Even tons, 1 to 50 inclusive.

1-10		11-20		21-30		31-40		41-50	
T	Am't	T	Am't	T	Am't	T	Am't	T	Am't
1	2.75	11	30.25	21	57.75	31	85.25	41	112.75
2	5.50	12	33.00	22	60.50	32	88.00	42	115.50
3	8.25	13	35.75	23	63.25	33	90.75	43	118.25
4	11.00	14	38.50	24	66.00	34	93.50	44	121.00
5	13.75	15	41.25	25	68.75	35	96.25	45	123.75
6	16.50	16	44.00	26	71.50	36	99.00	46	126.50
7	19.25	17	46.75	27	74.25	37	101.75	47	129.25
8	22.00	18	49.50	28	77.00	38	104.50	48	132.00
9	24.75	19	52.25	29	79.75	39	107.25	49	134.75
10	27.50	20	55.00	30	82.50	40	110.00	50	137.50
200	550	300	825	400	1100	500	1375	600	1650

—POUNDS—

2000	2100	2200	2300	2400		2500	2600	2700	2800	2900
		AMOUNT						AMOUNT		
2.75	2.89	3.03	3.16	3.30	5	3.44	3.58	3.71	3.85	3.99
2.76	2.89	3.03	3.17	3.31	5	3.44	3.58	3.72	3.86	3.99
2.76	2.90	3.04	3.18	3.31	10	3.45	3.59	3 73	3.86	4.00
2.77	2.91	3.05	3.18	3.32	15	3.46	3.60	3.73	3.87	4.01
2.78	2.92	3.05	3.19	3.33	20	3.47	3.60	3.74	3.88	4.02
2.78	2.92	3.06	3.20	3.33	25	3.47	3.61	3.75	3.88	4.02
2.79	2.93	3.07	3.20	3.34	30	3.48	3.62	3.75	3.89	4.03
2.80	2.94	3.07	3.21	3.35	35	3.49	3.62	3.76	3.90	4.04
2.81	2.94	3.08	3.22	3.36	40	3.49	3.63	3.77	3.91	4.04
2.81	2.95	3.09	3.22	3.36	45	3 50	3.64	3.77	3.91	4.05
2.82	2.96	3.09	3.23	3.37	50	3.51	3.64	3.78	3.92	4.06
2.83	2.96	3.10	3.24	3.38	55	3.51	3.65	3.79	3.93	4.06
2.83	2.97	3.11	3.25	3.38	60	3.52	3.66	3.80	3.93	4.07
2.84	2.98	3.11	3.25	3.39	65	3.53	3.66	3.80	3.94	4.08
2 85	2.98	3.12	3.26	3.40	70	3.53	3.67	3.81	3.95	4.08
2.85	2.99	3.13	3.27	3.40	75	3.54	3.68	3.82	3.95	4.09
2.86	3.00	3.14	3.27	3.41	80	3.55	3.69	3.82	3.96	4.10
2.87	3.00	3.14	3.28	3.42	85	3.55	3.69	3.83	3.97	4.10
2.87	3.01	3.15	3.29	3.42	90	3.56	3.70	3.84	3.97	4.11
2.88	3.02	3.16	3.29	3.43	95	3.57	3.71	3.84	3.98	4.12

—POUNDS—

3000	3100	3200	3300	3400		3500	3600	3700	3800	3900
		AMOUNT						AMOUNT		
4.13	4.26	4.40	4.54	4.68	5	4.81	4.95	5.09	5.23	5.36
4.13	4.27	4.41	4.54	4.68	5	4.82	4.96	5.09	5.23	5.37
4.14	4.28	4.41	4.55	4.69	10	4.83	4.96	5.10	5.24	5.38
4.15	4.28	4.42	4.56	4.70	15	4.83	4.97	5.11	5.25	5.38
4.15	4.29	4.43	4.57	4.70	20	4.84	4.98	5.12	5.25	5.39
4.16	4.30	4.43	4.57	4.71	25	4.85	4.98	5.12	5.26	5.40
4.17	4.30	4.44	4.58	4.72	30	4.85	4.99	5.13	5.27	5.40
4.17	4.31	4.45	4.59	4.72	35	4.86	5.00	5.14	5.27	5.41
4.18	4.32	4.46	4.59	4.73	40	4.87	5.01	5.14	5.28	5.42
4.19	4.32	4.46	4.60	4.74	45	4.87	5.01	5.15	5.29	5.42
4.19	4.33	4.47	4.61	4.74	50	4.88	5.02	5.16	5.29	5.43
4.20	4.34	4.48	4.61	4.75	55	4.89	5.03	5.16	5.30	5.44
4.21	4.35	4.48	4.62	4.76	60	4.90	5.03	5.17	5.31	5.45
4.21	4.35	4.49	4.63	4.76	65	4.90	5.04	5.18	5.31	5.45
4.22	4.36	4.50	4.63	4.77	70	4.91	5.05	5.18	5.32	5.46
4.23	4.37	4.50	4.64	4.78	75	4.92	5.05	5.19	5.33	5.47
4.24	4.37	4.51	4.65	4.79	80	4.92	5.06	5.20	5.34	5.47
4.24	4.38	4.52	4.65	4.79	85	4.93	5.07	5.20	5.34	5.48
4.25	4.39	4.52	4.66	4.80	90	4.94	5.07	5.21	5.35	5.49
4.26	4.39	4.53	4.67	4.81	95	4.94	5.08	5.22	5.36	5.49

Even tons, 51 to 100 inclusive.

51-60		61-70		71-80		81-90		91-100	
T	Am't	T	Am't	T	Am't	T	Am't	T	Am't
51	140.25	61	167.75	71	195.25	81	222.75	91	250.25
52	143.00	62	170.50	72	198.00	82	225.50	92	253.00
53	145.75	63	173.25	73	200.75	83	228.25	93	255.75
54	148.50	64	176.00	74	203.50	84	231.00	94	258.50
55	151.25	65	178.75	75	206.25	85	233.75	95	261.25
56	154.00	66	181.50	76	209.00	86	236.50	96	264.00
57	156.75	67	184.25	77	211.75	87	239.25	97	266.75
58	159.50	68	187.00	78	214.50	88	242.00	98	269.50
59	162.25	69	189.75	79	217.25	89	244.75	99	272.25
60	165.00	70	192.50	80	220.00	90	247.50	100	275.00

700	1925	800	2200	900	2475	1000	2750	1100	3025

POUNDS

Under 100	100	200	300	400		500	600	700	800	900
	AMOUNT						AMOUNT			
	.15	.30	.45	.60		.75	.90	1.05	1.20	1.35
.01	.16	.31	.46	.61	5	.76	.91	1.06	1.21	1.36
.02	.17	.32	.47	.62	10	.77	.92	1.07	1.22	1.37
.02	.17	.32	.47	.62	15	.77	.92	1.07	1.22	1.37
.03	.18	.33	.48	.63	20	.78	.93	1.08	1.23	1.38
.04	.19	.34	.49	.64	25	.79	.94	1.09	1.24	1.39
.05	.20	.35	.50	.65	30	.80	.95	1.10	1.25	1.40
.05	.20	.35	.50	.65	35	.80	.95	1.10	1.25 ·	1.40
.06	.21	.36	.51	.66	40	.81	.96	1.11	1.26	1.41
.07	.22	.37	.52	.67	45	.82	.97	1.12	1.27	1.42
.08	.23	.38	.53	.68	50	.83	.98	1.13	1.28	1.43
.08	.23	.38	.53	.68	55	.83	.98	1.13	1.28	1.43
.09	.24	.39	.54	.69	60	.84	.99	1.14	1.29	1.44
.10	.25	.40	.55	.70	65	.85	1.00	1.15	1.30	1.45
.11	.26	.41	.56	.71	70	.86	1.01	1.16	1.31	1.46
.11	.26	.41	.56	.71	75	.86	1.01	1.16	1.31	1.46
.12	.27	.42	.57	.72	80	.87	1.02	1.17	1.32	1.47
.13	.28	.43	.58	.73	85	.88	1.03	1.18	1.33	1.48
.14	.29	.44	.59	.74	90	.89	1.04	1.19	1.34	1.49
.14	.29	.44	.59	.74	95	.89	1.04	1.19	1.34	1.49

POUNDS

1000	1100	1200	1300	1400		1500	1600	1700	1800	1900
	AMOUNT						AMOUNT			
1.50	1.65	1.80	1.95	2.10		2.25	2.40	2.55	2.70	2.85
1.51	1.66	1.81	1.96	2.11	5	2.26	2.41	2.56	2.71	2.86
1.52	1.67	1.82	1.97	2.12	10	2.27	2.42	2.57	2.72	2.87
1.52	1.67	1.82	1.97	2.12	15	2.27	2.42	2.57	2.72	2.87
1.53	1.68	1.83	1.98	2.13	20	2.28	2.43	2.58	2.73	2.88
1.54	1.69	1.84	1.99	2.14	25	2.29	2.44	2.59	2.74	2.89
1.55	1.70	1.85	2.00	2.15	30	2.30	2.45	2.60	2.75	2.90
1.55	1.70	1.85	2.00	2.15	35	2.30	2.45	2.60	2.75	2.90
1.56	1.71	1.86	2.01	2.16	40	2.31	2.46	2.61	2.76	2.91
1.57	1.72	1.87	2.02	2.17	45	2.32	2.47	2.62	2.77	2.92
1.58	1.73	1.88	2.03	2.18	50	2.33	2.48	2.63	2.78	2.93
1.58	1.73	1.88	2.03	2.18	55	2.33	2.48	2.63	2.78	2.93
1.59	1.74	1.89	2.04	2.19	60	2.34	2.49	2.64	2.79	2.94
1.60	1.75	1.90	2.05	2.20	65	2.35	2.50	2.65	2.80	2.95
1.61	1.76	1.91	2.06	2.21	70	2.36	2.51	2.66	2.81	2.96
1.61	1.76	1.91	2.06	2.21	75	2.36	2.51	2.66	2.81	2.96
1.62	1.77	1.92	2.07	2.22	80	2.37	2.52	2.67	2.82	2.97
1.63	1.78	1.93	2.08	2.23	85	2.38	2.53	2.68	2.83	2.98
1.64	1.79	1.94	2.09	2.24	90	2.39	2.54	2.69	2.84	2.99
1.64	1.79	1.94	2.09	2.24	95	2.39	2.54	2.69	2.84	2.99

Even tons, 1 to 50 inclusive.

1-10		11-20		21-30		31-40		41-50	
T	Am't	T	Am't	T	Am't	T	Am't	T	Am't
1	3.00	11	33.00	21	63.00	31	93.00	41	123.00
2	6.00	12	36.00	22	66.00	32	96.00	42	126.00
3	9.00	13	39.00	23	69.00	33	99.00	43	129.00
4	12.00	14	42.00	24	72.00	34	102.00	44	132.00
5	15.00	15	45.00	25	75.00	35	105.00	45	135.00
6	18.00	16	48.00	26	78.00	36	108.00	46	138.00
7	21.00	17	51.00	27	81.00	37	111.00	47	141.00
8	24.00	18	54.00	28	84.00	38	114.00	48	144.00
9	27.00	19	57.00	29	87.00	39	117.00	49	147.00
10	30.00	20	60.00	30	90.00	40	120.00	50	150.00
200	600	**300**	900	**400**	1200	**500**	1500	**600**	1800

------ POUNDS ------

2000	2100	2200	2300	2400		2500	2600	2700	2800	2900
		—AMOUNT—						—AMOUNT—		
3.00	3.15	3.30	3.45	3.60		3.75	3.90	4.05	4.20	4.35
3.01	3.16	3.31	3.46	3.61	5	3.76	3.91	4.06	4.21	4.36
3.02	3.17	3.32	3.47	3.62	10	3.77	3.92	4.07	4.22	4.37
3.02	3.17	3.32	3.47	3.62	15	3.77	3.92	4.07	4.22	4.37
3.03	3.18	3.33	3.48	3.63	20	3.78	3.93	4.08	4.23	4.38
3.04	3.19	3.34	3.49	3.64	25	3.79	3.94	4.09	4.24	4.39
3.05	3.20	3.35	3.50	3.65	30	3.80	3.95	4.10	4.25	4.40
3.05	3.20	3.35	3.50	3.65	35	3.80	3.95	4.10	4.25	4.40
3.06	3.21	3.36	3.51	3.66	40	3.81	3.96	4.11	4.26	4.41
3.07	3.22	3.37	3.52	3.67	45	3.82	3.97	4.12	4.27	4.42
3.08	3.23	3.38	3.53	3.68	50	3.83	3.98	4.13	4.28	4.43
3.08	3.23	3.38	3.53	3.68	55	3.83	3.98	4.13	4.28	4.43
3.09	3.24	3.39	3.54	3.69	60	3.84	3.99	4.14	4.29	4.44
3.10	3.25	3.40	3.55	3.70	65	3.85	4.00	4.15	4.30	4.45
3.11	3.26	3.41	3.56	3.71	70	3.86	4.01	4.16	4.31	4.46
3.11	3.26	3.41	3.56	3.71	75	3.86	4.01	4.16	4.31	4.46
3.12	3.27	3.42	3.57	3.72	80	3.87	4.02	4.17	4.32	4.47
3.13	3.28	3.43	3.58	3.73	85	3.88	4.03	4.18	4.33	4.48
3.14	3.29	3.44	3.59	3.74	90	3.89	4.04	4.19	4.34	4.49
3.14	3.29	3.44	3.59	3.74	95	3.89	4.04	4.19	4.34	4.49

------ POUNDS ------

3000	3100	3200	3300	3400		3500	3600	3700	3800	3900
		—AMOUNT—						—AMOUNT—		
4.50	4.65	4.80	4.95	5.10		5.25	5.40	5.55	5.70	5.85
4.51	4.66	4.81	4.96	5.11	5	5.26	5.41	5.56	5.71	5.86
4.52	4.67	4.82	4.97	5.12	10	5.27	5.42	5.57	5.72	5.87
4.52	4.67	4.82	4.97	5.12	15	5.27	5.42	5.57	5.72	5.87
4.53	4.68	4.83	4.98	5.13	20	5.28	5.43	5.58	5.73	5.88
4.54	4.69	4.84	4.99	5.14	25	5.29	5.44	5.59	5.74	5.89
4.55	4.70	4.85	5.00	5.15	30	5.30	5.45	5.60	5.75	5.90
4.55	4.70	4.85	5.00	5.15	35	5.30	5.45	5.60	5.75	5.90
4.56	4.71	4.86	5.01	5.16	40	5.31	5.46	5.61	5.76	5.91
4.57	4.72	4.87	5.02	5.17	45	5.32	5.47	5.62	5 77	5.92
4.58	4.73	4.88	5.03	5.18	50	5.33	5.48	5.63	5.78	5.93
4.58	4.73	4.88	5.03	5.18	55	5.33	5.48	5.63	5.78	5.93
4.59	4.74	4.89	5.04	5.19	60	5.34	5.49	5.64	5.79	5.94
4.60	4.75	4.90	5.05	5.20	65	5.35	5.50	5.65	5.80	5.95
4.61	4.76	4.91	5.06	5.21	70	5.36	5.51	5.66	5.81	5.96
4.61	4.76	4.91	5.06	5.21	75	5.36	5.51	5.66	5.81	5.96
4.62	4.77	4.92	5.07	5.22	80	5.37	5.52	5.67	5.82	5.97
4.63	4.78	4.93	5.08	5.23	85	5.38	5.53	5.68	5.83	5.98
4.64	4.79	4.94	5.09	5.24	90	5.39	5.54	5.69	5.84	5.99
4.64	4.79	4.94	5.09	5.24	95	5.39	5.54	5.69	5.84	5.99

Even tons, 51 to 100 inclusive.

	51-60		61-70		71-80		81-90		91-100
T	Am't	T	Am't	T	Am't	T	Am't	T	Am't
51	153.00	61	183.00	71	213.00	81	243.00	91	273.00
52	156.00	62	186.00	72	216.00	82	246.00	92	276.00
53	159.00	63	189.00	73	219.00	83	249.00	93	279.00
54	162.00	64	192.00	74	222.00	84	252.00	94	282.00
55	165.00	65	195.00	75	225.00	85	255.00	95	285.00
56	168.00	66	198.00	76	228.00	86	258.00	96	288.00
57	171.00	67	201.00	77	231.00	87	261.00	97	291.00
58	174.00	68	204.00	78	234.00	88	264.00	98	294.00
59	177.00	69	207.00	79	237.00	89	267.00	99	297.00
60	180.00	70	210.00	80	240.00	90	270.00	100	300.00

700	2100	800	2400	900	2700	1000	3000	1100	3300

POUNDS

Under 100	100	200	300	400		500	600	700	800	900
	.16	.33	.49	.65		.81	.98	1.14	1.30	1.46
.01	.17	.33	.50	.66	5	.82	.98	1.15	1.31	1.47
.02	.18	.34	.50	.67	10	.83	.99	1.15	1.32	1.48
.02	.19	.35	.51	.67	15	.84	1.00	1.16	1.32	1.49
.03	.20	.36	.52	.68	20	.85	1.01	1.17	1.33	1.50
.04	.20	.37	.53	.69	25	.85	1.02	1.18	1.34	1.50
.05	.21	.37	.54	.70	30	.86	1.02	1.19	1.35	1.51
.06	.22	.38	.54	.71	35	.87	1.03	1.19	1.36	1.52
.07	.23	.39	.55	.72	40	.88	1.04	1.20	1.37	1.53
.07	.24	.40	.56	.72	45	.89	1.05	1.21	1.37	1.54
.08	.24	.41	.57	.73	50	.89	1.06	1.22	1.38	1.54
.09	.25	.41	.58	.74	55	.90	1.06	1.23	1.39	1.55
.10	.26	.42	.59	.75	60	.91	1.07	1.24	1.40	1.56
.11	.27	.43	.59	.76	65	.92	1.08	1.24	1.41	1.57
.11	.28	.44	.60	.76	70	.93	1.09	1.25	1.41	1.58
.12	.28	.45	.61	.77	75	.93	1.10	1.26	1.42	1.58
.13	.29	.46	.62	.78	80	.94	1.11	1.27	1.43	1.59
.14	.30	.46	.63	.79	85	.95	1.11	1.28	1.44	1.60
.15	.31	.47	.63	.80	90	.96	1.12	1.28	1.45	1.61
.15	.32	.48	.64	.80	95	.97	1.13	1.29	1.45	1.62

POUNDS

1000	1100	1200	1300	1400		1500	1600	1700	1800	1900
1.63	1.79	1.95	2.11	2.28		2.44	2.60	2.76	2.93	3.09
1.63	1.80	1.96	2.12	2.28	5	2.45	2.61	2.77	2.93	3.10
1.64	1.80	1.97	2.13	2.29	10	2.45	2.62	2.78	2.94	3.10
1.65	1.81	1.97	2.14	2.30	15	2.46	2.62	2.79	2.95	3.11
1.66	1.82	1.98	2.15	2.31	20	2.47	2.63	2.80	2.96	3.12
1.67	1.83	1.99	2.15	2.32	25	2.48	2.64	2.80	2.97	3.13
1.67	1.84	2.00	2.16	2.32	30	2.49	2.65	2.81	2.97	3.14
1.68	1.84	2.01	2.17	2.33	35	2.49	2.66	2.82	2.98	3.14
1.69	1.85	2.02	2.18	2.34	40	2.50	2.67	2.83	2.99	3.15
1.70	1.86	2.02	2.19	2.35	45	2.51	2.67	2.84	3.00	3.16
1.71	1.87	2.03	2.19	2.36	50	2.52	2.68	2.84	3.01	3.17
1.71	1.88	2.04	2.20	2.36	55	2.53	2.69	2.85	3.01	3.18
1.72	1.89	2.05	2.21	2.37	60	2.54	2.70	2.86	3.02	3.19
1.73	1.89	2.06	2.22	2.38	65	2.54	2.71	2.87	3.03	3.19
1.74	1.90	2.06	2.23	2.39	70	2.55	2.71	2.88	3.04	3.20
1.75	1.91	2.07	2.23	2.40	75	2.56	2.72	2.88	3.05	3.21
1.76	1.92	2.08	2.24	2.41	80	2.57	2.73	2.89	3.06	3.22
1.76	1.93	2.09	2.25	2.41	85	2.58	2.74	2.90	3.06	3.23
1.77	1.93	2.10	2.26	2.42	90	2.58	2.75	2.91	3.07	3.23
1.78	1.94	2.10	2.27	2.43	95	2.59	2.75	2.92	3.08	3.24

Even tons, 1 to 50 inclusive.

1-10		11-20		21-30		31-40		41-50	
T	Am't	T	Am't	T	Am't	T	Am't	T	Am't
1	3.25	11	35.75	21	68.25	31	100.75	41	133.25
2	6.50	12	39.00	22	71.50	32	104.00	42	136.50
3	9.75	13	42.25	23	74.75	33	107.25	43	139.75
4	13.00	14	45.50	24	78.00	34	110.50	44	143.00
5	16.25	15	48.75	25	81.25	35	113.75	45	146.25
6	19.50	16	52.00	26	84.50	36	117.00	46	149.50
7	22.75	17	55.25	27	87.75	37	120.25	47	152.75
8	26.00	18	58.50	28	91.00	38	123.50	48	156.00
9	29.25	19	61.75	29	94.25	39	126.75	49	159.25
10	32.50	20	65.00	30	97.50	40	130.00	50	162.50
200	650	300	975	400	1300	500	1625	600	1950

POUNDS

2000	2100	2200	2300	2400		2500	2600	2700	2800	2900
		AMOUNT						AMOUNT		
3.25	3.41	3.58	3.74	3.90		4.06	4.23	4.39	4.55	4.71
3.26	3.42	3.58	3.75	3.91	5	4.07	4.23	4.40	4.56	4.72
3.27	3.43	3.59	3.75	3.92	10	4.08	4.24	4.40	4.57	4.73
3.27	3.44	3.60	3.76	3.92	15	4.09	4.25	4.41	4.57	4.74
3.28	3.45	3.61	3.77	3.93	20	4.10	4.26	4.42	4.58	4.75
3.29	3.45	3.62	3.78	3.94	25	4.10	4.27	4.43	4.59	4.75
3.30	3.46	3.62	3.79	3.95	30	4.11	4.27	4.44	4.60	4.76
3.31	3.47	3.63	3.79	3.96	35	4.12	4.28	4.44	4.61	4.77
3.32	3.48	3.64	3.80	3.97	40	4.13	4.29	4.45	4.62	4.78
3.32	3.49	3.65	3.81	3.97	45	4.14	4.30	4.46	4.62	4.79
3.33	3.49	3.66	3.82	3.98	50	4.14	4.31	4.47	4.63	4.79
3.34	3.50	3.66	3.83	3.99	55	4.15	4.31	4.48	4.64	4.80
3.35	3.51	3.67	3.84	4.00	60	4.16	4.32	4.49	4.65	4.81
3.36	3.52	3.68	3.84	4.01	65	4.17	4.33	4.49	4.66	4.82
3.36	3.53	3.69	3.85	4.01	70	4.18	4.34	4.50	4.66	4.83
3.37	3.53	3.70	3.86	4.02	75	4.18	4.35	4.51	4.67	4.83
3.38	3.54	3.71	3.87	4.03	80	4.19	4.36	4.52	4.68	4.84
3.39	3.55	3.71	3.88	4.04	85	4.20	4.36	4.53	4.69	4.85
3.40	3.56	3.72	3.88	4.05	90	4.21	4.37	4.53	4.70	4.86
3.40	3.57	3.73	3.89	4.05	95	4.22	4.38	4.54	4.70	4.87

POUNDS

3000	3100	3200	3300	3400		3500	3600	3700	3800	3900
		AMOUNT						AMOUNT		
4.88	5.04	5.20	5.36	5.53		5.69	5.85	6.01	6.18	6.34
4.88	5.05	5.21	5.37	5.53	5	5.70	5.86	6.02	6.18	6.35
4.89	5.05	5.22	5.38	5.54	10	5.70	5.87	6.03	6.19	6.35
4.90	5.06	5.22	5.39	5.55	15	5.71	5.87	6.04	6.20	6.36
4.91	5.07	5.23	5.40	5.56	20	5.72	5.88	6.05	6.21	6.37
4.92	5.08	5.24	5.40	5.57	25	5.73	5.89	6.05	6.22	6.38
4.92	5.09	5.25	5.41	5.57	30	5.74	5.90	6.06	6.22	6.39
4.93	5.09	5.26	5.42	5.58	35	5.74	5.91	6.07	6.23	6.39
4.94	5.10	5.27	5.43	5.59	40	5.75	5.92	6.08	6.24	6.40
4.95	5.11	5.27	5.44	5.60	45	5.76	5.92	6.09	6.25	6.41
4.96	5.12	5.28	5.44	5.61	50	5.77	5.93	6.09	6.26	6.42
4.96	5.13	5.29	5.45	5.61	55	5.78	5.94	6.10	6.26	6.43
4.97	5.14	5.30	5.46	5.62	60	5.79	5.95	6.11	6.27	6.44
4.98	5.14	5.31	5.47	5.63	65	5.79	5.96	6.12	6.28	6.44
4.99	5.15	5.31	5.48	5.64	70	5.80	5.96	6.13	6.29	6.45
5.00	5.16	5.32	5.48	5.65	75	5.81	5.97	6.13	6.30	6.46
5.01	5.17	5.33	5.49	5.66	80	5.82	5.98	6.14	6.31	6.47
5.01	5.18	5.34	5.50	5.66	85	5.83	5.99	6.15	6.31	6.48
5.02	5.18	5.35	5.51	5.67	90	5.83	6.00	6.16	6.32	6.48
5.03	5.19	5.35	5.52	5.68	95	5.84	6.00	6.17	6.33	6.49

Even tons, 51 to 100 inclusive.

51-60		61-70		71-80		81-90		91-100	
T	Am't	T	Am't	T	Am't	T	Am't	T	Am't
51	165.75	61	198.25	71	230.75	81	263.25	91	295.75
52	169.00	62	201.50	72	234.00	82	266.50	92	299.00
53	172.25	63	204.75	73	237.25	83	269.75	93	302.25
54	175.50	64	208.00	74	240.50	84	273.00	94	305.50
55	178.75	65	211.25	75	243.75	85	276.25	95	308.75
56	182.00	66	214.50	76	247.00	86	279.50	96	312.00
57	185.25	67	217.75	77	250.25	87	282.75	97	315.25
58	188.50	68	221.00	78	253.50	88	286.00	98	318.50
59	191.75	69	224.25	79	256.75	89	289.25	99	321.75
60	195.00	70	227.50	80	260.00	90	292.50	100	325.00

700	2275	800	2600	900	2925	1000	3250	1100	3575

POUNDS

Under 100	100	200	300	400		500	600	700	800	900
	.18	.35	.53	.70		.88	1.05	1.23	1.40	1.58
.01	.18	.36	.53	.71	5	.88	1.06	1.23	1.41	1.58
.02	.19	.37	.54	.72	10	.89	1.07	1.24	1.42	1.59
.03	.20	.38	.55	.73	15	.90	1.08	1.25	1.43	1.60
.04	.21	.39	.56	.74	20	.91	1.09	1.26	1.44	1.61
.04	.22	.39	.57	.74	25	.92	1.09	1.27	1.44	1.62
.05	.23	.40	.58	.75	30	.93	1.10	1.28	1.45	1.63
.06	.24	.41	.59	.76	35	.94	1.11	1.29	1.46	1.64
.07	.25	.42	.60	.77	40	.95	1.12	1.30	1.47	1.65
.08	.25	.43	.60	.78	45	.95	1.13	1.30	1.48	1.65
.09	.26	.44	.61	.79	50	.96	1.14	1.31	1.49	1.66
.10	.27	.45	.62	.80	55	.97	1.15	1.32	1.50	1.67
.11	.28	.46	.63	.81	60	.98	1.16	1.33	1.51	1.68
.11	.29	.46	.64	.81	65	.99	1.16	1.34	1.51	1.69
.12	.30	.47	.65	.82	70	1.00	1.17	1.35	1.52	1.70
.13	.31	.48	.66	.83	75	1.01	1.18	1.36	1.53	1.71
.14	.32	.49	.67	.84	80	1.02	1.19	1.37	1.54	1.72
.15	.32	.50	.67	.85	85	1.02	1.20	1.37	1.55	1.72
.16	.33	.51	.68	.86	90	1.03	1.21	1.38	1.56	1.73
.17	.34	.52	.69	.87	95	1.04	1.22	1.39	1.57	1.74

POUNDS

1000	1100	1200	1300	1400		1500	1600	1700	1800	1900
1.75	1.93	2.10	2.28	2.45		2.63	2.80	2.98	3.15	3.33
1.76	1.93	2.11	2.28	2.46	5	2.63	2.81	2.98	3.16	3.33
1.77	1.94	2.12	2.29	2.47	10	2.64	2.82	2.99	3.17	3.34
1.78	1.95	2.13	2.30	2.48	15	2.65	2.83	3.00	3.18	3.35
1.79	1.96	2.14	2.31	2.49	20	2.66	2.84	3.01	3.19	3.36
1.79	1.97	2.14	2.32	2.49	25	2.67	2.84	3.02	3.19	3.37
1.80	1.98	2.15	2.33	2.50	30	2.68	2.85	3.03	3.20	3.38
1.81	1.99	2.16	2.34	2.51	35	2.69	2.86	3.04	3.21	3.39
1.82	2.00	2.17	2.35	2.52	40	2.70	2.87	3.05	3.22	3.40
1.83	2.00	2.18	2.35	2.53	45	2.70	2.88	3.05	3.23	3.40
1.84	2.01	2.19	2.36	2.54	50	2.71	2.89	3.06	3.24	3.41
1.85	2.02	2.20	2.37	2.55	55	2.72	2.90	3.07	3.25	3.42
1.86	2.03	2.21	2.38	2.56	60	2.73	2.91	3.08	3.26	3.43
1.86	2.04	2.21	2.39	2.56	65	2.74	2.91	3.09	3.26	3.44
1.87	2.05	2.22	2.40	2.57	70	2.75	2.92	3.10	3.27	3.45
1.88	2.06	2.23	2.41	2.58	75	2.76	2.93	3.11	3.28	3.46
1.89	2.07	2.24	2.42	2.59	80	2.77	2.94	3.12	3.29	3.47
1.90	2.07	2.25	2.42	2.60	85	2.77	2.95	3.12	3.30	3.47
1.91	2.08	2.26	2.43	2.61	90	2.78	2.96	3.13	3.31	3.48
1.92	2.09	2.27	2.44	2.62	95	2.79	2.97	3.14	3.32	3.49

Even tons, 1 to 50 inclusive.

1-10		11-20		21-30		31-40		41-50	
T	Am't	T	Am't	T	Am't	T	Am't	T	Am't
1	3.50	11	38.50	21	73.50	31	108.50	41	143.50
2	7.00	12	42.00	22	77.00	32	112.00	42	147.00
3	10.50	13	45.50	23	80.50	33	115.50	43	150.50
4	14.00	14	49.00	24	84.00	34	119.00	44	154.00
5	17.50	15	52.50	25	87.50	35	122.50	45	157.50
6	21.00	16	56.00	26	91.00	36	126.00	46	161.00
7	24.50	17	59.50	27	94.50	37	129.50	47	164.50
8	28.00	18	63.00	28	98.00	38	133.00	48	168.00
9	31.50	19	66.50	29	101.50	39	136.50	49	171.50
10	35.00	20	70.00	30	105.00	40	140.00	50	175.00

200	700	300	1050	400	1400	500	1750	600	2100

(30)

POUNDS

2000	2100	2200	2300	2400		2500	2600	2700	2800	2900
		AMOUNT						AMOUNT		
3.50	3.68	3.85	4.03	4.20		4.38	4.55	4.73	4.90	5.08
3.51	3.68	3.86	4.03	4.21	5	4.38	4.56	4.73	4.91	5.08
3.52	3.69	3.87	4.04	4.22	10	4.39	4.57	4.74	4.92	5.09
3.53	3.70	3.88	4.05	4.23	15	4.40	4.58	4.75	4.93	5.10
3.54	3.71	3.89	4.06	4.24	20	4.41	4.59	4.76	4.94	5.11
3.54	3.72	3.89	4.07	4.24	25	4.42	4.59	4.77	4.91	5.12
3.55	3.73	3.90	4.08	4.25	30	4.43	4.60	4.78	4.95	5.13
3.56	3.74	3.91	4.09	4.26	35	4.44	4.61	4.79	4.96	5.14
3.57	3.75	3.92	4.10	4.27	40	4.45	4.62	4.80	4.97	5.15
3.58	3.75	3.93	4.10	4.28	45	4.45	4.63	4.80	4.98	5.15
3.59	3.76	3.94	4.11	4.29	50	4.46	4.64	4.81	4.99	5.16
3.60	3.77	3.95	4.12	4.30	55	4.47	4.65	4.82	5.00	5.17
3.61	3.78	3.96	4.13	4.31	60	4.48	4.66	4.83	5.01	5.18
3.61	3.79	3.96	4.14	4.31	65	4.49	4.66	4.84	5.01	5.19
3.62	3.80	3.97	4.15	4.32	70	4.50	4.67	4.85	5.02	5.20
3 63	3.81	3.98	4.16	4.33	75	4.51	4.68	4.86	5.03	5.21
3.64	3.82	3.99	4.17	4.34	80	4.52	4.69	4.87	5.04	5.22
3.65	3.82	4.00	4.17	4.35	85	4.52	4.70	4.87	5.05	5.22
3.66	3.83	4.01	4.18	4.36	90	4.53	4.71	4.88	5.06	5.23
3.67	3.84	4.02	4.19	4.37	95	4.54	4.72	4.89	5.07	5.24

POUNDS

3000	3100	3200	3300	3400		3500	3600	3700	3800	3900
		AMOUNT						AMOUNT		
5.25	5.43	5.60	5.78	5.95		6.13	6.30	6.48	6.65	6.83
5.26	5.43	5.61	5.78	5.96	5	6.13	6.31	6.48	6.66	6.83
5.27	5.44	5.62	5.79	5.97	10	6.14	6.32	6.49	6.67	6.84
5.28	5.45	5.63	5.80	5.98	15	6.15	6.33	6.50	6.68	6.85
5.29	5.46	5.64	5.81	5.99	20	6.16	6.34	6.51	6.69	6.86
5.29	5.47	5.64	5.82	5.99	25	6.17	6.34	6.52	6.69	6.87
5.30	5.48	5.65	5.83	6.00	30	6.18	6.35	6.53	6.70	6.88
5.31	5.49	5.66	5.84	6.01	35	6.19	6.36	6.54	6.71	6.89
5.32	5.50	5.67	5.85	6.02	40	6.20	6.37	6.55	6.72	6.90
5.33	5.50	5.68	5.85	6.03	45	6.20	6.38	6.55	6.73	6.90
5.34	5.51	5.69	5.86	6.04	50	6.21	6.39	6.56	6.74	6.91
5.35	5.52	5.70	5.87	6.05	55	6.22	6.40	6.57	6.75	6.92
5.36	5.53	5.71	5.88	6.06	60	6.23	6.41	6.58	6.76	6.93
5.36	5.54	5.71	5.89	6.06	65	6.24	6.41	6.59	6.76	6.94
5.37	5.55	5.72	5.90	6.07	70	6.25	6.42	6.60	6.77	6.95
5.38	5.56	5.73	5.91	6.08	75	6.26	6.43	6.61	6.78	6.96
5.39	5.57	5.74	5.92	6.09	80	6.27	6.44	6.62	6.79	6.97
5.40	5.57	5.75	5.92	6.10	85	6.27	6.45	6.62	6.80	6.97
5.41	5.58	5.76	5.93	6.11	90	6.28	6.46	6.63	6.81	6.98
5.42	5.59	5.77	5.94	6.12	95	6.29	6.47	6.64	6.82	6.99

Even tons, 51 to 100 inclusive.

51-60		61-70		71-80		81-90		91-100	
T	Am't	T	Am't	T	Am't	T	Am't	T	Am't
51	178.50	61	213.50	71	248.50	81	283.50	91	318.50
52	182.00	62	217.00	72	252.00	82	287.00	92	322.00
53	185.50	63	220.50	73	255.50	83	290.50	93	325.50
54	189.00	64	224.00	74	259.00	84	294.00	94	329.00
55	192.50	65	227.50	75	262.50	85	297.50	95	332.50
56	196.00	66	231.00	76	266.00	86	301.00	96	336.00
57	199.50	67	234.50	77	269.50	87	304.50	97	339.50
58	203.00	68	238.00	78	273.00	88	308.00	98	343.00
59	206.50	69	241.50	79	276.50	89	311.50	99	346.50
60	210.00	70	245.00	80	280.00	90	315.00	100	350.00

700	2450	800	2800	900	3150	1000	3500	1100	3850

POUNDS

Under 100	100	200	300	400		500	600	700	800	900
	AMOUNT						AMOUNT			
	.19	.38	.56	.75		.94	1.13	1.31	1.50	1.69
.01	.20	.38	.57	.76	5	.95	1.13	1.32	1.51	1.70
.02	.21	.39	.58	.77	10	.96	1.14	1.33	1.52	1.71
.03	.22	.40	.59	.78	15	.97	1.15	1.34	1.53	1.72
.04	.23	.41	.60	.79	20	.98	1.16	1.35	1.54	1.73
.05	.23	.42	.61	.80	25	.98	1.17	1.36	1.55	1.73
.06	.24	.43	.62	.81	30	.99	1.18	1.37	1.56	1.74
.07	.25	.44	.63	.82	35	1.00	1.19	1.38	1.57	1.75
.08	.26	.45	.64	.83	40	1.01	1.20	1.39	1.58	1.76
.08	.27	.46	.65	.83	45	1.02	1.21	1.40	1.58	1.77
.09	.28	.47	.66	.84	50	1.03	1.22	1.41	1.59	1.78
.10	.29	.48	.67	.85	55	1.04	1.23	1.42	1.60	1.79
.11	.30	.49	.68	.86	60	1.05	1.24	1.43	1.61	1.80
.12	.31	.50	.68	.87	65	1.06	1.25	1.43	1.62	1.81
.13	.32	.51	.69	.88	70	1.07	1.26	1.44	1.63	1.82
.14	.33	.52	.70	.89	75	1.08	1.27	1.45	1.64	1.83
.15	.34	.53	.71	.90	80	1.09	1.28	1.46	1.65	1.84
.16	.35	.53	.72	.91	85	1.10	1.28	1.47	1.66	1.85
.17	.36	.54	.73	.92	90	1.11	1.29	1.48	1.67	1.86
.18	.37	.55	.74	.93	95	1.12	1.30	1.49	1.68	1.87

POUNDS

1000	1100	1200	1300	1400		1500	1600	1700	1800	1900
		AMOUNT						AMOUNT		
1.88	2.06	2.25	2.44	2.63		2.81	3.00	3.19	3.38	3.56
1.88	2.07	2.26	2.45	2.63	5	2.82	3.01	3.20	3.38	3.57
1.89	2.08	2.27	2.46	2.64	10	2.83	3.02	3.21	3.39	3.58
1.90	2.09	2.28	2.47	2.65	15	2.84	3.03	3.22	3.40	3.59
1.91	2.10	2.29	2.48	2.66	20	2.85	3.04	3.23	3.41	3.60
1.92	2.11	2.30	2.48	2.67	25	2.86	3.05	3.23	3.42	3.61
1.93	2.12	2.31	2.49	2.68	30	2.87	3.06	3.24	3.43	3.62
1.94	2.13	2.32	2.50	2.69	35	2.88	3.07	3.25	3.44	3.63
1.95	2.14	2.33	2.51	2.70	40	2.89	3.08	3.26	3.45	3.64
1.96	2.15	2.33	2.52	2.71	45	2.90	3.08	3.27	3.46	3.65
1.97	2.16	2.34	2.53	2.72	50	2.91	3.09	3.28	3.47	3.66
1.98	2.17	2.35	2.54	2.73	55	2.92	3.10	3.29	3.48	3.67
1.99	2.18	2.36	2.55	2.74	60	2.93	3.11	3.30	3.49	3.68
2.00	2.18	2.37	2.56	2.75	65	2.93	3.12	3.31	3.50	3.68
2.01	2.19	2.38	2.57	2.76	70	2.94	3.13	3.32	3.51	3.69
2.02	2.20	2.39	2.58	2.77	75	2.95	3.14	3.33	3.52	3.70
2.03	2.21	2.40	2.59	2.78	80	2.96	3.15	3.34	3.53	3.71
2.03	2.22	2.41	2.60	2.78	85	2.97	3.16	3.35	3.53	3.72
2.04	2.23	2.42	2.61	2.79	90	2.98	3.17	3.36	3.54	3.73
2.05	2.24	2.43	2.62	2.80	95	2.99	3.18	3.37	3.55	3.74

Even tons, 1 to 50 inclusive.

1-10		11-20		21-30		31-40		41-50	
T	Am't	T	Am't	T	Am't	T	Am't	T	Am't
1	3.75	11	41.25	21	78.75	31	116.25	41	153.75
2	7.50	12	45.00	22	82.50	32	120.00	42	157.50
3	11.25	13	48.75	23	86.25	33	123.75	43	161.25
4	15.00	14	52.50	24	90.00	34	127.50	44	165.00
5	18.75	15	56.25	25	93.75	35	131.25	45	168.75
6	22.50	16	60.00	26	97.50	36	135.00	46	172.50
7	26.25	17	63.75	27	101.25	37	138.75	47	176.25
8	30.00	18	67.50	28	105.00	38	142.50	48	180.00
9	33.75	19	71.25	29	108.75	39	146.25	49	183.75
10	37.50	20	75.00	30	112.50	40	150.00	50	187.50

200	750	300	1125	400	1500	500	1875	600	2250

———— POUNDS ————

2000	2100	2200	2300	2400		2500	2600	2700	2800	2900
		AMOUNT						AMOUNT		
3.75	3.94	4.13	4.31	4.50		4.69	4.88	5.06	5.25	5.44
3.76	3.95	4.13	4.32	4.51	5	4.70	4.88	5.07	5.26	5.45
3.77	3.96	4.14	4.33	4.52	10	4.71	4.89	5.08	5.27	5.46
3.78	3.97	4.15	4.34	4.53	15	4.72	4.90	5.09	5.28	5.47
3.79	3.98	4.16	4.35	4.54	20	4.73	4.91	5.10	5.29	5.48
3.80	3.98	4.17	4.36	4.55	25	4.73	4.92	5.11	5.30	5.48
3.81	3.99	4.18	4.37	4.56	30	4.74	4.93	5.12	5.31	5.49
3.82	4.00	4.19	4.38	4.57	35	4.75	4.94	5.13	5.32	5.50
3.83	4.01	4.20	4.39	4.58	40	4.76	4.95	5.14	5.33	5.51
3.83	4.02	4.21	4.40	4.58	45	4.77	4.96	5.15	5.33	5.52
3.84	4.03	4.22	4.41	4.59	50	4.78	4.97	5.16	5.34	5.53
3.85	4.04	4.23	4.42	4.60	55	4.79	4.98	5.17	5.35	5.54
3.86	4.05	4.24	4.43	4.61	60	4.80	4.99	5.18	5.36	5.55
3.87	4.06	4.25	4.43	4.62	65	4.81	5.00	5.18	5.37	5.56
3.88	4.07	4.26	4.44	4.63	70	4.82	5.01	5.19	5.38	5.57
3.89	4.08	4.27	4.45	4.64	75	4.83	5.02	5.20	5.39	5.58
3.90	4.09	4.28	4.46	4.65	80	4.84	5.03	5.21	5.40	5.59
3.91	4.10	4.28	4.47	4.66	85	4.85	5.03	5.22	5.41	5.60
3.92	4.11	4.29	4.48	4.67	90	4.86	5.04	5.23	5.42	5.61
3.93	4.12	4.30	4.49	4.68	95	4.87	5.05	5.24	5.43	5.62

———— POUNDS ————

3000	3100	3200	3300	3400		3500	3600	3700	3800	3900
		AMOUNT						AMOUNT		
5.63	5.81	6.00	6.19	6.38		6.56	6.75	6.94	7.13	7.31
5.63	5.82	6.01	6.20	6.38	5	6.57	6.76	6.95	7.13	7.32
5.64	5.83	6.02	6.21	6.39	10	6.58	6.77	6.96	7.14	7.33
5.65	5.84	6.03	6.22	6.40	15	6.59	6.78	6.97	7.15	7.34
5.66	5.85	6.04	6.23	6.41	20	6.60	6.79	6.98	7.16	7.35
5.67	5.86	6.05	6.23	6.42	25	6.61	6.80	6.98	7.17	7.36
5.68	5.87	6.06	6.24	6.43	30	6.62	6.81	6.99	7.18	7.37
5.69	5.88	6.07	6.25	6.44	35	6.63	6.82	7.00	7.19	7.38
5.70	5.89	6.08	6.26	6.45	40	6.64	6.83	7.01	7.20	7.39
5.71	5.90	6.08	6.27	6.46	45	6.65	6.83	7.02	7.21	7.40
5.72	5.91	6.09	6.28	6.47	50	6.66	6.84	7.03	7.22	7.41
5.73	5.92	6.10	6.29	6.48	55	6.67	6.85	7.04	7.23	7.42
5.74	5.93	6.11	6.30	6.49	60	6.68	6.86	7.05	7.24	7.43
5.75	5.93	6.12	6.31	6.50	65	6.68	6.87	7.06	7.25	7.43
5.76	5.94	6.13	6.32	6.51	70	6.69	6.88	7.07	7.26	7.44
5.77	5.95	6.14	6.33	6.52	75	6.70	6.89	7.08	7.27	7.45
5.78	5.96	6.15	6.34	6.53	80	6.71	6.90	7.09	7.28	7.46
5.78	5.97	6.16	6.35	6.53	85	6.72	6.91	7.10	7.28	7.47
5.79	5.98	6.17	6.36	6.54	90	6.73	6.92	7.11	7.29	7.48
5.80	5.99	6.18	6.37	6.55	95	6.74	6.93	7.12	7.30	7.49

Even tons, 51 to 100 inclusive.

51-60		61-70		71-80		81-90		91-100	
T	Am't	T	Am't	T	Am't	T	Am't	T	Am't
51	191.25	61	228.75	71	266.25	81	303.75	91	341.25
52	195.00	62	232.50	72	270.00	82	307.50	92	345.00
53	198.75	63	236.25	73	273.75	83	311.25	93	348.75
54	202.50	64	240.00	74	277.50	84	315.00	94	352.50
55	206.25	65	243.75	75	281.25	85	318.75	95	356.25
56	210.00	66	247.50	76	285.00	86	322.50	96	360.00
57	213.75	67	251.25	77	288.75	87	326.25	97	363.75
58	217.50	68	255.00	78	292.50	88	330.00	98	367.50
59	221.25	69	258.75	79	296.25	89	333.75	99	371.25
60	225.00	70	262.50	80	300.00	90	337.50	100	375.00

700	2625	800	3000	900	3375	1000	3750	1100	4125

POUNDS

Under 100	100	200	300	400		500	600	700	800	900
	AMOUNT							AMOUNT		
	.20	.40	.60	.80		1.00	1.20	1.40	1.60	1.80
.01	.21	.41	.61	.81	5	1.01	1.21	1.41	1.61	1.81
.02	.22	.42	.62	.82	10	1.02	1.22	1.42	1.62	1.82
.03	.23	.43	.63	.83	15	1.03	1.23	1.43	1.63	1.83
.04	.24	.44	.64	.84	20	1.04	1.24	1.44	1.64	1.84
.05	.25	.45	.65	.85	25	1.05	1.25	1.45	1.65	1.85
.06	.26	.46	.66	.86	30	1.06	1.26	1.46	1.66	1.86
.07	.27	.47	.67	.87	35	1.07	1.27	1.47	1.67	1.87
.08	.28	.48	.68	.88	40	1.08	1.28	1.48	1.68	1.88
.09	.29	.49	.69	.89	45	1.09	1.29	1.49	1.69	1.89
.10	.30	.50	.70	.90	50	1.10	1.30	1.50	1.70	1.90
.11	.31	.51	.71	.91	55	1.11	1.31	1.51	1.71	1.91
.12	.32	.52	.72	.92	60	1.12	1.32	1.52	1.72	1.92
.13	.33	.53	.73	.93	65	1.13	1.33	1.53	1.73	1.93
.14	.34	.54	.74	.94	70	1.14	1.34	1.54	1.74	1.94
.15	.35	.55	.75	.95	75	1.15	1.35	1.55	1.75	1.95
.16	.36	.56	.76	.96	80	1.16	1.36	1.56	1.76	1.96
.17	.37	.57	.77	.97	85	1.17	1.37	1.57	1.77	1.97
.18	.38	.58	.78	.98	90	1.18	1.38	1.58	1.78	1.98
.19	.39	.59	.79	.99	95	1.19	1.39	1.59	1.79	1.99

POUNDS

1000	1100	1200	1300	1400		1500	1600	1700	1800	1900
	AMOUNT							AMOUNT		
2.00	2.20	2.40	2.60	2.80		3.00	3.20	3.40	3.60	3.80
2.01	2.21	2.41	2.61	2.81	5	3.01	3.21	3.41	3.61	3.81
2.02	2.22	2.42	2.62	2.82	10	3.02	3.22	3.42	3.62	3.82
2.03	2.23	2.43	2.63	2.83	15	3.03	3.23	3.43	3.63	3.83
2.04	2.24	2.44	2.64	2.84	20	3.04	3.24	3.44	3.64	3.84
2.05	2.25	2.45	2.65	2.85	25	3.05	3.25	3.45	3.65	3.85
2.06	2.26	2.46	2.66	2.86	30	3.06	3.26	3.46	3.66	3.86
2.07	2.27	2.47	2.67	2.87	35	3.07	3.27	3.47	3.67	3.87
2.08	2.28	2.48	2.68	2.88	40	3.08	3.28	3.48	3.68	3.88
2.09	2.29	2.49	2.69	2.89	45	3.09	3.29	3.49	3.69	3.89
2.10	2.30	2.50	2.70	2.90	50	3.10	3.30	3.50	3.70	3.90
2.11	2.31	2.51	2.71	2.91	55	3.11	3.31	3.51	3.71	3.91
2.12	2.32	2.52	2.72	2.92	60	3.12	3.32	3.52	3.72	3.92
2.13	2.33	2.53	2.73	2.93	65	3.13	3.33	3.53	3.73	3.93
2.14	2.34	2.54	2.74	2.94	70	3.14	3.34	3.54	3.74	3.94
2.15	2.35	2.55	2.75	2.95	75	3.15	3.35	3.55	3.75	3.95
2.16	2.36	2.56	2.76	2.96	80	3.16	3.36	3.56	3.76	3.96
2.17	2.37	2.57	2.77	2.97	85	3.17	3.37	3.57	3.77	3.97
2.18	2.38	2.58	2.78	2.98	90	3.18	3.38	3.58	3.78	3.98
2.19	2.39	2.59	2.79	2.99	95	3.19	3.39	3.59	3.79	3.99

Even tons, 1 to 50 inclusive.

1-10		11-20		21-30		31-40		41-50	
T	Am't	T	Am't	T	Am't	T	Am't	T	Am't
1	4.00	11	44.00	21	84.00	31	124.00	41	164.00
2	8.00	12	48.00	22	88.00	32	128.00	42	168.00
3	12.00	13	52.00	23	92.00	33	132.00	43	172.00
4	16.00	14	56.00	24	96.00	34	136.00	44	176.00
5	20.00	15	60.00	25	100.00	35	140.00	45	180.00
6	24.00	16	64.00	26	104.00	36	144.00	46	184.00
7	28.00	17	68.00	27	108.00	37	148.00	47	188.00
8	32.00	18	72.00	28	112.00	38	152.00	48	192.00
9	36.00	19	76.00	29	116.00	39	156.00	49	196.00
10	40.00	20	80.00	30	120.00	40	160.00	50	200.00

200	800	300	1200	400	1600	500	2000	600	2400

POUNDS

2000	2100	2200	2300	2400		2500	2600	2700	2800	2900
		AMOUNT						AMOUNT		
4.00	4.20	4.40	4.60	4.80		5.00	5.20	5.40	5.60	5.80
4.01	4.21	4.41	4.61	4.81	5	5.01	5.21	5.41	5.61	5.81
4.02	4.22	4.42	4.62	4.82	10	5.02	5.22	5.42	5.62	5.82
4.03	4.23	4.43	4.63	4.83	15	5.03	5.23	5.43	5.63	5.83
4.04	4.24	4.44	4.64	4.84	20	5.04	5.24	5.44	5.64	5 84
4.05	4.25	4.45	4.65	4.85	25	5.05	5.25	5.45	5.65	5.85
4.06	4.26	4.46	4.66	4.86	30	5.06	5.26	5.46	5.66	5.86
4.07	4.27	4.47	4.67	4.87	35	5.07	5.27	5.47	5.67	5.87
4.08	4.28	4.48	4.68	4.88	40	5.08	5.28	5.48	5.68	5.88
4.09	4.29	4.49	4.69	4.89	45	5.09	5.29	5.49	5.69	5.89
4.10	4.30	4.50	4.70	4.90	50	5.10	5.30	5.50	5.70	5.90
4.11	4.31	4.51	4.71	4.91	55	5.11	5.31	5.51	5.71	5.91
4.12	4.32	4.52	4.72	4.92	60	5.12	5.32	5.52	5.72	5.92
4.13	4.33	4.53	4.73	4.93	65	5.13	5.33	5.53	5.73	5.93
4.14	4.34	4.54	4.74	4.94	70	5.14	5.34	5.54	5.74	5.94
4.15	4.35	4.55	4.75	4.95	75	5.15	5.35	5.55	5.75	5.95
4.16	4.36	4.56	4.76	4.96	80	5 16	5.36	5.56	5.76	5.96
4.17	4.37	4.57	4.77	4.97	85	5.17	5.37	5.57	5.77	5.97
4.18	4.38	4.58	4.78	4.98	90	5.18	5.38	5.58	5.78	5.98
4.19	4.39	4.59	4.79	4.99	95	5.19	5.39	5.59	5.79	5.99

POUNDS

3000	3100	3200	3300	3400		3500	3600	3700	3800	3900
		AMOUNT						AMOUNT		
6.00	6.20	6.40	6.60	6.80		7.00	7.20	7.40	7.60	7.80
6.01	6.21	6.41	6.61	6.81	5	7.01	7.21	7.41	7.61	7.81
6.02	6.22	6.42	6.62	6.82	10	7.02	7.22	7.42	7.62	7.82
6.03	6.23	6.43	6.63	6.83	15	7.03	7.23	7.43	7.63	7.83
6.04	6.24	6.44	6.64	6.84	20	7.04	7.24	7.44	7.64	7.84
6.05	6.25	6.45	6.65	6.85	25	7.05	7.25	7.45	7.65	7.85
6.06	6.26	6.46	6.66	6.86	30	7.06	7.26	7.46	7.66	7.86
6.07	6.27	6.47	6.67	6.87	35	7.07	7.27	7.47	7.67	7.87
6.08	6.28	6.48	6.68	6.88	40	7.08	7.28	7.48	7.68	7.88
6.09	6.29	6.49	6.69	6.89	45	7.09	7.29	7.49	7.69	7.89
6.10	6.30	6.50	6.70	6.90	50	7.10	7.30	7.50	7.70	7.90
6.11	6.31	6.51	6.71	6.91	55	7.11	7.31	7.51	7.71	7 91
6.12	6.32	6.52	6.72	6.92	60	7.12	7.32	7.52	7.72	7.92
6.13	6.33	6.53	6.73	6.93	65	7.13	7.33	7.53	7.73	7.93
6.14	6.34	6.54	6.74	6.94	70	7.14	7.34	7.54	7.74	7.94
6.15	6.35	6.55	6.75	6.95	75	7.15	7.35	7.55	7.75	7.95
6.16	6.36	6.56	6.76	6.96	80	7.16	7.36	7.56	7.76	7.96
6.17	6.37	6.57	6.77	6.97	85	7.17	7.37	7.57	7.77	7.97
6.18	6.38	6.58	6.78	6.98	90	7.18	7.38	7.58	7.78	7.98
6.19	6.39	6.59	6.79	6.99	95	7.19	7.39	7.59	7.79	7.99

Even tons, 51 to 100 inclusive.

	51-60		61-70		71-80		81-90		91-100
T	Am't	T	Am't	T	Am't	T	Am't	T	Am't
51	204.00	61	244.00	71	284.00	81	324.00	91	364.00
52	208.00	62	248.00	72	288.00	82	328.00	92	368.00
53	212.00	63	252.00	73	292.00	83	332.00	93	372.00
54	216.00	64	256.00	74	296.00	84	336.00	94	376.00
55	220.00	65	260.00	75	300.00	85	340.00	95	380.00
56	224.00	66	264.00	76	304.00	86	344.00	96	384.00
57	228.00	67	268.00	77	308.00	87	348.00	97	388.00
58	232.00	68	272.00	78	312.00	88	352.00	98	392.00
59	236.00	69	276.00	79	316.00	89	356.00	99	396.00
60	240.00	70	280.00	80	320.00	90	360.00	100	400.00

700	2800	800	3200	900	3600	1000	4000	1100	4400

POUNDS

Under 100	100	200	300	400		500	600	700	800	900
	AMOUNT							AMOUNT		
	.21	.43	.64	.85		1.06	1.28	1.49	1.70	1.91
.01	.22	.44	.65	.86	5	1.07	1.29	1.50	1.71	1.92
.02	.23	.45	.66	.87	10	1.08	1.30	1.51	1.72	1.93
.03	.24	.46	.67	.88	15	1.09	1.31	1.52	1.73	1.94
.04	.26	.47	.68	.89	20	1.11	1.32	1.53	1.74	1.96
.05	.27	.48	.69	.90	25	1.12	1.33	1.54	1.75	1.97
.06	.28	.49	.70	.91	30	1.13	1.34	1.55	1.76	1.98
.07	.29	.50	.71	.92	35	1.14	1.35	1.56	1.77	1.99
.09	.30	.51	.72	.94	40	1.15	1.36	1.57	1.79	2.00
.10	.31	.52	.73	.95	45	1.16	1.37	1.58	1.80	2.01
.11	.32	.53	.74	.96	50	1.17	1.38	1.59	1.81	2.02
.12	.33	.54	.75	.97	55	1.18	1.39	1.60	1.82	2.03
.13	.34	.55	.77	.98	60	1.19	1.40	1.62	1.83	2.04
.14	.35	.56	.78	.99	65	1.20	1.41	1.63	1.84	2.05
.15	.36	.57	.79	1.00	70	1.21	1.42	1 64	1.85	2.06
.16	.37	.58	.80	1.01	75	1.22	1.43	1.65	1.86	2.07
.17	.38	.60	.81	1.02	80	1.23	1.45	1.66	1.87	2.08
.18	.39	.61	.82	1.03	85	1.24	1.46	1.67	1.88	2.09
.19	.40	.62	.83	1.04	90	1.25	1.47	1.68	1.89	2.10
.20	.41	.63	.84	1.05	95	1.26	1.48	1.69	1.90	2.11

POUNDS

1000	1100	1200	1300	1400		1500	1600	1700	1800	1900
	AMOUNT							AMOUNT		
2.13	2.34	2.55	2.76	2.98		3.19	3.40	3.61	3.83	4.04
2.14	2.35	2.56	2.77	2.99	5	3.20	3.41	3.62	3.84	4.05
2.15	2.36	2.57	2.78	3.00	10	3.21	3.42	3.63	3.85	4.06
2.16	2.37	2.58	2.79	3.01	15	3.22	3.43	3.64	3.86	4.07
2.17	2.38	2.59	2.81	3.02	20	3.23	3.44	3.66	3.87	4.08
2.18	2.39	2.60	2.82	3.03	25	3.24	3.45	3.67	3.88	4.09
2.19	2.40	2.61	2.83	3.04	30	3.25	3.46	3.68	3.89	4.10
2.20	2.41	2.62	2.84	3.05	35	3.26	3.47	3.69	3.90	4.11
2.21	2.42	2.64	2.85	3.06	40	3.27	3.49	3.70	3.91	4.12
2.22	2.43	2.65	2.86	3.07	45	3.28	3.50	3.71	3.92	4.13
2.23	2.44	2.66	2.87	3.08	50	3.29	3.51	3.72	3.93	4.14
2.24	2.45	2.67	2.58	3.09	55	3.30	3.52	3.73	3.94	4.15
2.25	2.47	2.68	2.89	3.10	60	3.32	3.53	3.74	3.95	4.17
2.26	2.48	2.69	2.90	3.11	65	3.33	3.54	3.75	3.96	4.18
2.27	2.49	2.70	2.91	3.12	70	3.34	3.55	3.76	3.97	4.19
2.28	2.50	2.71	2.92	3.13	75	3.35	3.56	3.77	3.98	4.20
2.30	2.51	2.72	2.93	3.15	80	3.36	3.57	3.78	4.00	4.21
2.31	2.52	2.73	2.94	3.16	85	3.37	3.58	3.79	4.01	4.22
2.32	2.53	2.74	2.95	3.17	90	3.38	3.59	3.80	4.02	4.23
2.33	2.54	2.75	2.96	3.18	95	3.39	3.60	3.81	4.03	4.24

Even tons, 1 to 50 inclusive.

1-10		11-20		21-30		31-40		41-50	
T	Am't	T	Am't	T	Am't	T	Am't	T	Am't
1	4.25	11	46.75	21	89.25	31	131.75	41	174.25
2	8.50	12	51.00	22	93.50	32	136.00	42	178.50
3	12.75	13	55.25	23	97.75	33	140.25	43	182.75
4	17.00	14	59.50	24	102.00	34	144.50	44	187.00
5	21.25	15	63.75	25	106.25	35	148.75	45	191.25
6	25.50	16	68.00	26	110.50	36	153.00	46	195.50
7	29.75	17	72.25	27	114.75	37	157.25	47	199.75
8	34.00	18	76.50	28	119.00	38	161.50	48	204.00
9	38.25	19	80.75	29	123.25	39	165.75	49	208.25
10	42.50	20	85.00	30	127.50	40	170.00	50	212.50

200	850	300	1275	400	1700	500	2125	600	2550

POUNDS

2000	2100	2200	2300	2400		2500	2600	2700	2800	2900
		AMOUNT						AMOUNT		
4.25	4.46	4.68	4.89	5.10		5.31	5.53	5.74	5.95	6.16
4.26	4.47	4.69	4.90	5.11	5	5.32	5.54	5.75	5.96	6.17
4.27	4.48	4.70	4.91	5.12	10	5.33	5.55	5.76	5.97	6.18
4.28	4.49	4.71	4.92	5.13	15	5.34	5.56	5.77	5.98	6.19
4.29	4.51	4.72	4.93	5.14	20	5.36	5.57	5.78	5.99	6.21
4.30	4.52	4.73	4.94	5.15	25	5.37	5.58	5.79	6.00	6.22
4.31	4.53	4.74	4.95	5.16	30	5.38	5.59	5.80	6.01	6.23
4.32	4.54	4.75	4.96	5.17	35	5.39	5.60	5.81	6.02	6.24
4.34	4.55	4.76	4.97	5.19	40	5.40	5.61	5.82	6.04	6.25
4.35	4.56	4.77	4.98	5.20	45	5.41	5.62	5.83	6.05	6.26
4.36	4.57	4.78	4.99	5.21	50	5.42	5.63	5.84	6.06	6.27
4.37	4.58	4.79	5.00	5.22	55	5.43	5.64	5.85	6.07	6.28
4.38	4.59	4.80	5.02	5.23	60	5.44	5.65	5.87	6.08	6.29
4.39	4.60	4.81	5.03	5.24	65	5.45	5.66	5.88	6.09	6.30
4.40	4.61	4.82	5.04	5.25	70	5.46	5.67	5.89	6.10	6.31
4.41	4.62	4.83	5.05	5.26	75	5.47	5.68	5.90	6.11	6.32
4.42	4.63	4.85	5.06	5.27	80	5.48	5.70	5.91	6.12	6.33
4.43	4.64	4.86	5.07	5.28	85	5.49	5.71	5.92	6.13	6.34
4.44	4.65	4.87	5.08	5.29	90	5.50	5.72	5.93	6.14	6.35
4.45	4.66	4.88	5.09	5.30	95	5.51	5.73	5.94	6.15	6.36

POUNDS

3000	3100	3200	3300	3400		3500	3600	3700	3800	3900
		AMOUNT						AMOUNT		
6.38	6.59	6.80	7.01	7.23		7.44	7.65	7.86	8.08	8.29
6.39	6.60	6.81	7.02	7.24	5	7.45	7.66	7.87	8.09	8.30
6.40	6.61	6.82	7.03	7.25	10	7.46	7.67	7.88	8.10	8.31
6.41	6.62	6.83	7.04	7.26	15	7.47	7.68	7.89	8.11	8.32
6.42	6.63	6.84	7.06	7.27	20	7.48	7.69	7.91	8.12	8.33
6.43	6.64	6.85	7.07	7.28	25	7.49	7.70	7.92	8.13	8.34
6.44	6.65	6.86	7.08	7.29	30	7.50	7.71	7.93	8.14	8.35
6.45	6.66	6.87	7.09	7.30	35	7.51	7.72	7.94	8.15	8.36
6.46	6.67	6.89	7.10	7.31	40	7.52	7.74	7.95	8.16	8.37
6.47	6.68	6.90	7.11	7.32	45	7.53	7.75	7.96	8.17	8.38
6.48	6.69	6.91	7.12	7.33	50	7.54	7.76	7.97	8.18	8.39
6.49	6.70	6.92	7.13	7.34	55	7.55	7.77	7.98	8.19	8.40
6.50	6.72	6.93	7.14	7.35	60	7.57	7.78	7.99	8.20	8.42
6.51	6.73	6.94	7.15	7.36	65	7.58	7.79	8.00	8.21	8.43
6.52	6.74	6.95	7.16	7.37	70	7.59	7.80	8.01	8.22	8.44
6.53	6.75	6.96	7.17	7.38	75	7.60	7.81	8.02	8.23	8.45
6.55	6.76	6.97	7.18	7.40	80	7.61	7.82	8.03	8.25	8.46
6.56	6.77	6.98	7.19	7.41	85	7.62	7.83	8.04	8.26	8.47
6.57	6.78	6.99	7.20	7.42	90	7.63	7.84	8.05	8.27	8.48
6.58	6.79	7.00	7.21	7.43	95	7.64	7.85	8.06	8.28	8.49

Even tons, 51 to 100 inclusive.

51-60		61-70		71-80		81-90		91-100	
T	Am't	T	Am't	T	Am't	T	Am't	T	Am't
51	216.75	61	259.25	71	301.75	81	344.25	91	386.75
52	221.00	62	263.50	72	306.00	82	348.50	92	391.00
53	225.25	63	267.75	73	310.25	83	352.75	93	395.25
54	229.50	64	272.00	74	314.50	84	357.00	94	399.50
55	233.75	65	276.25	75	318.75	85	361.25	95	403.75
56	238.00	66	280.50	76	323.00	86	365.50	96	408.00
57	242.25	67	284.75	77	327.25	87	369.75	97	412.25
58	246.50	68	289.00	78	331.50	88	374.00	98	416.50
59	250.75	69	293.25	79	335.75	89	378.25	99	420.75
60	255.00	70	297.50	80	340.00	90	382.50	100	425.00

700	2975	800	3400	900	3825	1000	4250	1100	4675

4   (37)

POUNDS

Under 100	100	200	300	400		500	600	700	800	900
	.23	.45	.68	.90		1.13	1.35	1.58	1.80	2.03
.01	.24	.46	.69	.91	5	1.14	1.36	1.59	1.81	2.04
.02	.25	.47	.70	.92	10	1.15	1.37	1.60	1.82	2.05
.03	.26	.48	.71	.93	15	1.16	1.38	1.61	1.83	2.06
.05	.27	.50	.72	.95	20	1.17	1.40	1.62	1.85	2.07
.06	.28	.51	.73	.96	25	1.18	1.41	1.63	1.86	2.08
.07	.29	.52	.74	.97	30	1.19	1.42	1.64	1.87	2.09
.08	.30	.53	.75	.98	35	1.20	1.43	1.65	1.88	2.10
.09	.32	.54	.77	.99	40	1.22	1.44	1.67	1.89	2.12
.10	.33	.55	.78	1.00	45	1.23	1.45	1.68	1.90	2.13
.11	.34	.56	.79	1.01	50	1.24	1.46	1.69	1.91	2.14
.12	.35	.57	.80	1.02	55	1.25	1.47	1.70	1.92	2.15
.14	.36	.59	.81	1.04	60	1.26	1.49	1.71	1.94	2.16
.15	.37	.60	.82	1.05	65	1.27	1.50	1.72	1.95	2.17
.16	.38	.61	.83	1.06	70	1.28	1.51	1.73	1.96	2.18
.17	.39	.62	.84	1.07	75	1.29	1.52	1.74	1.97	2.19
.18	.41	.63	.86	1.08	80	1.31	1.53	1.76	1.98	2.21
.19	.42	.64	.87	1.09	85	1.32	1.54	1.77	1.99	2.22
.20	.43	.65	.88	1.10	90	1.33	1.55	1.78	2.00	2.23
.21	.44	.66	.89	1.11	95	1.34	1.56	1.79	2.01	2.24

POUNDS

1000	1100	1200	1300	1400		1500	1600	1700	1800	1900
2.25	2.48	2.70	2.93	3.15		3.38	3.60	3.83	4.05	4.28
2.26	2.49	2.71	2.94	3.16	5	3.39	3.61	3.84	4.06	4.29
2.27	2.50	2.72	2.95	3.17	10	3.40	3.62	3.85	4.07	4.30
2.28	2.51	2.73	2.96	3.18	15	3.41	3.63	3.86	4.08	4.31
2.30	2.52	2.75	2.97	3.20	20	3.42	3.65	3.87	4.10	4.32
2.31	2.53	2.76	2.98	3.21	25	3.43	3.66	3.88	4.11	4.33
2.32	2.54	2.77	2.99	3.22	30	3.44	3.67	3.89	4.12	4.34
2.33	2.55	2.78	3.00	3.23	35	3.45	3.68	3.90	4.13	4.35
2.34	2.57	2.79	3.02	3.24	40	3.47	3.69	3.92	4.14	4.37
2.35	2.58	2.80	3.03	3.25	45	3.48	3.70	3.93	4.15	4.38
2 36	2.59	2.81	3.04	3.26	50	3.49	3.71	3.94	4.16	4.39
2.37	2.60	2.82	3.05	3.27	55	3.50	3.72	3.95	4.17	4.40
2.39	2.61	2.84	3.06	3.29	60	3.51	3.74	3.96	4.19	4.41
2.40	2.62	2.85	3.07	3.30	65	3.52	3.75	3.97	4.20	4.42
2.41	2.63	2.86	3.08	3.31	70	3.53	3.76	3.98	4.21	4.43
2.42	2.64	2.87	3.09	3.32	75	3.54	3.77	3.99	4.22	4.44
2.43	2.66	2.88	3.11	3.33	80	3.56	3.78	4.01	4.23	4.46
2.44	2.67	2.89	3.12	3.34	85	3.57	3.79	4.02	4.24	4.47
2.45	2.68	2.90	3.13	3.35	90	3.58	3.80	4.03	4.25	4.48
2.46	2.69	2.91	3.14	3.36	95	3.59	3.81	4.04	4.26	4.49

Even tons, 1 to 50 inclusive.

1-10		11-20		21-30		31-40		41-50	
T	Am't	T	Am't	T	Am't	T	Am't	T	Am't
1	4.50	11	49.50	21	94.50	31	139.50	41	184.50
2	9.00	12	54.00	22	99.00	32	144.00	42	189.00
3	13.50	13	58.50	23	103.50	33	148.50	43	193.50
4	18.00	14	63.00	24	108.00	34	153.00	44	198.00
5	22.50	15	67.50	25	112.50	35	157.50	45	202.50
6	27.00	16	72.00	26	117.00	36	162.00	46	207.00
7	31.50	17	76.50	27	121.50	37	166.50	47	211.50
8	36.00	18	81.00	28	126.00	38	171.00	48	216.00
9	40.50	19	85.50	29	130.50	39	175.50	49	220.50
10	45.00	20	90.00	30	135.00	40	180.00	50	225.00
200	900	300	1350	400	1800	500	2250	600	2700

POUNDS

2000	2100	2200	2300	2400		2500	2600	2700	2800	2900
		AMOUNT						AMOUNT		
4.50	4.73	4.95	5.18	5.40		5.63	5.85	6.08	6.30	6.53
4.51	4.74	4.96	5.19	5.41	5	5.64	5.86	6.09	6.31	6.54
4.52	4.75	4.97	5.20	5.42	10	5.65	5.87	6.10	6.32	6.55
4.53	4.76	4.98	5.21	5.43	15	5.66	5.88	6.11	6.33	6.56
4.55	4.77	5.00	5.22	5.45	20	5.67	5.90	6.12	6.35	6.57
4.56	4.78	5.01	5.23	5.46	25	5.68	5.91	6.13	6.36	6.58
4.57	4.79	5.02	5.24	5.47	30	5.69	5.92	6.14	6.37	6.59
4.58	4.80	5.03	5.25	5.48	35	5.70	5.93	6.15	6.38	6.60
4.59	4.82	5.04	5.27	5.49	40	5.72	5.94	6.17	6.39	6.62
4.60	4.83	5.05	5.28	5.50	45	5.73	5.95	6.18	6.40	6.63
4.61	4.84	5.06	5.29	5.51	50	5.74	5.96	6.19	6.41	6.64
4.62	4.85	5.07	5.30	5.52	55	5.75	5.97	6.20	6.42	6.65
4.64	4.86	5.09	5.31	5.54	60	5.76	5.99	6.21	6.44	6.66
4.65	4.87	5.10	5.32	5.55	65	5.77	6.00	6.22	6.45	6.67
4.66	4.88	5.11	5.33	5.56	70	5.78	6.01	6.23	6.46	6.68
4.67	4.89	5.12	5.34	5.57	75	5.79	6.02	6.24	6.47	6.69
4.68	4.91	5.13	5.36	5.58	80	5.81	6.03	6.26	6.48	6.71
4.69	4.92	5.14	5.37	5.59	85	5.82	6.04	6.27	6.49	6.72
4.70	4.93	5.15	5.38	5.60	90	5.83	6.05	6.28	6.50	6.73
4.71	4.94	5.16	5.39	5.61	95	5.84	6.06	6.29	6.51	6.74

POUNDS

3000	3100	3200	3300	3400		3500	3600	3700	3800	3900
		AMOUNT						AMOUNT		
6.75	6.98	7.20	7.43	7.65		7.88	8.10	8.33	8.55	8.78
6.76	6.99	7.21	7.44	7.66	5	7.89	8.11	8.34	8.56	8.79
6.77	7.00	7.22	7.45	7.67	10	7.90	8.12	8.35	8.57	8.80
6.78	7.01	7.23	7.46	7.68	15	7.91	8.13	8.36	8.58	8.81
6.80	7.02	7.25	7.47	7.70	20	7.92	8.15	8.37	8.60	8.82
6.81	7.03	7.26	7.48	7.71	25	7.93	8.16	8.38	8.61	8.83
6.82	7.04	7.27	7.49	7.72	30	7.94	8.17	8.39	8.62	8.84
6.83	7.05	7.28	7.50	7.73	35	7.95	8.18	8.40	8.63	8.85
6.84	7.07	7.29	7.52	7.74	40	7.97	8.19	8.42	8.64	8.87
6.85	7.08	7.30	7.53	7.75	45	7.98	8.20	8.43	8.65	8.88
6.86	7.09	7.31	7.54	7.76	50	7.99	8.21	8.44	8.66	8.89
6.87	7.10	7.32	7.55	7.77	55	8.00	8.22	8.45	8.67	8.90
6.89	7.11	7.34	7.56	7.79	60	8.01	8.24	8.46	8.69	8.91
6.90	7.12	7.35	7.57	7.80	65	8.02	8.25	8.47	8.70	8.92
6.91	7.13	7.36	7.58	7.81	70	8.03	8.26	8.48	8.71	8.93
6.92	7.14	7.37	7.59	7.82	75	8.04	8.27	8.49	8.72	8.94
6.93	7.16	7.38	7.61	7.83	80	8.06	8.28	8.51	8.73	8.96
6.94	7.17	7.39	7.62	7.84	85	8.07	8.29	8.52	8.74	8.97
6.95	7.18	7.40	7.63	7.85	90	8.08	8.30	8.53	8.75	8.98
6.96	7.19	7.41	7.64	7.86	95	8.09	8.31	8.54	8.76	8.99

Even tons, 51 to 100 inclusive.

51-60		61-70		71-80		81-90		91-100	
T	Am't	T	Am't	T	Am't	T	Am't	T	Am't
51	229.50	61	274.50	71	319.50	81	364.50	91	409.50
52	234.00	62	279.00	72	324.00	82	369.00	92	414.00
53	238.50	63	283.50	73	328.50	83	373.50	93	418.50
54	243.00	64	288.00	74	333.00	84	378.00	94	423.00
55	247.50	65	292.50	75	337.50	85	382.50	95	427.50
56	252.00	66	297.00	76	342.00	86	387.00	96	432.00
57	256.50	67	301.50	77	346.50	87	391.50	97	436.50
58	261.00	68	306.00	78	351.00	88	396.00	98	441.00
59	265.50	69	310.50	79	355.50	89	400.50	99	445.50
60	270.00	70	315.00	80	360.00	90	405.00	100	450.00

700	3150	800	3600	900	4050	1000	4500	1100	4950

POUNDS

Under 100	100	200	300	400		500	600	700	800	900
	.24	.48	.71	.95		1.19	1.43	1.66	1.90	2.14
.01	.25	.49	.72	.96	5	1.20	1.44	1.67	1.91	2.15
.02	.26	.50	.74	.97	10	1.21	1.45	1.69	1.92	2.16
.03	.27	.51	.75	.99	15	1.22	1.46	1.70	1.94	2.17
.05	.29	.52	.76	1.00	20	1.24	1.47	1.71	1.95	2.19
.06	.30	.53	.77	1.01	25	1.25	1.48	1.72	1.96	2.20
.07	.31	.55	.78	1.02	30	1.26	1.50	1.73	1.97	2.21
.08	.32	.56	.80	1.03	35	1.27	1.51	1.75	1.98	2.22
.10	.33	.57	.81	1.05	40	1.28	1.52	1.76	2.00	2.23
.11	.34	.58	.82	1.06	45	1.29	1.53	1.77	2.01	2.24
.12	.36	.59	.83	1.07	50	1.31	1.54	1.78	2.02	2.26
.13	.37	.61	.84	1.08	55	1.32	1.56	1.79	2.03	2.27
.14	.38	.62	.86	1.09	60	1.33	1.57	1.81	2.04	2.28
.15	.39	.63	.87	1.10	65	1.34	1.58	1.82	2.05	2.29
.17	.40	.64	.88	1.12	70	1.35	1.59	1.83	2.07	2.30
.18	.42	.65	.89	1.13	75	1.37	1.60	1.84	2.08	2.32
.19	.43	.67	.90	1.14	80	1.38	1.62	1.85	2.09	2.33
.20	.44	.68	.91	1.15	85	1.39	1.63	1.86	2.10	2.34
.21	.45	.69	.93	1.16	90	1.40	1.64	1.88	2.11	2.35
.23	.46	.70	.94	1.18	95	1 41	1.65	1.89	2.13	2.36

POUNDS

1000	1100	1200	1300	1400		1500	1600	1700	1800	1900
2.38	2.61	2.85	3.09	3.33		3.56	3.80	4.04	4.28	4.51
2.39	2.62	2.86	3.10	3.34	5	3.57	3.81	4.05	4.29	4.52
2.40	2.64	2.87	3.11	3.35	10	3.59	3.82	4.06	4.30	4.54
2.41	2.65	2.89	3.12	3.36	15	3.60	3.84	4.07	4.31	4.55
2.42	2.66	2.90	3.14	3.37	20	3.61	3.85	4.09	4.32	4.56
2.43	2.67	2.91	3.15	3.38	25	3.62	3.86	4.10	4.33	4.57
2.45	2.68	2.92	3.16	3.40	30	3.63	3.87	4.11	4.35	4.58
2.46	2.70	2.93	3.17	3.41	35	3.65	3.88	4.12	4.36	4.60
2.47	2.71	2.95	3.18	3.42	40	3.66	3.90	4.13	4.37	4.61
2.48	2.72	2.96	3.19	3.43	45	3.67	3.91	4.14	4.38	4.62
2.49	2.73	2.97	3.21	3.44	50	3.68	3.92	4.16	4.39	4.63
2.51	2.74	2.98	3.22	3.46	55	3.69	3.93	4.17	4.41	4.64
2.52	2.76	2.99	3.23	3.47	60	3.71	3.94	4.18	4.42	4.66
2.53	2.77	3.00	3.24	3.48	65	3.72	3.95	4.19	4.43	4.67
2.54	2.78	3.02	3.25	3.49	70	3.73	3.97	4.20	4.44	4.68
2.55	2.79	3.03	3.27	3.50	75	3.74	3.98	4.22	4.45	4.69
2.57	2.80	3.04	3.28	3.52	80	3.75	3.99	4.23	4.47	4.70
2.58	2.81	3.05	3.29	3.53	85	3.76	4.00	4.24	4.48	4.71
2.59	2.83	3.06	3.30	3.54	90	3.78	4.01	4.25	4.49	4.73
2.60	2.84	3.08	3.31	3.55	95	3.79	4.03	4.26	4.50	4.74

Even tons, 1 to 50 inclusive.

1-10		11-20		21-30		31-40		41-50	
T	Am't	T	Am't	T	Am't	T	Am't	T	Am't
1	4.75	11	52.25	21	99.75	31	147.25	41	194.75
2	9.50	12	57.00	22	104.50	32	152.00	42	199.50
3	14.25	13	61.75	23	109.25	33	156.75	43	204.25
4	19.00	14	66.50	24	114.00	34	161.50	44	209.00
5	23.75	15	71.25	25	118.75	35	166.25	45	213.75
6	28.50	16	76.00	26	123.50	36	171.00	46	218.50
7	33.25	17	80.75	27	128.25	37	175.75	47	223.25
8	38.00	18	85.50	28	133.00	38	180.50	48	228.00
9	42.75	19	90.25	29	137.75	39	185.25	49	232.75
10	47.50	20	95.00	30	142.50	40	190.00	50	237.50
200	950	300	1425	400	1900	500	2375	600	2850

19c a bu. **$4.75 a T.** 23¾c a 100 lbs.

— POUNDS —

2000	2100	2200	2300	2400		2500	2600	2700	2800	2900
		AMOUNT						AMOUNT		
4.75	4.99	5.23	5.46	5.70		5.94	6.18	6.41	6.65	6.89
4.76	5.00	5.24	5.47	5.71	5	5.95	6.19	6.42	6.66	6.90
4.77	5.01	5.25	5.49	5.72	10	5.96	6.20	6.44	6.67	6.91
4.78	5.02	5.26	5.50	5.74	15	5.97	6.21	6.45	6.69	6.92
4.80	5.04	5.27	5.51	5.75	20	5.99	6.22	6.46	6.70	6.94
4.81	5.05	5.28	5.52	5.76	25	6.00	6.23	6.47	6.71	6.95
4.82	5.06	5.30	5.53	5.77	30	6.01	6.25	6.48	6.72	6.96
4.83	5.07	5.31	5.55	5.78	35	6.02	6.26	6.50	6.73	6.97
4.85	5.08	5.32	5.56	5.80	40	6.03	6.27	6.51	6.75	6.98
4.86	5.09	5.33	5.57	5.81	45	6.04	6.28	6.52	6.76	6.99
4.87	5.11	5.34	5.58	5.82	50	6.06	6.29	6.53	6.77	7.01
4.88	5.12	5.36	5.59	5.83	55	6.07	6.31	6.54	6.78	7.02
4.89	5.13	5.37	5.61	5.84	60	6.08	6.32	6.56	6.79	7.03
4.90	5.14	5.38	5.62	5.85	65	6.09	6.33	6.57	6.80	7.04
4.92	5.15	5.39	5.63	5.87	70	6.10	6.34	6.58	6.82	7.05
4.93	5.17	5.40	5.64	5.88	75	6.12	6.35	6.59	6.83	7.07
4.94	5.18	5.42	5.65	5.89	80	6.13	6.37	6.60	6.84	7.08
4.95	5.19	5.43	5.66	5.90	85	6.14	6.38	6.61	6.85	7.09
4.96	5.20	5.44	5.68	5.91	90	6.15	6.39	6.63	6.86	7.10
4.98	5.21	5.45	5.69	5.93	95	6.16	6.40	6.64	6.88	7.11

— POUNDS —

3000	3100	3200	3300	3400		3500	3600	3700	3800	3900
		AMOUNT						AMOUNT		
7.13	7.36	7.60	7.84	8.08		8.31	8.55	8.79	9.03	9.26
7.14	7.37	7.61	7.85	8.09	5	8.32	8.56	8.80	9.04	9.27
7.15	7.39	7.62	7.86	8.10	10	8.34	8.57	8.81	9.05	9.29
7.16	7.40	7.64	7.87	8.11	15	8.35	8.59	8.82	9.06	9.30
7.17	7.41	7.65	7.89	8.12	20	8.36	8.60	8.84	9.07	9.31
7.18	7.42	7.66	7.90	8.13	25	8.37	8.61	8.85	9.08	9.32
7.20	7.43	7.67	7.91	8.15	30	8.38	8.62	8.86	9.10	9.33
7.21	7.45	7.68	7.92	8.16	35	8.40	8.63	8.87	9.11	9.35
7.22	7.46	7.70	7.93	8.17	40	8.41	8.65	8.88	9.12	9.36
7.23	7.47	7.71	7.94	8.18	45	8.42	8.66	8.89	9.13	9.37
7.24	7.48	7.72	7.96	8.19	50	8.43	8.67	8.91	9.14	9.38
7.26	7.49	7.73	7.97	8.21	55	8.44	8.68	8.92	9.16	9.39
7.27	7.51	7.74	7.98	8.22	60	8.46	8.69	8.93	9.17	9.41
7.28	7.52	7.75	7.99	8.23	65	8.47	8.70	8.94	9.18	9.42
7.29	7.53	7 77	8.00	8 24	70	8.48	8.72	8.95	9.19	9.43
7.30	7.54	7 78	8.02	8.25	75	8.49	8.73	8.97	9.20	9.44
7.32	7.55	7.79	8.03	8.27	80	8.50	8.74	8.98	9.22	9.45
7.33	7.56	7.80	8.04	8.28	85	8.51	8.75	8.99	9.23	9.46
7.34	7.58	7.81	8.05	8.29	90	8.53	8.76	9.00	9.24	9.48
7.35	7.59	7.83	8.06	8.30	95	8.54	8.78	9.01	9.25	9.49

E–en tons, 51 to 100 inclusive.

51-60		61-70		71-80		81-90		91-100	
T	Am't	T	Am't	T	Am't	T	Am't	T	Am't
51	242.25	61	289.75	71	337.25	81	384.75	91	432.25
52	247.00	62	294.50	72	342.00	82	389.50	92	437.00
53	251.75	63	299.25	73	346.75	83	394.25	93	441.75
54	256.50	64	304.00	74	351.50	84	399.00	94	446.50
55	261.25	65	308.75	75	356.25	85	403.75	95	451.25
56	266 00	66	313.50	76	361.00	86	408.50	96	456.00
57	270.75	67	318.25	77	365.75	87	413.25	97	460.75
58	275.50	68	323.00	78	370.50	88	418.00	98	465.50
59	280.25	69	327.75	79	375.25	89	422.75	99	470.25
60	285.00	70	332.50	80	380.00	90	427.50	100	475.00

700	3325	800	3800	900	4275	1000	4750	1100	5225

(41)

20c a bu.   **$5.00 a T.**   **25c a 100** lbs.

POUNDS

Under 100	100	200	300	400		500	600	700	800	900
	AMOUNT						AMOUNT			
	.25	.50	.75	1.00		1.25	1.50	1.75	2.00	2.25
.01	.26	.51	.76	1.01	5	1.26	1.51	1.76	2.01	2.26
.03	.28	.53	.78	1.03	10	1.28	1.53	1.78	2.03	2.28
.04	.29	.54	.79	1.04	15	1.29	1.54	1.79	2.04	2.29
.05	.30	.55	.80	1.05	20	1.30	1.55	1.80	2.05	2.30
.06	.31	.56	.81	1.06	25	1.31	1.56	1.81	2.06	2.31
.08	.33	.58	.83	1.08	30	1.33	1.58	1.83	2.08	2.33
.09	.34	.59	.84	1.09	35	1.34	1.59	1.84	2.09	2.34
.10	.35	.60	.85	1.10	40	1.35	1.60	1.85	2.10	2.35
.11	.36	.61	.86	1.11	45	1.36	1.61	1.86	2.11	2.36
.13	.38	.63	.88	1.13	50	1.38	1.63	1.88	2.13	2.38
.14	.39	.64	.89	1.14	55	1.39	1.64	1.89	2.14	2.39
.15	.40	.65	.90	1.15	60	1.40	1.65	1.90	2.15	2.40
.16	.41	.66	.91	1.16	65	1.41	1.66	1.91	2.16	2.41
.18	.43	.68	.93	1.18	70	1.43	1.68	1.93	2.18	2.43
.19	.44	.69	.94	1.19	75	1.44	1.69	1.94	2.19	2.44
.20	.45	.70	.95	1.20	80	1.45	1.70	1.95	2.20	2.45
.21	.46	.71	.96	1.21	85	1.46	1.71	1.96	2.21	2.46
.23	.48	.73	.98	1.23	90	1.48	1.73	1.98	2.23	2.48
.24	.49	.74	.99	1.24	95	1.49	1.74	1.99	2.24	2.49

POUNDS

1000	1100	1200	1300	1400		1500	1600	1700	1800	1900
		AMOUNT						AMOUNT		
2.50	2.75	3.00	3.25	3.50		3.75	4.00	4.25	4.50	4.75
2.51	2.76	3.01	3.26	3.51	5	3.76	4.01	4.26	4.51	4.76
2.53	2.78	3.03	3.28	3.53	10	3.78	4.03	4.28	4.53	4.78
2.54	2.79	3.04	3.29	3.54	15	3.79	4.04	4.29	4.54	4.79
2.55	2.80	3.05	3.30	3.55	20	3.80	4.05	4.30	4.55	4.80
2.56	2.81	3.06	3.31	3.56	25	3.81	4.06	4.31	4.56	4.81
2.58	2.83	3.08	3.33	3.58	30	3.83	4.08	4.33	4.58	4.83
2.59	2.84	3.09	3.34	3.59	35	3.84	4.09	4.34	4.59	4.84
2.60	2.85	3.10	3.35	3.60	40	3.85	4.10	4.35	4.60	4.85
2.61	2.86	3.11	3.36	3.61	45	3.86	4.11	4.36	4.61	4.86
2.63	2.88	3.13	3.38	3.63	50	3.88	4.13	4.38	4.63	4.88
2.64	2.89	3.14	3.39	3.64	55	3.89	4.14	4.39	4.64	4.89
2.65	2.90	3.15	3.40	3.65	60	3.90	4.15	4.40	4.65	4.90
2.66	2.91	3.16	3.41	3.66	65	3.91	4.16	4.41	4.66	4.91
2.68	2.93	3.18	3.43	3.68	70	3.93	4.18	4.43	4.68	4.93
2.69	2.94	3.19	3.44	3.69	75	3.94	4.19	4.44	4.69	4.94
2.70	2.95	3.20	3.45	3.70	80	3.95	4.20	4.45	4.70	4.95
2.71	2.96	3.21	3.46	3.71	85	3.96	4.21	4.46	4.71	4.96
2.73	2.98	3.23	3.48	3.73	90	3.98	4.23	4.48	4.73	4.98
2.74	2.99	3.24	3.49	3.74	95	3.99	4.24	4.49	4.74	4.99

Even tons, 1 to 50 inclusive.

1-10		11-20		21-30		31-40		41-50	
T	Am't	T	Am't	T	Am't	T	Am't	T	Am't
1	5.00	11	55.00	21	105.00	31	155.00	41	205.00
2	10.00	12	60.00	22	110.00	32	160.00	42	210.00
3	15.00	13	65.00	23	115.00	33	165.00	43	215.00
4	20.00	14	70.00	24	120.00	34	170.00	44	220.00
5	25.00	15	75.00	25	125.00	35	175.00	45	225.00
6	30.00	16	80.00	26	130.00	36	180.00	46	230.00
7	35.00	17	85.00	27	135.00	37	185.00	47	235.00
8	40.00	18	90.00	28	140.00	38	190.06	48	240.00
9	45.00	19	95.00	29	145.00	39	195.00	49	245.00
10	50.00	20	100.00	30	150.00	40	200.00	50	250.00
200	1000	300	1500	400	2000	500	2500	600	3000

(42)

———— POUNDS ————

2000	2100	2200	2300	2400		2500	2600	2700	2800	2900
		AMOUNT						AMOUNT		
5.00	5.25	5.50	5.75	6.00		6.25	6.50	6.75	7.00	7.25
5.01	5.26	5.51	5.76	6.01	5	6.26	6.51	6.76	7.01	7.26
5.03	5.28	5.53	5.78	6.03	10	6.28	6.53	6.78	7.03	7.28
5.04	5.29	5.54	5.79	6.04	15	6.29	6.54	6.79	7.04	7.29
5.05	5.30	5.55	5.80	6.05	20	6.30	6.55	6.80	7.05	7.30
5.06	5.31	5.56	5.81	6.06	25	6.31	6.56	6.81	7.06	7.31
5.08	5.33	5.58	5.83	6.08	30	6.33	6.58	6.83	7.08	7.33
5.09	5.34	5.59	5.84	6.09	35	6.34	6.59	6.84	7.09	7.34
5.10	5.35	5.60	5.85	6.10	40	6.35	6.60	6.85	7.10	7.35
5.11	5.36	5.61	5.86	6.11	45	6.36	6.61	6.86	7.11	7.36
5.13	5.38	5.63	5.88	6.13	50	6.38	6.63	6.88	7.13	7.38
5.14	5.39	5.64	5.89	6.14	55	6.39	6.64	6.89	7.14	7.39
5.15	5.40	5.65	5.90	6.15	60	6.40	6.65	6.90	7.15	7.40
5.16	5.41	5.66	5.91	6.16	65	6.41	6.66	6.91	7.16	7.41
5.18	5.43	5.68	5.93	6.18	70	6.43	6.68	6.93	7.18	7.43
5.19	5.44	5.69	5.94	6.19	75	6.44	6.69	6.94	7.19	7.44
5.20	5.45	5.70	5.95	6.20	80	6.45	6.70	6.95	7.20	7.45
5.21	5.46	5.71	5.96	6.21	85	6.46	6.71	6.96	7.21	7.46
5.23	5.48	5.73	5.98	6.23	90	6.48	6.73	6.98	7.23	7.48
5.24	5.49	5.74	5.99	6.24	95	6.49	6.74	6.99	7.24	7.49

———— POUNDS ————

3000	3100	3200	3300	3400		3500	3600	3700	3800	3900
		AMOUNT						AMOUNT		
7.50	7.75	8.00	8.25	8.50		8.75	9.00	9.25	9.50	9.75
7.51	7.76	8.01	8.26	8.51	5	8.76	9.01	9.26	9.51	9.76
7.53	7.78	8.03	8.28	8.53	10	8.78	9.03	9.28	9.53	9.78
7.54	7.79	8.04	8.29	8.54	15	8.79	9.04	9.29	9.54	9.79
7.55	7.80	8.05	8.30	8.55	20	8.80	9.05	9.30	9.55	9.80
7.56	7.81	8.06	8.31	8.56	25	8.81	9.06	9.31	9.56	9.81
7.58	7.83	8.08	8.33	8.57	30	8.83	9.08	9.33	9.58	9.83
7.59	7.84	8.09	8.34	8.59	35	8.84	9.09	9.34	9.59	9.84
7.60	7.85	8.10	8.35	8.60	40	8.85	9.10	9.35	9.60	9.85
7.61	7.86	8.11	8.36	8.61	45	8.86	9.11	9.36	9.61	9.86
7.63	7.88	8.13	8.38	8.63	50	8.88	9.13	9.38	9.63	9.88
7.64	7.89	8.14	8.39	8.64	55	8.89	9.14	9.39	9.64	9.89
7.65	7.90	8.15	8.40	8.65	60	8.90	9.15	9.40	9.65	9.90
7.66	7.91	8.16	8.41	8.66	65	8.91	9.16	9.41	9.66	9.91
7.68	7.93	8.18	8.43	8.68	70	8.93	9.18	9.43	9.68	9.93
7.69	7.94	8.19	8.44	8.69	75	8.94	9.19	9.44	9.69	9.94
7.70	7.95	8.20	8.45	8.70	80	8.95	9.20	9.45	9.70	9.95
7.71	7.96	8.21	8.46	8.71	85	8.96	9.21	9.46	9.71	9.96
7.73	7.98	8.23	8.48	8.73	90	8.98	9.23	9.48	9.73	9.98
7.74	7.99	8.24	8.49	8.74	95	8.99	9.24	9.49	9.74	9.99

Even tons, 51 to 100 inclusive.

51-60		61-70		71-80		81-90		91-100	
T	Am't	T	Am't	T	Am't	T	Am't	T	Am't
51	255.00	61	305.00	71	355.00	81	405.00	91	455.00
52	260.00	62	310.00	72	360.00	82	410.00	92	460.00
53	265.00	63	315.00	73	365.00	83	415.00	93	465.00
54	270.00	64	320.00	74	370.00	84	420.00	94	470.00
55	275.00	65	325.00	75	375.00	85	425.00	95	475.00
56	280.00	66	330.00	76	380.00	86	430.00	96	480.00
57	285.00	67	335.00	77	385.00	87	435.00	97	485.00
58	290.00	68	340.00	78	390.00	88	440.00	98	490.00
59	295.00	69	345.00	79	395.00	89	445.00	99	495.00
60	300.00	70	350.00	80	400.00	90	450.00	100	500.00

700	3500	800	4000	900	4500	1000	5000	1100	5500

POUNDS

Under 100	100	200	300	400		500	600	700	800	900
	AMOUNT						AMOUNT			
	.26	.53	.79	1.05		1.31	1.58	1.84	2.10	2.36
.01	.28	.54	.80	1.06	5	1.33	1.59	1.85	2.11	2.38
.03	.29	.55	.81	1.08	10	1.34	1.60	1.86	2.13	2.39
.04	.30	.56	.83	1.09	15	1.35	1.61	1.88	2.14	2.40
.05	.32	.58	.84	1.10	20	1.37	1.63	1.89	2.15	2.42
.07	.33	.59	.85	1.12	25	1.38	1.64	1.90	2.17	2.43
.08	.34	.60	.87	1.13	30	1.39	1.65	1.92	2.18	2.44
.09	.35	.62	.88	1.14	35	1.41	1.67	1.93	2.19	2.45
.11	.37	.63	.89	1.16	40	1.42	1.68	1.94	2.21	2.47
.12	.38	.64	.91	1.17	45	1.43	1.69	1.96	2.22	2.48
.13	.39	.66	.92	1.18	50	1.44	1.71	1.97	2.23	2.49
.14	.41	.67	.93	1.19	55	1.46	1.72	1.98	2.24	2.51
.16	.42	.68	.95	1.21	60	1.47	1.73	2.00	2.26	2.52
.17	.43	.70	.96	1.22	65	1.48	1.75	2.01	2.27	2.53
.18	.45	.71	.97	1.23	70	1.50	1.76	2.02	2.28	2.55
.20	.46	.72	.99	1.25	75	1.51	1.77	2.03	2.30	2.56
.21	.47	.74	1.01	1.26	80	1.52	1.79	2.05	2.31	2.57
.22	.49	.75	1.02	1.27	85	1.54	1.80	2.06	2.32	2.59
.24	.50	.76	1.03	1.29	90	1.55	1.81	2.07	2.34	2.60
.25	.51	.77	1.04	1.30	95	1.56	1.82	2.09	2.35	2.61

POUNDS

1000	1100	1200	1300	1400		1500	1600	1700	1800	1900
AMOUNT							AMOUNT			
2.63	2.89	3.15	3.41	3.68		3.94	4.20	4.46	4.73	4.99
2.64	2.90	3.16	3.43	3.69	5	3.95	4.21	4.48	4.74	5.00
2.65	2.91	3.18	3.44	3.70	10	3.96	4.23	4.49	4.75	5.01
2.66	2.93	3.19	3.45	3.71	15	3.98	4.24	4.50	4.76	5.03
2.68	2.94	3.20	3.47	3.73	20	3.99	4.25	4.52	4.78	5.04
2.69	2.95	3.22	3.48	3.74	25	4.00	4.27	4.53	4.79	5.05
2.70	2.97	3.23	3.49	3.75	30	4.02	4.28	4.54	4.80	5.07
2.72	2.98	3.24	3.50	3.77	35	4.03	4.29	4.55	4.82	5.08
2.73	2.99	3.26	3.52	3.78	40	4.04	4.31	4.57	4.83	5.09
2.74	3.01	3.27	3.53	3.79	45	4.06	4.32	4.58	4.84	5.11
2.76	3.02	3.28	3.54	3.81	50	4.07	4.33	4.59	4.86	5.12
2.77	3.03	3.29	3.56	3.82	55	4.08	4.34	4.61	4.87	5.13
2.78	3.04	3.31	3.57	3.83	60	4.10	4.36	4.62	4.88	5.15
2.80	3.06	3.32	3.58	3.85	65	4.11	4.37	4.63	4.90	5.16
2.81	3.07	3.33	3.60	3.86	70	4.12	4.38	4.65	4.91	5.17
2.82	3.08	3.35	3.61	3.87	75	4.13	4.40	4.66	4.92	5.18
2.84	3.10	3.36	3.62	3.89	80	4.15	4.41	4.67	4.94	5.20
2.85	3.11	3.37	3.64	3.90	85	4.16	4.42	4.69	4.95	5.21
2.86	3.12	3.39	3.65	3.91	90	4.17	4.44	4.70	4.96	5.22
2.87	3.14	3.40	3.66	3.92	95	4.19	4.45	4.71	4.97	5.24

Even tons, 1 to 50 inclusive.

1-10		11-20		21-30		31-40		41-50	
T	Am't	T	Am't	T	Am't	T	Am't	T	Am't
1	5.25	11	57.75	21	110.25	31	162.75	41	215.25
2	10.50	12	63.00	22	115.50	32	168.00	42	220.50
3	15.75	13	68.25	23	120.75	33	173.25	43	225.75
4	21.00	14	73.50	24	126.00	34	178.50	44	231.00
5	26.25	15	78.75	25	131.25	35	183.75	45	236.25
6	31.50	16	84.00	26	136.50	36	189.00	46	241.50
7	36.75	17	89.25	27	141.75	37	194.25	47	246.75
8	42.00	18	94.50	28	147.00	38	199.50	48	252.00
9	47.25	19	99.75	29	152.25	39	204.75	49	257.25
10	52.50	20	105.00	30	157.50	40	210.00	50	262.50
200	1050	300	1575	400	2100	500	2625	600	3150

———— POUNDS ————

2000	2100	2200	2300	2400		2500	2600	2700	2800	2900
		AMOUNT						AMOUNT		
5.25	5.51	5.78	6.04	6.30		6.56	6.83	7.09	7.35	7.61
5.26	5.53	5.79	6.05	6.31	5	6.58	6.84	7.10	7.36	7.63
5.28	5.54	5.80	6.06	6.33	10	6.59	6.85	7.11	7.38	7.64
5.29	5.55	5.81	6.08	6.34	15	6.60	6.86	7.13	7.39	7.65
5.30	5.57	5.83	6.09	6.35	20	6.62	6.88	7.14	7.40	7.67
5.32	5.58	5.84	6.10	6.37	25	6.63	6.89	7.15	7.42	7.68
5 33	5.59	5.85	6.12	6.38	30	6.64	6.90	7.17	7.43	7.69
5.34	5.60	5.87	6.13	6.39	35	6.66	6.92	7.18	7.44	7.70
5.36	5.62	5.88	6.14	6.41	40	6.67	6.93	7.19	7.46	7.72
5.37	5.63	5.89	6.16	6.42	45	6.68	6.94	7.21	7.47	7.73
5.38	5.64	5.91	6.17	6.43	50	6.69	6.96	7.22	7.48	7.74
5.39	5.66	5.92	6.18	6.44	55	6.71	6.97	7.23	7.49	7.76
5.41	5.67	5.93	6.20	6.46	60	6.72	6.98	7.25	7.51	7.77
5.42	5.68	5.95	6.21	6.47	65	6.73	7.00	7.26	7.52	7.78
5.43	5.70	5.96	6.22	6.48	70	6.75	7.01	7.27	7.53	7.80
5.45	5.71	5.97	6.24	6.50	75	6.76	7.02	7.28	7.55	7.81
5.46	5.72	5.99	6.26	6.51	80	6.77	7.04	7.30	7.56	7.82
5.47	5.74	6.00	6.27	6.52	85	6.79	7.05	7.31	7.57	7.84
5.49	5.75	6.01	6.28	6.54	90	6.80	7.06	7.32	7.59	7.85
5.50	5.76	6.02	6.29	6.55	95	6.81	7.07	7.34	7.60	7.86

———— POUNDS ————

3000	3100	3200	3300	3400		3500	3600	3700	3800	3900
		AMOUNT						AMOUNT		
7.88	8.14	8.40	8.66	8.93		9.19	9.45	9.71	9.98	10.24
7.89	8.15	8.41	8.68	8.94	5	9.20	9.46	9.73	9.99	10.25
7.90	8.16	8.43	8.69	8.95	10	9.21	9.48	9.74	10.00	10.26
7.91	8.18	8.44	8.70	8.96	15	9.23	9.49	9.75	10.01	10.28
7.93	8.19	8.45	8.72	8.98	20	9.24	9.50	9.77	10.03	10.29
7.94	8.20	8.47	8.73	8.99	25	9.25	9.52	9.78	10.04	10.30
7.95	8.22	8.48	8.74	9.00	30	9.27	9.53	9.79	10.05	10.32
7.97	8.23	8.49	8.75	9.02	35	9.28	9.54	9.80	10.07	10.33
7.98	8.24	8.51	8.77	9.03	40	9.29	9.56	9.82	10.08	10.34
7.99	8.26	8.52	8.78	9.04	45	9.31	9.57	9.83	10.09	10.36
8.01	8.27	8.53	8.79	9.06	50	9.32	9.58	9.84	10.11	10.37
8.02	8.28	8.54	8.81	9.07	55	9.33	9.59	9.86	10.12	10.38
8.03	8.29	8.56	8.82	9.08	60	9.35	9.61	9.87	10.13	10.40
8.05	8.31	8.57	8.83	9.10	65	9.36	9.62	9.88	10.15	10.41
8.06	8.32	8.58	8.85	9.11	70	9.37	9.63	9.90	10.16	10.42
8.07	8.33	8.60	8.86	9.12	75	9.38	9.65	9.91	10.17	10.43
8.09	8.35	8.61	8.87	9.14	80	9.40	9.66	9.92	10.19	10.45
8.10	8.36	8.62	8.89	9.15	85	9.41	9.67	9.94	10.20	10.46
8.11	8.37	8.64	8.90	9.16	90	9.42	9.69	9.95	10.21	10.47
8.12	8.39	8.65	8.91	9.17	95	9.44	9.70	9.96	10.22	10.49

Even tons, 51 to 100 inclusive.

51-60		61-70		71-80		81-90		91-100	
T	Am't	T	Am't	T	Am't	T	Am't	T	Am't
51	267.75	61	320.25	71	372.75	81	425.25	91	477.75
52	273.00	62	325.50	72	378.00	82	430.50	92	483.00
53	278.25	63	330.75	73	383.25	83	435.75	93	488.25
54	283.50	64	336.00	74	388.50	84	441.00	94	493.50
55	288.75	65	341.25	75	393.75	85	446.25	95	498.75
56	294.00	66	346.50	76	399.00	86	451.50	96	504.00
57	299.25	67	351.75	77	404.25	87	456.75	97	509.25
58	304.50	68	357.00	78	409.50	88	462.00	98	514.50
59	309.75	69	362.25	79	414.75	89	467.25	99	519.75
60	315.00	70	367.50	80	420.00	90	472.50	100	525.00

700	3675	800	·4200	900	4725	1000	5250	1100	5775

————— POUNDS —————

Under 100	100	200	300	400		500	600	700	800	900
		AMOUNT						AMOUNT		
···	.28	.55	.83	1.10		1.38	1.65	1.93	2.20	2.48
.01	.29	.56	.84	1.11	5	1.39	1.66	1.94	2.21	2.49
.03	.30	.58	.85	1.13	10	1.40	1.68	1.95	2.23	2.50
.04	.32	.59	.87	1.14	15	1.42	1.69	1.97	2.24	2.52
.06	.33	.61	.88	1.16	20	1.43	1.71	1.98	2.26	2.53
.07	.34	.62	.89	1.17	25	1.44	1.72	1.99	2.27	2.54
.08	.36	.63	.91	1.18	30	1.46	1.73	2.01	2.28	2.56
.10	.37	.65	.92	1.20	35	1.47	1.75	2.02	2.30	2.57
.11	.39	.66	.94	1.21	40	1.49	1.76	2.04	2.31	2.59
.12	.40	.67	.95	1.22	45	1.50	1.77	2.05	2.32	2.60
.14	.41	.69	.96	1.24	50	1.51	1.79	2.06	2.34	2.61
.15	.43	.70	.98	1.25	55	1.53	1.80	2.08	2.35	2.63
.17	.44	.72	.99	1.27	60	1.54	1.82	2.09	2.37	2.64
.18	.45	.73	1.00	1.28	65	1.55	1.83	2.10	2.38	2.65
.19	.47	.74	1.02	1.29	70	1.57	1.84	2.12	2.39	2.67
.21	.48	.76	1.03	1.31	75	1.58	1.86	2.13	2.41	2.68
.22	.50	.77	1.05	1.32	80	1.60	1.87	2.15	2.42	2.70
.23	.51	.78	1.06	1.33	85	1.61	1.88	2.16	2.43	2.71
.25	.52	.80	1.07	1.35	90	1.62	1.90	2.17	2.45	2.72
.26	.54	.81	1.09	1.36	95	1.64	1.91	2.19	2.46	2.74

————— POUNDS —————

1000	1100	1200	1300	1400		1500	1600	1700	1800	1900
		AMOUNT						AMOUNT		
2.75	3.03	3.30	3.58	3.85		4.13	4.40	4.68	4.95	5.23
2.76	3.04	3.31	3.59	3.86	5	4.14	4.41	4.69	4.96	5.24
2.78	3.05	3.33	3.60	3.88	10	4.15	4.43	4.70	4.98	5.25
2.79	3.07	3.34	3.62	3.89	15	4.17	4.44	4.72	4.99	5.27
2.81	3.08	3.36	3.63	3.91	20	4.18	4.46	4.73	5.01	5.28
2.82	3.09	3.37	3.64	3.92	25	4.19	4.47	4.74	5.02	5.29
2.83	3.11	3.38	3.66	3.93	30	4.21	4.48	4.76	5.03	5.31
2.85	3.12	3.40	3.67	3.95	35	4.22	4.50	4.77	5.05	5.32
2.86	3.14	3.41	3.69	3.96	40	4.24	4.51	4.79	5.06	5.34
2.87	3.15	3.42	3.70	3.97	45	4.25	4.52	4.80	5.07	5.35
2.89	3.16	3.44	3.71	3.99	50	4.26	4.54	4.81	5.09	5.36
2.90	3.18	3.45	3.73	4.00	55	4.28	4.55	4.83	5.10	5.38
2.92	3.19	3.47	3.74	4.02	60	4.29	4.57	4.84	5.12	5.39
2.93	3.20	3.48	3.75	4.03	65	4.30	4.58	4.85	5.13	5.40
2.94	3.22	3.49	3.77	4.04	70	4.32	4.59	4.87	5.14	5.42
2.96	3.23	3.51	3.78	4.06	75	4.33	4.61	4.88	5.16	5.43
2.97	3.25	3.52	3.80	4.07	80	4.35	4.62	4.90	5.17	5.45
2.98	3.26	3.53	3.81	4.08	85	4.36	4.63	4.91	5.18	5.46
3.00	3.27	3.55	3.82	4.10	90	4.37	4.65	4.92	5.20	5.47
3.01	3.29	3.56	3.84	4.11	95	4.39	4.66	4.94	5.21	5.49

Even tons, 1 to 50 inclusive.

1-10		11-20		21-30		31-40		41-50	
T	Am't	T	Am't	T	Am't	T	Am't	T	Am't
1	5.50	11	60.50	21	115.50	31	170.50	41	225.50
2	11.00	12	66.00	22	121.00	32	176.00	42	231.00
3	16.50	13	71.50	23	126.50	33	181.50	43	236.50
4	22.00	14	77.00	24	132.00	34	187.00	44	242.00
5	27.50	15	82.50	25	137.50	35	192.50	45	247.50
6	33.00	16	88.00	26	143.00	36	198.00	46	253.00
7	38.50	17	93.50	27	148.50	37	203.50	47	258.50
8	44.00	18	99.00	28	154.00	38	209.00	48	264.00
9	49.50	19	104.50	29	159.50	39	214.50	49	269.50
10	55.00	20	110.00	30	165.00	40	220.00	50	275.00
200	1100	300	1650	400	2200	500	2750	600	3300

POUNDS

2000	2100	2200	2300	2400		2500	2600	2700	2800	2900
		AMOUNT						AMOUNT		
5.50	5.78	6.05	6.33	6.60		6.88	7.15	7.43	7.70	7.98
5.51	5.79	6.06	6.34	6.61	5	6.89	7.16	7.44	7.71	7.99
5.53	5.80	6.08	6.35	6.63	10	6.90	7.18	7.45	7.73	8.00
5.54	5.82	6.09	6.37	6.64	15	6.92	7.19	7.47	7.74	8.02
5.56	5.83	6.11	6.38	6.66	20	6.93	7.21	7.48	7.76	8.03
5.57	5.84	6.12	6.39	6.67	25	6.94	7.22	7.49	7.77	8.04
5.58	5.86	6.13	6.41	6.68	30	6.96	7.23	7.51	7.78	8.06
5.60	5.87	6.15	6.42	6.70	35	6.97	7.25	7.52	7.80	8.07
5.61	5.89	6.16	6.44	6.71	40	6.99	7.26	7.54	7.81	8.09
5.62	5.90	6.17	6.45	6.72	45	7.00	7.27	7.55	7.82	8.10
5.64	5.91	6.19	6.46	6.74	50	7.01	7.29	7.56	7.84	8.11
5.65	5.93	6.20	6.48	6.75	55	7.03	7.30	7.58	7.85	8.13
5.67	5.94	6.22	6.49	6.77	60	7.04	7.32	7.59	7.87	8.14
5.68	5.95	6.23	6.50	6.78	65	7.05	7.33	7.60	7.88	8.15
5.69	5.97	6.24	6.52	6.79	70	7.07	7.34	7.62	7.89	8.17
5.71	5.98	6.26	6.53	6.81	75	7.08	7.36	7.63	7.91	8.18
5.72	6.00	6.27	6.55	6.82	80	7.10	7.37	7.65	7.92	8.20
5.73	6.01	6.28	6.56	6.83	85	7.11	7.38	7.66	7.93	8.21
5.75	6.02	6.30	6.57	6.85	90	7.12	7.40	7.67	7.95	8.22
5.76	6 04	6.31	6.59	6.86	95	7.14	7.41	7.69	7.96	8.24

POUNDS

3000	3100	3200	3300	3400		3500	3600	3700	3800	3900
		AMOUNT						AMOUNT		
8.25	8.53	8.80	9.08	9.35		9.63	9.90	10.18	10.45	10.73
8.26	8.54	8.81	9.09	9.36	5	9.64	9.91	10.19	10.46	10.74
8.28	8.55	8.83	9.10	9.38	10	9.65	9.93	10.20	10.48	10.75
8.29	8.57	8.84	9.12	9.39	15	9.67	9.94	10.22	10.49	10.77
8.31	8.58	8.86	9.13	9.41	20	9.68	9.96	10.23	10.51	10.78
8.32	8.59	8.87	9.14	9.42	25	9.69	9.97	10.24	10.52	10.79
8.33	8.61	8.88	9.16	9.43	30	9.71	9.98	10.26	10.53	10.81
8.35	8.62	8.90	9.17	9.45	35	9.72	10.00	10.27	10.55	10.82
8.36	8.64	8.91	9.19	9.46	40	9.74	10.01	10.29	10.56	10.84
8.37	8.65	8.92	9.20	9.47	45	9.75	10.02	10.30	10.57	10.85
8.39	8.66	8.94	9.21	9.49	50	9.76	10.04	10.31	10.59	10.86
8.40	8.68	8.95	9.23	9.50	55	9.78	10.05	10.33	10.60	10.88
8.42	8.69	8.97	9.24	9.52	60	9.79	10.07	10.34	10.62	10.89
8.43	8.70	8.98	9.25	9.53	65	9.80	10.08	10.35	10.63	10.90
8.44	8.72	8.99	9.27	9.54	70	9.82	10.09	10.37	10.64	10.92
8.46	8.73	9.01	9.28	9.56	75	9.83	10.11	10.38	10.66	10.93
8.47	8.75	9.02	9.30	9.57	80	9.85	10.12	10.40	10.67	10.95
8.48	8.76	9.03	9.31	9.58	85	9.86	10.13	10.41	10.68	10.96
8.50	8.77	9.05	9.32	9.60	90	9.87	10.15	10.42	10.70	10.97
8.51	8.79	9.06	9.34	9.61	95	9.89	10.16	10.44	10.71	10.99

Even tons, 51 to 100 inclusive.

51-60		61-70		71-80		81-90		91-100	
T	Am't	T	Am't	T	Am't	T	Am't	T	Am't
51	280.50	61	335.50	71	390.50	81	445.50	91	500.50
52	286.00	62	341.00	72	396.00	82	451.00	92	506.00
53	291.50	63	346.50	73	401.50	83	456.50	93	511.50
54	297.00	64	352.00	74	407.00	84	462.00	94	517.00
55	302.50	65	357.50	75	412.50	85	467.50	95	522.50
56	308.00	66	363.00	76	418.00	86	473.00	96	528.00
57	313.50	67	368.50	77	423.50	87	478.50	97	533.50
58	319.00	68	374.00	78	429.00	88	484.00	98	539.00
59	324.50	69	379.50	79	434.50	89	489.50	99	544.50
60	330.00	70	385.00	80	440.00	90	495.00	100	550.00

700	3850	800	4400	900	4950	1000	5500	1100	6050

POUNDS

Under 100	100	200	300	400		500	600	700	800	90
	.29	.58	.86	1.15		1.44	1.73	2.01	2.30	2.59
.01	.30	.59	.88	1.16	5	1.45	1.74	2.03	2.31	2.60
.03	.32	.60	.89	1.18	10	1.47	1.75	2.04	2.33	2.62
.04	.33	.62	.91	1.19	15	1.48	1.77	2.06	2.34	2.63
.06	.35	.63	.92	1.21	20	1.50	1.78	2.07	2.36	2.65
.07	.36	.65	.93	1.22	25	1.51	1.80	2.08	2.37	2.66
.09	.37	.66	.95	1.24	30	1.52	1.81	2.10	2.39	2.67
.10	.39	.68	.96	1.25	35	1.54	1.83	2.11	2.40	2.69
.12	.40	.69	.98	1.27	40	1.55	1.84	2.13	2.42	2.70
.13	.42	.70	.99	1.28	45	1.57	1.85	2.14	2.43	2.72
.14	.43	.72	1.01	1.29	50	1.58	1.87	2.16	2.44	2.73
.16	.45	.73	1.02	1.31	55	1.60	1.88	2.17	2.46	2.75
.17	.46	.75	1.04	1.32	60	1.61	1.90	2.19	2.47	2.76
.19	.47	.76	1.05	1.34	65	1.62	1.91	2.20	2.49	2.77
.20	.49	.78	1.06	1.35	70	1.64	1.93	2.21	2.50	2.79
.22	.50	.79	1.08	1.37	75	1.65	1.94	2.23	2.52	2.80
.23	.52	.81	1.09	1.38	80	1.67	1.96	2.24	2.53	2.82
.24	.53	.82	1.11	1.39	85	1.68	1.97	2.26	2.54	2.83
.26	.55	.83	1.12	1.41	90	1.70	1.98	2.27	2.56	2.85
.27	.56	.85	1.14	1.42	95	1.71	2.00	2.29	2.57	2.86

POUNDS

1000	1100	1200	1300	1400		1500	1600	1700	1800	1900
2.88	3.16	3.45	3.74	4.03		4.31	4.60	4.89	5.18	5.46
2.89	3.18	3.46	3.75	4.04	5	4.33	4.61	4.90	5.19	5.48
2.90	3.19	3.48	3.77	4.05	10	4.34	4.63	4.92	5.20	5.49
2.92	3.21	3.49	3.78	4.07	15	4.36	4.64	4.93	5.22	5.51
2.93	3.22	3.51	3.80	4.08	20	4.37	4.66	4.95	5.23	5.52
2.95	3.23	3.52	3.81	4.10	25	4.38	4.67	4.96	5.25	5.53
2.96	3.25	3.54	3.82	4.11	30	4.40	4.69	4.97	5.26	5.55
2.98	3.26	3.55	3.84	4.13	35	4.41	4.70	4.99	5.28	5.56
2.99	3.28	3.57	3.85	4.14	40	4.43	4.72	5.00	5.29	5.58
3.00	3.29	3.58	3.87	4.15	45	4.44	4.73	5.02	5.30	5.59
3.02	3.31	3.59	3.88	4.17	50	4.46	4.74	5.03	5.32	5.61
3.03	3.32	3.61	3.90	4.18	55	4.47	4.76	5.05	5.33	5.62
3.05	3.34	3.62	3.91	4.20	60	4.49	4.77	5.06	5.35	5.64
3.06	3.35	3.64	3.92	4.21	65	4.50	4.79	5.07	5.36	5.65
3.08	3.36	3.65	3.94	4.23	70	4.51	4.80	5.09	5.38	5.66
3.09	3.38	3.67	3.95	4.24	75	4.53	4.82	5.10	5.39	5.68
3.11	3.39	3.68	3.97	4.26	80	4.54	4.83	5.12	5.41	5.69
3.12	3.41	3.69	3.98	4.27	85	4.56	4.84	5.13	5.42	5.71
3.13	3.42	3.71	4.00	4.28	90	4.57	4.86	5.15	5.43	5.72
3.15	3.44	3.72	4.01	4.30	95	4.59	4.87	5.16	5.45	5.74

Even tons, 1 to 50 inclusive.

1-10		11-20		21-30		31-40		41-50	
T	Am't	T	Am't	T	Am't	T	Am't	T	Am't
1	5.75	11	63.25	21	120.75	31	178.25	41	235.75
2	11.50	12	69.00	22	126.50	32	184.00	42	241.50
3	17.25	13	74.75	23	132.25	33	189.75	43	247.25
4	23.00	14	80.50	24	138.00	34	195.50	44	253.00
5	28.75	15	86.25	25	143.75	35	201.25	45	258.75
6	34.50	16	92.00	26	149.50	36	207.00	46	264.50
7	40.25	17	97.75	27	155.25	37	212.75	47	270.25
8	46.00	18	103.50	28	161.00	38	218.50	48	276.00
9	51.75	19	109.25	29	166.75	39	224.25	49	281.75
10	57.50	20	115.00	30	172.50	40	230.00	50	287.50
200	1150	300	1725	400	2300	500	2875	600	3450

——————————— POUNDS ———————————

2000	2100	2200	2300	2400		2500	2600	2700	2800	2900
		AMOUNT						AMOUNT		
5.75	6.04	6.33	6.61	6.90		7.19	7.48	7.76	8.05	8.34
5.76	6.05	6.34	6.63	6.91	5	7.20	7.49	7.78	8.06	8.35
5.78	6.07	6.35	6.64	6.93	10	7.22	7.50	7.79	8.08	8.37
5.79	6.08	6.37	6.66	6.94	15	7.23	7.52	7.81	8.09	8.38
5.81	6.10	6.38	6.67	6.96	20	7.25	7.53	7.82	8.11	8.40
5.82	6.11	6.40	6.68	6.97	25	7.26	7.55	7.83	8.12	8.41
5.84	6.12	6.41	6.70	6.99	30	7.27	7.56	7.85	8.14	8.42
5.85	6.14	6.43	6.71	7.00	35	7.29	7.58	7.86	8.15	8.44
5.87	6.15	6.44	6.73	7.02	40	7.30	7.59	7.88	8.17	8.45
5.88	6.17	6.45	6.74	7.03	45	7.32	7.60	7.89	8.18	8.47
5.89	6.18	6.47	6.76	7.04	50	7.33	7.62	7.91	8.19	8.48
5.91	6.20	6.48	6.77	7.06	55	7.35	7.63	7.92	8.21	8.50
5.92	6.21	6.50	6.79	7.07	60	7.36	7.65	7.94	8.22	8.51
5.94	6.22	6.51	6.80	7.09	65	7.37	7.66	7.95	8.24	8.52
5.95	6.24	6.53	6.81	7.10	70	7.39	7.68	7 96	8.25	8.54
5.97	6.25	6.54	6.83	7.12	75	7.40	7.69	7.98	8.27	8.55
5.98	6.27	6.56	6.84	7.13	80	7.42	7.71	7.99	8.28	8.57
5.99	6.28	6.57	6.86	7.14	85	7.43	7.72	8.01	8.29	8.58`
6.01	6.30	6.58	6.87	7.16	90	7.45	7.73	8.02	8.31	8.60
6.02	6.31	6.60	6.89	7.17	95	7.46	7.75	8.04	8.32	8.61

——————————— POUNDS ———————————

3000	3100	3200	3300	3400		3500	3600	3700	3800	3900
		AMOUNT						AMOUNT		
8.63	8.91	9.20	9.49	9.78		10.06	10.35	10.64	10.93	11.21
8.64	8.93	9.21	9.50	9.79	5	10.08	10.36	10.65	10.94	11.23
8.65	8.94	9.23	9.52	9.80	10	10.09	10.38	10.67	10.95	11.24
8.67	8.95	9.24	9.53	9.82	15	10.11	10.39	10.68	10.97	11.26
8.68	8.97	9.26	9.55	9.83	20	10.12	10.41	10.70	10.98	11.27
8.70	8.98	9.27	9.56	9.85	25	10.13	10.42	10.71	11.00	11.28
8.71	9.00	9.29	9.57	9.86	30	10.15	10.44	10.72	11.01	11.30
8.73	9.01	9.30	9.59	9.88	35	10.16	10.45	10.74	11.03	11.31
8.74	9.03	9.32	9.60	9.89	40	10.18	10.47	10.75	11.04	11.33
8.75	9.04	9.33	9.62	9.90	45	10.19	10.48	10.77	11.05	11.34
8.77	9.06	9.34	9.63	9.92	50	10.21	10.49	10.78	11.07	11.36
8.78	9.07	9.36	9.65	9.93	55	10.22	10.51	10.80	11.08	11.37
8.80	9.09	9.37	9.66	9.95	60	10.24	10.52	10.81	11.10	11.39
8.81	9.10	9.39	9.67	9.96	65	10.25	10.54	10.82	11.11	11.40
8.83	9.11	9.40	9.69	9.98	70	10.26	10.55	10.84	11.13	11.41
8.84	9.13	9.42	9.70	9.99	75	10.28	10.57	10.85	11.14	11.43
8.86	9.14	9.43	9.72	10.01	80	10.29	10.58	10.87	11.16	11.44
8.87	9.16	9.44	9.73	10.02	85	10.31	10.59	10.88	11.17	11.46
8.88	9.17	9.46	9.75	10.03	90	10.32	10.61	10.90	11.18	11.47
8.90	9.19	9.47	9.76	10.05	95	10.34	10.62	10.91	11.20	11.49

Even tons, 51 to 100 inclusive.

51-60		61-70		71-80		81-90		91-100	
T	Am't	T	Am't	T	Am't	T	Am't	T	Am't
51	293.25	61	350.75	71	408.25	81	465.75	91	523.25
52	299.00	62	356.50	72	414.00	82	471.50	92	529.00
53	304.75	63	362.25	73	419.75	83	477.25	93	534.75
54	310.50	64	368.00	74	425.50	84	483.00	94	540.50
55	316.25	65	373.75	75	431.25	85	488.75	95	546.25
56	322.00	66	379.50	76	437.00	86	494.50	96	552.00
57	327.75	67	385.25	77	442.75	87	500.25	97	557.75
58	333.50	68	391.00	78	448.50	88	506.00	98	563.50
59	339.25	69	396.75	79	454.25	89	511.75	99	569.25
60	345.00	70	402.50	80	460.00	90	517.50	100	575.00

700	4025	800	4600	900	5175	1000	5750	1100	6325

POUNDS

Under 100	100	200	300	400		500	600	700	800	900
	.30	.60	.90	1.20		1.50	1.80	2.10	2.40	2.70
.02	.32	.62	.92	1.22	5	1.52	1.82	2.12	2.42	2.72
.03	.33	.63	.93	1.23	10	1.53	1.83	2.13	2.43	2.73
.05	.35	.65	.95	1.25	15	1.55	1.85	2.15	2.45	2.75
.06	.36	.66	.96	1.26	20	1.56	1.86	2.16	2.46	2.76
.08	.38	.68	.98	1.28	25	1.58	1.88	2.18	2.48	2.78
.09	.39	.69	.99	1.29	30	1.59	1.89	2.19	2.49	2.79
.11	.41	.71	1.01	1.31	35	1.61	1.91	2.21	2.51	2.81
.12	.42	.72	1.02	1.32	40	1.62	1.92	2.22	2.52	2.82
.14	.44	.74	1.04	1.34	45	1.64	1.94	2.24	2.54	2.84
.15	.45	.75	1.05	1.35	50	1.65	1.95	2.25	2.55	2.85
.17	.47	.77	1.07	1.37	55	1.67	1.97	2.27	2.57	2.87
.18	.48	.78	1.08	1.38	60	1.68	1.98	2.28	2.58	2.88
.20	.50	.80	1.10	1.40	65	1.70	2.00	2.30	2.60	2.90
.21	.51	.81	1.11	1.41	70	1.71	2.01	2.31	2.61	2.91
.23	.53	.83	1.13	1.43	75	1.73	2.03	2.33	2.63	2.93
.24	.54	.84	1.14	1.44	80	1.74	2.04	2.34	2.64	2.94
.26	.56	.86	1.16	1.46	85	1.76	2.06	2.36	2.66	2.96
.27	.57	.87	1.17	1.47	90	1.77	2.07	2.37	2.67	2.97
.29	.59	.89	1.19	1.49	95	1.79	2.09	2.39	2.69	2.99

POUNDS

1000	1100	1200	1300	1400		1500	1600	1700	1800	1900
3.00	3.30	3.60	3.90	4.20		4.50	4.80	5.10	5.40	5.70
3.02	3.32	3.62	3.92	4.22	5	4.52	4.82	5.12	5.42	5.72
3.03	3.33	3.63	3.93	4.23	10	4.53	4.83	5.13	5.43	5.73
3.05	3.35	3.65	3.95	4.25	15	4.55	4.85	5.15	5.45	5.75
3.06	3.36	3.66	3.96	4.26	20	4.56	4.86	5.16	5.46	5.76
3.08	3.38	3.68	3.98	4.28	25	4.58	4.88	5.18	5.48	5.78
3.09	3.39	3.69	3.99	4.29	30	4.59	4.89	5.19	5.49	5.79
3.11	3.41	3.71	4.01	4.31	35	4.61	4.91	5.21	5.51	5.81
3.12	3.42	3.72	4.02	4.32	40	4.62	4.92	5.22	5.52	5.82
3.14	3.44	3.74	4.04	4.34	45	4.64	4.94	5.24	5.54	5.84
3.15	3.45	3.75	4.05	4.35	50	4.65	4.95	5.25	5.55	5.85
3.17	3.47	3.77	4.07	4.37	55	4.67	4.97	5.27	5.57	5.87
3.18	3.48	3.78	4.08	4.38	60	4.68	4.98	5.28	5.58	5.88
3.20	3.50	3.80	4.10	4.40	65	4.70	5.00	5.30	5.60	5.90
3.21	3.81	3.81	4.11	4.41	70	4.71	5.01	5.31	5.61	5.91
3.23	3.53	3.83	4.13	4.43	75	4.73	5.03	5.33	5.63	5.93
3.24	3.54	3.84	4.14	4.44	80	4.74	5.04	5.34	5.64	5.94
3.26	3.56	3.86	4.16	4.46	85	4.76	5.06	5.36	5.66	5.96
3.27	3.57	3.87	4.17	4.47	90	4.77	5.07	5.37	5.67	5.97
3.29	3.59	3.89	4.19	4.49	95	4.79	5.09	5.39	5.69	5.99

Even tons, 1 to 50 inclusive.

T	Am't	T	Am't	T	Am't	T	Am't	T	Am't
1	6.00	11	66.00	21	126.00	31	186.00	41	246.00
2	12.00	12	72.00	22	132.00	32	192.00	42	252.00
3	18.00	13	78.00	23	138.00	33	198.00	43	258.00
4	24.00	14	84.00	24	144.00	34	204.00	44	264.00
5	30.00	15	90.00	25	150.00	35	210.00	45	270.00
6	36.00	16	96.00	26	156.00	36	216.00	46	276.00
7	42.00	17	102.00	27	162.00	37	222.00	47	282.00
8	48.00	18	108.00	28	168.00	38	228.00	48	288.00
9	54.00	19	114.00	29	174.00	39	234.00	49	294.00
10	60.00	20	120.00	30	180.00	40	240.00	50	300.00

200	1200	300	1800	400	2400	500	3000	600	3600

--- POUNDS ---

2000	2100	2200	2300	2100		2500	2600	2700	2800	2900
		AMOUNT						AMOUNT		
6.00	6.30	6.60	6.90	7.20		7.50	7.80	8.10	8.40	8.70
6.02	6.32	6.62	6.92	7.22	5	7.52	7.82	8.12	8.42	8.72
6.03	6.33	6.63	6.93	7.23	10	7.53	7.83	8.13	8.43	8.73
6.05	6.35	6.65	6.95	7.25	15	7.55	7.85	8.15	8.45	8.75
6.06	6.36	6.66	6.96	7.26	20	7.56	7.86	8.16	8.46	8.76
6.08	6.38	6.68	6.98	7.28	25	7.58	7.88	8.18	8.48	8.78
6.09	6.39	6.69	6.99	7.29	30	7.59	7.89	8.19	8.49	8.79
6.11	6.41	6.71	7.00	7.31	35	7.61	7.91	8.21	8.51	8.81
6.12	6.42	6.72	7.02	7.32	40	7.62	7.92	8.22	8.52	8.82
6.14	6.44	6.74	7.04	7.34	45	7.64	7.94	8.24	8.54	8.84
6.15	6.45	6.75	7.05	7.35	50	7.65	7.95	8.25	8.55	8.85
6.17	6.47	6.77	7.07	7.37	55	7.67	7.97	8.27	8.57	8.87
6.18	6.48	6.78	7.08	7.38	60	7.68	7.98	8.28	8.58	8.88
6.20	6.50	6.80	7.10	7.40	65	7.70	8.00	8.30	8.60	8.90
6.21	6.51	6.81	7.11	7.41	70	7.71	8.01	8.31	8.61	8.91
6.23	6.53	6.83	7.13	7.43	75	7.73	8.03	8.33	8.63	8.93
6.24	6.54	6.84	7.14	7.44	80	7.74	8.04	8.34	8.64	8.94
6.26	6.56	6.86	7.16	7.46	85	7.76	8.06	8.36	8.66	8.96
6.27	6.57	6.87	7.17	7.47	90	7.77	8.07	8.37	8.67	8.97
6.29	6.59	6.89	7.19	7.49	95	7.79	8.09	8.39	8.69	8.99

--- POUNDS ---

3000	3100	3200	3300	3400		3500	3600	3700	3800	3900
		AMOUNT						AMOUNT		
9.00	9.30	9.60	9.90	10.20		10.50	10.80	11.10	11.40	11.70
9.02	9.32	9.62	9.92	10.22	5	10.52	10.82	11.12	11.42	11.72
9.03	9.33	9.63	9.93	10.23	10	10.53	10.83	11.13	11.43	11.73
9.05	9.35	9.65	9.95	10.25	15	10.55	10.85	11.15	11.45	11.75
9.06	9.36	9.66	9.96	10.26	20	10.56	10.86	11.16	11.46	11.76
9.08	9.38	9.68	9.98	10.28	25	10.58	10.88	11.18	11.48	11.78
9.09	9.39	9.69	9.99	10.29	30	10.59	10.89	11.19	11.49	11.79
9.11	9.41	9.71	10.01	10.31	35	10.61	10.91	11.21	11.51	11.81
9.12	9.42	9.72	10.02	10.32	40	10.62	10.92	11.22	11.52	11.82
9.14	9.44	9.74	10.04	10.34	45	10.64	10.94	11.24	11.54	11.84
9.15	9.45	9.75	10.05	10.35	50	10.65	10.95	11.25	11.55	11.85
9.17	9.47	9.77	10.07	10.37	55	10.67	10.97	11.27	11.57	11.87
9.18	9.48	9.78	10.08	10.38	60	10.68	10.98	11.28	11.58	11.88
9.20	9.50	9.80	10.10	10.40	65	10.70	11.00	11.30	11.60	11.90
9.21	9.51	9.81	10.11	10.41	70	10.71	11.01	11.31	11.61	11.91
9.23	9.53	9.83	10.13	10.43	75	10.73	11.03	11.33	11.63	11.93
9.24	9.54	9.84	10.14	10.44	80	10.74	11.04	11.34	11.64	11.94
9.26	9.56	9.86	10.16	10.46	85	10.76	11.06	11.36	11.66	11.96
9.27	9.57	9.87	10.17	10.47	90	10.77	11.07	11.37	11.67	11.97
9.29	9.59	9.89	10.19	10.49	95	10.79	11.09	11.39	11.69	11.99

Even tons, 51 to 100 inclusive.

51-60		61-70		71-80		81-90		91-100	
T	Am't	T	Am't	T	Am't	T	Am't	T	Am't
51	306 00	61	366.00	71	426.00	81	486.00	91	546.00
52	312.00	62	372.00	72	432.00	82	492.00	92	552.00
53	318.00	63	378.00	73	438.00	83	498.00	93	558.00
54	324.00	64	384.00	74	444.00	84	504.00	94	564.00
55	330.00	65	390.00	75	450.00	85	510.00	95	570.00
56	336.00	66	396.00	76	456.00	86	516.00	96	576.00
57	342.00	67	402.00	77	462.00	87	522.00	97	582.00
58	348.00	68	408.00	78	468.00	88	528.00	98	588.00
59	354.00	69	414.00	79	474.00	89	534.00	99	594.00
60	360.00	70	420.00	80	480.00	90	540.00	100	600.00

700	4200	800	4800	900	5400	1000	6000	1100	6600

25c a bu. $6.25 a T.   31¼c a 100 lbs.

POUNDS

Under 100	100	200	300	400		500	600	700	800	900
	AMOUNT					AMOUNT				
	.31	.63	.94	1.25		1.56	1.88	2.19	2.50	2.81
.02	.33	.64	.95	1.27	5	1.58	1.89	2.20	2.52	2.83
.03	.34	.66	.97	1.28	10	1.59	1.91	2.22	2.53	2.84
.05	.36	.67	.98	1.30	15	1.61	1.92	2.23	2.55	2.86
.06	.38	.69	1.00	1.31	20	1.63	1.94	2.25	2.56	2.88
.08	.39	.70	1.02	1.33	25	1.64	1.95	2.27	2.58	2.89
.09	.41	.72	1.03	1.34	30	1.66	1.97	2.28	2.59	2.91
.11	.42	.73	1.05	1.36	35	1.67	1.98	2.30	2.61	2.92
.13	.44	.75	1.06	1.38	40	1.69	2.00	2.31	2.63	2.94
.14	.45	.77	1.08	1.39	45	1.70	2.02	2.33	2.64	2.95
.16	.47	.78	1.09	1.41	50	1.72	2.03	2.34	2.66	2.97
.17	.48	.80	1.11	1.42	55	1.73	2.05	2.36	2.67	2.98
.19	.50	.81	1.13	1.44	60	1.75	2.06	2.38	2.69	3.00
.20	.52	.83	1.14	1.45	65	1.77	2.08	2.39	2.70	3.02
.22	.53	.84	1.16	1.47	70	1.78	2.09	2.41	2.72	3 03
.23	.55	.86	1.17	1.48	75	1.80	2.11	2.42	2.73	3.05
.25	.56	.88	1.19	1.50	80	1.81	2.13	2.44	2.75	3.06
.27	.58	.89	1.20	1.52	85	1.83	2.14	2.45	2.77	3.08
.28	.59	.91	1.22	1.53	90	1.84	2.16	2.47	2.78	3.09
.30	.61	.92	1.23	1.55	95	1.86	2.17	2.48	2.80	3.11

POUNDS

1000	1100	1200	1300	1400		1500	1600	1700	1800	1900
	AMOUNT					AMOUNT				
3.13	3.44	3.75	4.06	4.38		4.69	5.00	5.31	5.63	5.94
3.14	3.45	3.77	4.08	4.39	5	4.70	5.02	5.33	5.64	5.95
3.16	3.47	3.78	4.09	4.41	10	4.72	5.03	5.34	5.66	5.97
3.17	3.48	3.80	4.11	4.42	15	4.73	5.05	5.36	5.67	5.98
3.19	3.50	3.81	4.13	4.44	20	4.75	5.06	5.38	5.69	6.00
3.20	3.52	3.83	4.14	4.45	25	4.77	5.08	5.39	5.70	6.02
3.22	3.53	3.84	4.16	4.47	30	4.78	5.09	5.41	5.72	6.03
3.23	3.55	3.86	4.17	4.48	35	4.80	5.11	5.42	5.73	6.05
3.25	3.56	3.88	4.19	4.50	40	4.81	5.13	5.44	5.75	6.06
3.27	3.58	3.89	4.20	4.52	45	4.83	5.14	5 45	5.77	6.08
3.28	3.59	3.91	4.22	4.53	50	4.84	5.16	5.47	5.78	6.09
3.30	3.61	3.92	4.23	4.55	55	4.86	5.17	5.48	5.80	6.11
3.31	3.63	3.94	4.25	4.56	60	4.88	5.19	5.50	5.81	6.13
3.33	3 64	3.95	4.27	4.58	65	4.89	5.20	5.52	5.83	6.14
3.34	3.66	3.97	4.28	4.59	70	4.91	5.22	5.53	5.84	6 16
3.36	3.67	3.98	4.30	4.61	75	4.92	5.23	5.55	5.86	6.17
3.38	3.69	4.00	4.31	4.63	80	4.94	5.25	5.56	5.88	6.19
3.39	3.70	4.02	4.33	4.64	85	4.95	5.27	5.58	5.89	6.20
3.41	3.72	4.03	4.34	4.66	90	4.97	5.28	5.59	5.91	6.22
3.42	3.73	4.05	4.36	4.67	95	4.98	5.30	5.61	5.92	6.23

Even tons, 1 to 50 inclusive.

1-10		11-20		21-30		31-40		41-50	
T	Am't	T	Am't	T	Am't	T	Am't	T	Am't
1	6.25	11	68.75	21	131.25	31	193.75	41	256.25
2	12.50	12	75.00	22	137.50	32	200.00	42	262.50
3	18.75	13	81.25	23	143.75	33	206.25	43	268.75
4	25.00	14	87.50	24	150.00	34	212.50	44	275.00
5	31.25	15	93.75	25	156.25	35	218.75	45	281.25
6	37.50	16	100.00	26	162.50	36	225.00	46	287.50
7	43.75	17	106.25	27	168.75	37	231.25	47	293.75
8	50.00	18	112.50	28	175.00	38	237.50	48	300.00
9	56.25	19	118.75	29	181.25	39	243.75	49	306.25
10	62.50	20	125.00	30	187.50	40	250.00	50	312.50
200	1250	300	1875	400	2500	500	3125	600	3750

———— POUNDS ————

2000	2100	2200	2300	2400		2500	2600	2700	2800	2900
		—AMOUNT—						—AMOUNT—		
6.25	6.56	6.88	7.19	7.50		7.81	8.13	8.44	8.75	9.06
6.27	6.58	6.89	7.20	7.52	5	7.83	8.14	8.45	8.77	9.08
6.28	6.59	6.91	7.22	7.53	10	7.84	8.16	8.47	8.78	9.09
6.30	6.61	6.92	7.23	7.55	15	7.86	8.17	8.48	8.80	9.11
6.31	6.63	6.94	7.25	7.56	20	7.88	8.19	8.50	8.81	9.13
6.33	6.64	6.95	7.27	7.58	25	7.89	8.20	8.52	8.83	9.14
6.34	6.66	6.97	7.28	7.59	30	7.91	8.22	8.53	8.84	9.16
6.36	6.67	6.98	7.30	7.61	35	7.92	8.23	8.55	8.86	9.17
6.38	6.69	7.00	7.31	7.63	40	7.94	8.25	8.56	8.88	9.19
6.39	6.70	7.02	7.33	7.64	45	7.95	8.27	8.58	8.89	9.20
6.41	6.72	7.03	7.34	7.66	50	7.97	8.28	8.59	8.91	9.22
6.42	6.73	7.05	7.36	7.67	55	7.98	8.30	8.61	8.92	9.23
6.44	6.75	7.06	7.38	7.69	60	8.00	8.31	8.63	8.94	9.25
6.45	6.77	7.08	7.39	7.70	65	8.02	8.33	8.64	8.95	9.27
6.47	6.78	7.09	7.41	7.72	70	8.03	8.34	8.66	8.97	9.28
6.48	6.80	7.11	7.42	7.73	75	8.05	8.36	8.67	8.98	9.30
6.50	6.81	7.13	7.44	7.75	80	8.06	8.38	8.69	9.00	9.31
6.52	6.83	7.14	7.45	7.77	85	8.08	8.39	8.70	9.02	9.33
6.53	6.84	7.16	7.47	7.78	90	8.09	8.41	8.72	9.03	9.34
6.55	6.86	7.17	7.48	7.80	95	8.11	8.42	8.73	9.05	9.36

———— POUNDS ————

3000	3100	3200	3300	3400		3500	3600	3700	3800	3900
		—AMOUNT—						—AMOUNT—		
9.38	9.69	10.00	10.31	10.63		10.94	11.25	11.56	11.88	12.19
9.39	9.70	10.02	10.33	10.64	5	10.95	11.27	11.58	11.89	12.20
9.41	9.72	10.03	10.34	10.66	10	10.97	11.28	11.59	11.91	12.22
9.42	9.73	10.05	10.36	10.67	15	10.98	11.30	11.61	11.92	12.23
9.44	9.75	10.06	10.38	10.69	20	11.00	11.31	11.63	11.94	12.25
9.45	9.77	10.08	10.39	10.70	25	11.02	11.33	11.64	11.95	12.27
9.47	9.78	10.09	10.41	10.72	30	11.03	11.34	11.66	11.97	12.28
9.48	9.80	10.11	10.42	10.73	35	11.05	11.36	11.67	11.98	12.30
9.50	9.81	10.13	10.44	10.75	40	11.06	11.38	11.69	12.00	12.31
9.52	9.83	10.14	10.45	10.77	45	11.08	11.39	11.70	12.02	12.33
9.53	9.84	10.16	10.47	10.78	50	11.09	11.41	11.72	12.03	12.34
9.55	9.86	10.17	10.48	10.80	55	11.11	11.42	11.73	12.05	12.36
9.56	9.88	10.19	10.50	10.81	60	11.13	11.44	11.75	12.06	12.38
9.58	9.89	10.20	10.52	10.83	65	11.14	11.45	11.77	12.08	12.39
9.59	9.91	10.22	10.53	10.84	70	11.16	11.47	11.78	12.09	12.41
9.61	9.92	10.23	10.55	10.86	75	11.17	11.48	11.80	12.11	12.42
9.63	9.94	10.25	10.56	10.88	80	11.19	11.50	11.81	12.13	12.44
9.64	9.95	10.27	10.58	10.89	85	11.20	11.52	11.83	12.14	12.45
9.66	9.97	10.28	10.59	10.91	90	11.22	11.53	11.84	12.16	12.47
9.67	9.98	10.30	10.61	10.92	95	11.23	11.55	11.86	12.17	12.48

Even tons, 51 to 100 inclusive.

51-60		61-70		71-80		81-90		91-100	
T	Am't	T	Am't	T	Am't	T	Am't	T	Am't
51	318.75	61	381.25	71	443.75	81	506.25	91	568.75
52	325.00	62	387.50	72	450.00	82	512.50	92	575.00
53	331.25	63	393.75	73	456.25	83	518.75	93	581.25
54	337.50	64	400.00	74	462.50	84	525.00	94	587.50
55	343.75	65	406.25	75	468.75	85	531.25	95	593.75
56	350.00	66	412.50	76	475.00	86	537.50	96	600.00
57	356.25	67	418.75	77	481.25	87	543.75	97	606.25
58	362.50	68	425.00	78	487.50	88	550.00	98	612.50
59	368.75	69	431.25	79	493.75	89	556.25	99	618.75
60	375.00	70	437.50	80	500.00	90	562.50	100	625.00

700	4375	800	5000	900	5625	1000	6250	1100	6875

POUNDS

Under 100	100	200	300	400		500	600	700	800	900
	.33	.65	.98	1.30		1.63	1.95	2.28	2.60	2.93
.02	.34	.67	.99	1.32	5	1.64	1.97	2.29	2.62	2.94
.03	.36	.68	1.01	1.33	10	1.66	1.98	2.31	2.63	2.96
.05	.37	.70	1.02	1.35	15	1.67	2.00	2.32	2.65	2.97
.07	.39	.72	1.04	1.37	20	1.69	2.02	2.34	2.67	2.99
.08	.41	.73	1.06	1.38	25	1.71	2.03	2.36	2.68	3.01
.10	.42	.75	1.07	1.40	30	1.72	2.05	2.37	2.70	3.02
.11	.44	.76	1.09	1.41	35	1.74	2.06	2.39	2.71	3.04
.13	.46	.78	1.11	1.43	40	1.76	2.08	2.41	2.73	3.06
.15	.47	.80	1.12	1.45	45	1.77	2.10	2.42	2.75	3.07
.16	.49	.81	1.14	1.46	50	1.79	2.11	2.44	2.76	3.09
.18	.50	.83	1.15	1.48	55	1.80	2.13	2.45	2.78	3.10
.20	.52	.85	1.17	1.50	60	1.82	2.15	2.47	2.80	3.12
.21	.54	.86	1.19	1.51	65	1.84	2.16	2.49	2.81	3.14
.23	.55	.88	1.20	1.53	70	1 85	2.18	2.50	2.83	3.15
.24	.57	.89	1.22	1.54	75	1.87	2.19	2.52	2.84	3.17
.26	.59	.91	1.24	1.56	80	1.89	2.21	2.54	2.86	3.19
.28	.60	.93	1.25	1.58	85	1.90	2.23	2.55	2.88	3.20
.29	.62	.94	1.27	1.59	90	1.92	2.24	2.57	2.89	3.22
.31	.63	.96	1.28	1.61	95	1.93	2.26	2 58	2.91	3.23

POUNDS

1000	1100	1200	1300	1400		1500	1600	1700	1800	1900
3.25	3.58	3.90	4.23	4.55		4.88	5.20	5.53	5.85	6.18
3.27	3.59	3.92	4.24	4.57	5	4.89	5.22	5.54	5.87	6.19
3.28	3.61	3.93	4.26	4.58	10	4.91	5.23	5.56	5.88	6.21
3.30	3.62	3.95	4.27	4.60	15	4.92	5.25	5.57	5.90	6.22
3.32	3.64	3.97	4.29	4.62	20	4.94	5.27	5.59	5.92	6.24
3.33	3.66	3.98	4.31	4.63	25	4.96	5.28	5.61	5.93	6.26
3.35	3.67	4.00	4.32	4.65	30	4.97	5.30	5.62	5.95	6.27
3.36	3.69	4.01	4.34	4.66	35	4.99	5.31	5.64	5.96	6.29
3.38	3.71	4.03	4.36	4.68	40	5.01	5.33	5.66	5.98	6.31
3.40	3.72	4.05	4.37	4.70	45	5.02	5.35	5.67	6.00	6.32
3.41	3 74	4.06	4.39	4.71	50	5.04	5.36	5.69	6.01	6.34
3.43	3.75	4.08	4.40	4.73	55	5.05	5.38	5.70	6.03	6.35
3.45	3.77	4.10	4.42	4.75	60	5.07	5.40	5.72	6.05	6.37
3.46	3.79	4.11	4.44	4.76	65	5.09	5.41	5.74	6.06	6.39
3.48	3.80	4.13	4.45	4.78	70	5.10	5.43	5.75	6.08	6.40
3.49	3.82	4.14	4.47	4.79	75	5.12	5.44	5.77	6.09	6.42
3.51	3.84	4.16	4.49	4.81	80	5.14	5.46	5.79	6.11	6.44
3.53	3.85	4.18	4.50	4.83	85	5.15	5.48	5.80	6.13	6.45
3.54	3.87	4.19	4.52	4.84	90	5.17	5.49	5.82	6.14	6.47
3.56	3.88	4.21	4.53	4.86	95	5.18	5.51	5.83	6.16	6.48

Even tons, 1 to 50 inclusive.

1-10		11-20		21-30		31-40		41-50	
T	Am't	T	Am't	T	Am't	T	Am't	T	Am't
1	6.50	11	71.50	21	136.50	31	201.50	41	266.50
2	13.00	12	78.00	22	143.00	32	208.00	42	273.00
3	19.50	13	84.50	23	149.50	33	214.50	43	279.50
4	26.00	14	91.00	24	156.00	34	221.00	44	286.00
5	32.50	15	97.50	25	162.50	35	227.50	45	292.50
6	39.00	16	104.00	26	169.00	36	234.00	46	299.00
7	45.50	17	110.50	27	175.50	37	240.50	47	305.50
8	52.00	18	182.00	28	182.00	38	247.00	48	312.00
9	58.50	19	123.50	29	188.50	39	253.50	49	318.50
10	65 00	20	130.00	30	195.00	40	260.00	50	325.00

200	1300	300	1950	400	2600	500	3250	600	3900

— POUNDS —

2000	2100	2200	2300	2400		2500	2600	2700	2800	2900
		AMOUNT						AMOUNT		
6.50	6.83	7.15	7.48	7.80		8.13	8.45	8.78	9.10	9.43
6.52	6.84	7.17	7.49	7.82	5	8.14	8.47	8.79	9.12	9.44
6.53	6.86	7.18	7.51	7.83	10	8.16	8.48	8.81	9.13	9.46
6.55	6.87	7.20	7.52	7.85	15	8.17	8.50	8.82	9.15	9.47
6.57	6.89	7.22	7.54	7.87	20	8.19	8.52	8.84	9.17	9.49
6.58	6.91	7.23	7.56	7.98	25	8.21	8.53	8.86	9.18	9.51
6.60	6.92	7.25	7.57	7.90	30	8.22	8.55	8.87	9.20	9.52
6.61	6.94	7.26	7.59	7.91	35	8.24	8.56	8.89	9.21	9.54
6.63	6.96	7.28	7.61	7.93	40	8.26	8.58	8.91	9.23	9.56
6.65	6.97	7.30	7.62	7.95	45	8.27	8.60	8.92	9.25	9.57
6.66	6.99	7.31	7.64	7.96	50	8.29	8.61	8.94	9.26	9.59
6.68	7.00	7.33	7.65	7.98	55	8.30	8.63	8.95	9.28	9.60
6.70	7.02	7.35	7.67	8.00	60	8.32	8.65	8.97	9.30	9.62
6.71	7.04	7.36	7.69	8.01	65	8.34	8.66	8.99	9.31	9.64
6.73	7.05	7.38	7.70	8.03	70	8.35	8.68	9.00	9.33	9.65
6.74	7.07	7.39	7.72	8.04	75	8.37	8.69	9.02	9.34	9.67
6.76	7.09	7.41	7.74	8.06	80	8.39	8.71	9.04	9.36	9.69
6.78	7.10	7.43	7.75	8.08	85	8.40	8.73	9.05	9.38	9.70
6.79	7.12	7.44	7.77	8.09	90	8.42	8.74	9.07	9.39	9.72
6.81	7.13	7.46	7.78	8.11	95	8.43	8.76	9.08	9.41	9.73

— POUNDS —

3000	3100	3200	3300	3400		3500	3600	3700	3800	3900
		AMOUNT						AMOUNT		
9.75	10.08	10.40	10.73	11.05		11.38	11.70	12.03	12.35	12.68
9.77	10.09	10.42	10.74	11.07	5	11.39	11.72	12.04	12.37	12.69
9.78	10.11	10.43	10.76	11.08	10	11.41	11.73	12.06	12.38	12.71
9.80	10.12	10.45	10.77	11.10	15	11.42	11.75	12.07	12.40	12.72
9.82	10.14	10.47	10.79	11.12	20	11.44	11.77	12.09	12.42	12.74
9.83	10.16	10.48	10.81	11.13	25	11.46	11.78	12.11	12.43	12.76
9.85	10.17	10.50	10.82	11.15	30	11.47	11.80	12.12	12.45	12.77
9.86	10.19	10.51	10.84	11.16	35	11.49	11.81	12.14	12.46	12.79
9.88	10.21	10.53	10.86	11.18	40	11.51	11.83	12.16	12.48	12.81
9.90	10.22	10.55	10.87	11.20	45	11.52	11.85	12.17	12.50	12.82
9.91	10.24	10.56	10.89	11.21	50	11.54	11.86	12.19	12.51	12.84
9.93	10.25	10.58	10.90	11.23	55	11.55	11.88	12.20	12.53	12.85
9.95	10.27	10.60	10.92	11.25	60	11.57	11.90	12.22	12.55	12.87
9.96	10.29	10.61	10.94	11.26	65	11.59	11.91	12.24	12.56	12.89
9.98	10.30	10.63	10.95	11.28	70	11.60	11.93	12.25	12.58	12.90
9.99	10.32	10.64	10.97	11.29	75	11.62	11.94	12.27	12.59	12.92
10.01	10.34	10.66	10.99	11.31	80	11.64	11.96	12.29	12.61	12.94
10.03	10.35	10.68	11.00	11.33	85	11.65	11.98	12.30	12.63	12.95
10.04	10.37	10.69	11.02	11.34	90	11.67	11.99	12.32	12.64	12.97
10.06	10.38	10.71	11.03	11.36	95	11.68	12.01	12.33	12.66	12.98

Even tons, 51 to 100 inclusive.

51-60		61-70		71-80		81-90		91-100	
T	Am't	T	Am't	T	Am't	T	Am't	T	Am't
51	331.50	61	396.50	71	461.50	81	526.50	91	591.50
52	338.00	62	403.00	72	468.00	82	533.00	92	598.00
53	344.50	63	409.50	73	474.50	83	539.50	93	604.50
54	351.00	64	416.00	74	481.00	84	546.00	94	611.00
55	357.50	65	422.50	75	487.50	85	552.50	95	617.50
56	364.00	66	429.00	76	494.00	86	559.00	96	624.00
57	370.50	67	435.50	77	500.50	87	565.50	97	630.50
58	377.00	68	442.00	78	507.00	88	572.00	98	637.00
59	383.50	69	448.50	79	513.50	89	578.50	99	643.50
60	390.00	70	455.00	80	520.00	90	585.00	100	650.00

700	4550	800	5200	900	5850	1000	6500	1100	7150

──────── POUNDS ────────

Under 100	100	200	300	400		500	600	70C	800	900
	.34	.68	1.01	1.35		1.69	2.03	2.36	2.70	3.04
.02	.35	.69	1.03	1.37	5	1.70	2.04	2.38	2.72	3.05
.03	.37	.71	1.05	1.38	10	1.72	2.06	2.40	2.73	3.07
.05	.39	.73	1.06	1.40	15	1.74	2.08	2.41	2.75	3.09
.07	.41	.74	1.08	1.42	20	1.76	2.09	2.43	2.77	3.11
.08	.42	.76	1.10	1.43	25	1.77	2.11	2.45	2.78	3.12
.10	.44	.78	1.11	1.45	30	1.79	2.13	2.46	2.80	3.14
.12	.46	.79	1.13	1.47	35	1.81	2.14	2.48	2.82	3.16
.14	.47	.81	1.15	1.49	40	1.82	2.16	2.50	2.84	3.17
.15	.49	.83	1.16	1.50	45	1.84	2.18	2.51	2.85	3.19
.17	.51	.84	1.18	1.52	50	1.86	2.19	2.53	2.87	3.21
.19	.52	.86	1.20	1.54	55	1.87	2.21	2.55	2.89	3.22
.20	.54	.88	1.22	1.55	60	1.89	2.23	2.57	2.90	3.24
.22	.56	.89	1.23	1.57	65	1.91	2.24	2.58	2.92	3.26
.24	.57	.91	1.25	1.59	70	1.92	2.26	2.60	2.94	3.27
.25	.59	.93	1.27	1.60	75	1.94	2.28	2.62	2.95	3.29
.27	.61	.95	1.28	1.62	80	1.96	2.30	2.63	2.97	3.31
.29	.62	.96	1.30	1.64	85	1.97	2.31	2.65	2.99	3.32
.30	.64	.98	1.32	1.65	90	1.99	2.33	2.67	3.00	3.34
.32	.66	1.00	1.33	1.67	95	2.01	2.35	2.68	3.02	3.36

──────── POUNDS ────────

1000	1100	1200	1300	1400		1500	1600	1700	1800	1900
3.38	3.71	4.05	4.39	4.73		5.06	5.40	5.74	6.08	6.41
3.39	3.73	4.07	4.40	4.74	5	5.08	5.42	5.75	6.09	6.43
3.41	3.75	4.08	4.42	4.76	10	5.10	5.43	5.77	6.11	6.45
3.43	3.76	4.10	4.44	4.78	15	5.11	5.45	5.79	6.13	6.46
3.44	3.78	4.12	4.46	4.79	20	5.13	5.47	5.81	6.14	6.48
3.46	3.80	4.13	4.47	4.81	25	5.15	5.48	5.82	6.16	6.50
3.48	3.81	4.15	4.49	4.83	30	5.16	5.50	5.84	6.18	6.51
3.49	3.83	4.17	4.51	4.84	35	5.18	5.52	5.86	6.19	6.53
3.51	3.85	4.19	4.52	4.86	40	5.20	5.54	5.87	6.21	6.55
3.53	3.86	4.20	4.54	4.88	45	5.21	5.55	5.89	6.23	6.56
3.54	3.88	4.22	4.56	4.89	50	5.23	5.57	5.91	6.24	6.58
3.56	3.90	4.24	4.57	4.91	55	5.25	5.59	5.92	6.26	6.60
3.58	3.92	4.25	4.59	4.93	60	5.27	5.60	5.94	6.28	6.62
3.59	3.93	4.27	4.61	4.94	65	5.28	5.62	5.96	6.29	6.63
3.61	3.95	4.29	4.62	4.96	70	5.30	5.64	5.97	6.31	6.65
3.63	3.97	4.30	4.64	4.98	75	5.32	5.65	5.99	6.33	6.67
3.65	3.98	4.32	4.66	5.00	80	5.33	5.67	6.01	6.35	6.68
3.66	4.00	4.34	4.67	5.01	85	5.35	5.69	6.02	6.36	6.70
3.68	4.02	4.35	4.69	5.03	90	5.37	5.70	6.04	6.38	6.72
3.70	4.03	4.37	4.71	5.05	95	5.38	5.72	6.06	6.40	6.73

Even tons, 1 to 50 inclusive.

1-10		11-20		21-30		31-40		41-50	
T	Am't	T	Am't	T	Am't	T	Am't	T	Am't
1	6.75	11	74.25	21	141.75	31	209.25	41	276.75
2	13.50	12	81.00	22	148.50	32	216.00	42	283.50
3	20.25	13	87.75	23	155.25	33	222.75	43	290.25
4	27.00	14	94.50	24	162.00	34	229.50	44	297.00
5	33.75	15	101.25	25	168.75	35	236.25	45	303.75
6	40.50	16	108.00	26	175.50	36	243.00	46	310.50
7	47.25	17	114.75	27	182.25	37	249.75	47	317.25
8	54.00	18	121.50	28	189.00	38	256.50	48	324.00
9	60.75	19	128.25	29	195.75	39	263.25	49	330.75
10	67.50	20	135.00	30	202.50	40	270.00	50	337.50

200	1350	300	2025	400	2700	500	3375	600	4050

─────────── POUNDS ───────────

2000	2100	2200	2300	2400		2500	2600	2700	2800	2900
AMOUNT						AMOUNT				
6.75	7.09	7.43	7.76	8.10		8.44	8.78	9.11	9.45	9.79
6.77	7.10	7.44	7.78	8.12	5	8.45	8.79	9.13	9.47	9.80
6.78	7.12	7.46	7.80	8.13	10	8.47	8.81	9.15	9.48	9.82
6.80	7.14	7.48	7.81	8.15	15	8.49	8.83	9.16	9.50	9.84
6.82	7.16	7.49	7.83	8.17	20	8.51	8.84	9.18	9.52	9.86
6.83	7.17	7.51	7.85	8.18	25	8.52	8.86	9.20	9.53	9.87
6.85	7.19	7.53	7.86	8.20	30	8.54	8.88	9.21	9.55	9.89
6.87	7.21	7.54	7.88	8.22	35	8.56	8.89	9.23	9.57	9.91
6.89	7.22	7.56	7.90	8.24	40	8.57	8.91	9.25	9.59	9.92
6.90	7.24	7.58	7.91	8.25	45	8.59	8.93	9.26	9.60	9.94
6.92	7.26	7.59	7.93	8.27	50	8.61	8.94	9.28	9.62	9.96
6.94	7.27	7.61	7.95	8.29	55	8.62	8.96	9.30	9.64	9.97
6.95	7.29	7.63	7.97	8.30	60	8.64	8.98	9.32	9.65	9.99
6.97	7.31	7.64	7.98	8.32	65	8.66	8.99	9.33	9.67	10.01
6.99	7.32	7.66	8.00	8.34	70	8.67	9.01	9.35	9.69	10.02
7.00	7.34	7.68	8.02	8.35	75	8.69	9.03	9.37	9.70	10.04
7.02	7.36	7.70	8.03	8.37	80	8.71	9.05	9.38	9.72	10.06
7.04	7.37	7.71	8.05	8.39	85	8.72	9.06	9.40	9.74	10.07
7.05	7.39	7.73	8.07	8.40	90	8.74	9.08	9.42	9.75	10.09
7.07	7.41	7.75	8.08	8.42	95	8.76	9.10	9.43	9.77	10.11

─────────── POUNDS ───────────

3000	3100	3200	3300	3400		3500	3600	3700	3800	3900
AMOUNT						AMOUNT				
10.13	10.46	10.80	11.14	11.48		11.81	12.15	12.49	12.83	13.16
10.15	10.48	10.82	11.15	11.49	5	11.83	12.17	12.50	12.84	13.18
10.16	10.50	10.83	11.17	11.51	10	11.85	12.18	12.52	12.86	13.20
10.18	10.51	10.85	11.19	11.53	15	11.86	12.20	12.54	12.88	13.21
10.19	10.53	10.87	11.21	11.54	20	11.88	12.22	12.56	12.89	13.23
10.21	10.55	10.88	11.22	11.56	25	11.90	12.23	12.57	12.91	13.25
10.23	10.56	10.90	11.24	11.58	30	11.91	12.25	12.59	12.93	13.26
10.24	10.58	10.92	11.26	11.59	35	11.93	12.27	12.61	12.94	13.28
10.26	10.60	10.94	11.27	11.61	40	11.95	12.29	12.62	12.96	13.30
10.28	10.61	10.95	11.29	11.63	45	11.96	12.30	12.64	12.98	13.31
10.29	10.63	10.97	11.31	11.64	50	11.98	12.32	12.66	12.99	13.33
10.31	10.65	10.99	11.32	11.66	55	12.00	12.34	12.67	13.01	13.35
10.33	10.67	11.00	11.34	11.68	60	12.02	12.35	12.69	13.03	13.37
10.34	10.68	11.02	11.36	11.69	65	12.03	12.37	12.71	13.04	13.38
10.36	10.70	11.04	11.37	11.71	70	12.05	12.39	12.72	13.06	13.40
10.38	10.72	11.05	11.39	11.73	75	12.07	12.40	12.74	13.08	13.42
10.40	10.73	11.07	11.41	11.75	80	12.08	12.42	12.76	13.10	13.43
10.41	10.75	11.09	11.42	11.76	85	12.10	12.44	12.77	13.11	13.45
10.43	10.77	11.10	11.44	11.78	90	12.12	12.45	12.79	13.13	13.47
10.45	10.78	11.12	11.46	11.80	95	12.13	12.47	12.81	13.15	13.48

Even tons, 51 to 100 inclusive.

51-60		61-70		71-80		81-90		91-100	
T	Am't	T	Am't	T	Am't	T	Am't	T	Am't
51	344.25	61	411.75	71	479.25	81	546.75	91	614.25
52	351.00	62	418.50	72	486.00	82	553.50	92	621.00
53	357.75	63	425.25	73	492.75	83	560.25	93	627.75
54	364.50	64	432.00	74	499.50	84	567.00	94	634.50
55	371.25	65	438.75	75	506.25	85	573.75	95	641.25
56	378.00	66	445.50	76	513.00	86	580.50	96	648.00
57	384.75	67	452.25	77	519.75	87	587.25	97	654.75
58	391.50	68	459.00	78	526.50	88	594.00	98	661.50
59	398.25	69	465.75	79	533.25	89	600.75	99	668.25
60	405.00	70	472.50	80	540.00	90	607.50	100	675.00

700	4725	800	5400	900	6075	1000	6750	1100	7425

28c a bu.   **$7.00 a T.**   35c a 100 lbs.

POUNDS

Under 100	100	200	300	400		500	600	700	800	900
	AMOUNT						AMOUNT			
	.35	.70	1.05	1.40		1.75	2.10	2.45	2.80	3.15
02	.37	.72	1.07	1.42	5	1.77	2.12	2.47	2.82	3.17
.04	.39	.74	1.09	1.44	10	1.79	2.14	2.49	2.84	3.19
.05	.40	.75	1.10	1.45	15	1.80	2.15	2.50	2.85	3.20
.07	.42	.77	1.12	1.47	20	1.82	2.17	2.52	2.87	3.22
.09	.44	.79	1.14	1.49	25	1.84	2.19	2.54	2.89	3.24
.11	.46	.81	1.16	1.51	30	1.86	2.21	2.56	2.91	3.26
.12	.47	.82	1.17	1.52	35	1.87	2.22	2.57	2.92	3.27
.14	.49	.84	1.19	1.54	40	1.89	2.24	2.59	2.94	3.29
.16	.51	.86	1.21	1.56	45	1.91	2.26	2.61	2.96	3.31
.18	.53	.88	1.23	1.58	50	1.93	2.28	2.63	2.98	3.33
.19	.54	.89	1.24	1.59	55	1.94	2.29	2.64	2.99	3.34
.21	.56	.91	1.26	1.61	60	1.96	2.31	2.66	3.01	3.36
.23	.58	.93	1.28	1.63	65	1.98	2.33	2.68	3.03	3.38
.25	.60	.95	1.30	1.65	70	2.00	2.35	2.70	3.05	3.40
.26	.61	.96	1.31	1.66	75	2.01	2.36	2.71	3.06	3.41
.28	.63	.98	1.33	1.68	80	2.03	2.38	2.73	3.08	3.43
.30	.65	1.00	1.35	1.70	85	2.05	2.40	2.75	3.10	3.45
.32	.67	1.02	1.37	1.72	90	2.07	2.42	2.77	3.12	3.47
.33	.68	1.03	1.38	1.73	95	2.08	2.43	2.78	3.13	3.48

POUNDS

1000	1100	1200	1300	1400		1500	1600	1700	1800	1900
	AMOUNT						AMOUNT			
3.50	3.85	4.20	4.55	4.90		5.25	5.60	5.95	6.30	6.65
3.52	3.87	4.22	4.57	4.92	5	5.27	5.62	5.97	6.32	6.67
3.54	3.89	4.24	4.59	4.94	10	5.29	5.64	5.99	6.34	6.69
3.55	3.90	4.25	4.60	4.95	15	5.30	5.65	6.00	6.35	6.70
3.57	3.92	4.27	4.62	4.97	20	5.32	5.67	6.02	6.37	6.72
3.59	3.94	4.29	4.64	4.99	25	5.34	5.69	6.04	6.39	6.74
3.61	3.96	4.31	4.66	5.01	30	5.36	5.71	6.06	6.41	6.76
3.62	3.97	4.32	4.67	5.02	35	5.37	5.72	6.07	6.42	6.77
3.64	3.99	4.34	4.69	5.04	40	5.39	5.74	6.09	6.44	6.79
3.66	4.01	4.36	4.71	5.06	45	5.41	5.76	6.11	6.46	6.81
3.68	4.03	4.38	4.73	5.08	50	5.43	5.78	6.13	6.48	6.83
3.69	4.04	4.39	4.74	5.09	55	5.44	5.79	6.14	6.49	6.84
3.71	4.06	4.41	4.76	5.11	60	5.46	5.81	6.16	6.51	6.86
3.73	4.08	4.43	4.78	5.13	65	5.48	5.83	6.18	6.53	6.88
3.75	4.10	4.45	4.80	5.15	70	5.50	5.85	6.20	6.55	6.90
3.76	4.11	4.46	4.81	5.16	75	5.51	5.86	6.21	6.56	6.91
3.78	4.13	4.48	4.83	5.18	80	5.53	5.88	6.23	6.58	6.93
3.80	4.15	4.50	4.85	5.20	85	5.55	5.90	6.25	6.60	6.95
3.82	4.17	4.52	4.87	5.22	90	5.57	5.92	6.27	6.62	6.97
3.83	4.18	4.53	4.88	5.23	95	5.58	5.93	6.28	6.63	6.98

Even tons, 1 to 50 inclusive.

1-10		11-20		21-30		31-40		41-50	
T	Am't	T	Am't	T	Am't	T	Am't	T	Am't
1	7.00	11	77.00	21	147.00	31	217.00	41	287.00
2	14.00	12	84.00	22	154.00	32	224.00	42	294.00
3	21.00	13	91.00	23	161.00	33	231.00	43	301.00
4	28.00	14	98.00	24	168.00	34	238.00	44	308.00
5	35.00	15	105.00	25	175.00	35	245.00	45	315.00
6	42.00	16	112.00	26	182.00	36	252.00	46	322.00
7	49.00	17	119.00	27	189.00	37	259.00	47	329.00
8	56.00	18	126.00	28	196.00	38	266.00	48	336.00
9	63.00	19	133.00	29	203.00	39	273.00	49	343.00
10	70.00	20	140.00	30	210.00	40	280.00	50	350.00

200	1400	300	2100	400	2800	500	3500	600	4200

———— POUNDS ————

2000	2100	2200	2300	2400		2500	2660	2700	2800	2900
	AMOUNT						AMOUNT			
7.00	7.35	7.70	8.05	8.40		8.75	9.10	9.45	9.80	10.15
7.02	7.37	7.72	8.07	8.42	5	8.77	9.12	9.47	9.82	10.17
7.04	7.39	7.74	8.09	8.44	10	8.79	9.14	9.49	9.84	10.19
7.05	7.40	7.75	8.10	8.45	15	8.80	9.15	9.50	9.85	10.20
7.07	7.42	7.77	8.12	8.47	20	8.82	9.17	9.52	9.87	10.22
7.09	7.44	7.79	8.14	8.49	25	8.84	9.19	9.54	9.89	10.24
7.11	7.46	7.81	8.16	8.51	30	8.86	9.21	9.56	9.91	10.26
7.12	7.47	7.82	8.17	8.52	35	8.87	9.22	9.57	9.92	10.27
7.14	7.49	7.84	8.19·	8.54	40	8.89	9.24	9.59	9.94	10.29
7.16	7.51	7.86	8.21	8.56	45	8.91	9.26	9.61	9.96	10.31
7.18	7.53	7.88	8.23	8.58	50	8.93	9.28	9.63	9.98	10.33
7.19	7.54	7.89	8.24	8.59	55	8.94	9.29	9.64	9.99	10.34
7.21	7.56	7.91	8.26	8.61	60	8.96	9.31	9.66	10.01	10.36
7.23	7.58	7.93	8.28	8.63	65	8.98	9.33	9.68	10.03	10.38
7.25	7.60	7.95	8.30	8.65	70	9.00	9.35	9.70	10.05	10.40
7.26	7.61	7.96	8.31	8.66	75	9.01	9.36	9.71	10.06	10.41
7.28	7.63	7.98	8.33	8.68	80	9.03	9.38	9.73	10.08	10.43
7.30	7.65	8.00	8.35	8.70	85	9.05	9.40	9.75	10.10	10.45
7.32	7.67	8.02	8.37	8.72	90	9.07	9.42	9.77	10.12	10.47
7.33	7.68	8.03	8.38	8.73	95	9.08	9.43	9.78	10.13	10.48

———— POUNDS ————

3000	3100	3200	3300	3400		3500	3600	3700	3800	3900
	AMOUNT						AMOUNT			
10.50	10.85	11.20	11.55	11.90		12.25	12.60	12.95	13.30	13.65
10.52	10.87	11.22	11.57	11.92	5	12.27	12.62	12.96	13.32	13.67
10.54	10.89	11.24	11.59	11.94	10	12.29	12.64	12.99	13.34	13.69
10.55	10.90	11.25	11.60	11.95	15	12.30	12.65	13.00	13.35	13.70
10.57	10.92	11.27	11.62	11.97	20	12.32	12 67	13.02	13.37	13.72
10.59	10.94	11.29	11.64	11.99	25	12.34	12.69	13.04	13.39	13.74
10.61	10.96	11.31	11.66	12.01	30	12.36	12.71	13.06	13.41	13.76
10.62	10.97	11.32	11.67	12.02	35	12.37	12.72	13.07	13.42	13.77
10.64	10.99	11.34	11.69	12.04	40	12.39	12.74	13.09	13.44	13.79
10.66	11.01	11.36	11.71	12.06	45	12.41	12.76	13.11	13.46	13.81
10.68	11.03	11.38	11.73	12.08	50	12.43	12.78	13.13	13.48	13.83
10.69	11.04	11.39	11.74	12.09	55	12.44	12.79	13.14	13.49	13.84
10.71	11.06	11.41	11.76	12.11	60	12.46	12.81	13.16	13.51	13.86
10.73	11.08	11.43	11.78	12.13	65	12.48	12.83	13.18	13.53	13.88
10.75	11.10	11.45	11.80	12.15	70	12.50	12.85	13.20	13.55	13.90
10.76	11.11	11.46	11.81	12.16	75	12.51	12.86	13.21	13.56	13.91
10.78	11.13	11.48	11.83	12.18	80	12.53	12.88	13.23	13.58	13.93
10.80	11.15	11.50	11.85	12.20	85	12.55	12.90	18.25	13.60	13.95
10.82	11.17	11.52	11.87	12.22	90	12.57	12.92	13.27	13.62	13.97
10.83	11.18	11.53	11.88	12.23	95	12.58	12.93	13.28	13.63	13.98

Even tons, 51 to 100 inclusive.

51-60		61-70		71-80		81-90		91-100	
T	Am't	T	Am't	T	Am't	T	Am't	T	Am't
51	357.00	61	427.00	71	497.00	81	567.00	91	637.00
52	364.00	62	434.00	72	504.00	82	574.00	92	644.00
53	371.00	63	441.00	73	511.00	83	581.00	93	651.00
54	378.00	64	448.00	74	518.00	84	588.00	94	658.00
55	385.00	65	455.00	75	525.00	85	595.00	95	665.00
56	392.00	66	462.00	76	532.00	86	602.00	96	672.00
57	399.00	67	469.00	77	539.00	87	609.00	97	679.00
58	406.00	68	476.00	78	546.00	88	616.00	98	686.00
59	413.00	69	483.00	79	553.00	89	623.00	99	693.00
60	420.00	70	490.00	80	560.00	90	630.00	100	700.00

700	4900	800	5600	900	6300	1000	7000	1100	7700

(59)

POUNDS

Under 100	100	200	300	400		500	600	700	800	900
	.36	.73	1.09	1.45		1.81	2.18	2.54	2.90	3.26
.02	.38	.74	1.11	1.47	5	1.83	2.19	2.56	2.92	3.28
.04	.40	.76	1.12	1.49	10	1.85	2.21	2.57	2.94	3.30
.05	.42	.78	1.14	1.50	15	1.87	2.23	2.59	2.95	3.32
.07	.44	.80	1.16	1.52	20	1.89	2.25	2.61	2.97	3.34
.09	.45	.82	1.18	1.54	25	1.90	2.27	2.63	2.99	3.35
.11	.47	.83	1.20	1.56	30	1.92	2.28	2.65	3.01	3.37
.13	.49	.85	1.21	1.58	35	1.94	2.30	2.66	3.03	3.39
.15	.51	.87	1.23	1.60	40	1.96·	2.32	2.68	3.05	3.41
.16	.53	.89	1.25	1.61	45	1.98	2.34	2.70	3.06	3.43
.18	.54	.91	1.27	1.63	50	1.99	2.36	2.72	3.08	3.44
.20	.56	.92	1.29	1.65	55	2.01	2.37	2.74	3.10	3.46
.22	.58	.94	1.31	1.67	60	2.03	2.39	2.76	3.12	3.48
.24	.60	.96	1.32	1.69	65	2.05	2.41	2.77	3.14	3.50
.25	.62	.98	1.34	1.70	70	2.07	2.43	2.79	3.15	3.52
.27	.63	1.00	1.36	1.72	75	2.08	2.45	2.81	3.17	3.53
.29	.65	1.02	1.38	1.74	80	2.10	2.47	2.83	3.19	3.55
.31	.67	1.03	1.40	1.76	85	2.12	2.48	2.85	3.21	3.57
.33	.69	1.05	1.41	1.78	90	2.14	2.50	2.86	3.23	3.59
.34	.71	1.07	1.43	1.79	95	2.16	2.52	2.88	3.24	3.61

POUNDS

1000	1100	1200	1300	1400		1500	1600	1700	1800	1900
3.63	3.99	4.35	4.71	5.08		5.44	5.80	6.16	6.53	6.89
3.64	4.01	4.37	4.73	5.09	5	5.46	5.82	6.18	6.54	6.91
3.66	4.02	4.39	4.75	5.11	10	5.47	5.84	6.20	6.56	6.92
3.68	4.04	4.40	4.77	5.13	15	5.49	5.85	6.22	6.58	6.94
3.70	4.06	4.42	4.79	5.15	20	5.51	5.87	6.24	6.60	6.96
3.72	4.08	4.44	4.80	5.17	25	5.53	5.89	6.25	6.62	6.98
3.73	4.10	4.46	4.82	5.18	30	5.55	5.91	6.27	6.63	7.00
3.75	4.11	4.48	4.84	5.20	35	5.56	5.93	6.29	6.65	7.01
3.77	4.13	4.50	4.86	5.22	40	5.58	5.95	6.31	6.67	7.03
3.79	4.15	4.51	4.88	5.24	45	5.60	5.96	6.33	6.69	7.05
3.81	4.17	4.53	4.89	5.26	50	5.62	5.98	6.34	6.71	7.07
3.82	4.19	4.55	4.91	5.27	55	5.64	6.00	6.36	6.72	7.09
3.84	4.21	4.57	4.93	5.29	60	5.66	6.02	6.38	6.74	7.11
3.86	4.22	4.59	4.95	5.31	65	5.67	6.04	6.40	6.76	7.12
3.88	4.24	4.60	4.97	5.33	70	5.69	6.05	6.42	6.78	7.14
3.90	4.26	4.62	4.98	5.35	75	5.71	6.07	6.43	6.80	7.16
3.92	4.28	4.64	5.00	5.37	80	5.73	6.09	6.45	6.82	7.18
3.93	4.30	4.66	5.02	5.38	85	5.75	6.11	6.47	6.83	7.20
3.95	4.31	4.68	5.04	5.40	90	5.76	6.13	6.49	6.85	7.21
3.97	4.33	4.69	5.06	5.42	95	5.78	6.14	6.51	6.87	7.23

Even tons, 1 to 50 inclusive.

1-10		11-20		21-30		31-40		41-50	
T	Am't	T	Am't	T	Am't	T	Am't	T	Am't
1	7.25	11	79.75	21	152.25	31	224.75	41	297.25
2	14.50	12	87.00	22	159.50	32	232.00	42	304.50
3	21.75	13	94.25	23	166.75	33	239.25	43	311.75
4	29.00	14	101.50	24	174.00	34	246.50	44	319.00
5	36.25	15	108.75	25	181.25	35	253.75	45	326.25
6	43.50	16	116.00	26	188.50	36	261.00	46	333.50
7	50.75	17	123.25	27	195.75	37	268.25	47	340.75
8	58.00	18	130.50	28	203.00	38	275.50	48	348.00
9	65.25	19	137.75	29	210.25	39	282.75	49	355.25
10	72.50	20	145.00	30	217.50	40	290.00	50	362.50
200	1450	300	2175	400	2900	500	3625	600	4350

———POUNDS———

2000	2100	2200	2300	2400		2500	2600	2700	2800	2900
		AMOUNT						AMOUNT		
7.25	7.61	7.98	8.34	8.70		9.06	9.43	9.79	10.15	10.51
7.27	7.63	7.99	8.36	8.72	5	9.08	9.44	9.81	10.17	10.53
7.29	7.65	8.01	8.37	8.74	10	9.10	9.46	9.82	10.19	10.55
7.30	7.67	8.03	8.39	8.75	15	9.12	9.48	9.84	10.20	10.57
7.32	7.69	8.05	8.41	8.77	20	9.14	9.50	9.86	10.22	10.59
7.34	7.70	8.07	8.43	8.79	25	9.15	9.52	9.88	10.24	10.60
7.36	7.72	8.08	8.45	8.81	30	9.17	9.53	9.90	10.26	10.62
7.38	7.74	8.10	8.46	8.83	35	9.19	9.55	9.91	10.28	10.64
7.40	7.76	8.12	8.48	8.85	40	9.21	9.57	9.93	10.30	10.66
7.41	7.78	8.14	8.50	8.86	45	9.23	9.59	9.95	10.31	10.68
7.43	7.79	8.16	8.52	8.88	50	9.24	9.61	9.97	10.33	10.69
7.45	7.81	8.17	8.54	8.90	55	9.26	9.62	9.99	10.35	10.71
7.47	7.83	8.19	8.56	8.92	60	9.28	9.64	10.01	10.37	10.73
7.49	7.85	8.21	8.57	8.94	65	9.30	9.66	10.02	10.39	10.75
7.50	7.87	8.23	8.59	8.95	70	9.32	9.68	10.04	10.40	10.77
7.52	7.88	8.25	8.61	8.97	75	9.33	9.70	10.06	10.42	10.78
7.54	7.90	8.27	8.63	8.99	80	9.35	9.72	10.08	10.44	10.80
7.56	7.92	8.28	8.65	9.01	85	9.37	9.73	10.10	10.46	10.82
7.58	7.94	8.30	8.66	9.03	90	9.39	9.75	10.11	10.48	10.84
7.59	7.96	8.32	8.68	9.04	95	9.41	9.77	10.13	10.49	10.86

———POUNDS———

3000	3100	3200	3300	3400		3500	3600	3700	3800	3900
		AMOUNT						AMOUNT		
10.88	11.24	11.60	11.96	12.33		12.69	13.05	13.41	13.78	14.14
10.89	11.26	11.62	11.98	12.34	5	12.71	13.07	13.43	13.79	14.16
10.91	11.27	11.64	12.00	12.36	10	12.72	13.09	13.45	13.81	14.17
10.93	11.29	11.65	12.02	12.38	15	12.74	13.10	13.47	13.83	14.19
10.95	11.31	11.67	12.04	12.40	20	12.76	13.12	13.49	13.85	14.21
10.97	11.33	11.69	12.05	12.42	25	12.78	13.14	13.50	13.87	14.23
10.98	11.35	11.71	12.07	12.43	30	12.80	13.16	13.52	13.88	14.25
11.00	11.36	11.73	12.09	12.45	35	12.81	13.18	13.54	13.90	14.26
11.02	11.38	11.75	12.11	12.47	40	12.83	13.20	13.56	13.92	14.28
11.04	11.40	11.76	12.13	12.49	45	12.85	13.21	13.58	13.94	14.30
11.06	11.42	11.78	12.14	12.51	50	12.87	13.23	13.59	13.96	14.32
11.07	11.44	11.80	12.16	12.52	55	12.89	13.25	13.61	13.97	14.34
11.09	11.46	11.82	12.18	12.54	60	12.91	13.27	13.63	13.99	14.36
11.11	11.47	11.84	12.20	12.56	65	12.92	13.29	13.65	14.01	14.37
11.13	11.49	11.85	12.22	12.58	70	12.94	13.30	13.67	14.03	14.39
11.15	11.51	11.87	12.23	12.60	75	12.96	13.32	13.68	14.05	14.41
11.17	11.53	11.89	12.25	12.62	80	12.98	13.34	13.70	14.07	14.43
11.18	11.55	11.91	12.27	12.63	85	13.00	13.36	13.72	14.08	14.45
11.20	11.56	11.93	12.29	12.65	90	13.01	13.38	13.74	14.10	14.46
11.22	11.58	11.94	12.31	12.67	95	13.03	13.39	13.76	14.12	14.48

Even tons, 51 to 100 inclusive.

51-60		61-70		71-80		81-90		91-100	
T	Am't	T	Am't	T	Am't	T	Am't	T	Am't
51	369.75	61	442.25	71	514.75	81	587.25	91	659.75
52	377.00	62	449.50	72	522.00	82	594.50	92	667.00
53	384.25	63	456.75	73	529.25	83	601.75	93	674.25
54	391.50	64	464.00	74	536.50	84	609.00	94	681.50
55	398.75	65	471.25	75	543.75	85	616.25	95	688.75
56	406.00	66	478.50	76	551.00	86	623.50	96	696.00
57	413.25	67	485.75	77	558.25	87	630.75	97	703.25
58	420.50	68	493.00	78	565.50	88	638.00	98	710.50
59	427.75	69	500.25	79	572.75	89	645.25	99	717.75
60	435.00	70	507.50	80	580.00	90	652.50	100	725.00

700	5075	800	5800	900	6525	1000	7250	1100	7975

6

POUNDS

Under 100	100	200	300	400		500	600	700	800	900
		AMOUNT						AMOUNT		
	.38	.75	1.13	1.50		1.88	2.25	2.63	3.00	3.38
.02	.39	.77	1.14	1.52	5	1.89	2.27	2.64	3.02	3.39
.04	.41	.79	1.16	1.54	10	1.91	2.29	2.66	3.04	3.41
.06	.43	.81	1.18	1.56	15	1.93	2.31	2.68	3.06	3.43
.08	.45	.83	1.20	1.58	20	1.95	2.33	2.70	3.08	3.45
.09	.47	.84	1.22	1.59	25	1.97	2.34	2.72	3.09	3.47
.11	.49	.86	1.24	1.61	30	1.99	2.36	2.74	3.11	3.49
.13	.51	.88	1.26	1.63	35	2.01	2.38	2.76	3.13	3.51
.15	.53	.90	1.28	1.65	40	2.03	2.40	2.78	3.15	3.53
.17	.54	.92	1.29	1.67	45	2.04	2.42	2.79	3.17	3.54
.19	.56	.94	1.31	1.69	50	2.06	2.44	2.81	3.19	3.56
.21	.58	.96	1.33	1.71	55	2.08	2.46	2.83	3.21	3.58
.23	.60	.98	1.35	1.73	60	2.10	2.48	2.85	3.23	3.60
.24	.62	.99	1.37	1.74	65	2.12	2.49	2.87	3.24	3.62
.26	.64	1.01	1.39	1.76	70	2.14	2.51	2.89	3.26	3.64
.28	.66	1.03	1.41	1.78	75	2.16	2.53	2.91	3.28	3.66
.30	.68	1.05	1.43	1.80	80	2.18	2.55	2.93	3.30	3.68
.32	.69	1.07	1.44	1.82	85	2.19	2.57	2.94	3.32	3.69
.34	.71	1.09	1.46	1.84	90	2.21	2.59	2.96	3.34	3.71
.36	.73	1.11	1.48	1.86	95	2.23	2.61	2.98	3.36	3.73

POUNDS

1000	1100	1200	1300	1400		1500	1600	1700	1800	1900
		AMOUNT						AMOUNT		
3.75	4.13	4.50	4.88	5.25		5.63	6.00	6.38	6.75	7.13
3.77	4.14	4.52	4.89	5.27	5	5.64	6.02	6.39	6.77	7.14
3.79	4.16	4.54	4.91	5.29	10	5.66	6.04	6.41	6.79	7.16
3.81	4.18	4.56	4.93	5.31	15	5.68	6.06	6.43	6.81	7.18
3.83	4.20	4.58	4.95	5.33	20	5.70	6.08	6.45	6.83	7.20
3.84	4.22	4.59	4.97	5.34	25	5.72	6.09	6.47	6.84	7.22
3.86	4.24	4.61	4.99	5.36	30	5.74	6.11	6.49	6.86	7.24
3.88	4.26	4.63	5.01	5.38	35	5.76	6.13	6.51	6.88	7.26
3.90	4.28	4.65	5.03	5.40	40	5.78	6.15	6.53	6.90	7.28
3.92	4.29	4.67	5.04	5.42	45	5.79	6.17	6.54	6.92	7.29
3.94	4.31	4.69	5.06	5.44	50	5.81	6.19	6.56	6.94	7.31
3.96	4.33	4.71	5.08	5.46	55	5.83	6.21	6.58	6.96	7.33
3.98	4.35	4.73	5.10	5.48	60	5.85	6.23	6.60	6.98	7.35
3.99	4.37	4.74	5.12	5.49	65	5.87	6.24	6.62	6.99	7.37
4.01	4.39	4.76	5.14	5.51	70	5.89	6.26	6.64	7.01	7.39
4.03	4.41	4.78	5.16	5.53	75	5.91	6.28	6.66	7.03	7.41
4.05	4.43	4.80	5.18	5.55	80	5.93	6.30	6.68	7.05	7.43
4.07	4.44	4.82	5.19	5.57	85	5.94	6.32	6.69	7.07	7.44
4.09	4.46	4.84	5.21	5.59	90	5.96	6.34	6.71	7.09	7.46
4.11	4.48	4.86	5.23	5.61	95	5.98	6.36	6.73	7.11	7.48

Even tons, 1 to 50 inclusive.

1-10		11-20		21-30		31-40		41-50	
T	Am't	T	Am't	T	Am't	T	Am't	T	Am't
1	7.50	11	82.50	21	157.50	31	232.50	41	307.50
2	15.00	12	90.00	22	165.00	32	240.00	42	315.00
3	22.50	13	97.50	23	172.50	33	247.50	43	322.50
4	30.00	14	105.00	24	180.00	34	255.00	44	330.00
5	37.50	15	112.50	25	187.50	35	262.50	45	337.50
6	45.00	16	120.00	26	195.00	36	270.00	46	345.00
7	52.50	17	127.50	27	202.50	37	277.50	47	352.50
8	60.00	18	135.00	28	210.00	38	285.00	48	360.00
9	67.50	19	142.50	29	217.50	39	292.50	49	367.50
10	75.00	20	150.00	30	225.00	40	300.00	50	375.00

200	1500	300	2250	400	3000	500	3750	600	4500

——— Pounds ———

2000	2100	2200	2300	2400		2500	2600	2700	2800	2900
		AMOUNT						AMOUNT		
7.50	7.88	8.25	8.63	9.00		9.38	9.75	10.13	10.50	10.88
7.52	7.89	8.27	8.64	9.02	5	9.39	9.77	10.14	10.52	10.89
7.54	7.91	8.29	8.66	9.04	10	9.41	9.79	10.16	10.54	10.91
7.56	7.93	8.31	8.68	9.06	15	9.43	9.81	10.18	10.56	10.93
7.58	7.95	8.33	8.70	9.08	20	9.45	9.83	10.20	10.58	10.95
7.59	7.97	8.34	8.72	9.09	25	9.47	9.84	10.22	10.59	10.97
7.61	7.99	8.36	8.74	9.11	30	9.49	9.86	10.24	10.61	10.99
7.63	8.01	8.38	8.76	9.13	35	9.51	9.88	10.26	10.63	11.01
7.65	8.03	8.40	8.78	9.15	40	9.53	9.90	10.28	10.65	11.03
7.67	8.04	8.42	8.79	9.17	45	9.54	9.92	10.29	10.67	11.04
7.69	8.06	8.44	8.81	9.19	50	9.56	9.94	10.31	10.69	11.06
7.71	8.08	8.46	8.83	9.21	55	9.58	9.96	10.33	10.71	11.08
7.73	8.10	8.48	8.85	9.23	60	9.60	9.98	10.35	10.73	11.10
7.74	8.12	8.49	8.87	9.24	65	9.62	9.99	10.37	10.74	11.12
7.76	8.14	8.51	8.89	9.26	70	9.64	10.01	10.39	10.76	11.14
7.78	8.16	8.53	8.91	9.28	75	9.66	10.03	10.41	10.78	11.16
7.80	8.18	8.55	8.93	9.30	80	9.68	10.05	10.43	10.80	11.18
7.82	8.19	8.57	8.94	9.32	85	9.69	10.07	10.44	10.82	11.19
7.84	8.21	8.59	8.96	9.34	90	9.71	10.09	10.46	10.84	11.21
7.86	8.23	8.61	8.98	9.36	95	9.73	10.11	10.48	10.86	11.23

——— Pounds ———

3000	3100	3200	3300	3400		3500	3600	3700	3800	3900
		AMOUNT						AMOUNT		
11.25	11.63	12.00	12.38	12.75		13.13	13.50	13.88	14.25	14.63
11.27	11.64	12.02	12.39	12.77	5	13.14	13.52	13.89	14.27	14.64
11.29	11.66	12.04	12.41	12.79	10	13.16	13.54	13.91	14.29	14.66
11.31	11.68	12.06	12.43	12.81	15	13.18	13.56	13.93	14.31	14.68
11.33	11.70	12.08	12.45	12.83	20	13.20	13.58	13.95	14.33	14.70
11.34	11.72	12.09	12.47	12.84	25	13.22	13.59	13.97	14.34	14.72
11.36	11.74	12.11	12.49	12.86	30	13.24	13.61	13.99	14.36	14.74
11.38	11.76	12.13	12.51	12.88	35	13.26	13.63	14.01	14.38	14.76
11.40	11.78	12.15	12.53	12.90	40	13.28	13.65	14.03	14.40	14.78
11.42	11.79	12.17	12.54	12.92	45	13.29	13.67	14.04	14.42	14.79
11.44	11.81	12.19	12.56	12.94	50	13.31	13.69	14.06	14.44	14.81
11.46	11.83	12.21	12.58	12.96	55	13.33	13.71	14.08	14.46	14.83
11.48	11.85	12.23	12.60	12.98	60	13.35	13.73	14.10	14.48	14.85
11.49	11.87	12.24	12.62	12.99	65	13.37	13.74	14.12	14.49	14.87
11.51	11.89	12.26	12.64	13.01	70	13.39	13.76	14.14	14.51	14.89
11.53	11.91	12.28	12.66	13.03	75	13.41	13.78	14.16	14.53	14.91
11.55	11.93	12.30	12.68	13.05	80	13.43	13.80	14.18	14.55	14.93
11.57	11.94	12.32	12.69	13.07	85	13.44	13.82	14.19	14.57	14.94
11.59	11.96	12.34	12.71	13.09	90	13.46	13.84	14.21	14.59	14.96
11.61	11.98	12.36	12.73	13.11	95	13.48	13.86	14.23	14.61	14.98

Even tons, 51 to 100 inclusive.

51-60		61-70		71-80		81-90		91-100	
T	Am't	T	Am't	T	Am't	T	Am't	T	Am't
51	382.50	61	457.50	71	532.50	81	607.50	91	682.50
52	390.00	62	465.00	72	540.00	82	615.00	92	690.00
53	397.50	63	472.50	73	547.50	83	622.50	93	697.50
54	405.00	64	480.00	74	555.00	84	630.00	94	705.00
55	412.50	65	487.50	75	562.50	85	637.50	95	712.50
56	420.00	66	495.00	76	570.00	86	645.00	96	720.00
57	427.50	67	502.50	77	577.50	87	652.50	97	727.50
58	435.00	68	510.00	78	585.00	88	660.00	98	735.00
59	442.50	69	517.50	79	592.50	89	667.50	99	742.50
60	450.00	70	525.00	80	600.00	90	675.00	100	750.00
700	5250	800	6000	900	6750	1000	7500	1100	8250

POUNDS

Under 100	100	200	300	400		500	600	700	800	900
	AMOUNT							AMOUNT		
	.39	.78	1.16	1.55		1.94	2.33	2.71	3.10	3.49
.02	.41	.79	1.18	1.57	5	1.96	2.34	2.73	3.12	3.51
.04	.43	.81	1.20	1.59	10	1.98	2.36	2.75	3.14	3.53
.06	.45	.83	1.22	1.61	15	2.00	2.38	2.77	3.16	3.55
.08	.47	.85	1.24	1.63	20	2.02	2.40	2.79	3.18	3.57
.10	.48	.87	1.26	1.65	25	2.03	2.42	2.81	3.20	3.58
.12	.50	.89	1.28	1.67	30	2.05	2.44	2.83	3.22	3.60
.14	.52	.91	1.30	1.69	35	2.07	2.46	2.85	3.24	3.62
.16	.54	.93	1.32	1.71	40	2.09	2.48	2.87	3.26	3.64
.17	.56	.95	1.34	1.72	45	2.11	2.50	2.89	3.27	3.66
.19	.58	.97	1.36	1.74	50	2.13	2.52	2.91	3.29	3.68
.21	.60	.99	1.38	1.76	55	2.15	2.54	2.93	3.31	3.70
.23	.62	1.01	1.40	1.78	60	2.17	2.56	2.95	3.33	3.72
.25	.64	1.03	1.41	1.80	65	2.19	2.58	2.96	3.35	3.74
.27	.66	1.05	1.43	1.82	70	2.21	2.60	2.98	3.37	3.76
.29	.68	1.07	1.45	1.84	75	2.23	2.62	3.00	3.39	3.78
.31	.70	1.09	1.47	1.86	80	2.25	2.64	3.02	3.41	3.80
.33	.72	1.10	1.49	1.88	85	2.27	2.65	3.04	3.43	3.82
.35	.74	1.12	1.51	1.90	90	2.29	2.67	3.06	3.45	3.84
.37	.76	1.14	1.53	1.92	95	2.31	2.69	3.08	3.47	3.86

POUNDS

1000	1100	1200	1300	1400		1500	1600	1700	1800	1900
	AMOUNT							AMOUNT		
3.88	4.26	4.65	5.04	5.43		5.81	6.20	6.59	6.98	7.36
3.89	4.28	4.67	5.06	5.44	5	5.83	6.22	6.61	6.99	7.38
3.91	4.30	4.69	5.08	5.46	10	5.85	6.24	6.63	7.01	7.40
3.93	4.32	4.71	5.10	5.48	15	5.87	6.26	6.65	7.03	7.42
3.95	4.34	4.73	5.12	5.50	20	5.89	6.28	6.67	7.05	7.44
3.97	4.36	4.75	5.13	5.52	25	5.91	6.30	6.68	7.07	7.46
3.99	4.38	4.77	5.15	5.54	30	5.93	6.32	6.70	7.09	7.48
4.01	4.40	4.79	5.17	5.56	35	5.95	6.34	6.72	7.11	7.50
4.03	4.42	4.81	5.19	5.58	40	5.97	6.36	6.74	7.13	7.52
4.05	4.44	4.82	5.21	5.60	45	5.99	6.37	6.76	7.15	7.54
4.07	4.46	4.84	5.23	5.62	50	6.01	6.39	6.78	7.17	7.56
4.09	4.48	4.86	5.25	5.64	55	6.03	6.41	6.80	7.19	7.58
4.11	4.50	4.88	5.27	5.66	60	6.05	6.43	6.82	7.21	7.60
4.13	4.51	4.90	5.29	5.68	65	6.06	6.45	6.84	7.23	7.61
4.15	4.53	4.92	5.31	5.70	70	6.08	6.47	6.86	7.25	7.63
4.17	4.55	4.94	5.33	5.72	75	6.10	6.49	6.88	7.27	7.65
4.19	4.57	4.96	5.35	5.74	80	6.12	6.51	6.90	7.29	7.67
4.20	4.59	4.98	5.37	5.75	85	6.14	6.53	6.92	7.30	7.69
4.22	4.61	5.00	5.39	5.77	90	6.16	6.55	6.94	7.32	7.71
4.24	4.63	5.02	5.41	5.79	95	6.18	6.57	6.96	7.34	7.73

Even tons, 1 to 50 inclusive.

1-10		11-20		21-30		31-40		41-50	
T	Am't	T	Am't	T	Am't	T	Am't	T	Am't
1	7.75	11	85.25	21	162.75	31	240.25	41	317.75
2	15.50	12	93.00	22	170.50	32	248.00	42	325.50
3	23.25	13	100.75	23	178.25	33	255.75	43	333.25
4	31.00	14	108.50	24	186.00	34	263.50	44	341.00
5	38.75	15	116.25	25	193.75	35	271.25	45	348.75
6	46.50	16	124.00	26	201.50	36	279.00	46	356.50
7	54.25	17	131.75	27	209.25	37	286.75	47	364.25
8	62.00	18	139.50	28	217.00	38	294.50	48	372.00
9	69.75	19	147.25	29	224.75	39	302.25	49	379.75
10	77.50	20	155.00	30	232.50	40	310.00	50	387.50

200	1550	300	2325	400	3100	500	3875	600	4650

—————— POUNDS ——————

2000	2100	2200	2300	2400		2500	2600	2700	2800	2900
		—AMOUNT—					—AMOUNT—			
7.75	8.14	8.53	8.91	9.30		9.69	10.08	10.46	10.85	11.24
7.77	8.16	8.54	8.93	9.32	5	9.71	10.09	10.48	10.87	11.26
7.79	8.18	8.56	8.95	9.34	10	9.73	10.11	10.50	10.89	11.28
7.81	8.20	8.58	8.97	9.36	15	9.75	10.13	10.52	10.91	11.30
7.83	8.22	8.60	8.99	9.38	20	9.77	10.15	10.54	10.93	11.32
7.85	8.23	8.62	9.01	9.40	25	9.78	10.17	10.56	10.95	11.33
7.87	8.25	8.64	9.03	9.42	30	9.80	10.19	10.58	10.97	11.35
7.89	8.27	8.66	9.05	9.44	35	9.82	10.21	10.60	10.99	11.37
7.91	8.29	8.68	9.07	9.46	40	9.84	10.23	10.62	11.01	11.39
7.92	8.31	8.70	9.09	9.47	45	9.86	10.25	10.64	11.02	11.41
7.94	8.33	8.72	9.11	9.49	50	9.88	10.27	10.66	11.04	11.43
7.96	8.35	8.74	9.13	9.51	55	9.90	10.29	10.68	11.06	11.45
7.98	8.37	8.76	9.15	9.53	60	9.92	10.31	10.70	11.08	11.47
8.00	8.39	8.78	9.16	9.55	65	9.94	10.33	10.71	11.10	11.49
8.02	8.41	8.80	9.18	9.57	70	9.96	10.35	10.73	11.12	11.51
8.04	8.43	8.82	9.20	9.59	75	9.98	10.37	10.75	11.14	11.53
8.06	8.45	8.84	9.22	9.61	80	10.00	10.39	10.77	11.16	11.55
8.08	8.47	8.85	9.24	9.63	85	10.02	10.40	10.79	11.18	11.57
8.10	8.49	8.87	9.26	9.65	90	10.04	10.42	10.81	11.20	11.59
8.12	8.51	8.89	9.28	9.67	95	10.06	10.44	10.83	11.22	11.61

—————— POUNDS ——————

3000	3100	3200	3300	3400		3500	3600	3700	3800	3900
		—AMOUNT—					—AMOUNT—			
11.63	12.01	12.40	12.79	13.18		13.56	13.95	14.34	14.73	15.11
11.64	12.03	12.42	12.81	13.19	5	13.58	13.97	14.36	14.74	15.13
11.66	12.05	12.44	12.83	13.21	10	13.60	13.99	14.38	14.76	15.15
11.68	12.07	12.46	12.85	13.23	15	13.62	14.01	14.40	14.78	15.17
11.70	12.09	12.48	12.87	13.25	20	13.64	14.03	14.42	14.80	15.19
11.72	12.11	12.50	12.88	13.27	25	13.66	14.05	14.43	14.82	15.21
11.74	12.13	12.52	12.90	13.29	30	13.68	14.07	14.45	14.84	15.23
11.76	12.15	12.54	12.92	13.31	35	13.70	14.09	14.47	14.86	15.25
11.78	12.17	12.56	12.94	13.33	40	13.72	14.11	14.49	14.88	15.27
11.80	12.19	12.57	12.96	13.35	45	13.74	14.12	14.51	14.90	15.29
11.82	12.21	12.59	12.98	13.37	50	13.76	14.14	14.53	14.92	15.31
11.84	12.23	12.61	13.00	13.39	55	13.78	14.16	14.55	14.94	15.33
11.86	12.25	12.63	13.02	13.41	60	13.80	14.18	14.57	14.96	15.35
11.88	12.26	12.65	13.04	13.43	65	13.81	14.20	14.59	14.98	15.36
11.90	12.28	12.67	13.06	13.45	70	13.83	14.22	14.61	15.00	15.38
11.92	12.30	12.69	13.08	13.47	75	13.85	14.24	14.63	15.02	15.40
11.94	12.32	12.71	13.10	13.49	80	13.87	14.26	14.65	15.04	15.42
11.95	12.34	12.73	13.12	13.50	85	13.89	14.28	14.67	15.05	15.44
11.97	12.36	12.75	13.14	13.52	90	13.91	14.30	14.69	15.07	15.46
11.99	12.38	12.77	13.16	13.54	95	13.93	14.32	14.71	15.09	15.48

Even tons, 51 to 100 inclusive.

51-60		61-70		71-80		81-90		91-100	
T	Am't	T	Am't	T	Am't	T	Am't	T	Am't
51	395.25	61	472.75	71	550.25	81	627.75	91	705.25
52	403.00	62	480.50	72	558.00	82	635.50	92	713.00
53	410.75	63	488.25	73	565.75	83	643.25	93	720.75
54	418.50	64	496.00	74	573.50	84	651.00	94	728.50
55	426.25	65	503.75	75	581.25	85	658.75	95	736.25
56	434.00	66	511.50	76	589.00	86	666.50	96	744.00
57	441.75	67	519.25	77	596.75	87	674.25	97	751.75
58	449.50	68	527.00	78	604.50	88	682.00	98	759.50
59	457.25	69	534.75	79	612.25	89	689.75	99	767.25
60	465.00	70	542.50	80	620.00	90	697.50	100	775.00

700	5425	800	6200	900	6975	1000	7750	1100	8525

— POUNDS —

Under 100	100	200	300	400		500	600	700	800	900
	.40	.80	1.20	1.60		2.00	2.40	2.80	3.20	3.60
.02	.42	.82	1.22	1.62	5	2.02	2.42	2.82	3.22	3.62
.04	.44	.84	1.24	1.64	10	2.04	2.44	2.84	3.24	3.64
.06	.46	.86	1.26	1.66	15	2.06	2.46	2.86	3.26	3.66
.08	.48	.88	1.28	1.68	20	2.08	2.48	2.88	3.28	3.68
.10	.50	.90	1.30	1.70	25	2.10	2.50	2.90	3.30	3.70
.12	.52	.92	1.32	1.72	30	2.12	2.52	2.92	3.32	3.72
.14	.54	.94	1.34	1.74	35	2.14	2.54	2.94	3.34	3.74
.16	.56	.96	1.36	1.76	40	2.16	2.56	2.96	3.36	3.76
.18	.58	.98	1.38	1.78	45	2.18	2.58	2.98	3.38	3.78
.20	.60	1.00	1.40	1.80	50	2.20	2.60	3.00	3.40	3.80
.22	.62	1.02	1.42	1.82	55	2.22	2.62	3.02	3.42	3.82
.24	.64	1.04	1.44	1.84	60	2.24	2.64	3.04	3.44	3.84
.26	.66	1.06	1.46	1.86	65	2.26	2.66	3.06	3.46	3.86
.28	.68	1.08	1.48	1.88	70	2.28	2.68	3.08	3.48	3.88
.30	.70	1.10	1.50	1.90	75	2.30	2.70	3.10	3.50	3.90
.32	.72	1.12	1.52	1.92	80	2.32	2.72	3.12	3.52	3.92
.34	.74	1.14	1.54	1.94	85	2.34	2.74	3.14	3.54	3.94
.36	.76	1.16	1.56	1.96	90	2.36	2.76	3.16	3.56	3.96
.38	.78	1.18	1.58	1.98	95	2.38	2.78	3.18	3.58	3.98

— POUNDS —

1000	1100	1200	1300	1400		1500	1600	1700	1800	1900
4.00	4.40	4.80	5.20	5.60		6.00	6.40	6.80	7.20	7.60
4.02	4.42	4.82	5.22	5.62	5	6.02	6.42	6.82	7.22	7.62
4.04	4.44	4.84	5.24	5.64	10	6.04	6.44	6.84	7.24	7.64
4.06	4.46	4.86	5.26	5.66	15	6.06	6.46	6.86	7.26	7.66
4.08	4.48	4.88	5.28	5.68	20	6.08	6.48	6.88	7.28	7.68
4.10	4.50	4.90	5.30	5.70	25	6.10	6.50	6.90	7.30	7.70
4.12	4.52	4.92	5.32	5.72	30	6.12	6.52	6.92	7.32	7.72
4.14	4.54	4.94	5.34	5.74	35	6.14	6.54	6.94	7.34	7.74
4.16	4.56	4.96	5.36	5.76	40	6.16	6.56	6.96	7.36	7.76
4.18	4.58	4.98	5.38	5.78	45	6.18	6.58	6.98	7.38	7.78
4.20	4.60	5.00	5.40	5.80	50	6.20	6.60	7.00	7.40	7.80
4.22	4.62	5.02	5.42	5.82	55	6.22	6.62	7.02	7.42	7.82
4.24	4.64	5.04	5.44	5.84	60	6.24	6.64	7.04	7.44	7.84
4.26	4.66	5.06	5.46	5.86	65	6.26	6.66	7.06	7.46	7.86
4.28	4.68	5.08	5.48	5.88	70	6.28	6.68	7.08	7.48	7.88
4.30	4.70	5.10	5.50	5.90	75	6.30	6.70	7.10	7.50	7.90
4.32	4.72	5.12	5.52	5.92	80	6.32	6.72	7.12	7.52	7.92
4.34	4.74	5.14	5.54	5.94	85	6.34	6.74	7.14	7.54	7.94
4.36	4.76	5.16	5.56	5.96	90	6.36	6.76	7.16	7.56	7.96
4.38	4.78	5.18	5.58	5.98	95	6.38	6.78	7.18	7.58	7.98

Even tons, 1 to 50 inclusive.

1-10		11-20		21-30		31-40		41-50	
T	Am't	T	Am't	T	Am't	T	Am't	T	Am't
1	8.00	11	88.00	21	168.00	31	248.00	41	328.00
2	16.00	12	96.00	22	176.00	32	256.00	42	336.00
3	24.00	13	104.00	23	184.00	33	264.00	43	344.00
4	32.00	14	112.00	24	192.00	34	272.00	44	352.00
5	40.00	15	120.00	25	200.00	35	280.00	45	360.00
6	48.00	16	128.00	26	208.00	36	288.00	46	368.00
7	56.00	17	136.00	27	216.00	37	296.00	47	376.00
8	64.00	18	144.00	28	224.00	38	304.00	48	384.00
9	72.00	19	152.00	29	232.00	39	312.00	49	392.00
10	80.00	20	160.00	30	240.00	40	320.00	50	400.00
200	1600	300	2400	400	3200	500	4000	600	4800

———POUNDS———

2000	2100	2200	2300	2400		2500	2600	2700	2800	2900
		AMOUNT						AMOUNT		
8.00	8.40	8.80	9.20	9.60		10.00	10.40	10.80	11.20	11.60
8.02	8.42	8.82	9.22	9.62	5	10.02	10.42	10.82	11.22	11.62
8.04	8.44	8.84	9.24	9.64	10	10.04	10.44	10.84	11.24	11.64
8.06	8.46	8.86	9.26	9.66	15	10.06	10.46	10.86	11.26	11.66
8.08	8.48	8.88	9.28	9.68	20	10.08	10.48	10.88	11.28	11.68
8.10	8.50	8.90	9.30	9.70	25	10.10	10.50	10.90	11.30	11.70
8.12	8.52	8.92	9.32	9.72	30	10.12	10.52	10.92	11.32	11.72
8.14	8.54	8.94	9.34	9.74	35	10.14	10.54	10.94	11.34	11.74
8.16	8.56	8.96	9.36	9.76	40	10.16	10.56	10.96	11.36	11.76
8.18	8.58	8.98	9.38	9.78	45	10.18	10.58	10.98	11.38	11.78
8.20	8.60	9.00	9.40	9.80	50	10.20	10.60	11.00	11.40	11.80
8.22	8.62	9.02	9.42	9.82	55	10.22	10.62	11.02	11.42	11.82
8.24	8.64	9.04	9.44	9.84	60	10.24	10.64	11.04	11.44	11.84
8.26	8.66	9.06	9.46	9.86	65	10.26	10.66	11.06	11.46	11.86
8.28	8.68	9.08	9.48	9.88	70	10.28	10.68	11.08	11.48	11.88
8.30	8.70	9.10	9.50	9.90	75	10.30	10.70	11.10	11.50	11.90
8.32	8.72	9.12	9.52	9.92	80	10.32	10.72	11.12	11.52	11.92
8.34	8.74	9.14	9.54	9.94	85	10.34	10.74	11.14	11.54	11.94
8.36	8.76	9.16	9.56	9.96	90	10.36	10.76	11.16	11.56	11.96
8.38	8.78	9.18	9.58	9.98	95	10.38	10.78	11.18	11.58	11.98

———POUNDS———

3000	3100	3200	3300	3400		3500	3600	3700	3800	3900
		AMOUNT						AMOUNT		
12.00	12.40	12.80	13.20	13.60		14.00	14.40	14.80	15.20	15.60
12.02	12.42	12.82	13.22	13.62	5	14.02	14.42	14.82	15.22	15.62
12.04	12.44	12.84	13.24	13.64	10	14.04	14.44	14.84	15.24	15.64
12.06	12.46	12.86	13.26	13.66	15	14.06	14.46	14.86	15.26	15.66
12.08	12.48	12.88	13.28	13.68	20	14.08	14.48	14.88	15.28	15.68
12.10	12.50	12.90	13.30	13.70	25	14.10	14.50	14.90	15.30	15.70
12.12	12.52	12.92	13.32	13.72	30	14.12	14.52	14.92	15.32	15.72
12.14	12.54	12.94	13.34	13.74	35	14.14	14.54	14.94	15.34	15.74
12.16	12.56	12.96	13.36	13.76	40	14.16	14.56	14.96	15.36	15.76
12.18	12.58	12.98	13.38	13.78	45	14.18	14.58	14.98	15.38	15.78
12.20	12.60	13.00	13.40	13.80	50	14.20	14.60	15.00	15.40	15.80
12.22	12.62	13.02	13.42	13.82	55	14.22	14.62	15.02	15.42	15.82
12.24	12.64	13.04	13.44	13.84	60	14.24	14.64	15.04	15.44	15.84
12.26	12.66	13.06	13.46	13.86	65	14.26	14.66	15.06	15.46	15.86
12.28	12.68	13.08	13.48	13.88	70	14.28	14.68	15.08	15.48	15.88
12.30	12.70	13.10	13.50	13.90	75	14.30	14.70	15.10	15.50	15.90
12.32	12.72	13.12	13.52	13.92	80	14.32	14.72	15.12	15.52	15.92
12.34	12.74	13.14	13.54	13.94	85	14.34	14.74	15.14	15.54	15.94
12.36	12.76	13.16	13.56	13.96	90	14.36	14.76	15.16	15.56	15.96
12.38	12.78	13.18	13.58	13.98	95	14.38	14.78	15.18	15.58	15.98

Even tons, 51 to 100 inclusive.

\ 51-60		61-70		71-80		81-90		91-100	
T	Am't	T	Am't	T	Am't	T	Am't	T	Am't
51	408.00	61	488.00	71	568.00	81	648.00	91	728.00
52	416.00	62	496.00	72	576.00	82	656.00	92	736.00
53	424.00	63	504.00	73	584.00	83	664.00	93	744.00
54	432.00	64	512.00	74	592.00	84	672.00	94	752.00
55	440.00	65	520.00	75	600.00	85	680.00	95	760.00
56	448.00	66	528.00	76	608.00	86	688.00	96	768.00
57	456.00	67	536.00	77	616.00	87	696.00	97	776.00
58	464.00	68	544.00	78	624.00	88	704.00	98	784.00
59	472.00	69	552.00	79	632.00	89	712.00	99	792.00
60	480.00	70	560.00	80	640.00	90	720.00	100	800.00

700	5600	800	6400	900	7200	1000	8000	1100	8800

POUNDS

Under 100	100	200	300	400		500	600	700	800	900
	.41	.83	1.24	1.65		2.06	2.48	2.89	3.30	3.71
.02	.43	.85	1.26	1.67	5	2.08	2.50	2.91	3.32	3.73
.04	.45	.87	1.28	1.69	10	2.10	2.52	2.93	3.34	3.75
.06	.47	.89	1.30	1.71	15	2.12	2.54	2.95	3.36	3.77
.08	.50	.91	1.32	1.73	20	2.15	2.56	2.97	3.38	3 80
.10	.52	.93	1.34	1.75	25	2.17	2.58	2.99	3.40	3.82
.12	.54	.95	1.36	1.77	30	2.19	2.60	3.01	3.42	3.84
.14	.56	97	1.38	1.79	35	2.21	2.62	3.03	3.44	3.86
.17	.58	.99	1.40	1.82	40	2.23	2.64	3.05	3.47	3.88
.19	.60	1.01	1.42	1.84	45	2.25	2.66	3.07	3.49	3.90
.21	.62	1.03	1.44	1.86	50	2.27	2.68	3.09	3.51	3.92
.23	.64	1.05	1.46	1.88	55	2.29	2.70	3.11	3.53	3.94
.25	.66	1.07	1.49	1.90	60	2.31	2.72	3.14	3.55	3.96
.27	.68	1.09	1.51	1.92	65	2.33	2.74	3.16	3.57	3.98
.29	.70	1.11	1.53	1.94	70	2.35	2.76	3.18	3.59	4.00
.31	.72	1.13	1.55	1.96	75	2.37	2.78	3.20	3.61	4.02
.33	.74	1.16	1.57	1.98	80	2.39	2.81	3.22	3.63	4.04
.35	.76	1.18	1.59	2.00	85	2.41	2.83	3.24	3.65	4.06
.37	.78	1.20	1.61	2.02	90	2.43	2.85	3.26	3.67	4.08
.39	.80	1.22	1.63	2.04	95	2.45	2.87	3.28	3.69	4.10

POUNDS

1000	1100	1200	1300	1400		1500	1600	1700	1800	1900
4.13	4.54	4.95	5.36	5.78		6.19	6.60	7.01	7.43	7.84
4.15	4.56	4.97	5.38	5.80	5	6.21	6.62	7.03	7.45	7.86
4.17	4.58	4.99	5.40	5.82	10	6.23	6.64	7.05	7.47	7.88
4.19	4.60	5.01	5.42	5.84	15	6.25	6.66	7.07	7.49	7.90
4.21	4.62	5.03	5.45	5.86	20	6.27	6.68	7.10	7.51	7.92
4.23	4.64	5.05	5.47	5.88	25	6.29	6.70	7.12	7.53	7.94
4.25	4.66	5.07	5.49	5.90	30	6.31	6.72	7.14	7.55	7.96
4.27	4.68	5.09	5.51	5.92	35	6.33	6.74	7.16	7.57	7.98
4.29	4.70	5.12	5.53	5.94	40	6.35	6.77	7.18	7.59	8.00
4.31	4.72	5.14	5.55	5.96	45	6.37	6.79	7.20	7.61	8.02
4.33	4.74	5.16	5.57	5.98	50	6.39	6.81	7.22	7.63	8.04
4.35	4.76	5.18	5.59	6.00	55	6.41	6.83	7.24	7.65	8.06
4.37	4.79	5.20	5.61	6.02	60	6.44	6.85	7.26	7.67	8.09
4.39	4.81	5.22	5.63	6.04	65	6.46	6.87	7.28	7.69	8.11
4.41	4.83	5.24	5.65	6.06	70	6.48	6.89	7.30	7.71	8.13
4.43	4.85	5.26	5.67	6.08	75	6.50	6.91	7.32	7.73	8.15
4.46	4.87	5.28	5.69	6.11	80	6.52	6.93	7.34	7.76	8.17
4.48	4.89	5.30	5.71	6.13	85	6.54	6.95	7.36	7.78	8.19
4.50	4.91	5.32	5.73	6.15	90	6.56	6.97	7.38	7.80	8.21
4.52	4.93	5.34	5.75	6.17	95	6.58	6.99	7.40	7.82	8.23

Even tons, 1 to 50 inclusive.

1-10		11-20		21-30		31-40		41-50	
T	Am't	T	Am't	T	Am't	T	Am't	T	Am't
1	8.25	11	90.75	21	173.25	31	255.75	41	338.25
2	16.50	12	99.00	22	181.50	32	264.00	42	346.50
3	24.75	13	107.25	23	189.75	33	272.25	43	354.75
4	33.00	14	115.50	24	198.00	34	280.50	44	363.00
5	41.25	15	123 75	25	206.25	35	288.75	45	371.25
6	49.50	16	132.00	26	214.50	36	297.00	46	379.50
7	57.75	17	140.25	27	222.75	37	305.25	47	387.75
8	66.00	18	148.50	28	231.00	38	313.50	48	396.00
9	74.25	19	156.75	29	239.25	39	321.75	49	404.25
10	82.50	20	165.00	30	247.50	40	330.00	50	412.50
200	1650	300	2475	400	3300	500	4125	600	4950

POUNDS

2000	2100	2200	2300	2400		2500	2600	2700	2800	2900
		—Amount—						—Amount—		
8.25	8.66	9.08	9.49	9.90		10.31	10.73	11.14	11.55	11.96
8.27	8.68	9.10	9.51	9.92	5	10.33	10.75	11.16	11.57	11.98
8.29	8.70	9.12	9.53	9.94	10	10.35	10.77	11.18	11.59	12.00
8.31	8.72	9.14	9.55	9.96	15	10.37	10.79	11.20	11.61	12.02
8.33	8.75	9.16	9.57	9.98	20	10.40	10.81	11.22	11.63	12.05
8.35	8.77	9.18	9.59	10.00	25	10.42	10.83	11.24	11.65	12.07
8.37	8.79	9.20	9.61	10.02	30	10.44	10.85	11.26	11.67	12.09
8.39	8.81	9.22	9.63	10.04	35	10.46	10.87	11.28	11.69	12.11
8.42	8.83	9.24	9.65	10.07	40	10.48	10.89	11.30	11.72	12.13
8.44	8.85	9.26	9.67	10.09	45	10.50	10.91	11.32	11.74	12.15
8.46	8.87	9.28	9.69	10.11	50	10.52	10.93	11.34	11.76	12.17
8.48	8.89	9.30	9.71	10.13	55	10.54	10.95	11.36	11.78	12.19
8.50	8.91	9.32	9.74	10.15	60	10.56	10.97	11.39	11.80	12.21
8.52	8.93	9.34	9.76	10.17	65	10.58	10.99	11.41	11.82	12.23
8.54	8.95	9.36	9.78	10.19	70	10.60	11.01	11.43	11.84	12.25
8.56	8.97	9.38	9.80	10.21	75	10.62	11.03	11.45	11.86	12.27
8.58	8.99	9.41	9.82	10.23	80	10.64	11.06	11.47	11.88	12.29
8.60	9.01	9.43	9.84	10.25	85	10.66	11.08	11.49	11.90	12.31
8.62	9.03	9.45	9.86	10.27	90	10.68	11.10	11.51	11.92	12.33
8.64	9.05	9.47	9.88	10.29	95	10.70	11.12	11.53	11.94	12.35

POUNDS

3000	3100	3200	3300	3400		3500	3600	3700	3800	3900
		—Amount—						—Amount—		
12.38	12.79	13.20	13.61	14.03		14.44	14.85	15.26	15.68	16.09
12.40	12.81	13.22	13.63	14.05	5	14.46	14.87	15.28	15.70	16.11
12.42	12.83	13.24	13.65	14.07	10	14.48	14.89	15.30	15.72	16.13
12.44	12.85	13.26	13.67	14.09	15	14.50	14.91	15.32	15.74	16.15
12.46	12.87	13.28	13.70	14.11	20	14.52	14.93	15.35	15.76	16.17
12.48	12.89	13.30	13.72	14.13	25	14.54	14.95	15.37	15.78	16.19
12.50	12.91	13.32	13.74	14.15	30	14.56	14.97	15.39	15.80	16.21
12.52	12.93	13.34	13.76	14.17	35	14.58	14.99	15.41	15.82	16.23
12.54	12.95	13.37	13.78	14.19	40	14.60	15.02	15.43	15.84	16.25
12.56	12.97	13.39	13.80	14.21	45	14.62	15.04	15.45	15.86	16.27
12.58	12.99	13.41	13.82	14.23	50	14.64	15.06	15.47	15.88	16.29
12.60	13.01	13.43	13.84	14.25	55	14.66	15.08	15.49	15.90	16.31
12.62	13.04	13.45	13.86	14.27	60	14.69	15.10	15.51	15.92	16.34
12.64	13.06	13.47	13.88	14.29	65	14.71	15.12	15.53	15.94	16.36
12.66	13.08	13.49	13.90	14.31	70	14.73	15.14	15.55	15.96	16.38
12.68	13.10	13.51	13.92	14.33	75	14.75	15.16	15.57	15.98	16.40
12.71	13.12	13.53	13.94	14.36	80	14.77	15.18	15.59	16.01	16.42
12.73	13.14	13.55	13.96	14.38	85	14.79	15.20	15.61	16.03	16.44
12.75	13.16	13.57	13.98	14.40	90	14.81	15.22	15.63	16.05	16.46
12.77	13.18	13.59	14.00	14.42	95	14.83	15.24	15.65	16.07	16.48

Even tons, 51 to 100 inclusive.

51-60		61-70		71-80		81-90		91-100	
T	Am't	T	Am't	T	Am't	T	Am't	T	Am't
51	420.75	61	503.25	71	585.75	81	668.25	91	750.75
52	429.00	62	511.50	72	594.00	82	676.50	92	759.00
53	437.25	63	519.75	73	602.25	83	684.75	93	767.25
54	445.50	64	528.00	74	610.50	84	693.00	94	775.50
55	453.75	65	536.25	75	618.75	85	701.25	95	783.75
56	462.00	66	544.50	76	627.00	86	709.50	96	792.00
57	470.25	67	552.75	77	635.25	87	717.75	97	800.25
58	478.50	68	561.00	78	643.50	88	726.00	98	808.50
59	486.75	69	569.25	79	651.75	89	734.25	99	816.75
60	495.00	70	577.50	80	660.00	90	742.50	100	825.00

700	5775	800	6600	900	7425	1000	8250	1100	9075

POUNDS

Under 100	100	200	300	400		500	600	700	800	900
		AMOUNT						AMOUNT		
	.43	.85	1.28	1.70		2.13	2.55	2.98	3.40	3.83
.02	.45	.87	1.30	1.72	5	2.15	2.57	3.00	3.42	3.85
.04	.47	.89	1.32	1.74	10	2.17	2.59	3.02	3.44	3.87
.06	.49	.91	1.34	1.76	15	2.19	2.61	3.04	3.46	3.89
.09	.51	.94	1.36	1.79	20	2.21	2.64	3.06	3.49	3.91
.11	.53	.96	1.38	1.81	25	2.23	2.66	3.08	3.51	3.93
.13	.55	.98	1.40	1.83	30	2.25	2.68	3.10	3.53	3.95
.15	.57	1.00	1.42	1.85	35	2.27	2.70	3.12	3.55	3.97
.17	.60	1.02	1.45	1.87	40	2.30	2.72	3.15	3.57	4.00
.19	.62	1.04	1.47	1.89	45	2.32	2.74	3.17	3.59	4.02
.21	.64	1.06	1.49	1.91	50	2.34	2.76	3.19	3.61	4.04
.23	.66	1.08	1.51	1.93	55	2.36	2.78	3.21	3.63	4.06
.26	.68	1.11	1.53	1.96	60	2.38	2.81	3.23	3.66	4.08
.28	.70	1.13	1.55	1.98	65	2.40	2.83	3.25	3.68	4.10
.30	.72	1.15	1.57	2.00	70	2.42	2.85	3.27	3.70	4.12
.32	.74	1.17	1.59	2.02	75	2.44	2.87	3.29	3.72	4.14
.34	.77	1.19	1.62	2.04	80	2.47	2.89	3.32	3.74	4.17
.36	.79	1.21	1.64	2.06	85	2.49	2.91	3.34	3.76	4.19
.38	.81	1.23	1.66	2.08	90	2.51	2.93	3.36	3.78	4.21
.40	.83	1.25	1.68	2.10	95	2.53	2.95	3.38	3.80	4.23

POUNDS

1000	1100	1200	1300	1400		1500	1600	1700	1800	1900
		AMOUNT						AMOUNT		
4.25	4.68	5.10	5.53	5.95		6.38	6.80	7.23	7.65	8.08
4.27	4.70	5.12	5.55	5.97	5	6.40	6.82	7.25	7.67	8.10
4.29	4.72	5.14	5.57	5.99	10	6.42	6.84	7.27	7.69	8.12
4.31	4.74	5.16	5.59	6.01	15	6.44	6.86	7.29	7.71	8.14
4.34	4.76	5.19	5.61	6.04	20	6.46	6.89	7.31	7.74	8.16
4.36	4.78	5.21	5.63	6.06	25	6.48	6.91	7.33	7.76	8.18
4.38	4.80	5.23	5.65	6.08	30	6.50	6.93	7.35	7.78	8.20
4.40	4.82	5.25	5.67	6.10	35	6.52	6.95	7.37	7.80	8.22
4.42	4.85	5.27	5.70	6.12	40	6.55	6.97	7.40	7.82	8.25
4.44	4.87	5.29	5.72	6.14	45	6.57	6.99	7.42	7.84	8.27
4.46	4.89	5.31	5.74	6.16	50	6.59	7.01	7.44	7.86	8.29
4.48	4.91	5.33	5.76	6.18	55	6.61	7.03	7.46	7.88	8.31
4.51	4.93	5.36	5.78	6.21	60	6.63	7.06	7.48	7.91	8.33
4.53	4.95	5.38	5.80	6.23	65	6.65	7.08	7.50	7.93	8.35
4.55	4.97	5.40	5.82	6.25	70	6.67	7.10	7.52	7.95	8.37
4.57	4.99	5.42	5.84	6.27	75	6.69	7.12	7.54	7.97	8.39
4.59	5.02	5.44	5.87	6.29	80	6.72	7.14	7.57	7.99	8.42
4.61	5.04	5.46	5.89	6.31	85	6.74	7.16	7.59	8.01	8.44
4.63	5.06	5.48	5.91	6.33	90	6.76	7.18	7.61	8.03	8.46
4.65	5.08	5.50	5.93	6.35	95	6.78	7.20	7.63	8.05	8.48

Even tons, 1 to 50 inclusive.

1-10		11-20		21-30		31-40		41-50	
T	Am't	T	Am't	T	Am't	T	Am't	T	Am't
1	8.50	11	93.50	21	178.50	31	263.50	41	348.50
2	17.00	12	102.00	22	187 00	32	272.00	42	357.00
3	25.50	13	110.50	23	195.50	33	280.50	43	365.50
4	34.00	14	119.00	24	204.00	34	289.00	44	374.00
5	42.50	15	127.50	25	212.50	35	297.50	45	382.50
6	51.00	16	136.00	26	221.00	36	306.00	46	391.00
7	59.50	17	144.50	27	229.50	37	314.50	47	399.50
8	68.00	18	153.00	28	238.00	38	323.00	48	408.00
9	76.50	19	161.50	29	246.50	39	331.50	49	416.50
10	85.00	20	170.00	30	255.00	40	340.00	50	425.00
200	1700	300	2550	400	3400	500	4250	600	5100

——— POUNDS ———

2000	2100	2200	2300	2400		2500	2600	2700	2800	2900
		AMOUNT						AMOUNT		
8.50	8.93	9.35	9.78	10.20	·	10.63	11.05	11.48	11.90	12.33
8.52	8.95	9.37	9.80	10.22	5	10.65	11.07	11.50	11.92	12.35
8.54	8.97	9.39	9.82	10.24	10	10.67	11.09	11.52	11.94	12.37
8.56	8.99	9.41	9.84	10.26	15	10.69	11.11	11.54	11.96	12.39
8.59	9.01	9.44	9.86	10.29	20	10.71	11.14	11.56	11.99	12.41
8.61	9.03	9.46	9.88	10.31	25	10.73	11.16	11.58	12.01	12.43
8.63	9.05	9.48	9.90	10.33	30	10.75	11.18	11.60	12.03	12.45
8.65	9.07	9.50	9.92	10.35	35	10.77	11.20	11.62	12.05	12.47
8.67	9.10	9.52	9.95	10.37	40	10.80	11.22	11.65	12.07	12.50
8.69	9.12	9.54	9.97	10.39	45	10.82	11.24	11.67	12.09	12.52
8.71	9.14	9.56	9.99	10.41	50	10.84	11.26	11.69	12.11	12.54
8.73	9.16	9.58	10.01	10.43	55	10.86	11.28	11.71	12.13	12.56
8.76	9.18	9.61	10.03	10.46	60	10.88	11.31	11.73	12.16	12.58
8.78	9.20	9.63	10.05	10.48	65	10.90	11.33	11.75	12.18	12.60
8.80	9.22	9.65	10.07	10.50	70	10.92	11.35	11.77	12.20	12.62
8.82	9.24	9.67	10.09	10.52	75	10.94	11.37	11.79	12.22	12.64
8.84	9.27	9.69	10.12	10.54	80	10.97	11.39	11.82	12.24	12.67
8.86	9.29	9.71	10.14	10.56	85	10.99	11.41	11.84	12.26	12.69
8.88	9.31	9.73	10.16	10.58	90	11.01	11.43	11.86	12.28	12.71
8.90	9.33	9.75	10.18	10.60	95	11.03	11.45	11.88	12.30	12.73

——— POUNDS ———

3000	3100	3200	3300	3400		3500	3600	3700	3800	3900
		AMOUNT						AMOUNT		
12.75	13.18	13.60	14.03	14.45		14.88	15.30	15.73	16.15	16.58
12.77	13.20	13.62	14.05	14.47	5	14.90	15.32	15.75	16.17	16.60
12.79	13.22	13.64	14.07	14.49	10	14.92	15.34	15.77	16.19	16.62
12.81	13.24	13.66	14.09	14.51	15	14.94	15.36	15.79	16.21	16.64
12.84	13.26	13.69	14.11	14.54	20	14.96	15.39	15.81	16.24	16.66
12.86	13.28	13.71	14.13	14.56	25	14.98	15.41	15.83	16.26	16.68
12.88	13.30	13.73	14.15	14.58	30	15.00	15.43	15.85	16.28	16.70
12.90	13.32	13.75	14.17	14.60	35	15.02	15.45	15.87	16.30	16.72
12.92	13.35	13.77	14.20	14.62	40	15.05	15.47	15.90	16.32	16.75
12.94	13.37	13.79	14.22	14.64	45	15.07	15.49	15.92	16.34	16.77
12.96	13.39	13.81	14.24	14.66	50	15.09	15.51	15.94	16.36	16.79
12.98	13.41	13.83	14.26	14.68	55	15.11	15.53	15.96	16.38	16.81
13.01	13.43	13.86	14.28	14.71	60	15.13	15.56	15.98	16.41	16.83
13.03	13.45	13.88	14.30	14.73	65	15.15	15.58	16.00	16.43	16.85
13.05	13 47	13.90	14.32	14.75	70	15.17	15.60	16.02	16.45	16.87
13.07	13.49	13.92	14.34	14.77	75	15.19	15.62	16.04	16.47	16.89
13.09	13.52	13.94	14.37	14.79	80	15.22	15.64	16.07	16.49	16.92
13.11	13.54	13.96	14.39	14.81	85	15.24	15.66	16.09	16.51	16.94
13.13	13.56	13.98	14.41	14.83	90	15.26	15.68	16.11	16.53	16.96
13.15	13.58	14.00	14.43	14.85	95	15.28	15.70	16.13	16.55	16.98

Even tons, 51 to 100 inclusive.

51-60		61-70		71-80		81-90		91-100	
T	Am't	T	Am't	T	Am't	T	Am't	T	Am't
51	433.50	61	518.50	71	603.50	81	688.50	91	773.50
52	442.00	62	527.00	72	612.00	82	697.00	92	782.00
53	450.50	63	535.50	73	620.50	83	705.50	93	790.50
54	459.00	64	544.00	74	629.00	84	714.00	94	799.00
55	467.50	65	552.50	75	637.50	85	722.50	95	807.50
56	476.00	66	561.00	76	646.00	86	731.00	96	816.00
57	484.50	67	569.50	77	654.50	87	739.50	97	824.50
58	493.00	68	578.00	78	663.00	88	748.00	98	833.00
59	501.50	69	586.50	79	671.50	89	756.50	99	841.50
60	510.00	70	595.00	80	680.00	90	765.00	100	850.00

700	5950	800	6800	900	7650	1000	8500	1100	9350

POUNDS

Under 100	100	200	300	400		500	600	700	800	900
	AMOUNT						AMOUNT			
	.44	.88	1.31	1.75		2.19	2.63	3.06	3.50	3.94
.02	.46	.90	1.33	1.77	5	2.21	2.65	3.08	3.52	3.96
.04	.48	.92	1.36	1.79	10	2.23	2.67	3.11	3.54	3.98
.07	.50	.94	1.38	1.82	15	2.25	2.69	3.13	3.57	4.00
.09	.53	.96	1.40	1.84	20	2.28	2.71	3.15	3.59	4.03
.11	.55	.98	1.42	1.86	25	2.30	2.73	3.17	3.61	4.05
.13	.57	1.01	1.44	1.88	30	2.32	2.76	3.19	3.63	4.07
.15	.59	1.03	1.47	1.90	35	2.34	2.78	3.22	3.65	4.09
.18	.61	1.05	1.49	1.93	40	2.36	2.80	3.24	3.68	4.11
.20	.63	1.07	1.51	1.95	45	2.38	2.82	3.26	3.70	4.13
.22	.66	1.09	.1.53	1.97	50	2.41	2.84	3.28	3.72	4.16
.24	.68	1.12	1.55	1.99	55	2.43	2.87	3.30	3.74	4.18
.26	.70	1.14	1.58	2.01	60	2.45	2.89	3.33	3.76	4.20
.28	.72	1.16	1.60	2.03	65	2.47	2.91	3.35	3.78	4.22
.31	.74	1.18	1.62	2.06	70	2.49	2.93	3.37	3.81	4.24
.33	.77	1.20	1.64	2.08	75	2.52	2.95	3.39	3.83	4.27
.35	.79	1.23	1.66	2.10	80	2.54	2.98	3.41	3.85	4.29
.37	.81	1.25	1.68	2.12	85	2.56	3.00	3.43	3.87	4.31
.39	.83	1.27	1.71	2.14	90	2.58	3.02	3.46	3.89	4.33
.42	.85	1.29	1.73	2.17	95	2.60	3.04	3.48	3.92	4.35

POUNDS

1000	1100	1200	1300	1400		1500	1600	1700	1800	1900
	AMOUNT						AMOUNT			
4.38	4.81	5.25	5.69	6.13		6.56	7.00	7.44	7.88	8.31
4.40	4.83	5.27	5.71	6.15	5	6.58	7.02	7.46	7.90	8.33
4.42	4.86	5.29	5.73	6.17	10	6.61	7.04	7.48	7.92	8.36
4.44	4.88	5.32	5.75	6.19	15	6.63	7.07	7.50	7.94	8.38
4.46	4.90	5.34	5.78	6.21	20	6.65	7.09	7.53	7.96	8.40
4.48	4.92	5.36	5.80	6.23	25	6.67	7.11	7.55	7.98	8.42
4.51	4.94	5.38	5.82	6.26	30	6.69	7.13	7.57	8.01	8.44
4.53	4.97	5.40	5.84	6.28	35	6.72	7.15	7.59	8.03	8.47
4.55	4.99	5.43	5.86	6.30	40	6.74	7.18	7.61	8.05	8.49
4.57	5.01	5.45	5.88	6.32	45	6.76	7.20	7.63	8.07	8.51
4.59	5.03	5.47	5.91	6.34	50	6.78	7.22	7.66	8.09	8.53
4.62	5.05	5.49	5.93	6.37	55	6.80	7.24	7.68	8.12	8.55
4.64	5.08	5.51	5.95	6.39	60	6.83	7.26	7.70	8.14	8.58
4.66	5.10	5.53	5.97	6.41	65	6.85	7.28	7.72	8.16	8.60
4.68	5.12	5.56	5.99	6.43	70	6.87	7.31	7.74	8.18	8.62
4.70	5.14	5.58	6.02	6.45	75	6.89	7.33	7.77	8.20	8.64
4.73	5.16	5.60	6.04	6.48	80	6.91	7.35	7.79	8.23	8.66
4.75	5.18	5.62	6.06	6.50	85	6.93	7.37	7.81	8.25	8.68
4.77	5.21	5.64	6.08	6.52	90	6.96	7.39	7.83	8.27	8.71
4.79	5.23	5.67	6.10	6.54	95	6.98	7.42	7.85	8.29	8.73

Even tons, 1 to 50 inclusive.

1-10		11-20		21-30		31-40		41-50	
T	Am't	T	Am't	T	Am't	T	Am't	T	Am't
1	8.75	11	96.25	21	183.75	31	271.25	41	358.75
2	17.50	12	105.00	22	192.50	32	280.00	42	367.50
3	26.25	13	113.75	23	201.25	33	288.75	43	376.25
4	35.00	14	122.50	24	210.00	34	297.50	44	385.00
5	43.75	15	131.25	25	218.75	35	306.25	45	393.75
6	52.50	16	140.00	26	227.50	36	315.00	46	402.50
7	61.25	17	148.75	27	236.25	37	323.75	47	411.25
8	70.00	18	157.50	28	245.00	38	332.50	48	420.00
9	78.75	19	166.25	29	253.75	39	341.25	49	428.75
10	87.50	20	175.00	30	262.50	40	350.00	50	437.50

200	1750	300	2625	400	3500	500	4375	600	5250

---POUNDS---

2000	2100	2200	2300	2400		2500	2600	2700	2800	2900
		AMOUNT						AMOUNT		
8.75	9.19	9.63	10.06	10.50		10.94	11.38	11.81	12.25	12.69
8.77	9.21	9.65	10.08	10.52	5	10.96	11.40	11.83	12.27	12.71
8.79	9.23	9.67	10.11	10.54	10	10.98	11.42	11.86	12.29	12.73
8.82	9.25	9.69	10.13	10.57	15	11.00	11.44	11.88	12.32	12.75
8.84	9.28	9.71	10.15	10.59	20	11.03	11.46	11.90	12.34	12.78
8.86	9.30	9.73	10.17	10.61	25	11.05	11.48	11.92	12.36	12.80
8.88	9.32	9.76	10.19	10.63	30	11.07	11.51	11.94	12.38	12.82
8.90	9.34	9.78	10.22	10.65	35	11.09	11.53	11.97	12.40	12.84
8.93	9.36	9.80	10.24	10.68	40	11.11	11.55	11.99	12.43	12.86
8.95	9.38	9.82	10.26	10.70	45	11.13	11.57	12.01	12.45	12.88
8.97	9.41	9.84	10.28	10.72	50	11.16	11.59	12.03	12.47	12.91
8.99	9.43	9.87	10.30	10.74	55	11.18	11.62	12.05	12.49	12.93
9.01	9.45	9.89	10.33	10.76	60	11.20	11.64	12.08	12.51	12.95
9.03	9.47	9.91	10.35	10.78	65	11.22	11.66	12.10	12.53	12.97
9.06	9.49	9.93	10.37	10.81	70	11.24	11.68	12.12	12.56	12.99
9.08	9.52	9.95	10.39	10.83	75	11.27	11.70	12.14	12.58	13.02
9.10	9.54	9.98	10.41	10.85	80	11.29	11.73	12.16	12.60	13.04
9.12	9.56	10.00	10.43	10.87	85	11.31	11.75	12.18	12.62	13.06
9.14	9.58	10.02	10.46	10.89	90	11.33	11.77	12.21	12.64	13.08
9.17	9.60	10.04	10.48	10.92	95	11.35	11.79	12.23	12.67	13.10

---POUNDS---

3000	3100	3200	3300	3400		3500	3600	3700	3800	3900
		AMOUNT						AMOUNT		
13.13	13.56	14.00	14.44	14.88		15.31	15.75	16.19	16.63	17.06
13.15	13.58	14.02	14.46	14.90	5	15.33	15.77	16.21	16.65	17.08
13.17	13.61	14.04	14.48	14.92	10	15.36	15.79	16.23	16.67	17.11
13.19	13.63	14.06	14.50	14.94	15	15.38	15.82	16.25	16.69	17.13
13.21	13.65	14.09	14.53	14.96	20	15.40	15.84	16.28	16.71	17.15
13.23	13.67	14.11	14.55	14.98	25	15.42	15.86	16.30	16.73	17.17
13.26	13.69	14.13	14.57	15.01	30	15.44	15.88	16.32	16.76	17.19
13.28	13.72	14.15	14.59	15.03	35	15.47	15.90	16.34	16.78	17.22
13.30	13.74	14.18	14.61	15.05	40	15.49	15.93	16.36	16.80	17.24
13.32	13.76	14.20	14.63	15.07	45	15.51	15.95	16.38	16.82	17.26
13.34	13.78	14.22	14.66	15.09	50	15.53	15.97	16.41	16.84	17.28
13.37	13.80	14.24	14.68	15.12	55	15.55	15.99	16.43	16.87	17.30
13.39	13.83	14.26	14.70	15.14	60	15.58	16.01	16.45	16.89	17.33
13.41	13.85	14.28	14.72	15.16	65	15.60	16.03	16.47	16.91	17.35
13.43	13.87	14.31	14.74	15.18	70	15.62	16.06	16.49	16.93	17.37
13.45	13.89	14.33	14.77	15.20	75	15.64	16.08	16.52	16.95	17.39
13.48	13.91	14.35	14.79	15.23	80	15.66	16.10	16.54	16.98	17.41
13.50	13.93	14.37	14.81	15.25	85	15.68	16.12	16.56	17.00	17.43
13.52	13.96	14.39	14.83	15.27	90	15.71	16.14	16.58	17.02	17.46
13.54	13.98	14.42	14.85	15.29	95	15.73	16.17	16.60	17.04	17.48

Even tons, 51 to 100 inclusive.

51-60		61-70		71-80		81-90		91-100	
T	Am't	T	Am't	T	Am't	T	Am't	T	Am't
51	446.25	61	533.75	71	621.25	81	708.75	91	796.25
52	455.00	62	542.50	72	630.00	82	717.50	92	805.00
53	463.75	63	551.25	73	638.75	83	726.25	93	813.75
54	472.50	64	560.00	74	647.50	84	735.00	94	822.50
55	481.25	65	568.75	75	656.25	85	743.75	95	831.25
56	490.00	66	577.50	76	665.00	86	752.50	96	840.00
57	498.75	67	586.25	77	673.75	87	761.25	97	848.75
58	507.50	68	595.00	78	682.50	88	770.00	98	857.50
59	516.25	69	603.75	79	691.25	89	778.75	99	866.25
60	525.00	70	612.50	80	700.00	90	787.50	100	875.00

700	6125	800	7000	900	7875	1000	8750	1100	9625

7 (73)

------ POUNDS ------

Under 100	100	200	300	400		500	600	700	800	900
	.45	.90	1.35	1.80		2.25	2.70	3.15	3.60	4.05
.02	.47	.92	1.37	1.82	5	2.27	2.72	3.17	3.62	4.07
.05	.50	.95	1.40	1.85	10	2.30	2.75	3.20	3.65	4.10
.07	.52	.97	1.42	1.87	15	2.32	2.77	3.22	3.67	4.12
.09	.54	.99	1.44	1.89	20	2.34	2.79	3.24	3.69	4.14
.11	.56	1.01	1.46	1.91	25	2.36	2.81	3.26	3.71	4.16
.14	.59	1.04	1.49	1.94	30	2.39	2.84	3.29	3.74	4.19
.16	.61	1.06	1.51	1.96	35	2.41	2.86	3.31	3.76	4.21
.18	.63	1.08	1.53	1.98	40	2.43	2.88	3.33	3.78	4.23
.20	.65	1.10	1.55	2.00	45	2.45	2.90	3.35	3.80	4.25
.23	.68	1.13	1.58	2.03	50	2.48	2.93	3.38	3.83	4.28
.25	.70	1.15	1.60	2.05	55	2.50	2.95	3.40	3.85	4.30
.27	.72	1.17	1.62	2.07	60	2.52	2.97	3.42	3.87	4.32
.29	.74	1.19	1.64	2.09	65	2.54	2.99	3.44	3.89	4.34
.32	.77	1.22	1.67	2.12	70	2.57	3.02	3.47	3.92	4.37
.34	.79	1.24	1.69	2.14	75	2.59	3.04	3.49	3.94	4.39
.36	.81	1.26	1.71	2.16	80	2.61	3.06	3.51	3.96	4.41
.38	.83	1.28	1.73	2.18	85	2.63	3.08	3.53	3.98	4.43
.41	.86	1.31	1.76	2.21	90	2.66	3.11	3.56	4.01	4.46
.43	.88	1.33	1.78	2.23	95	2.68	3.13	3.58	4.03	4.48

------ POUNDS ------

1000	1100	1200	1300	1400		1500	1600	1700	1800	1900
4.50	4.95	5.40	5.85	6.30		6.75	7.20	7.65	8.10	8.55
4.52	4.97	5.42	5.87	6.32	5	6.77	7.22	7.67	8.12	8.57
4.55	5.00	5.45	5.90	6.35	10	6.80	7.25	7.70	8.15	8.60
4.57	5.02	5.47	5.92	6.37	15	6.82	7.27	7.72	8.17	8.62
4.59	5.04	5.49	5.94	6.39	20	6.84	7.29	7.74	8.19	8.64
4.61	5.06	5.51	5.96	6.41	25	6.86	7.31	7.76	8.21	8.66
4.64	5.09	5.54	5.99	6.44	30	6.89	7.34	7.79	8.24	8.69
4.66	5.11	5.56	6.01	6.46	35	6.91	7.36	7.81	8.26	8.71
4.68	5.13	5.58	6.03	6.48	40	6.93	7.38	7.83	8.28	8.73
4.70	5.15	5.60	6.05	6.50	45	6.95	7.40	7.85	8.30	8.75
4.73	5.18	5.63	6.08	6.53	50	6.98	7.43	7.88	8.33	8.78
4.75	5.20	5.65	6.10	6.55	55	7.00	7.45	7.90	8.35	8.80
4.77	5.22	5.67	6.12	6.57	60	7.02	7.47	7.92	8.37	8.82
4.79	5.24	5.69	6.14	6.59	65	7.04	7.49	7.94	8.39	8.84
4.82	5.27	5.72	6.17	6.62	70	7.07	7.52	7.97	8.42	8.87
4.84	5.29	5.74	6.19	6.64	75	7.09	7.54	7.99	8.44	8.89
4.86	5.31	5.76	6.21	6.66	80	7.11	7.56	8.01	8.46	8.91
4.88	5.33	5.78	6.23	6.68	85	7.13	7.58	8.03	8.48	8.93
4.91	5.36	5.81	6.26	6.71	90	7.16	7.61	8.06	8.51	8.96
4.93	5.38	5.83	6.28	6.73	95	7.18	7.63	8.08	8.53	8.98

Even tons, 1 to 50 inclusive.

1-10		11-20		21-30		31-40		41-50	
T	Am't	T	Am't	T	Am't	T	Am't	T	Am't
1	9.00	11	99.00	21	189.00	31	279.00	41	369.00
2	18.00	12	108.00	22	198.00	32	288.00	42	378.00
3	27.00	13	117.00	23	207.00	33	297.00	43	387.00
4	36.00	14	126.00	24	216.00	34	306.00	44	396.00
5	45.00	15	135.00	25	225.00	35	315.00	45	405.00
6	54.00	16	144.00	26	234.00	36	324.00	46	414.00
7	63.00	17	153.00	27	243.00	37	333.00	47	423.00
8	72.00	18	162.00	28	252.00	38	342.00	48	432.00
9	81.00	19	171.00	29	261.00	39	351.00	49	441.00
10	90.00	20	180.00	30	270.00	40	360.00	50	450.00

200	1800	300	2700	400	3600	500	4500	600	5400

$9.00 a T.

-------POUNDS-------

2000	2100	2200	2300	2400		2500	2600	2700	2800	2900
		--AMOUNT--					--AMOUNT--			
9.00	9.45	9.90	10.35	10.80		11.25	11.70	12.15	12.60	13.05
9.02	9.47	9.92	10.37	10.82	5	11.27	11.72	12.17	12.62	13.07
9.05	9.50	9.95	10.40	10.85	10	11.30	11.75	12.20	12.65	13.10
9.07	9.52	9.97	10.42	10.87	15	11.32	11.77	12.22	12.67	13.12
9.09	9.54	9.99	10.44	10.89	20	11.34	11.79	12.24	12.69	13.14
9.11	9.56	10.01	10.46	10.91	25	11.36	11.81	12.26	12.71	13.16
9.14	9.59	10.04	10.49	10.94	30	11.39	11.84	12.29	12.74	13.19
9.16	9.61	10.06	10.51	10.96	35	11.41	11.86	12.31	12.76	13.21
9.18	9.63	10.08	10.53	10.98	40	11.43	11.88	12.33	12.78	13.23
9.20	9.65	10.10	10.55	11.00	45	11.45	11.90	12.35	12.80	13.25
9.23	9.68	10.13	10.58	11.03	50	11.48	11.93	12.38	12.83	13.28
9.25	9.70	10.15	10.60	11.05	55	11.50	11.95	12.40	12.85	13.30
9.27	9.72	10.17	10.62	11.07	60	11.52	11.97	12.42	12.87	13.32
0.29	9.74	10.19	10.64	11.09	65	11.54	11.99	12.44	12.89	13.34
9.32	9.77	10.22	10.67	11.12	70	11.57	12.02	12.47	12.92	13.37
9.34	9.79	10.24	10.69	11.14	75	11.59	12.04	12.49	12.94	13.39
9.36	9.81	10.26	10.71	11.16	80	11.61	12.06	12.51	12.96	13.41
9.38	9.83	10.28	10.73	11.18	85	11.63	12.08	12.53	12.98	13.43
9.41	9.86	10.31	10.76	11.21	90	11.66	12.11	12.56	13.01	13.46
9.43	9.88	10.33	10.78	11.23	95	11.68	12.13	12.58	13.03	13.48

-------POUNDS-------

3000	3100	3200	3300	3400		3500	3600	3700	3800	3900
		--AMOUNT--					--AMOUNT--			
13.50	13.95	14.40	14.85	15.30		15.75	16.20	16.65	17.10	17.55
13.52	13.97	14.42	14.87	15.32	5	15.77	16.22	16.67	17.12	17.57
13.55	14.00	14.45	14.90	15.35	10	15.80	16.25	16.70	17.15	17.60
13.57	14.02	14.47	14.92	15.37	15	15.82	16.27	16.72	17.17	17.62
13.59	14.04	14.49	14.94	15.39	20	15.84	16.29	16.74	17.19	17.64
13.61	14.06	14.51	14.96	15.41	25	15.86	16.31	16.76	17.21	17.66
13.64	14.09	14.54	14.99	15.44	30	15.89	16.34	16.79	17.24	17.69
13.66	14.11	14.56	15.01	15.46	35	15.91	16.36	16.81	17.26	17.71
13.68	14.13	14.58	15.03	15.48	40	15.93	16.38	16.83	17.28	17.73
13.70	14.15	14.60	15.05	15.50	45	15.95	16.40	16.85	17.30	17.75
13.73	14.18	14.63	15.08	15.53	50	15.98	16.43	16.88	17.33	17.78
13.75	14.20	14.65	15.10	15.55	55	16.00	16.45	16.90	17.35	17.80
13.77	14.22	14.67	15.12	15.57	60	16.02	16.47	16.92	17.37	17.82
13.79	14.24	14.69	15.14	15.59	65	16.04	16.49	16.94	17.39	17.84
13.82	14.27	14.72	15.17	15.62	70	16.07	16.52	16.97	17.42	17.87
13.84	14.29	14.74	15.19	15.64	75	16.09	16.54	16.99	17.44	17.89
13.86	14.31	14.76	15.21	15.66	80	16.11	16.56	17.01	17.46	17.91
13.88	14.33	14.78	15.23	15.68	85	16.13	16.58	17.03	17.48	17.93
13.91	14.36	14.81	15.26	15.71	90	16.16	16.61	17.06	17.51	17.96
13.93	14.38	14.83	15.28	15.73	95	16.18	16.63	17.08	17.53	17.98

Even tons, 51 to 100 inclusive.

51-60		61-70		71-80		81-90		91-100	
T	Am't	T	Am't	T	Am't	T	Am't	T	Am't
51	459.00	61	549.00	71	639.00	81	729.00	91	819.00
52	468.00	62	558.00	72	648.00	82	738.00	92	828.00
53	477.00	63	567.00	73	657.00	83	747.00	93	837.00
54	486.00	64	576.00	74	666.00	84	756.00	94	846.00
55	495.00	65	585.00	75	675.00	85	765.00	95	855.00
56	504.00	66	594.00	76	684.00	86	774.00	96	864.00
57	513.00	67	603.00	77	693.00	87	783.00	97	873.00
58	522.00	68	612.00	78	702.00	88	792.00	98	882.00
59	531.00	69	621.00	79	711.00	89	801.00	99	891.00
60	540.00	70	630.00	80	720.00	90	810.00	100	900.00

700	6300	800	7200	900	8100	1000	9000	1100	9900

POUNDS

Under 100	100	200	300	400		500	600	700	800	900
	.46	.93	1.39	1.85		2.31	2.78	3.24	3.70	4.16
.02	.49	.95	1.41	1.87	5	2.34	2.80	3.26	3.72	4.19
.05	.51	.97	1.43	1.90	10	2.36	2.82	3.28	3.75	4.21
.07	.53	.99	1.46	1.92	15	2.38	2.84	3.31	3.77	4.23
.09	.56	1.02	1.48	1.94	20	2.41	2.87	3.33	3.79	4.26
.12	.58	1.04	1.50	1.97	25	2.43	2.89	3.35	3.82	4.28
.14	.60	1.06	1.53	1.99	30	2.45	2.91	3.38	3.84	4.30
.16	.62	1.09	1.55	2.01	35	2.47	2.94	3.40	3.86	4.32
.19	.65	1.11	1.57	2.04	40	2.50	2.96	3.42	3.89	4.35
.21	.67	1.13	1.60	2.06	45	2.52	2.98	3.45	3.91	4.37
.23	.69	1.16	1.62	2.08	50	2.54	3.01	3.47	3.93	4.39
.25	.72	1.18	1.64	2.10	55	2.57	3.03	3.49	3.95	4.42
.28	.74	1.20	1.67	2.13	60	2.59	3.05	3.52	3.98	4.44
.30	.76	1.23	1.69	2.15	65	2.61	3.08	3.54	4.00	4.46
.32	.79	1.25	1.71	2.17	70	2.64	3.10	3.56	4.02	4.49
.35	.81	1.27	1.73	2.20	75	2.66	3.12	3.58	4.05	4.51
.37	.83	1.30	1.76	2.22	80	2.68	3.15	3.61	4.07	4.53
.39	.86	1.32	1.78	2.24	85	2.71	3.17	3.63	4.09	4.56
.42	.88	1.34	1.80	2.27	90	2.73	3.19	3.65	4.12	4.58
.44	.90	1.36	1.83	2.29	95	2.75	3.21	3.68	4.14	4.60

POUNDS

1000	1100	1200	1300	1400		1500	1600	1700	1800	1900
4.63	5.09	5.55	6.01	6.48		6.94	7.40	7.86	8.33	8.79
4.65	5.11	5.57	6.04	6.50	5	6.96	7.42	7.89	8.35	8.81
4.67	5.13	5.60	6.06	6.52	10	6.98	7.45	7.91	8.37	8.83
4.69	5.16	5.62	6.08	6.54	15	7.01	7.47	7.93	8.39	8.86
4.72	5.18	5.64	6.11	6.57	20	7.03	7.49	7.96	8.42	8.88
4.74	5.20	5.67	6.13	6.59	25	7.05	7.52	7.98	8.44	8.90
4.76	5.23	5.69	6.15	6.61	30	7.08	7.54	8.00	8.46	8.93
4.79	5.25	5.71	6.17	6.64	35	7.10	7.56	8.02	8.49	8.95
4.81	5.27	5.74	6.20	6.66	40	7.12	7.59	8.05	8.51	8.97
4.83	5.30	5.76	6.22	6.68	45	7.15	7.61	8.07	8.53	9.00
4.86	5.32	5.78	6.24	6.71	50	7.17	7.63	8.09	8.56	9.02
4.88	5.34	5.80	6.27	6.73	55	7.19	7.65	8.12	8.58	9.04
4.90	5.37	5.83	6.29	6.75	60	7.22	7.68	8.14	8.60	9.07
4.93	5.39	5.85	6.31	6.78	65	7.24	7.70	8.16	8.63	9.09
4.95	5.41	5.87	6.34	6.80	70	7.26	7.72	8.19	8.65	9.11
4.97	5.43	5.90	6.36	6.82	75	7.28	7.75	8.21	8.67	9.13
5.00	5.46	5.92	6.38	6.85	80	7.31	7.77	8.23	8.70	9.16
5.02	5.48	5.94	6.41	6.87	85	7.33	7.79	8.26	8.72	9.18
5.04	5.50	5.97	6.43	6.89	90	7.35	7.82	8.28	8.74	9.20
5.06	5.53	5.99	6.45	6.91	95	7.38	7.84	8.30	8.76	9.23

Even tons, 1 to 50 inclusive.

1-10		11-20		21-30		31-40		41-50	
T	Am't	T	Am't	T	Am't	T	Am't	T	Am't
1	9.25	11	101.75	21	194.25	31	286.75	41	379.25
2	18.50	12	111.00	22	203.50	32	296.00	42	388.50
3	27.75	13	120.25	23	212.75	33	305.25	43	397.75
4	37.00	14	129.50	24	222.00	34	314.50	44	407.00
5	46.25	15	138.75	25	231.25	35	323.75	45	416.25
6	55.50	16	148.00	26	240.50	36	333.00	46	425.50
7	64.75	17	157.25	27	249.75	37	342.25	47	434.75
8	74.00	18	166.50	28	259.00	38	351.50	48	444.00
9	83.25	19	175.75	29	268.25	39	360.75	49	453.25
10	92.50	20	185.00	30	277.50	40	370.00	50	462.50

200	1850	300	2775	400	3700	500	4625	600	5550

——— POUNDS ———

2000	2100	2200	2300	2400		2500	2600	2700	2800	2900
		—AMOUNT—					—AMOUNT—			
9.25	9.71	10.18	10.64	11.10		11.56	12.03	12.49	12.95	13.41
9.27	9.74	10.20	10.66	11.12	5	11.59	12.05	12.51	12.97	13.44
9.30	9.76	10.22	10.68	11.15	10	11.61	12.07	12.53	13.00	13.46
9.32	9.78	10.24	10.71	11.17	15	11.63	12.09	12.56	13.02	13.48
9.34	9.81	10.27	10.73	11.19	20	11.66	12.12	12.58	13.04	13.51
9.37	9.83	10.29	10.75	11.21	25	11.68	12.14	12.60	13.07	13.53
9.39	9.85	10.31	10.78	11.24	30	11.70	12.16	12.63	13.09	13.55
9.41	9.87	10.34	10.80	11.26	35	11.72	12.19	12.65	13.11	13.57
9.44	9.90	10.36	10.82	11.29	40	11.75	12.21	12.67	13.14	13.60
9.46	9.92	10.38	10.85	11.31	45	11.77	12.23	12.70	13.16	13.62
9.48	9.94	10.41	10.87	11.33	50	11.79	12.26	12.72	13.18	13.64
9.50	9.97	10.43	10.89	11.35	55	11.82	12.28	12.74	13.20	13.67
9.53	9.99	10.45	10.92	11.38	60	11.84	12.30	12.77	13.23	13.69
9.55	10.01	10.48	10.94	11.40	65	11.86	12.33	12.79	13.25	13.71
9.57	10.04	10.50	10.96	11.42	70	11.89	12.35	12.81	13.27	13.74
9.60	10.06	10.52	10.98	11.45	75	11.91	12.37	12.83	13.30	13.76
9.62	10.08	10.55	11.01	11.47	80	11.93	12.40	12.86	13.32	13.78
9.64	10.11	10.57	11.03	11.49	85	11.96	12.42	12.88	13.34	13.81
9.67	10.13	10.59	11.05	11.52	90	11.98	12.44	12.90	13.37	13.83
9.69	10.15	10.61	11.08	11.54	95	12.00	12.46	12.93	13.39	13.85

——— POUNDS ———

3000	3100	3200	3300	3400		3500	3600	3700	3800	3900
		—AMOUNT—					—AMOUNT—			
13.88	14.34	14.80	15.26	15.73		16.19	16.65	17.11	17.58	18.04
13.90	14.36	14.82	15.29	15.75	5	16.21	16.67	17.14	17.60	18.06
13.92	14.38	14.85	15.31	15.77	10	16.23	16.70	17.16	17.62	18.08
13.94	14.41	14.87	15.33	15.79	15	16.26	16.72	17.18	17.64	18.11
13.97	14.43	14.89	15.36	15.82	20	16.28	16.74	17.21	17.67	18.13
13.99	14.45	14.92	15.38	15.84	25	16.30	16.77	17.23	17.69	18.15
14.01	14.48	14.94	15.40	15.86	30	16.33	16.79	17.25	17.71	18.18
14.04	14.50	14.96	15.42	15.89	35	16.35	16.81	17.27	17.74	18.20
14.06	14.52	14.99	15.45	15.91	40	16.37	16.84	17.30	17.76	18.22
14.08	14.55	15.01	15.47	15.93	45	16.40	16.86	17.32	17.78	18.25
14.11	14.57	15.03	15.49	15.96	50	16.42	16.88	17.34	17.81	18.27
14.13	14.59	15.05	15.52	15.98	55	16.44	16.90	17.37	17.83	18.29
14.15	14.62	15.08	15.54	16.00	60	16.47	16.93	17.39	17.85	18.32
14.18	14.64	15.10	15.56	16.03	65	16.49	16.95	17.41	17.88	18.34
14.20	14.66	15.12	15.59	16.05	70	16.51	16.97	17.44	17.90	18.36
14.22	14.68	15.15	15.61	16.07	75	16.53	17.00	17.46	17.92	18.38
14.25	14.71	15.17	15.63	16.10	80	16.56	17.02	17.48	17.95	18.41
14.27	14.73	15.19	15.66	16.12	85	16.58	17.04	17.51	17.97	18.43
14.29	14.75	15.22	15.68	16.14	90	16.60	17.07	17.53	17.99	18.45
14.31	14.78	15.24	15.70	16.16	95	16.63	17.09	17.55	18.01	18.48

Even tons, 51 to 100 inclusive.

51-60		61-70		71-80		81-90		91-100	
T	Am't	T	Am't	T	Am't	T	Am't	T	Am't
51	471.75	61	564.25	71	656.25	81	749.25	91	841.75
52	481.00	62	573.50	72	666.00	82	758.50	92	851.00
53	490.25	63	582.75	73	675.25	83	767.75	93	860.25
54	499.50	64	592.00	74	684.50	84	777.00	94	869.50
55	508.75	65	601.25	75	693.75	85	786.25	95	878.75
56	518.00	66	610.50	76	703.00	86	795.50	96	888.00
57	527.25	67	619.75	77	712.25	87	804.75	97	897.25
58	536.50	68	629.00	78	721.50	88	814.00	98	906.50
59	545.75	69	638.25	79	730.75	89	823.25	99	915.75
60	555.00	70	647.50	80	740.00	90	832.50	100	925.00

700	6475	800	7400	900	8325	1000	9250	1100	10175

POUNDS

Under 100	100	200	300	400		500	600	700	800	900
	.48	.95	1.43	1.90		2.38	2.85	3.33	3.80	4.28
.02	.50	.97	1.45	1.92	5	2.40	2.87	3.35	3.82	4.30
.05	.52	1.00	1.47	1.95	10	2.42	2.90	3.37	3.85	4.32
.07	.55	1.02	1.50	1.97	15	2.45	2.92	3.40	3.87	4.35
.10	.57	1.05	1.52	2.00	20	2.47	2.95	3.42	3.90	4.37
.12	.59	1.07	1.54	2.02	25	2.49	2.97	3.44	3.92	4.39
.14	.62	1.09	1.57	2.04	30	2.52	2.99	3.47	3.94	4.42
.17	.64	1.12	1.59	2.07	35	2.54	3.02	3.49	3.97	4.44
.19	.67	1.14	1.62	2.09	40	2.57	3.04	3.52	3.99	4.47
.21	.69	1.16	1.64	2.11	45	2.59	3.06	3.54	4.01	4.49
.24	.71	1.19	1.66	2.14	50	2.61	3.09	3.56	4.04	4.51
.26	.74	1.21	1.69	2.16	55	2.64	3.11	3.59	4.06	4.54
.29	.76	1.24	1.71	2.19	60	2.66	3.14	3.61	4.09	4.56
.31	.78	1.26	1.73	2.21	65	2.68	3.16	3.63	4.11	4.58
.33	.81	1.28	1.76	2.23	70	2.71	3.18	3.66	4.13	4.61
.36	.83	1.31	1.78	2.26	75	2.73	3.21	3.68	4.16	4.63
.38	.86	1.33	1.81	2.28	80	2.76	3.23	3.71	4.18	4.66
.40	.88	1.35	1.83	2.30	85	2.78	3.25	3.73	4.20	4.68
.43	.90	1.38	1.85	2.33	90	2.80	3.28	3.75	4.23	4.70
.45	.93	1.40	1.88	2.35	95	2.83	3.30	3.78	4.25	4.73

POUNDS

1000	1100	1200	1300	1400		1500	1600	1700	1800	1900
4.75	5.23	5.70	6.18	6.65		7.13	7.60	8.08	8.55	9.03
4.77	5.25	5.72	6.20	6.67	5	7.15	7.62	8.10	8.57	9.05
4.80	5.27	5.75	6.22	6.70	10	7.17	7.65	8.12	8.60	9.07
4.82	5.30	5.77	6.25	6.72	15	7.20	7.67	8.15	8.62	9.10
4.85	5.32	5.80	6.27	6.75	20	7.22	7.70	8.17	8.65	9.12
4.87	5.34	5.82	6.29	6.77	25	7.24	7.72	8.19	8.67	9.14
4.89	5.37	5.84	6.32	6.79	30	7.27	7.74	8.22	8.69	9.17
4.92	5.39	5.87	6.34	6.82	35	7.29	7.77	8.24	8.72	9.19
4.94	5.42	5.89	6.37	6.84	40	7.32	7.79	8.27	8.74	9.22
4.96	5.44	5.91	6.39	6.86	45	7.34	7.81	8.29	8.76	9.24
4.99	5.46	5.94	6.41	6.89	50	7.36	7.84	8.31	8.79	9.26
5.01	5.49	5.96	6.44	6.91	55	7.39	7.86	8.34	8.81	9.29
5.04	5.51	5.99	6.46	6.94	60	7.41	7.89	8.36	8.84	9.31
5.06	5.53	6.01	6.48	6.96	65	7.43	7.91	8.38	8.86	9.33
5.08	5.56	6.03	6.51	6.98	70	7.46	7.93	8.41	8.88	9.36
5.11	5.58	6.06	6.53	7.01	75	7.48	7.96	8.43	8.91	9.38
5.13	5.61	6.08	6.56	7.03	80	7.51	7.98	8.46	8.93	9.41
5.15	5.63	6.10	6.58	7.05	85	7.53	8.00	8.48	8.95	9.43
5.18	5.65	6.13	6.60	7.08	90	7.55	8.03	8.50	8.98	9.45
5.20	5.68	6.15	6.63	7.10	95	7.58	8.05	8.53	9.00	9.48

Even tons, 1 to 50 inclusive.

T	Am't	T	Am't	T	Am't	T	Am't	T	Am't
1	9.50	11	104.50	21	199.50	31	294.50	41	389.50
2	19.00	12	114.00	22	209.00	32	304.00	42	399.00
3	28.50	13	123.50	23	218.50	33	313.50	43	408.50
4	38.00	14	133.00	24	228.00	34	323.00	44	418.00
5	47.50	15	142.50	25	237.50	35	332.50	45	427.50
6	57.00	16	152.00	26	247.00	36	342.00	46	437.00
7	66.50	17	161.50	27	256.50	37	351.50	47	446.50
8	76.00	18	171.00	28	266.00	38	361.00	48	456.00
9	85.50	19	180.50	29	275.50	39	370.50	49	465.50
10	95.00	20	190.00	30	285.00	40	380.00	50	475.00

200	1900	300	2850	400	3800	500	4750	600	5700

POUNDS

2000	2100	2200	2300	2400		2500	2600	2700	2800	2900
		AMOUNT						AMOUNT		
9.50	9.98	10.45	10.93	11.40		11.88	12.35	12.83	13.30	13.78
9.52	10.00	10.47	10.95	11.42	5	11.90	12.37	12.85	13.32	13.80
9.55	10.02	10.50	10.97	11.45	10	11.92	12.40	12.87	13.35	13.82
9.57	10.05	10.52	11.00	11.47	15	11.95	12.42	12.90	13.37	13.85
9.60	10.07	10.55	11.02	11.50	20	11.97	12.45	12.92	13.40	13.87
9.62	10.09	10.57	11.04	11.52	25	11.99	12.47	12.94	13.42	13.89
9.64	10.12	10.59	11.07	11.54	30	12.02	12.49	12.97	13.44	13.92
9.67	10.14	10.62	11.09	11.57	35	12.04	12.52	12.99	13.47	13.94
9.69	10.17	10.64	11.12	11.59	40	12.07	12.54	13.02	13.49	13.97
9.71	10.19	10.66	11.14	11.61	45	12.09	12.56	13.04	13.51	13.99
9.74	10.21	10.69	11.16	11.64	50	12.11	12.59	13.06	13.54	14.01
9.76	10.24	10.71	11.19	11.66	55	12.14	12.61	13.09	13.56	14.04
9.79	10.26	10.74	11.21	11.69	60	12.16	12.64	13.11	13.59	14.06
9.81	10.28	10.76	11.23	11.71	65	12.18	12.66	13.13	13.61	14.08
9.83	10.31	10.78	11.26	11.73	70	12.21	12.68	13.16	13.63	14.11
9.86	10.33	10.81	11.28	11.76	75	12.23	12.71	13.18	13.66	14.13
9.88	10.36	10.83	11.31	11.78	80	12.26	12.73	13.21	13.68	14.16
9.90	10.38	10.85	11.33	11.80	85	12.28	12.75	13.23	13.70	14.18
9.93	10.40	10.88	11.35	11.83	90	12.30	12.78	13.25	13.73	14.20
9.95	10.43	10.90	11.38	11.85	95	12.33	12.80	13.28	13.75	14.23

POUNDS

3000	3100	3200	3300	3400		3500	3600	3700	3800	3900
		AMOUNT						AMOUNT		
14.25	14.73	15.20	15.68	16.15		16.63	17.10	17.58	18.05	18.53
14.27	14.75	15.22	15.70	16.17	5	16.65	17.12	17.60	18.07	18.55
14.30	14.77	15.25	15.72	16.20	10	16.67	17.15	17.62	18.10	18.57
14.32	14.80	15.27	15.75	16.22	15	16.70	17.17	17.65	18.12	18.60
14.35	14.82	15.30	15.77	16.25	20	16.72	17.20	17.67	18.15	18 62
14.37	14.84	15.32	15.79	16.27	25	16.74	17.22	17.69	18.17	18.64
14.39	14.87	15.34	15.82	16.29	30	16.77	17.24	17.72	18.19	18.67
14.42	14.89	15.37	15.84	16.32	35	16.79	17.27	17.74	18.22	18.69
14.44	14.92	15.39	15.87	16.34	40	16.82	17.29	17.77	18.24	18.72
14.46	14.94	15.41	15.89	16.36	45	16.84	17.31	17.79	18.26	18.74
14.49	14.96	15.44	15.91	16.39	50	16.86	17.34	17.81	18.29	18.76
14.51	14.99	15.46	15.94	16.41	55	16.89	17.36	17.84	18.31	18.79
14.54	15.01	15.49	15.96	16.44	60	16.91	17.39	17.86	18.34	18.81
14.56	15.03	15.51	15.98	16.46	65	16.93	17.41	17.88	18.36	18.83
14.58	15.06	15.53	16.01	16.48	70	16.96	17.43	17.91	18.38	18.86
14.61	15.08	15.56	16.03	16.51	75	16.98	17.46	17.93	18.41	18.88
14.63	15.11	15.58	16.06	16.53	80	17.01	17.48	17.96	18.43	18.91
14.65	15.13	15.60	16.08	16.55	85	17.03	17.50	17.98	18.45	18.93
14.68	15.15	15.63	16.10	16.58	90	17.05	17.53	18.00	18.48	18.95
14.70	15.18	15.65	16.13	16.60	95	17.08	17.55	18.03	18.50	18.98

Even tons, 51 to 100 inclusive.

	51-60		61-70		71-80		81-90		91-100
T	Am't	T	Am't	T	Am't	T	Am't	T	Am't
51	484.50	61	579.50	71	674.50	81	769.50	91	864.50
52	494.00	62	589.00	72	684.00	82	779.00	92	874.00
53	503.50	63	598.50	73	693.50	83	788.50	93	883.50
54	513.00	64	608.00	74	703.00	84	798.00	94	893.00
55	522.50	65	617.50	75	712.50	85	807.50	95	902.50
56	532.00	66	627.00	76	722.00	86	817.00	96	912.00
57	541.50	67	636.50	77	731.50	87	826.50	97	921.50
58	551.00	68	646.00	78	741.00	88	836 00	98	931.00
59	560.50	69	655.50	79	750.50	89	845.50	99	940.50
60	570.00	70	665.00	80	760.00	90	855.00	100	950.00

700	6650	800	7600	900	8550	1000	9500	1100	10450

POUNDS

Under 100	100	200	300	400		500	600	700	800	900
	.49	.98	1.46	1.95		2.44	2.93	3.41	3.90	4.39
.02	.51	1.00	1.49	1.97	5	2.46	2.95	3.44	3.92	4.41
.05	.54	1.02	1.51	2.00	10	2.49	2.97	3.46	3.95	4.44
.07	.56	1.05	1.54	2.02	15	2.51	3.00	3.49	3.97	4.46
.10	.59	1.07	1.56	2.05	20	2.54	3.02	3.51	4.00	4.49
.12	.61	1.10	1.58	2.07	25	2.56	3.05	3.53	4.02	4.51
.15	.63	1.12	1.61	2.10	30	2.58	3.07	3.56	4.05	4.53
.17	.66	1.15	1.63	2.12	35	2.61	3.10	3.58	4.07	4.56
.20	.68	1.17	1.66	2.15	40	2.63	3.12	3.61	4.10	4.58
.22	.71	1.19	1.68	2.17	45	2.66	3.14	3.63	4.12	4.61
.24	.73	1.22	1.71	2.19	50	2.68	3.17	3.66	4.14	4.63
.27	.76	1.24	1.73	2.22	55	2.71	3.19	3.68	4.17	4.66
.29	.78	1.27	1.76	2.24	60	2.73	3.22	3.71	4.19	4.68
.32	.80	1.29	1.78	2.27	65	2.75	3.24	3.73	4.22	4.70
.34	.83	1.32	1.80	2.29	70	2.78	3.27	3.75	4.24	4.73
.37	.85	1.34	1.83	2.32	75	2.80	3.29	3.78	4.27	4.75
.39	.88	1.37	1.85	2.34	80	2.83	3.32	3.80	4.29	4.78
.41	.90	1.39	1.88	2.36	85	2.85	3.34	3.83	4.31	4.80
.44	.93	1.41	1.90	2.39	90	2.88	3.36	3.85	4.34	4.83
.46	.95	1.44	1.93	2.41	95	2.90	3.39	3.88	4.36	4.85

POUNDS

1000	1100	1200	1300	1400		1500	1600	1700	1800	1900
4.88	5.36	5.85	6.34	6.83		7.31	7.80	8.29	8.78	9.26
4.90	5.39	5.87	6.36	6.85	5	7.34	7.82	8.31	8.80	9.29
4.92	5.41	5.90	6.39	6.87	10	7.36	7.85	8.34	8.82	9.31
4.95	5.44	5.92	6.41	6.90	15	7.39	7.87	8.36	8.85	9.34
4.97	5.46	5.95	6.44	6.92	20	7.41	7.90	8.39	8.87	9.36
5.00	5.48	5.97	6.46	6.95	25	7.43	7.92	8.41	8.90	9.38
5.02	5.51	6.00	6.48	6.97	30	7.46	7.95	8.43	8.92	9.41
5.05	5.53	6.02	6.51	7.00	35	7.48	7.97	8.46	8.95	9.43
5.07	5.56	6.05	6.53	7.02	40	7.51	8.00	8.48	8.97	9.46
5.09	5.58	6.07	6.56	7.04	45	7.53	8.02	8.51	8.99	9.48
5.12	5.61	6.09	6.58	7.07	50	7.56	8.04	8.53	9.02	9.51
5.14	5.63	6.12	6.61	7.09	55	7.58	8.07	8.56	9.04	9.53
5.17	5.66	6.14	6.63	7.12	60	7.61	8.09	8.58	9.07	9.56
5.19	5.68	6.17	6.65	7.14	65	7.63	8.12	8.60	9.09	9.58
5.22	5.70	6.19	6.68	7.17	70	7.65	8.14	8.63	9.12	9.60
5.24	5.73	6.22	6.70	7.19	75	7.68	8.17	8.65	9.14	9.63
5.27	5.75	6.24	6.73	7.22	80	7.70	8.19	8.68	9.17	9.65
5.29	5.78	6.26	6.75	7.24	85	7.73	8.21	8.70	9.19	9.68
5.31	5.80	6.29	6.78	7.26	90	7.75	8.24	8.73	9.21	9.70
5.34	5.83	6.31	6.80	7.29	95	7.78	8.26	8.75	9.24	9.73

Even tons, 1 to 50 inclusive.

1-10		11-20		21-30		31-40		41-50	
T	Am't	T	Am't	T	Am't	T	Am't	T	Am't
1	9.75	11	107.25	21	204.75	31	302.25	41	399.75
2	19.50	12	117.00	22	214.50	32	312.00	42	409.50
3	29.25	13	126.75	23	224.25	33	321.75	43	419.25
4	39.00	14	136.50	24	234.00	34	331.50	44	429.00
5	48.75	15	146.25	25	243.75	35	341.25	45	438.75
6	58.50	16	156.00	26	253.50	36	351.00	46	448.50
7	68.25	17	165.75	27	263.25	37	360.75	47	458.25
8	78.00	18	175.50	28	273.00	38	370.50	48	468.00
9	87.75	19	185.25	29	282.75	39	380.25	49	477.75
10	97.50	20	195.00	30	292.50	40	390.00	50	487.50
200	1950	300	2925	400	3900	500	4875	600	5850

POUNDS

2000	2100	2200	2300	2400		2500	2600	2700	2800	2900
		AMOUNT						AMOUNT		
9.75	10.24	10.73	11.21	11.70		12.19	12.68	13.16	13.65	14.14
9.77	10.26	10.75	11.24	11.72	5	12.21	12.70	13.19	13.67	14.16
9.80	10.29	10.77	11.26	11.75	10	12.24	12.72	13.21	13.70	14.19
9.82	10.31	10.80	11.29	11.77	15	12.26	12.75	13.24	13.72	14.21
9.85	10.34	10.82	11.31	11.80	20	12.29	12.77	13.26	13.75	14.24
9.87	10.36	10.85	11.33	11.82	25	12.31	12.80	13.28	13.77	14.26
9.90	10.38	10.87	11.36	11.85	30	12.33	12.82	13.31	13.80	14.28
9.92	10.41	10.90	11.38	11.87	35	12.36	12.85	13.33	13.82	14.31
9.95	10.43	10.92	11.41	11.90	40	12.38	12.87	13.36	13.85	14.33
9.97	10.46	10.94	11.43	11.92	45	12.41	12.89	13.38	13.87	14.36
9.99	10.48	10.97	11.46	11.94	50	12.43	12.92	13.41	13.89	14.38
10.02	10.51	10.99	11.48	11.97	55	12.46	12.94	13.43	13.92	14.41
10.04	10.53	11.02	11.51	11.99	60	12.48	12.97	13.46	13.94	14.43
10.07	10.55	11.04	11.53	12.02	65	12.50	12.99	13.48	13.97	14.45
10.09	10.58	11.07	11.55	12.04	70	12.53	13.02	13.50	13.99	14.48
10.12	10.60	11.09	11.58	12.07	75	12.55	13.04	13.53	14.02	14.50
10.14	10.63	11.12	11.60	12.09	80	12.58	13.07	13.55	14.04	14.53
10.16	10.65	11.14	11.63	12.11	85	12.60	13.09	13.58	14.06	14.55
10.19	10.68	11.16	11.65	12.14	90	12.63	13.11	13.60	14.09	14.58
10.21	10.70	11.19	11.68	12.16	95	12.65	13.14	13.63	14.11	14.60

POUNDS

3000	3100	3200	3300	3400		3500	3600	3700	3800	3900
		AMOUNT						AMOUNT		
14.63	15.11	15.60	16.09	16.58		17.06	17.55	18.04	18.53	19.01
14.65	15.14	15.62	16.11	16.60	5	17.09	17.57	18.06	18.55	19.04
14.67	15.16	15.65	16.14	16.62	10	17.11	17.60	18.09	18.57	19.06
14.70	15.19	15.67	16.16	16.65	15	17.14	17.62	18.11	18.60	19.09
14.72	15.21	15.70	16.19	16.67	20	17.16	17.65	18.14	18.62	19.11
14.75	15.23	15.72	16.21	16.70	25	17.18	17.67	18.16	18.65	19.13
14.77	15.26	15.75	16.23	16.72	30	17.21	17.70	18.18	18.67	19.16
14.80	15.28	15.77	16.26	16.75	35	17.23	17.72	18.21	18.70	19.18
14.82	15.31	15.80	16.28	16.77	40	17.26	17.75	18.23	18.72	19.21
14.84	15.33	15.82	16.31	16.79	45	17.28	17.77	18.26	18.74	19.23
14.87	15.36	15.84	16.33	16.82	50	17.31	17.79	18.28	18.77	19.26
14.89	15.38	15.87	16.36	16.84	55	17.33	17.82	18.31	18.79	19.28
14.92	15.41	15.89	16.38	16.87	60	17.36	17.84	18.33	18.82	19.31
14.94	15.43	15.92	16.40	16.89	65	17.38	17.87	18.35	18.84	19.33
14.97	15.45	15.94	16.43	16.92	70	17.40	17.89	18.38	18.87	19.35
14.99	15.48	15.97	16.45	16.94	75	17.43	17.92	18.40	18.89	19.38
15.02	15.50	15.99	16.48	16.97	80	17.45	17.94	18.43	18.92	19.40
15.04	15.53	16.01	16.50	16.99	85	17.48	17.96	18.45	18.94	19.43
15.06	15.55	16.04	16.53	17.01	90	17.50	17.99	18.48	18.96	19.45
15.09	15.58	16.06	16.55	17.04	95	17.53	18.01	18.50	18.99	19.48

Even tons, 51 to 100 inclusive.

51-60		61-70		71-80		81-90		91-100	
T	Am't	T	Am't	T	Am't	T	Am't	T	Am't
51	497.25	61	594.75	71	692.25	81	789.75	91	887.25
52	507.00	62	604.50	72	702.00	82	799.50	92	897.00
53	516.75	63	614.25	73	711.75	83	809.25	93	906.75
54	526.50	64	624.00	74	721.50	84	819.00	94	916.50
55	536.25	65	633.75	75	731.25	85	828.75	95	926.25
56	546.00	66	643.50	76	741.00	86	838.50	96	936.00
57	555.75	67	653.25	77	750.75	87	848.25	97	945.75
58	565.50	68	663.00	78	760.50	88	858.00	98	955.50
59	575.25	69	672.75	79	770.25	89	867.75	99	965.25
60	585.00	70	682.50	80	780.00	90	877.50	100	975.00

700	6825	800	7800	900	8775	1000	9750	1100	10725

POUNDS

Under 100	100	200	300	400		500	600	700	800	900
	Amount							Amount		
	.50	1.00	1.50	2.00		2.50	3.00	3.50	4.00	4.50
.03	.53	1.03	1.53	2.03	5	2.53	3.03	3.53	4.03	4.53
.05	.55	1.05	1.55	2.05	10	2.55	3.05	3.55	4.05	4.55
.08	.58	1.08	1.58	2.08	15	2.58	3.08	3.58	4.08	4.58
.10	.60	1.10	1.60	2.10	20	2.60	3.10	3.60	4.10	4.60
.13	.63	1.13	1.63	2.13	25	2.63	3.13	3.63	4.13	4.63
.15	.65	1.15	1.65	2.15	30	2.65	3.15	3.65	4.15	4.65
.18	.68	1.18	1.68	2.18	35	2.68	3.18	3.68	4.18	4.68
.20	.70	1.20	1.70	2.20	40	2.70	3.20	3.70	4.20	4.70
.23	.73	1.23	1.73	2.23	45	2.73	3.23	3.73	4.23	4.73
.25	.75	1.25	1.75	2.25	50	2.75	3.25	3.75	4.25	4.75
.28	.78	1.28	1.78	2.28	55	2.78	3.28	3.78	4.28	4.78
.30	.80	1.30	1.80	2.30	60	2.80	3.30	3.80	4.30	4.80
.33	.83	1.33	1.83	2.33	65	2.83	3.33	3.83	4.33	4.83
.35	.85	1.35	1.85	2.35	70	2.85	3.35	3.85	4.35	4.85
.38	.88	1.38	1.88	2.38	75	2.88	3.38	3.88	4.38	4.88
.40	.90	1.40	1.90	2.40	80	2.90	3.40	3.90	4.40	4.90
.43	.93	1.43	1.93	2.43	85	2.93	3.43	3.93	4.43	4.93
.45	.95	1.45	1.95	2.45	90	2.95	3.45	3.95	4.45	4.95
.48	.98	1.48	1.98	2.48	95	2.98	3.48	3.98	4.48	4.98

POUNDS

1000	1100	1200	1300	1400		1500	1600	1700	1800	1900
	Amount							Amount		
5.00	5.50	6.00	6.50	7.00		7.50	8.00	8.50	9.00	9.50
5.03	5.53	6.03	6.53	7.03	5	7.53	8.03	8.53	9.03	9.53
5.05	5.55	6.05	6.55	7.05	10	7.55	8.05	8.55	9.05	9.55
5.08	5.58	6.08	6.58	7.08	15	7.58	8.08	8.58	9.08	9.58
5.10	5.60	6.10	6.60	7.10	20	7.60	8.10	8.60	9.10	9.60
5.13	5.63	6.13	6.63	7.13	25	7.63	8.13	8.63	9.13	9.63
5.15	5.65	6.15	6.65	7.15	30	7.65	8.15	8.65	9.15	9.65
5.18	5.68	6.18	6.68	7.18	35	7.68	8.18	8.68	9.18	9.68
5.20	5.70	6.20	6.70	7.20	40	7.70	8.20	8.70	9.20	9.70
5.23	5.73	6.23	6.73	7.23	45	7.73	8.23	8.73	9.23	9.73
5.25	5.75	6.25	6.75	7.25	50	7.75	8.25	8.75	9.25	9.75
5.28	5.78	6.28	6.78	7.28	55	7.78	8.28	8.78	9.28	9.78
5.30	5.80	6.30	6.80	7.30	60	7.80	8.30	8.80	9.30	9.80
5.33	5.83	6.33	6.83	7.33	65	7.83	8.33	8.83	9.33	9.83
5.35	5.85	6.35	6.85	7.35	70	7.85	8.35	8.85	9.35	9.85
5.38	5.88	6.38	6.88	7.38	75	7.88	8.38	8.88	9.38	9.88
5.40	5.90	6.40	6.90	7.40	80	7.90	8.40	8.90	9.40	9.90
5.43	5.93	6.43	6.93	7.43	85	7.93	8.43	8.93	9.43	9.93
5.45	5.95	6.45	6.95	7.45	90	7.95	8.45	8.95	9.45	9.95
5.48	5.98	6.48	6.98	7.48	95	7.98	8.48	8.98	9.48	9.98

Even tons, 1 to 50 inclusive.

1-10		11-20		21-30		31-40		41-50	
T	Am't	T	Am't	T	Am't	T	Am't	T	Am't
1	10.00	11	110.00	21	210.00	31	310.00	41	410.00
2	20.00	12	120.00	22	220.00	32	320.00	42	420.00
3	30.00	13	130.00	23	230.00	33	330.00	43	430.00
4	40.00	14	140.00	24	240.00	34	340.00	44	440.00
5	50.00	15	150.00	25	250.00	35	350.00	45	450.00
6	60.00	16	160.00	26	260.00	36	360.00	46	460.00
7	70.00	17	170.00	27	270.00	37	370.00	47	470.00
8	80.00	18	180.00	28	280.00	38	380.00	48	480.00
9	90.00	19	190.00	29	290.00	39	390.00	49	490.00
10	100.00	20	200.00	30	300.00	40	400.00	50	500.00

200	2000	300	3000	400	4000	500	5000	600	6000

40c a bu.   **$10.00 a T.**   50c a 100 lbs.

POUNDS

2000	2100	2200	2300	2400		2500	2600	2700	2800	2900
		AMOUNT						AMOUNT		
10.00	10.50	11.00	11.50	12.00		12.50	13.00	13.50	14.00	14.50
10.03	10.53	11.03	11.53	12.03	5	12.53	13.03	13.53	14.03	14.53
10.05	10.55	11.05	11.55	12.05	10	12.55	13.05	13.55	14.05	14.55
10.08	10.58	11.08	11.58	12.08	15	12.58	13.08	13.58	14.08	14.58
10.10	10.60	11.10	11.60	12.10	20	12.60	13.10	13.60	14.10	14.60
10.13	10.63	11.13	11.63	12.13	25	12.63	13.13	13.63	14.13	14.63
10.15	10.65	11.15	11.65	12.15	30	12.65	13.15	13.65	14.15	14.65
10.18	10.68	11.18	11.68	12.18	35	12.68	13.18	13.68	14.18	14.68
10.20	10.70	11.20	11.70	12.20	40	12.70	13.20	13.70	14.20	14.70
10.23	10.73	11.23	11.73	12.23	45	12.73	13.23	13.73	14.23	14.73
10.25	10.75	11.25	11.75	12.25	50	12.75	13.25	13.75	14.25	14.75
10.28	10.78	11.28	11.78	12.28	55	12.78	13.28	13.78	14.28	14.78
10.30	10.80	11.30	11.80	12.30	60	12.80	13.30	13.80	14.30	14.80
10.33	10.83	11.33	11.83	12.33	65	12.83	13.33	13.83	14.33	14.83
10.35	10.85	11.35	11.85	12.35	70	12.85	13.35	13.85	14.35	14.85
10.38	10.88	11.38	11.88	12.38	75	12.88	13.38	13.88	14.38	14.88
10.40	10.90	11.40	11.90	12.40	80	12.90	13.40	13.90	14.40	14.90
10.43	10.93	11.43	11.93	12.43	85	12.93	13.43	13.93	14.43	14.93
10.45	10.95	11.45	11.95	12.45	90	12.95	13.45	13.95	14.45	14.95
10.48	10.98	11.48	11.98	12.48	95	12.98	13.48	13.98	14.48	14.98

POUNDS

3000	3100	3200	3300	3400		3500	3600	3700	3800	3900
		AMOUNT						AMOUNT		
15.00	15.50	16.00	16.50	17.00		17.50	18.00	18.50	19.00	19.50
15.03	15.53	16.03	16.53	17.03	5	17.53	18.03	18.53	19.03	19.53
15.05	15.55	16.05	16.55	17.05	10	17.55	18.05	18.55	19.05	19.55
15.08	15.58	16.08	16.58	17.08	15	17.58	18.08	18.58	19.08	19.58
15.10	15.60	16.10	16.60	17.10	20	17.60	18.10	18.60	19.10	19.60
15.13	15.63	16.13	16.63	17.13	25	17.63	18.13	18.63	19.13	19.63
15.15	15.65	16.15	16.65	17.15	30	17.65	18.15	18.65	19.15	19.65
15.18	15.68	16.18	16.68	17.18	35	17.68	18.18	18.68	19.18	19.68
15.20	15.70	16.20	16.70	17.20	40	17.70	18.20	18.70	19.20	19.70
15.23	15.73	16.23	16.73	17.23	45	17.73	18.23	18.73	19.23	19.73
15.25	15.75	16.25	16.75	17.25	50	17.75	18.25	18.75	19.25	19.75
15.28	15.78	16.28	16.78	17.28	55	17.78	18.28	18.78	19.28	19.78
15.30	15.80	16.30	16.80	17.30	60	17.80	18.30	18.80	19.30	19.80
15.33	15.83	16.33	16.83	17.33	65	17.83	18.33	18.83	19.33	19.83
15.35	15.85	16.35	16.85	17.35	70	17.85	18.35	18.85	19.35	19.85
15.38	15.88	16.38	16.88	17.38	75	17.88	18.38	18.88	19.38	19.88
15.40	15.90	16.40	16.90	17.40	80	17.90	18.40	18.90	19.40	19.90
15.43	15.93	16.43	16.93	17.43	85	17.93	18.43	18.93	19.43	19.93
15.45	15.95	16.45	16.95	17.45	90	17.95	18.45	18.95	19.45	19.95
15.48	15.98	16.48	16.98	17.48	95	17.98	18.48	18.98	19.48	19.98

Even tons, 51 to 100 inclusive.

51-60		61-70		71-80		81-90		91-100	
T	Am't	T	Am't	T	Am't	T	Am't	T	Am't
51	510.00	61	610.00	71	710.00	81	810.00	91	910.00
52	520.00	62	620.00	72	720.00	82	820.00	92	920.00
53	530.00	63	630.00	73	730.00	83	830.00	93	930.00
54	540.00	64	640.00	74	740.00	84	840.00	94	940.00
55	550.00	65	650.00	75	750.00	85	850.00	95	950.00
56	560.00	66	660.00	76	760.00	86	860.00	96	960.00
57	570.00	67	670.00	77	770.00	87	870.00	97	970.00
58	580.00	68	680.00	78	780.00	88	880.00	98	980.00
59	590.00	69	690.00	79	790.00	89	890.00	99	990.00
60	600.00	70	700.00	80	800.00	90	900.00	100	1000.00

700	7000	800	8000	900	9000	1000	10000	1100	11000

— POUNDS —

Under 100	100	200	300	400		500	600	700	800	900
	AMOUNT							AMOUNT		
	.51	1.03	1.54	2.05		2.56	3.08	3.59	4.10	4.61
.03	.54	1.05	1.56	2.08	5	2.59	3.10	3.61	4.13	4.64
.05	.56	1.08	1.59	2.10	10	2.61	3.13	3.64	4.15	4.66
.08	.59	1.10	1.61	2.13	15	2.64	3.15	3.66	4.18	4.69
.10	.62	1.13	1.64	2.15	20	2.67	3.18	3.69	4.20	4.72
.13	.64	1.15	1.67	2.18	25	2.69	3.20	3.72	4.23	4.74
.15	.67	1.18	1.69	2.20	30	2.72	3.23	3.74	4.25	4.77
.18	.69	1.20	1.72	2.23	35	2.74	3.25	3 77	4.28	4.79
.21	.72	1.23	1.74	2.26	40	2.77	3.28	3.79	4.31	4.82
.23	.74	1.26	1.77	2.28	45	2.79	3.31	3.82	4.33	4.84
.26	.77	1.28	1.79	2.31	50	2.82	3.33	3.84	4.36	4.87
.28	.79	1.31	1.82	2.33	55	2.84	3.36	3.87	4.38	4.89
.31	.82	1.33	1.85	2.36	60	2.87	3.38	3.90	4.41	4.92
.33	.84	1.36	1.87	2.38	65	2.90	3.41	3.92	4.43	4.94
.36	.87	1.38	1.90	2.41	70	2.92	3.43	3.95	4.46	4.97
.38	.90	1.41	1.92	2.43	75	2.95	3.46	3.97	4.48	5.00
.41	.92	1.44	1.95	2.46	80	2.97	3.49	4.00	4.51	5.02
.43	.95	1.46	1.97	2.49	85	3.00	3.51	4.02	4.53	5.05
.46	.97	1.49	2.00	2.51	90	3.02	3.54	4.05	4.56	5.07
.48	1.00	1.51	2.02	2.54	95	3 05	3.56	4.07	4.58	5.10

— POUNDS —

1000	1100	1200	1300	1400		1500	1600	1700	1800	1900
	AMOUNT							AMOUNT		
5.13	5.64	6.15	6.66	7.18		7.69	8.20	8.71	9.23	9.74
5.15	5.66	6.18	6.69	7.20	5	7 71	8.23	8.74	9.25	9.76
5.18	5.69	6.20	6.71	7.23	10	7.74	8.25	8.76	9.28	9.79
5.20	5.71	6.23	6.74	7.25	15	7.76	8.28	8.79	9.30	9.81
5.23	5.74	6.25	6.77	7.28	20	7.79	8.30	8.82	9.33	9.84
5.25	5.77	6.28	6.79	7.30	25	7.82	8.33	8.84	9.35	9.87
5.28	5.79	6.30	6.82	7.33	30	7.84	8.35	8.87	9.38	9.89
5.30	5.82	6.33	6.84	7.35	35	7.87	8.38	8.89	9.40	9.92
5.33	5.84	6.36	6.87	7.38	40	7.89	8.41	8.92	9.43	9.94
5.36	5.87	6.38	6.89	7.41	45	7.92	8.43	8.94	9.46	9.97
5.38	5.89	6.41	6.92	7.43	50	7.94	8.46	8.97	9.48	9.99
5.41	5.92	6.43	6.94	7.46	55	7.97	8.48	8.99	9.51	10.02
5.43	5.95	6.46	6.97	7.48	60	8.00	8.51	9.02	9.53	10.05
5.46	5.97	6.48	7.00	7.51	65	8.02	8.53	9.04	9.56	10.07
5.48	6.00	6.51	7.02	7.53	70	8.05	8.56	9.07	9.58	10.10
5.51	6.02	6.53	7.05	7.56	75	8.07	8.58	9.10	9.61	10.12
5.54	6.05	6.56	7.07	7.59	80	8.10	8.61	9.12	9.64	10.15
5.56	6.07	6.59	7.10	7.61	85	8.12	8.63	9.15	9.66	10.17
5.59	6.10	6.61	7.12	7.64	90	8.15	8.66	9.17	9.69	10.20
5.61	6.12	6.64	7.15	7.66	95	8.17	8.68	9.20	9.71	10.22

Even tons, 1 to 50 inclusive.

1-10		11-20		21-30		31-40		41-50	
T	Am't	T	Am't	T	Am't	T	Am't	T	Am't
1	10.25	11	112.75	21	215.25	31	317.75	41	420.25
2	20.50	12	123.00	22	225.50	32	328.00	42	430.50
3	30.75	13	133.25	23	235.75	33	338.25	43	440.75
4	41.00	14	143.50	24	246.00	34	348.50	44	451.00
5	51.25	15	153.75	25	256.25	35	358.75	45	461.25
6	61.50	16	164.00	26	266.50	36	369.00	46	471.50
7	71.75	17	174.25	27	276.75	37	379.25	47	481.75
8	82.00	18	184.50	28	287.00	38	389.50	48	492.00
9	92.25	19	194.75	29	297.25	39	399.75	49	502.25
10	102.50	20	205.00	30	307.50	40	410.00	50	512.50

200	2050	300	3075	400	4100	500	5125	600	6150

--------POUNDS--------

2000	2100	2200	2300	2400		2500	2600	2700	2800	2900
		—AMOUNT—					—AMOUNT—			
10.25	10.76	11.28	11.79	12.30		12.81	13.33	13.84	14.35	14.86
10.28	10.79	11.30	11.81	12.33	5	12.84	13.35	13.86	14.38	14.89
10.30	10.81	11.33	11.84	12.35	10	12.86	13.38	13.89	14.40	14.91
10.33	10.84	11.35	11.86	12.38	15	12.89	13.40	13.91	14.43	14.94
10.35	10.87	11.38	11.89	12.40	20	12.92	13.43	13.94	14.45	14.97
10.38	10.89	11.40	11.92	12.43	25	12.94	13.45	13.97	14.48	14.99
10.40	10.92	11.43	11.94	12.45	30	12.97	13.48	13.99	14.50	15.02
10.43	10.94	11.45	11.97	12.48	35	12.99	13.50	14.02	14.53	15.04
10.46	10.97	11.48	11.99	12.51	40	13.02	13.53	14.04	14.56	15.07
10 48	10.99	11.51	12.02	12.53	45	13.04	13.56	14.07	14.58	15.09
10.51	11.02	11.53	12.04	12.56	50	13.07	13.58	14.09	14.61	15.12
10.53	11.04	11.56	12.07	12.58	55	13.09	13.61	14.12	14.63	15.14
10.56	11.07	11.58	12.10	12.61	60	13.12	13.63	14.15	14.66	15.17
10.58	11.09	11.61	12.12	12.63	65	13.15	13.66	14.17	14.68	15.19
10.61	11.12	11.63	12.15	12.66	70	13.17	13.68	14.20	14.71	15.22
10.63	11.15	11.66	12.17	12.68	75	13.20	13.71	14.22	14.73	15.25
10.66	11.17	11.69	12.20	12.71	80	13.22	13.74	14.25	14.76	15.27
10.68	11.20	11.71	12.22	12.74	85	13.25	13.76	14.27	14.78	15.30
10.71	11.22	11.74	12.25	12.76	90	13.27	13.79	14.30	14.81	15.32
10.73	11.25	11.76	12.27	15.79	95	13.30	13.81	14.32	14.83	15.35

--------POUNDS--------

3000	3100	3200	3300	3400		3500	3600	3700	3800	3900
		—AMOUNT—					—AMOUNT—			
15.38	15.89	16.40	16.91	17.43		17.94	18.45	18.96	19.48	19.99
15.40	15.91	16.43	16.94	17.45	5	17.96	18.48	18.99	19.50	20.01
15.43	15.94	16.45	16.96	17.48	10	17.99	18.50	19.01	19.53	20.04
15.45	15.96	16.48	16.99	17.50	15	18.01	18.53	19.04	19.55	20.06
15.48	15.99	16.50	17.02	17.53	20	18.04	18.55	19.07	19.58	20.09
15.50	16.02	16.53	17.04	17.55	25	18.07	18.58	19.09	19.60	20.12
15.53	16.04	16.55	17.07	17.58	30	18.09	18.60	19.12	19.63	20.14
15.55	16.07	16.58	17.09	17.60	35	18.12	18.63	19.14	19.65	20.17
15.58	16.09	16.61	17.12	17.63	40	18.14	18.66	19.17	19.68	20.19
15.61	16.12	16.63	17.14	17.66	45	18.17	18.68	19.19	19.71	20.22
15.63	16.14	16.66	17.17	17.68	50	18.19	18.71	19.22	19.73	20.24
15.66	16.17	16.68	17.19	17.71	55	18.22	18.73	19.24	19.76	20.27
15.68	16.20	16.71	17.22	17.73	60	18.25	18.76	19.27	19.78	20.30
15.71	16.22	16.73	17.25	17.76	65	18.27	18.78	19.29	19.81	20.32
15.73	16.25	16.76	17.27	17.78	70	18.30	18.81	19.32	19.83	20.35
15.76	16.27	16.78	17.30	17.81	75	18.32	18.83	19.35	19.86	20.37
15.79	16.30	16.81	17.32	17.84	80	18.35	18.86	19.37	19.89	20.40
15.81	16.32	16.84	17.35	17.86	85	18.37	18.88	19.40	19.91	20.42
15.84	16.35	16.86	17.37	17.89	90	18.40	18.91	19.42	19.94	20.45
15.86	16.37	16.89	17.40	17.91	95	18.42	18.93	19.45	19.96	20.47

Even tons, 51 to 100 inclusive.

51-60		61-70		71-80		81-90		91-100	
T	Am't	T	Am't	T	Am't	T	Am't	T	Am't
51	522.75	61	625.25	71	727.75	81	830.25	91	932.75
52	533.00	62	635.50	72	738.00	82	840.50	92	943.00
53	543.25	63	645.75	73	748.25	83	850.75	93	953.25
54	553.50	64	656.00	74	758.50	84	861.00	94	963.50
55	563.75	65	666.25	75	768.75	85	871.25	95	973.75
56	574.00	66	676.50	76	779.00	86	881.50	96	984.00
57	584.25	67	686.75	77	789.25	87	891.75	97	994.25
58	594.50	68	697.00	78	799.50	88	902.00	98	1004.50
59	604.75	69	707.25	79	809.75	89	912.25	99	1014.75
60	615.00	70	717.50	80	820.00	90	922.50	100	1025.00
700	7175	800	8200	900	9225	1000	10250	1100	11275

POUNDS

Under 100	100	200	300	400		500	600	700	800	900
	.53	1.05	1.58	2.10		2.63	3.15	3.68	4.20	4.73
.03	.55	1.08	1.60	2.13	5	2.65	3.18	3.70	4.23	4.75
.05	.58	1.10	1.63	2.15	10	2.68	3.20	3.73	4.25	4.78
.08	.60	1.13	1.65	2.18	15	2.70	3.23	3.75	4.28	4.80
.11	.63	1.16	1.68	2.21	20	2.73	3.26	3.78	4.31	4.83
.13	.66	1.18	1.71	2.23	25	2.76	3.28	3.81	4.33	4.86
.16	.68	1.21	1.73	2.26	30	2.78	3.31	3.83	4.36	4.88
.18	.71	1.23	1.76	2.28	35	2.81	3.33	3.86	4.38	4.91
.21	.74	1.26	1.79	2.31	40	2.84	3.36	3.89	4.41	4.94
.24	.76	1.29	1.81	2.34	45	2.86	3.39	3.91	4.44	4.96
.26	.79	1.31	1.84	2.36	50	2.89	3.41	3.94	4.46	4.99
.29	.81	1.34	1.86	2.39	55	2.91	3.44	3.96	4.49	5.01
.32	.84	1.37	1.89	2.42	60	2.94	3.47	3.99	4.52	5.04
.34	.87	1.39	1.92	2.44	65	2.97	3.49	4.02	4.54	5.07
.37	.89	1.42	1.94	2.47	70	2.99	3.52	4.04	4.57	5.09
.39	.92	1.44	1.97	2.49	75	3.02	3.54	4.07	4.59	5.12
.42	.95	1.47	2.00	2.52	80	3.05	3.57	4.10	4.62	5.15
.45	.97	1.50	2.02	2.55	85	3.07	3.60	4.12	4.65	5.17
.47	1.00	1.52	2.05	2.57	90	3.10	3.62	4.15	4.67	5.20
.50	1.02	1.55	2.07	2.60	95	3.12	3.65	4.17	4.70	5.22

POUNDS

1000	1100	1200	1300	1400		1500	1600	1700	1800	1900
5.25	5.78	6.30	6.83	7.35		7.88	8.40	8.93	9.45	9.98
5.28	5 80	6.33	6.85	7.38	5	7.90	8.43	8.95	9.48	10.00
5.30	5.83	6.35	6.88	7.40	10	7.93	8.45	8.98	9.50	10.03
5.33	5.85	6.38	6.90	7.43	15	7.95	8.48	9.00	9.53	10.05
5.36	5.88	6.41	6.93	7.46	20	7.98	8.51	9.03	9.56	10.08
5.38	5.91	6.43	6.96	7.48	25	8.01	8.53	9.06	9.58	10.11
5.41	5.93	6.46	6.98	7.51	30	8.03	8.56	9.08	9.61	10.13
5.43	5.96	6.48	7.01	7.53	35	8.06	8.58	9.11	9.63	10.16
5.46	5.99	6.51	7.04	7.56	40	8.09	8.61	9.14	9.66	10.19
5.49	6.01	6.54	7.06	7.59	45	8.11	8.64	9.16	9.69	10.21
5.51	6.04	6.56	7.09	7.61	50	8.14	8.66	9.19	9.71	10.24
5.54	6.06	6.59	7.11	7.64	55	8.16	8.69	9.21	9.74	10.26
5.57	6.09	6.62	7.14	7.67	60	8.19	8.72	9.24	9.77	10.29
5.59	6.12	6.64	7.17	7.69	65	8.22	8.74	9.27	9.79	10.32
5.62	6.14	6.67	7.19	7.72	70	8.24	8.77	9.29	9.82	10.34
5.64	6.17	6.69	7.22	7.74	75	8.27	8.79	9.32	9.84	10.37
5.67	6.20	6.72	7.25	7.77	80	8.30	8.82	9.35	9.87	10.40
5.70	6.22	6.75	7.27	7.80	85	8.32	8.85	9.37	9.90	10.42
5.72	6.25	6.77	7.30	7.82	90	8.35	8.87	9.40	9.92	10.45
5.75	6.27	6.80	7.32	7.85	95	8.37	8.90	9.42	9.95	10.47

Even tons, 1 to 50 inclusive.

T	Am't	T	Am't	T	Am't	T	Am't	T	Am't
1	10.50	11	115.50	21	220.50	31	325.50	41	430.50
2	21.00	12	126.00	22	231.00	32	336.00	42	441.00
3	31.50	13	136.50	23	241.50	33	346.50	43	451.50
4	42.00	14	147.00	24	252.00	34	357.00	44	462.00
5	52.50	15	157.50	25	262.50	35	367.50	45	472.50
6	63.00	16	168.00	26	273.00	36	378.00	46	483.00
7	73.50	17	178.50	27	283.50	37	388.50	47	493.50
8	84.00	18	189.00	28	294.00	38	399.00	48	504.00
9	94.50	19	199.50	29	304.50	39	409.50	49	514.50
10	105.00	20	210.00	30	315.00	40	420.00	50	525.00

200	2100	300	3150	400	4200	500	5250	600	6300

------POUNDS------

2000	2100	2200	2300	2400		2500	2600	2700	2800	2900
		—AMOUNT—					—AMOUNT—			
10.50	11.03	11.55	12.08	12.60		13.13	13.65	14.18	14.70	15.23
10.53	11.05	11.58	12.10	12.63	5	13.15	13.68	14.20	14.73	15.25
10.55	11.08	11.60	12.13	12.65	10	13.18	13.70	14.23	14.75	15.28
10.58	11.10	11.63	12.15	12.68	15	13.20	13.73	14.25	14.78	15.30
10.61	11.13	11.66	12.18	12.71	20	13.23	13.76	14.28	14.81	15.33
10.63	11.16	11.68	12.21	12.73	25	13.26	13.78	14.31	14.83	15.36
10.66	11.18	11.71	12.23	12.76	30	13.28	13.81	14.33	14.86	15.38
10.68	11.21	11.73	12.26	12.78	35	13.31	13.83	14.36	14.88	15.41
10.71	11.24	11.76	12.29	12.81	40	13.34	13.86	14.39	14.91	15.44
10.74	11.26	11.79	12.31	12.84	45	13.36	13.89	14.41	14.94	15.46
10.76	11.29	11.81	12.34	12.86	50	13.39	13.91	14.44	14.96	15.49
10.79	11.31	11.84	12.36	12.89	55	13.41	13.94	14.46	14.99	15.51
10.82	11.34	11.87	12.39	12.92	60	13.44	13.97	14.49	15.02	15.54
10.84	11.37	11.89	12.42	12.94	65	13.47	13.99	14.52	15.04	15.57
10.87	11.39	11.92	12.44	12.97	70	13.49	14.02	14.54	15.07	15.59
10.89	11.42	11.94	12.47	12.99	75	13.52	14.04	14.57	15.09	15.62
10.92	11.45	11.97	12.50	13.02	80	13.55	14.07	14.60	15.12	15.65
10.95	11.47	12.00	12.52	13.05	85	13.57	14.10	14.62	15.15	15.67
10.97	11.50	12.02	12.55	13.07	90	13.60	14.12	14.65	15.17	15.70
11.00	11.52	12.05	12.57	13.10	95	13.62	14.15	14.67	15.20	15.72

------POUNDS------

3000	3100	3200	3300	3400		3500	3600	3700	3800	3900
		—AMOUNT—					—AMOUNT—			
15.75	16.28	16.80	17.33	17.85		18.38	18.90	19.43	19.95	20.48
15.78	16.30	16.83	17.35	17.88	5	18.40	18.93	19.45	19.98	20.50
15.80	16.33	16.85	17.38	17.90	10	18.43	18.95	19.48	20.00	20.53
15.83	16.35	16.88	17.40	17.93	15	18.45	18.98	19.50	20.03	20.55
15.86	16.38	16.91	17.43	17.96	20	18.48	19.01	19.53	20.06	20.58
15.88	16.41	16.93	17.46	17.98	25	18.51	19.03	19.56	20.08	20,61
15.91	16.43	16.96	17.48	18.01	30	18.53	19.06	19.58	20.11	20.63
15.93	16.46	16.98	17.51	18.03	35	18.56	19.08	19.61	20.13	20.66
15.96	16.49	17.01	17.54	18.06	40	18.59	19.11	19.64	20.16	20.69
15.99	16.51	17.04	17.56	18.09	45	18.61	19.14	19.66	20.19	20.71
16.01	16.54	17.06	17.59	18.11	50	18.64	19.16	19.69	20.21	20.74
16.04	16.56	17.09	17.61	18.14	55	18.66	19.19	19.71	20.24	20.76
16.07	16.59	17.12	17.64	18.17	60	18.69	19.22	19.74	20.27	20.79
16.09	16.62	17.14	17.67	18.19	65	18.72	19.24	19.77	20.29	20.82
16.12	16.64	17.17	17.69	18.22	70	18.74	19.27	19.79	20.32	20.84
16.14	16.67	17.19	17.72	18.24	75	18.77	19.29	19.82	20.34	20.87
16.17	16.70	17.22	17.75	18.27	80	18.80	19.32	19.85	20.37	20.90
16.20	16.72	17.25	17.77	18.30	85	18.82	19.35	19.87	20.40	20.92
16.22	16.75	17.27	17.80	18.32	90	18.85	19.37	19.90	20.42	20.95
16.25	16.77	17.30	17.82	18.35	95	18.87	19.40	19.92	20.45	20.97

Even tons, 51 to 100 inclusive.

51-60		61-70		71-80		81-90		91-100	
T	Am't	T	Am't	T	Am't	T	Am't	T	Am't
51	535.50	61	640.50	71	745.50	81	850.50	91	955.50
52	546.00	62	651.00	72	756.00	82	861.00	92	966.00
53	556.50	63	661.50	73	766.50	83	871.50	93	976.50
54	567.00	64	672.00	74	777.00	84	882.00	94	987.00
55	577.50	65	682.50	75	787.50	85	892.50	95	997.50
56	588.00	66	693.00	76	798.00	86	903.00	96	1008.00
57	598.50	67	703.50	77	808.50	87	913.50	97	1018.50
58	609.00	68	714.00	78	819.00	88	924.00	98	1029.00
59	619.50	69	724.50	79	829.50	89	934.50	99	1039.50
60	630.00	70	735.00	80	840.00	90	945.00	100	1050.00

700	7350	800	8400	900	9450	1000	10500	1100	11550

POUNDS

Under 100	100	200	300	400		500	600	700	800	900
		AMOUNT						AMOUNT		
	.54	1.08	1.61	2.15		2.69	3.23	3.76	4.30	4.84
.03	.56	1.10	1.64	2.18	5	2.71	3.25	3.79	4.33	4.86
.05	.59	1.13	1.67	2.20	10	2.74	3.28	3.82	4.35	4.89
.08	.62	1.16	1.69	2.23	15	2.77	3.31	3.84	4.38	4.92
.11	.65	1.18	1.72	2.26	20	2.80	3.33	3.87	4.41	4.95
.13	.67	1.21	1.75	2.28	25	2.82	3.36	3.90	4.43	4.97
.16	.70	1.24	1.77	2.31	30	2.85	3.39	3.92	4.46	5.00
.19	.73	1.26	1.80	2.34	35	2.88	3.41	3.95	4.49	5.03
.22	.75	1.29	1.83	2.37	40	2.90	3.44	3.98	4.52	5.05
.24	.78	1.32	1.85	2.39	45	2.93	3.47	4.00	4.54	5.08
.27	.81	1.34	1.88	2.42	50	2.96	3.49	4.03	4.57	5.11
.30	.83	1.37	1.91	2.45	55	2.98	3.52	4.06	4.60	5.13
.32	.86	1.40	1.94	2.47	60	3.01	3.55	4.09	4.62	5.16
.35	.89	1.42	1.96	2.50	65	3.04	3.57	4.11	4.65	5.19
.38	.91	1.45	1.99	2.53	70	3.06	3.60	4.14	4.68	5.21
.40	.94	1.48	2.02	2.55	75	3.09	3.63	4.17	4.70	5.24
.43	.97	1.51	2.04	2.58	80	3.12	3.66	4.19	4.73	5.27
.46	.99	1.53	2.07	2.61	85	3.14	3.68	4.22	4.76	5.29
.48	1.02	1.56	2.10	2.63	90	3.17	3.71	4.25	4.78	5.32
.51	1.05	1.59	2.12	2.66	95	3.20	3.74	4.27	4.81	5.35

POUNDS

1000	1100	1200	1300	1400		1500	1600	1700	1800	1900
		AMOUNT						AMOUNT		
5.38	5.91	6.45	6.99	7.53		8.06	8.60	9.14	9.68	10.21
5.40	5.94	6.48	7.01	7.55	5	8.09	8.63	9.16	9.70	10.24
5.43	5.97	6.50	7.04	7.58	10	8.12	8.65	9.19	9.73	10.27
5.46	5.99	6.53	7.07	7.61	15	8.14	8.68	9.22	9.76	10.29
5.48	6.02	6.56	7.10	7.63	20	8.17	8.71	9.25	9.78	10.32
5.51	6.05	6.58	7.12	7.66	25	8.20	8.73	9.27	9.81	10.35
5.54	6.07	6.61	7.15	7.69	30	8.22	8.76	9.30	9.84	10.37
5.56	6.10	6.64	7.18	7.71	35	8.25	8.79	9.33	9.86	10.40
5.59	6.13	6.67	7.20	7.74	40	8.28	8.82	9.35	9.89	10.43
5.62	6.15	6.69	7.23	7.77	45	8.30	8.84	9.38	9.92	10.45
5.64	6.18	6.72	7.26	7.79	50	8.33	8.87	9.41	9.94	10.48
5.67	6.21	6.75	7.28	7.82	55	8.36	8.90	9.43	9.97	10.51
5.70	6.24	6.77	7.31	7.85	60	8.39	8.92	9.46	10.00	10.54
5.72	6.26	6.80	7.34	7.87	65	8.41	8.95	9.49	10.02	10.56
5.75	6.29	6.83	7.36	7.90	70	8.44	8.98	9.51	10.05	10.59
5.78	6.32	6.85	7.39	7.93	75	8.47	9.00	9.54	10.08	10.62
5.81	6.34	6.88	7.42	7.96	80	8.49	9.03	9.57	10.11	10.64
5.83	6.37	6.91	7.44	7.98	85	8.52	9.06	9.59	10.13	10.67
5.86	6.40	6.93	7.47	8.01	90	8.55	9.08	9.62	10.16	10.70
5.89	6.42	6.96	7.50	8.04	95	8.57	9.11	9.65	10.19	10.72

Even tons, 1 to 50 inclusive.

1-10		11-20		21-30		31-40		41-50	
T	Am't	T	Am't	T	Am't	T	Am't	T	Am't
1	10.75	11	118.25	21	225.75	31	333.25	41	440.75
2	21.50	12	129.00	22	236.50	32	344.00	42	451.50
3	32.25	13	139.75	23	247.25	33	354.75	43	462.25
4	43.00	14	150.50	24	258.00	34	365.50	44	473.00
5	53.75	15	161.25	25	268.75	35	376.25	45	483.75
6	64.50	16	172.00	26	279.50	36	387.00	46	494.50
7	75.25	17	182.75	27	290.25	37	397.75	47	505.25
8	86.00	18	193.50	28	301.00	38	408.50	48	516.00
9	96.75	19	204.25	29	311.75	39	419.25	49	526.75
10	107.50	20	215.00	30	322.50	40	430.00	50	537.50

200	2150	300	3225	400	4300	500	5375	600	6450

2000	2100	2200	2300	2400		2500	2600	2700	2800	2900
		AMOUNT						AMOUNT		
10.75	11.29	11.83	12.36	12.90		13.44	13.98	14.51	15.05	15.59
10.78	11.31	11.85	12.39	12.93	5	13.46	14.00	14.54	15.08	15.61
10.80	11.34	11.88	12.42	12.95	10	13.49	14.03	14.57	15.10	15.64
10.83	11.37	11.91	12.44	12.98	15	13.52	14.06	14.59	15.13	15.67
10.86	11.40	11.93	12.47	13.01	20	13.55	14.08	14.62	15.16	15.70
10.88	11.42	11.96	12.50	13.03	25	13.57	14.11	14.65	15.18	15.72
10.91	11.45	11.99	12.52	13.06	30	13.60	14.14	14.67	15.21	15.75
10.94	11.48	12.01	12.55	13.09	35	13.63	14.16	14.70	15.24	15.78
10.97	11.50	12.04	12.58	13.12	40	13.65	14.19	14.73	15.27	15.80
10.99	11.53	12.07	12.60	13.14	45	13.68	14.22	14.75	15.29	15.83
11.02	11.56	12.09	12.63	13.17	50	13.71	14.24	14.78	15.32	15.86
11.05	11.58	12.12	12.66	13.20	55	13.73	14.27	14.81	15.35	15.88
11.07	11.61	12.15	12.69	13.22	60	13.76	14.30	14.84	15.37	15.91
11.10	11.64	12.17	12.71	13.25	65	13.79	14.32	14.86	15.40	15.94
11.13	11.66	12.20	12.74	13.28	70	13.81	14.35	14.89	15.43	15.96
11.15	11.69	12.23	12.77	13.30	75	13.84	14.38	14.92	15.45	15.99
11.18	11.72	12.26	12.79	13.33	80	13.87	14.41	14.94	15.48	16.02
11.21	11.74	12.28	12.82	13.36	85	13.89	14.43	14.97	15.51	16.04
11.23	11.77	12.31	12.85	13.38	90	13.92	14.46	15.00	15.53	16.07
11.26	11.80	12.34	12.87	13.41	95	13.95	14.49	15.02	15.56	16.10

3000	3100	3200	3300	3400	POUNDS	3500	3600	3700	3800	3900
		AMOUNT						AMOUNT		
16.13	16.66	17.20	17.74	18.28		18.81	19.35	19.89	20.43	20.96
16.15	16.69	17.23	17.76	18.30	5	18.84	19.38	19.91	20.45	20.99
16.18	16.72	17.25	17.79	18.33	10	18.87	19.40	19.94	20.48	21.02
16.21	16.74	17.28	17.82	18.36	15	18.89	19.43	19.97	20.51	21.04
16.23	16.77	17.31	17.85	18.38	20	18.92	19.46	20.00	20.53	21.07
16.26	16.80	17.33	17.87	18.41	25	18.95	19.48	20.02	20.56	21.10
16.29	16.82	17.36	17.90	18.44	30	18.97	19.51	20.05	20.59	21.12
16.31	16.85	17.39	17.93	18.46	35	19.00	19.54	20.08	20.61	21.15
16.34	16.88	17.42	17.95	18.49	40	19.03	19.57	20.10	20.64	21.18
16.37	16.90	17.44	17.98	18.52	45	19.05	19.59	20.13	20.67	21.20
16.39	16.93	17.47	18.01	18.54	50	19.08	19.62	20.16	20.69	21.23
16.42	16.96	17.50	18.03	18.57	55	19.11	19.65	20.18	20.72	21.26
16.45	16.99	17.52	18.06	18.60	60	19.14	19.67	20.21	20.75	21.29
16.47	17.01	17.55	18.09	18.62	65	19.16	19.70	20.24	20.77	21.31
16.50	17.04	17.58	18.11	18.65	70	19.19	19.73	20.26	20.80	21.34
16.53	17.07	17.60	18.14	18.68	75	19.22	19.75	20.29	20.83	21.37
16.56	17.09	17.63	18.17	18.71	80	19.24	19.78	20.32	20.86	21.39
16.58	17.12	17.66	18.19	18.73	85	19.27	19.81	20.34	20.88	21.42
16.61	17.15	17.68	18.22	18.76	90	19.30	19.83	20.37	20.91	21.45
16.64	17.17	17.71	18.25	18.79	95	19.32	19.86	20.40	20.94	21.47

Even tons, 51 to 100 inclusive.

51-60		61-70		71-80		81-90		91-100	
T	Am't	T	Am't	T	Am't	T	Am't	T	Am't
51	548.25	61	655.75	71	763.25	81	870.75	91	978.25
52	559.00	62	666.50	72	774.00	82	881.50	92	989.00
53	569.75	63	677.25	73	784.75	83	892.25	93	999.75
54	580.50	64	688.00	74	795.50	84	903.00	94	1010.50
55	591.25	65	698.75	75	806.25	85	913.75	95	1021.25
56	602.00	66	709.50	76	817.00	86	924.50	96	1032.00
57	612.75	67	720.25	77	827.75	87	935.25	97	1042.75
58	623.50	68	731.00	78	838.50	88	946.00	98	1053.50
59	634.25	69	741.75	79	849.25	89	956.75	99	1064.25
60	645.00	70	752.50	80	860.00	90	967.50	100	1075.00

700	7525	800	8600	900	9675	1000	10750	1100	11825

—————— POUNDS ——————

Under 100	100	200	300	400		500	600	700	800	900
		AMOUNT						AMOUNT		
	.55	1.10	1.65	2.20		2.75	3.30	3.85	4.40	4.95
.03	.58	1.13	1.68	2.23	5	2.78	3.33	3.88	4.43	4.98
.06	.61	1.16	1.71	2.26	10	2.81	3.36	3.91	4.46	5.01
.08	.63	1.18	1.73	2.28	15	2.83	3.38	3.93	4.48	5.03
.11	.66	1.21	1.76	2.31	20	2.86	3.41	3.96	4.51	5.06
.14	.69	1.24	1.79	2.34	25	2.89	3.44	3.99	4.54	5.09
.17	.72	1.27	1.82	2.37	30	2.92	3.47	4.02	4.57	5.12
.19	.74	1.29	1.84	2.39	35	2.94	3.49	4.04	4.59	5.14
.22	.77	1.32	1.87	2.42	40	2.97	3.52	4.07	4.62	5.17
.25	.80	1.35	1.90	2.45	45	3.00	3.55	4.10	4.65	5.20
.28	.83	1.38	1.93	2.48	50	3.03	3.58	4.13	4.68	5.23
.30	.85	1.40	1.95	2.50	55	3.05	3.60	4.15	4.70	5.25
.33	.88	1.43	1.98	2.53	60	3.08	3.63	4.18	4.73	5.28
.36	.91	1.46	2.01	2.56	65	3.11	3.66	4.21	4.76	5.31
.39	.94	1.49	2.04	2.59	70	3.14	3.69	4.24	4.79	5.34
.41	.96	1.51	2.06	2.61	75	3.16	3.71	4.26	4.81	5.36
.44	.99	1.54	2.09	2.64	80	3.19	3.74	4.29	4.84	5.39
.47	1.02	1.57	2.12	2.67	85	3.22	3.77	4.32	4.87	5.42
.50	1.05	1.60	2.15	2.70	90	3.25	3.80	4.35	4.90	5.45
.52	1.07	1.62	2.17	2.72	95	3.27	3.82	4.37	4.92	5.47

—————— POUNDS ——————

1000	1100	1200	1300	1400		1500	1600	1700	1800	1900
		AMOUNT						AMOUNT		
5.50	6.05	6.60	7.15	7.70		8.25	8.80	9.35	9.90	10.45
5.53	6.08	6.63	7.18	7.73	5	8.28	8.83	9.38	9.93	10.48
5.56	6.11	6.66	7.21	7.76	10	8.31	8.86	9.41	9.96	10.51
5.58	6.13	6.68	7.23	7.78	15	8.33	8.88	9.43	9.98	10.53
5.61	6.16	6.71	7.26	7.81	20	8.36	8.91	9.46	10.01	10.56
5.64	6.19	6.74	7.29	7.84	25	8.39	8.94	9.49	10.04	10.59
5.67	6.22	6.77	7.32	7.87	30	8.42	8.97	9.52	10.07	10.62
5.69	6.24	6.79	7.34	7.89	35	8.44	8.99	9.54	10.09	10.64
5.72	6.27	6.82	7.37	7.92	40	8.47	9.02	9.57	10.12	10.67
5.75	6.30	6.85	7.40	7.95	45	8.50	9.05	9.60	10.15	10.70
5.78	6.33	6.88	7.43	7.98	50	8.53	9.08	9.63	10.18	10.73
5.80	6.35	6.90	7.45	8.00	55	8.55	9.10	9.65	10.20	10.75
5.83	6.38	6.93	7.48	8.03	60	8.58	9.13	9.68	10.23	10.78
5.86	6.41	6.96	7.51	8.06	65	8.61	9.16	9.71	10.26	10.81
5.89	6.44	6.99	7.54	8.09	70	8.64	9.19	9.74	10.29	10.84
5.91	6.46	7.01	7.56	8.11	75	8.66	9.21	9.76	10.31	10.86
5.94	6.49	7.04	7.59	8.14	80	8.69	9.24	9.79	10.34	10.89
5.97	6.52	7.07	7.62	8.17	85	8.72	9.27	9.82	10.37	10.92
6.00	6.55	7.10	7.65	8.20	90	8.75	9.30	9.85	10.40	10.95
6.02	6.57	7.12	7.67	8.22	95	8.77	9.32	9.87	10.42	10.97

Even tons, 1 to 50 inclusive.

1-10		11-20		21-30		31-40		41-50	
T	Am't	T	Am't	T	Am't	T	Am't	T	Am't
1	11.00	11	121.00	21	231.00	31	341.00	41	451.00
2	22.00	12	132.00	22	242.00	32	352.00	42	462.00
3	33.00	13	143.00	23	253.00	33	363.00	43	473.00
4	44.00	14	154.00	24	264.00	34	374.00	44	484.00
5	55.00	15	165.00	25	275.00	35	385.00	45	495.00
6	66.00	16	176.00	26	286.00	36	396.00	46	506.00
7	77.00	17	187.00	27	297.00	37	407.00	47	517.00
8	88.00	18	198.00	28	308.00	38	418.00	48	528.00
9	99.00	19	209.00	29	319.00	39	429.00	49	539.00
10	110.00	20	220.00	30	330.00	40	440.00	50	550.00

200	2200	300	3300	400	4400	500	5500	600	6600

—Pounds—

2000	2100	2200	2300	2400	lbs	2500	2600	2700	2800	2900
11.00	**11.55**	12.10	**12.65**	13.20		13.75	**14.30**	14.85	**15.40**	15.95
11.03	**11.58**	12.13	**12.68**	13.23	5	13.78	**14.33**	14.88	**15.43**	15.98
11.06	**11.61**	12.16	**12.71**	13.26	10	13.81	**14.36**	14.91	**15.46**	16.01
11.08	**11.63**	12.18	**12.73**	13.28	15	13.83	**14.38**	14.93	**15.48**	16.03
11.11	**11.66**	12.21	**12.76**	13.31	20	13.86	**14.41**	14.96	**15.51**	16.06
11.14	**11.69**	12.24	**12.79**	13.34	25	13.89	**14.44**	14.99	**15.54**	16.09
11.17	**11.72**	12.27	**12.82**	13.37	30	13.92	**14.47**	15.02	**15.57**	16.12
11.19	**11.74**	12.29	**12.84**	13.39	35	13.94	**14.49**	15.04	**15.59**	16.14
11.22	**11.77**	12.32	**12.87**	13.42	40	13.97	**14.52**	15.07	**15.62**	16.17
11.25	**11.80**	12.35	**12.90**	13.45	45	14.00	**14.55**	15.10	**15.65**	16.20
11.28	**11.83**	12.38	**12.93**	13.48	50	14.03	**14.58**	15.13	**15.68**	16.23
11.30	**11.85**	12.40	**12.95**	13.50	55	14.05	**14.60**	15.15	**15.70**	16.25
11.33	**11.88**	12.43	**12.98**	13.53	60	14.08	**14.63**	15.18	**15.73**	16.28
11.36	**11.91**	12.46	**13.01**	13.56	65	14.11	**14.66**	15.21	**15.76**	16.31
11.39	**11.94**	12.49	**13.04**	13.59	70	14.14	**14.69**	15.24	**15.79**	16.34
11.41	**11.96**	12.51	**13.06**	13.61	75	14.16	**14.71**	15.26	**15.81**	16.36
11.44	**11.99**	12.54	**13.09**	13.64	80	14.19	**14.74**	15.29	**15.84**	16.39
11.47	**12.02**	12.57	**13.12**	13.67	85	14.22	**14.77**	15.32	**15.87**	16.42
11.50	**12.05**	12.60	**13.15**	13.70	90	14.25	**14.80**	15.35	**15.90**	16.45
11.52	**12.07**	12.62	**13.17**	13.72	95	14.27	**14.82**	15.37	**15.92**	16.47

—Pounds—

3000	3100	3200	3300	3400	lbs	3500	3600	3700	3800	3900
16.50	**17.05**	17.60	**18.15**	18.70		19.25	**19.80**	20.35	**20.90**	21.45
16.53	**17.08**	17.63	**18.18**	18.73	5	19.28	**19.83**	20.38	**20.93**	21.48
16.56	**17.11**	17.66	**18.21**	18.76	10	19.31	**19.86**	20.41	**20.96**	21.51
16.58	**17.13**	17.68	**18.23**	18.78	15	19.33	**19.88**	20.43	**20.98**	21.53
16.61	**17.16**	17.71	**18.26**	18.81	20	19.36	**19.91**	20.46	**21.01**	21.56
16.64	**17.19**	17.74	**18.29**	18.84	25	19.39	**19.94**	20.49	**21.04**	21.59
16.67	**17.22**	17.77	**18.32**	18.87	30	19.42	**19.97**	20.52	**21.07**	21.62
16.69	**17.24**	17.79	**18.34**	18.89	35	19.44	**19.99**	20.54	**21.09**	21.64
16.72	**17.27**	17.82	**18.37**	18.92	40	19.47	**20.02**	20.57	**21.12**	21.67
16.75	**17.30**	17.85	**18.40**	18.95	45	19.50	**20.05**	20.60	**21.15**	21.70
16.78	**17.33**	17.88	**18.43**	18.98	50	19.53	**20.08**	20.63	**21.18**	21.73
16.80	**17.35**	17.90	**18.45**	19.00	55	19.55	**20.10**	20.65	**21.20**	21.75
16.83	**17.38**	17.93	**18.48**	19.03	60	19.58	**20.13**	20.68	**21.23**	21.78
16.86	**17.41**	17.96	**18.51**	19.06	65	19.61	**20.16**	20.71	**21.26**	21.81
16.89	**17.44**	17.99	**18.54**	19.09	70	19.64	**20.19**	20.74	**21.29**	21.84
16.91	**17.46**	18.01	**18.56**	19.11	75	19.66	**20.21**	20.76	**21.31**	21.86
16.94	**17.49**	18.04	**18.59**	19.14	80	19.69	**20.24**	20.79	**21.34**	21.89
16.97	**17.52**	18.07	**18.62**	19.17	85	19.72	**20.27**	20.82	**21.37**	21.92
17.00	**17.55**	18.10	**18.65**	19.20	90	19.75	**20.30**	20.85	**21.40**	21.95
17.02	**17.57**	18.12	**18.67**	19.22	95	19.77	**20.32**	20.87	**21.42**	21.97

Even tons, 51 to 100 inclusive.

	51-60		61-70		71-80		81-90		91-100
T	Am't	T	Am't	T	Am't	T	Am't	T	Am't
51	561.00	61	671.00	71	781.00	81	891.00	91	1001.00
52	572.00	62	682.00	72	792.00	82	902.00	92	1012.00
53	583.00	63	693.00	73	803.00	83	913.00	93	1023.00
54	594.00	64	704.00	74	814.00	84	924.00	94	1034.00
55	605.00	65	715.00	75	825.00	85	935.00	95	1045.00
56	616.00	66	726.00	76	836.00	86	946.00	96	1056.00
57	627.00	67	737.00	77	847 00	87	957.00	97	1067.00
58	638.00	68	748.00	78	858.00	88	968.00	98	1078.00
59	649.00	69	759.00	79	869.00	89	979.00	99	1089.00
60	660.00	70	770.00	80	880.00	90	990 00	100	1100.00

700	7700	800	8800	900	9900	1000	11000	1100	12100

POUNDS

Under 100	100	200	300	400		500	600	700	800	900
		AMOUNT					AMOUNT			
	.56	1.13	1.69	2.25		2.81	3.38	3.94	4.50	5.06
.03	.59	1.15	1.72	2.28	5	2.84	3.40	3.97	4.53	5.09
.06	.62	1.18	1.74	2.31	10	2.87	3.43	3.99	4.56	5.12
.08	.65	1.21	1.77	2.33	15	2.90	3.46	4.02	4.58	5.15
.11	.68	1.24	1.80	2.36	20	2.93	3.49	4.05	4.61	5.18
.14	.70	1.27	1.83	2.39	25	2.95	3.52	4.08	4.64	5.20
.17	.73	1.29	1.86	2.42	30	2.98	3.54	4.11	4.67	5.23
.20	.76	1.32	1.88	2.45	35	3.01	3.57	4.13	4.70	5.26
.23	.79	1.35	1.91	2.48	40	3.04	3.60	4.16	4.73	5.29
.25	.82	1.38	1.94	2.50	45	3.07	3.63	4.19	4.75	5.32
.28	.84	1.41	1.97	2.53	50	3.09	3.66	4.22	4.78	5.34
.31	.87	1.43	2.00	2.56	55	3.12	3.68	4.25	4.81	5.37
.34	.90	1.46	2.03	2.59	60	3.15	3.71	4.28	4.84	5.40
.37	.93	1.49	2.05	2.62	65	3.18	3.74	4.30	4.87	5.43
.39	.96	1.52	2.08	2.64	70	3.21	3.77	4.33	4.89	5.46
.42	.98	1.55	2.11	2.67	75	3.23	3.80	4.36	4.92	5.48
.45	1.01	1.58	2.14	2.70	80	3.26	3.83	4.39	4.95	5.51
.48	1.04	1.60	2.17	2.73	85	3.29	3.85	4.42	4.98	5.54
.51	1.07	1.63	2.19	2.76	90	3.32	3.88	4.44	5.01	5.57
.53	1.10	1.66	2.22	2.78	95	3.35	3.91	4.47	5.03	5.60

POUNDS

1000	1100	1200	1300	1400		1500	1600	1700	1800	1900
		AMOUNT					AMOUNT			
5.63	6.19	6.75	7.31	7.88		8.44	9.00	9.56	10.13	10.69
5.65	6.22	6.78	7.34	7.90	5	8.47	9.03	9.59	10.15	10.72
5.68	6.24	6.81	7.37	7.93	10	8.49	9.06	9.62	10.18	10.74
5.71	6.27	6.83	7.40	7.96	15	8.52	9.08	9.65	10.21	10.77
5.74	6.30	6.86	7.43	7.99	20	8.55	9.11	9.68	10.24	10.80
5.77	6.33	6.89	7.45	8.02	25	8.58	9.14	9.70	10.27	10.83
5.79	6.36	6.92	7.48	8.04	30	8.61	9.17	9.73	10.29	10.86
5.82	6.38	6.95	7.51	8.07	35	8.63	9.20	9.76	10.32	10.88
5.85	6.41	6.98	7.54	8.10	40	8.66	9.23	9.79	10.35	10.91
5.88	6.44	7.00	7.57	8.13	45	8.69	9.25	9.82	10.38	10.94
5.91	6.47	7.03	7.59	8.16	50	8.72	9.28	9.84	10.41	10.97
5.93	6.50	7.06	7.62	8.18	55	8.75	9.31	9.87	10.43	11.00
5.96	6.53	7.09	7.65	8.21	60	8.78	9.34	9.90	10.46	11.03
5.99	6.55	7.12	7.68	8.24	65	8.80	9.37	9.93	10.49	11.05
6.02	6.58	7.14	7.71	8.27	70	8.83	9.39	9.96	10.52	11.08
6.05	6.61	7.17	7.73	8.30	75	8.86	9.42	9.98	10.55	11.11
6.08	6.64	7.20	7.76	8.33	80	8.89	9.45	10.01	10.58	11.14
6.10	6.67	7.23	7.79	8.35	85	8.92	9.48	10.04	10.60	11.17
6.13	6.69	7.26	7.82	8.38	90	8.94	9.51	10.07	10.63	11.19
6.16	6.72	7.28	7.85	8.41	95	8.97	9.53	10.10	10.66	11.22

Even tons, 1 to 50 inclusive.

1-10		11-20		21-30		31-40		41-50	
T	Am't	T	Am't	T	Am't	T	Am't	T	Am't
1	11.25	11	123.75	21	236.25	31	348.75	41	461.25
2	22.50	12	135.00	22	247.50	32	360.00	42	472.50
3	33.75	13	146.25	23	258.75	33	371.25	43	483.75
4	45.00	14	157.50	24	270.00	34	382.50	44	495.00
5	56.25	15	168.75	25	281.25	35	393.75	45	506.25
6	67.50	16	180.00	26	292.50	36	405.00	46	517.50
7	78.75	17	191.25	27	303.75	37	416.25	47	528.75
8	90.00	18	202.50	28	315.00	38	427.50	48	540.00
9	101.25	19	213.75	29	326.25	39	438.75	49	551.25
10	112.50	20	225.00	30	337.50	40	450.00	50	562.50
200	2250	300	3375	400	4500	500	5625	600	6750

POUNDS

2000	2100	2200	2300	2400		2500	2600	2700	2800	2900
		AMOUNT						AMOUNT		
11.25	11.81	12.38	12.94	13.50		14.06	14.63	15.19	15.75	16.31
11.28	11.84	12.40	12.97	13.53	5	14.09	14.65	15.22	15.78	16.34
11.31	11.87	12.43	12.99	13.56	10	14.12	14.68	15.24	15.81	16.37
11.33	11.90	12.46	13.02	13.58	15	14.15	14.71	15.27	15.83	16.40
11.36	11.93	12.49	13.05	13.61	20	14.18	14.74	15.30	15.86	16.43
11.39	11.95	12.52	13.08	13.64	25	14.20	14.77	15.33	15.89	16.45
11.42	11.98	12.54	13.11	13.67	30	14.23	14.79	15.36	15.92	16.48
11.45	12.01	12.57	13.13	13.70	35	14.26	14.82	15.38	15.95	16.51
11.48	12.04	12.60	13.16	13.73	40	14.29	14.85	15.41	15.98	16.54
11.50	12.07	12.63	13.19	13.75	45	14.32	14.88	15.44	16.00	16.57
11.53	12.09	12.66	13.22	13.78	50	14.34	14.91	15.47	16.03	16.59
11.56	12.12	12.68	13.25	13.81	55	14.37	14.93	15.50	16.06	16.62
11.59	12.15	12.71	13.28	13.84	60	14.40	14.96	15.53	16.09	16.65
11.62	12.18	12.74	13.30	13.87	65	14.43	14.99	15.55	16.12	16.68
11.64	12.21	12.77	13.33	13.89	70	14.46	15.02	15.58	16.14	16.71
11.67	12.23	12.80	13.36	13.92	75	14.48	15.05	15.61	16.17	16.73
11.70	12.26	12.83	13.39	13.95	80	14.51	15.08	15.64	16.20	16.76
11.73	12.29	12.85	13.42	13.98	85	14.54	15.10	15.67	16.23	16.79
11.76	12.32	12.88	13.44	14.01	90	14.57	15.13	15.69	16.26	16.82
11.78	12.35	12.91	13.47	14.03	95	14.60	15.16	15.72	16.28	16.85

POUNDS

3000	3100	3200	3300	3400		3500	3600	3700	3800	3900
		AMOUNT						AMOUNT		
16.88	17.44	18.00	18.56	19.13		19.69	20.25	20.81	21.38	21.94
16.90	17.47	18.03	18.59	19.15	5	19.72	20.28	20.84	21.40	21.97
16.93	17.49	18.06	18.62	19.18	10	19.74	20.31	20.87	21.43	21.99
16.96	17.52	18.08	18.65	19.21	15	19.77	20.33	20.90	21.46	22.02
16.99	17.55	18.11	18.68	19.24	20	19.80	20.36	20.93	21.49	22.05
17.02	17.58	18.14	18.70	19.27	25	19.83	20.39	20.95	21.52	22.08
17.04	17.61	18.17	18.73	19.29	30	19.86	20.42	20.98	21.54	22.11
17.07	17.63	18.20	18.76	19.32	35	19.88	20.45	21.01	21.57	22.13
17.10	17.66	18.23	18.79	19.35	40	19.91	20.48	21.04	21.60	22.16
17.13	17.69	18.25	18.82	19.38	45	19.94	20.50	21.07	21.63	22.19
17.16	17.72	18.28	18.84	19.41	50	19.97	20.53	21.09	21.66	22.22
17.18	17.75	18.31	18.87	19.43	55	20.00	20.56	21.12	21.68	22.25
17.21	17.78	18.34	18.90	19.46	60	20.03	20.59	21.15	21.71	22.28
17.24	17.80	18.37	18.93	19.49	65	20.05	20.62	21.18	21.74	22.30
17.27	17.83	18.39	18.96	19.52	70	20.08	20.64	21.21	21.77	22.33
17.30	17.86	18.42	18.98	19.55	75	20.11	20.67	21.23	21.80	22.36
17.33	17.89	18.45	19.01	19.58	80	20.14	20.70	21.26	21.83	22.39
17.35	17.92	18.48	19.04	19.60	85	20.17	20.73	21.29	21.85	22.42
17.38	17.94	18.51	19.07	19.63	90	20.19	20.76	21.32	21.88	22.44
17.41	17.97	18.53	19.10	19.66	95	20.22	20.78	21.35	21.91	22.47

Even tons, 51 to 100 inclusive.

51-60		61-70		71-80		81-90		91-100	
T	Am't	T	Am't	T	Am't	T	Am't	T	Am't
51	573.75	61	686.25	71	798.75	81	911.25	91	1023.75
52	585.00	62	697.50	72	810.00	82	922.50	92	1035.00
53	596.25	63	708.75	73	821.25	83	933.75	93	1046.25
54	607.50	64	720.00	74	832.50	84	945.00	94	1057.50
55	618.75	65	731.25	75	843.75	85	956.25	95	1068.75
56	630.00	66	742.50	76	855.00	86	967.50	96	1080.00
57	641.25	67	753.75	77	866.25	87	978.75	97	1091.25
58	652.50	68	765.00	78	877.50	88	990.00	98	1102.50
59	663.75	69	776.25	79	888.75	89	1001.25	99	1113.75
60	.675.00	70	787.50	80	900.00	90	1012.50	100	1125.00

700	7875	800	9000	900	10125	1000	11250	1100	12375

POUNDS

Under 100	100	200	300	400		500	600	700	800	900
			AMOUNT					AMOUNT		
	.58	1.15	1.73	2.30		2.88	3.45	4.03	4.60	5.18
.03	.60	1.18	1.75	2.33	5	2.90	3.48	4.05	4.63	5.20
.06	.63	1.21	1.78	2.36	10	2.93	3.51	4.08	4.66	5.23
.09	.66	1.24	1.81	2.39	15	2.96	3.54	4.11	4.69	5.26
.12	.69	1.27	1.84	2.42	20	2.99	3.57	4.14	4.72	5.29
.14	.72	1.29	1.87	2.44	25	3.02	3.59	4.17	4.74	5.32
.17	.75	1.32	1.90	2.47	30	3.05	3.62	4.20	4.77	5.35
.20	.78	1.35	1.93	2.50	35	3.08	3.65	4.23	4.80	5.38
.23	.81	1.38	1.96	2.53	40	3.11	3.68	4.26	4.83	5.41
.26	.83	1.41	1.98	2.56	45	3.13	3.71	4.28	4.86	5.43
.29	.86	1.44	2.01	2.59	50	3.16	3.74	4.31	4.89	5.46
.32	.89	1.47	2.04	2.62	55	3.19	3.77	4.34	4.92	5.49
.35	.92	1.50	2.07	2.65	60	3.22	3.80	4.37	4.95	5.52
.37	.95	1.52	2.10	2.67	65	3.25	3.82	4.40	4.97	5.55
.40	.98	1.55	2.13	2.70	70	3.28	3.85	4.43	5.00	5.58
.43	1.01	1.58	2.16	2.73	75	3.31	3.88	4.46	5.03	5.61
.46	1.04	1.61	2.19	2.76	80	3.34	3.91	4.49	5.06	5.64
.49	1.06	1.64	2.21	2.79	85	3.36	3.94	4.51	5.09	5.66
.52	1.09	1.67	2.24	2.82	90	3.39	3.97	4.54	5.12	5.69
.55	1.12	1.70	2.27	2.85	95	3.42	4.00	4.57	5.15	5.72

POUNDS

1000	1100	1200	1300	1400		1500	1600	1700	1800	1900
		AMOUNT						AMOUNT		
5.75	6.33	6.90	7.48	8.05		8.63	9.20	9.78	10.35	10.93
5.78	6.35	6.93	7.50	8.08	5	8.65	9.23	9.80	10.38	10.95
5.81	6.38	6.96	7.53	8.11	10	8 68	9.26	9.83	10.41	10.98
5.84	6.41	6.99	7.56	8.14	15	8.71	9.29	9.86	10.44	11.01
5.87	6.44	7.02	7.59	8.17	20	8.74	9.32	9.89	10.47	11.04
5.89	6.47	7.04	7.62	8.19	25	8.77	9.34	9.92	10.49	11.07
5.92	6.50	7.07	7.65	8.22	30	8.80	9.37	9.95	10.52	11.10
5.95	6.53	7.10	7.68	8.25	35	8.83	9.40	9.98	10.55	11.13
5.98	6.56	7.13	7.71	8.28	40	8.86	9.43	10.01	10.58	11.16
6.01	6.58	7.16	7.73	8.31	45	8.88	9.46	10.03	10.61	11.18
6.04	6.61	7.19	7.76	8.34	50	8.91	9.49	10.06	10.64	11.21
6.07	6.64	7.22	7.79	8.37	55	8.94	9.52	10.09	10.67	11.24
6.10	6.67	7.25	7.82	8.40	60	8.97	9.55	10.12	10.70	11.27
6.12	6.70	7.27	7.85	8.42	65	9.00	9.57	10.15	10.72	11.30
6.15	6.73	7.30	7.88	8.45	70	9.03	9.60	10.18	10.75	11.33
6.18	6.76	7.33	7.91	8.48	75	9.06	9.63	10.21	10.78	11.36
6.21	6.79	7.36	7.94	8.51	80	9.09	9.66	10.24	10.81	11.39
6.24	6.81	7.39	7.96	8.54	85	9.11	9.69	10.26	10.84	11.41
6.27	6.84	7.42	7.99	8.57	90	9.14	9.72	10.29	10.87	11.44
6.30	6.87	7.45	8.02	8.60	95	9.17	9.75	10.32	10.90	11.47

Even tons, 1 to 50 inclusive.

1-10 T	Am't	11-20 T	Am't	21-30 T	Am't	31-40 T	Am't	41-50 T	Am't
1	11.50	11	126.50	21	241.50	31	356.50	41	471.50
2	23.00	12	138.00	22	253.00	32	368.00	42	483.00
3	34.50	13	149.50	23	264.50	33	379.50	43	494.50
4	46.00	14	161.00	24	276.00	34	391.00	44	506.00
5	57.50	15	172.50	25	287.50	35	402.50	45	517.50
6	69.00	16	184.00	26	299.00	36	414.00	46	529.00
7	80.50	17	195.50	27	310.50	37	425.50	47	540.50
8	92.00	18	207.00	28	322.00	38	437.00	48	552.00
9	103.50	19	218.50	29	333.50	39	448.50	49	563.50
10	115.00	20	230.00	30	345.00	40	460.00	50	575.00

200	2300	300	3450	400	4600	500	5750	600	6900

-POUNDS-

2000	2100	2200	2300	2400		2500	2600	2700	2800	2900
		AMOUNT						AMOUNT		
11.50	12.08	12.65	13.23	13.80		14.38	14.95	15.53	16.10	16.68
11.53	12.10	12.68	13.25	13.83	5	14.40	14.98	15.55	16.13	16.70
11.56	12.13	12.71	13.28	13.86	10	14.43	15.01	15.58	16.16	16.73
11.59	12.16	12.74	13.31	13.89	15	14.46	15.04	15.61	16.19	16.76
11.62	12.19	12.77	13.34	13.92	20	14.49	15.07	15.64	16.22	16.79
11.64	12.22	12.79	13.37	13.94	25	14.52	15.09	15.67	16.24	16.82
11.67	12.25	12.82	13.40	13.97	30	14.55	15.12	15.70	16.27	16.85
11.70	12.28	12.85	13.43	14.00	35	14.58	15.15	15.73	16.30	16.88
11.73	12.31	12.88	13.46	14.03	40	14.61	15.18	15.76	16.33	16.91
11.76	12.33	12.91	13.48	14.06	45	14.63	15.21	15.78	16.36	16.93
11.79	12.36	12.94	13.51	14.09	50	14.66	15.24	15.81	16.39	16.96
11.82	12.39	12.97	13.54	14.12	55	14.69	15.27	15.84	16.42	16.99
11.85	12.42	13.00	13.57	14.15	60	14.72	15.30	15.87	16.45	17.02
11.87	12.45	13.02	13.60	14.17	65	14.75	15.32	15.90	16.47	17.05
11.90	12.48	13.05	13.63	14.20	70	14.78	15.35	15.93	16.50	17.08
11.93	12.51	13.08	13.66	14.23	75	14.81	15.38	15.96	16.53	17.11
11.96	12.54	13.11	13.69	14.26	80	14.84	15.41	15.99	16.56	17.14
11.99	12.56	13.14	13.71	14.29	85	14.86	15.44	16.01	16.59	17.16
12.02	12.59	13.17	13.74	14.32	90	14.89	15.47	16.04	16.62	17.19
12.05	12.62	13.20	13.77	14.35	95	14.92	15.50	16.07	16.65	17.22

-POUNDS-

3000	3100	3200	3300	3400		3500	3600	3700	3800	3900
		AMOUNT						AMOUNT		
17.25	17.83	18.40	18.98	19.55		20.13	20.70	21.28	21.85	22.43
17.28	17.85	18.43	19.00	19.58	5	20.15	20.73	21.30	21.88	22.45
17.31	17.88	18.46	19.03	19.61	10	20.18	20.76	21.33	21.91	22.48
17.34	17.91	18.49	19.06	19.64	15	20.21	20.79	21.36	21.94	22.51
17.37	17.94	18.52	19.09	19.67	20	20.24	20.82	21.39	21.97	22.54
17.39	17.97	18.54	19.12	19.69	25	20.27	20.84	21.42	21.99	22.57
17.42	18.00	18.57	19.15	19.72	30	20.30	20.87	21.45	22.02	22.60
17.45	18.03	18.60	19.18	19.75	35	20.33	20.90	21.48	22.05	22.63
17.48	18.06	18.63	19.21	19.78	40	20.36	20.93	21.51	22.08	22.66
17.51	18.08	18.66	19.23	19.81	45	20.38	20.96	21.53	22.11	22.68
17.54	18.11	18.69	19.26	19.84	50	20.41	20.99	21.56	22.14	22.71
17.57	18.14	18.72	19.29	19.87	55	20.44	21.02	21.59	22.17	22.74
17.60	18.17	18.75	19.32	19.90	60	20.47	21.05	21.62	22.20	22.77
17.62	18.20	18.77	19.35	19.92	65	20.50	21.07	21.65	22.22	22.80
17.65	13.23	18.80	19.38	19.95	70	20.53	21.10	21.68	22.25	22.83
17.68	18.26	18.83	19.41	19.98	75	20.56	21.13	21.71	22.28	22.86
17.71	18.29	18.86	19.44	20.01	80	20.59	21.16	21.74	22.31	22.89
17.74	18.31	18.89	19.46	20.04	85	20.61	21.19	21.76	22.34	22.91
17.77	18.34	18.92	19.49	20.07	90	20.64	21.22	21.79	22.37	22.94
17.80	18.37	18.95	19.52	20.10	95	20.67	21.25	21.82	22.40	22.97

Even tons, 51 to 100 inclusive.

51-60		61-70		71-80		81-90		91-100	
T	Am't	T	Am't	T	Am't	T	Am't	T	Am't
51	586.50	61	701.50	71	816.50	81	931.50	91	1046.50
52	598.00	62	713.00	72	828.00	82	943.00	92	1058.00
53	609.50	63	724.50	73	839.50	83	954.50	93	1069.50
54	621.00	64	736.00	74	851.00	84	966.00	94	1081.00
55	632.50	65	747.50	75	862.50	85	977.50	95	1092.50
56	644.00	66	759.00	76	874.00	86	989.00	96	1104.00
57	655.50	67	770.50	77	885.50	87	1000.50	97	1115.50
58	667.00	68	782.00	78	897.00	88	1012.00	98	1127.00
59	678.50	69	793.50	79	908.50	89	1023.50	99	1138.50
60	690.00	70	805.00	80	920.00	90	1035.00	100	1150.00

700	8050	800	9200	900	10350	1000	11500	1100	12650

POUNDS

Under 100	100	200	300	400		500	600	700	800	900
		AMOUNT						AMOUNT		
	.59	1.18	1.76	2.35		2.94	3.53	4.11	4.70	5.29
.03	.62	1.20	1.79	2.38	5	2.97	3.55	4.14	4.73	5.32
.06	.65	1.23	1.82	2.41	10	3.00	3.58	4.17	4.76	5.35
.09	.68	1.26	1.85	2.44	15	3.03	3.61	4.20	4.79	5.38
.12	.71	1.29	1.88	2.47	20	3.06	3.64	4.23	4.82	5.41
.15	.73	1.32	1.91	2.50	25	3.08	3.67	4.26	4.85	5.43
.18	.76	1.35	1.94	2.53	30	3.11	3.70	4.29	4.88	5.46
.21	.79	1.38	1.97	2.56	35	3.14	3.73	4.32	4.91	5.49
.24	.82	1.41	2.00	2.59	40	3.17	3.76	4.35	4.94	5.52
.26	.85	1.44	2.03	2.61	45	3.20	3.79	4.38	4.96	5.55
.29	.88	1.47	2.06	2.64	50	3.23	3.82	4.41	4.99	5.58
.32	.91	1.50	2.09	2.67	55	3.26	3.85	4.44	5.02	5.61
.35	.94	1.53	2.12	2.70	60	3.29	3.88	4.47	5.05	5.64
.38	.97	1.56	2.14	2.73	65	3.32	3.91	4.49	5.08	5.67
.41	1.00	1.59	2.17	2.76	70	3.35	3.94	4.52	5.11	5.70
.44	1.03	1.62	2.20	2.79	75	3.38	3.97	4.55	5.14	5.73
.47	1.06	1.65	2.23	2.82	80	3.41	4.00	4.58	5.17	5.76
.50	1.09	1.67	2.26	2.85	85	3.44	4.02	4.61	5.20	5.79
.53	1.12	1.70	2.29	2.88	90	3.47	4.05	4.64	5.23	5.82
.56	1.15	1.73	2.32	2.91	95	3.50	4.08	4.67	5.26	5.85

POUNDS

1000	1100	1200	1300	1400		1500	1600	1700	1800	1900
		AMOUNT						AMOUNT		
5.88	6.46	7.05	7.64	8.23		8.81	9.40	9.99	10.58	11.16
5.90	6.49	7.08	7.67	8.25	5	8.84	9.43	10.02	10.60	11.19
5.93	6.52	7.11	7.70	8.28	10	8.87	9.46	10.05	10.63	11.22
5.96	6.55	7.14	7.73	8.31	15	8.90	9.49	10.08	10.66	11.25
5.99	6.58	7.17	7.76	8.34	20	8.93	9.52	10.11	10.69	11.28
6.02	6.61	7.20	7.78	8.37	25	8.96	9.55	10.13	10.72	11.31
6.05	6.64	7.23	7.81	8.40	30	8.99	9.58	10.16	10.75	11.34
6.08	6.67	7.26	7.84	8.43	35	9.02	9.61	10.19	10.78	11.37
6.11	6.70	7.29	7.87	8.46	40	9.05	9.64	10.22	10.81	11.40
6.14	6.73	7.31	7.90	8.49	45	9.08	9.66	10.25	10.84	11.43
6.17	6.76	7.34	7.93	8.52	50	9.11	9.69	10.28	10.87	11.46
6.20	6.79	7.37	7.96	8.55	55	9.14	9.72	10.31	10.90	11.49
6.23	6.82	7.40	7.99	8.58	60	9.17	9.75	10.34	10.93	11.52
6.26	6.84	7.43	8.02	8.61	65	9.19	9.78	10.37	10.96	11.54
6.29	6.87	7.46	8.05	8.64	70	9.22	9.81	10.40	10.99	11.57
6.32	6.90	7.49	8.08	8.67	75	9.25	9.84	10.43	11.02	11.60
6.35	6.93	7.52	8.11	8.70	80	9.28	9.87	10.46	11.05	11.63
6.37	6.96	7.55	8.14	8.72	85	9.31	9.90	10.49	11.07	11.66
6.40	6.99	7.58	8.17	8.75	90	9.34	9.93	10.52	11.10	11.69
6.43	7.02	7.61	8.20	8.78	95	9.37	9.96	10.55	11.13	11.72

Even tons, 1 to 50 inclusive.

1-10		11-20		21-30		31-40		41-50	
T	Am't	T	Am't	T	Am't	T	Am't	T	Am't
1	11.75	11	129.25	21	246.75	31	364.25	41	481.75
2	23.50	12	141.00	22	258.50	32	376.00	42	493.50
3	35.25	13	152.75	23	270.25	33	387.75	43	505.25
4	47.00	14	164.50	24	282.00	34	399.50	44	517.00
5	58.75	15	176.25	25	293.75	35	411.25	45	528.75
6	70.50	16	188.00	26	305.50	36	423.00	46	540.50
7	82.25	17	199.75	27	317.25	37	434.75	47	552.25
8	94.00	18	211.50	28	329.00	38	446.50	48	564.00
9	105.75	19	223.25	29	340.75	39	458.25	49	575.75
10	117.50	20	235.00	30	352.50	40	470.00	50	587.50
200	2350	300	3525	400	4700	500	5875	600	7050

——POUNDS——

2000	2100	2200	2300	2400		2500	2600	2700	2800	2900
		AMOUNT					AMOUNT			
11.75	12.34	12.93	13.51	14.10		14.69	15.28	15.86	16.45	17.04
11.78	12.37	12.95	13.54	14.13	5	14.72	15.30	15.89	16.48	17.07
11.81	12.40	12.98	13.57	14.16	10	14.75	15.33	15.92	16.51	17.10
11.84	12.43	13.01	13.60	14.19	15	14.78	15.36	15.95	16.54	17.13
11.87	12.46	13.04	13.63	14.22	20	14.81	15.39	15.98	16.57	17.16
11.90	12.48	13.07	13.66	14.25	25	14.83	15.42	16.01	16.60	17.18
11.93	12.51	13.10	13.69	14.28	30	14.86	15.45	16.04	16.63	17.21
11.96	12.54	13.13	13.72	14.31	35	14.89	15.48	16.07	16.66	17.24
11.99	12.57	13.16	13.75	14.34	40	14.92	15.51	16.10	16.69	17.27
12.01	12.60	13.19	13.78	14.36	45	14.95	15.54	16.13	16.71	17.30
12.04	12.63	13 22	13.81	14.39	50	14.98	15.57	16.16	16.74	17.33
12.07	12.66	13.25	13.84	14.42	55	15.01	15.60	16.19	16.77	17.36
12.10	12.69	13.28	13.87	14.45	60	15.04	15.63	16.22	16.80	17.39
12.13	12.72	13.31	13.89	14.48	65	15.07	15.66	16.24	16.83	17.42
12.16	12.75	13.34	13.92	14.51	70	15.10	15.69	16.27	16.86	17.45
12.19	12.78	13.37	13.95	14.54	75	15.13	15.72	16.30	16.89	17.48
12.22	12.81	13.40	13.98	14.57	80	15.16	15.75	16.33	16.92	17.51
12.25	12.84	13.42	14.01	14.60	85	15.19	15.77	16.36	16.95	17.54
12.28	12.87	13.45	14.04	14.63	90	15.22	15.80	16.39	16.98	17.57
12.31	12.90	13.48	14.07	14.66	95	15.25	15.83	16.42	17.01	17 60

——POUNDS——

3000	3100	3200	3300	3400		3500	3600	3700	3800	3900
		AMOUNT					AMOUNT			
17.63	18.21	18.80	19.39	19.98		20.56	21.15	21.74	22.33	22.91
17.65	18.24	18.83	19.42	20.00	5	20.59	21.18	21.77	22.35	22.94
17.68	18.27	18.86	19.45	20.03	10	20.62	21.21	21.80	22.38	22.97
17.71	18.30	18.89	19.48	20.06	15	20.65	21.24	21.83	22.41	23.00
17.74	18.33	18.92	19.51	20.09	20	20.68	21.27	21.86	22.44	23.03
17.77	18.36	18.95	19.53	20.12	25	20.71	21.30	21.88	22.47	23.06
17.80	18.39	18.98	19.56	20.15	30	20.74	21.33	21.91	22.50	23.09
17.83	18.42	19.01	19.59	20.18	35	20.77	21.36	21.94	22.53	23.12
17.86	18.45	19.04	19.62	20.21	40	20.80	21.39	21.97	22.56	23.15
17.89	18.48	19.06	19.65	20.24	45	20.83	21.41	22.00	22.59	23.18
17.92	18.51	19.09	19.68	20.27	50	20.86	21.44	22.03	22.62	23.21
17.95	18.54	19.12	19.71	20.30	55	20.89	21.47	22.06	22.65	23.24
17.98	18.57	19.15	19.74	20.33	60	20.92	21.50	22.09	22.68	23.27
18.01	18.59	19.18	19.77	20.36	65	20.94	21.53	22.12	22.71	23.29
18.04	18.62	19.21	19.80	20.39	70	20.97	21.56	22.15	22.74	23.32
18.07	18.65	19.24	19.83	20.42	75	21.00	21.59	22.18	22.77	23.35
18.10	18.68	19.27	19.86	20.45	80	21.03	21.62	22.21	22.80	23.38
18.12	18.71	19.30	19.89	20.47	85	21.06	21.65	22.24	22.82	23.41
18.15	18.74	19.33	19.92	20.50	90	21.09	21.68	22.27	22.85	23.44
18.18	18.77	19.36	19.95	20.53	95	21.12	21.71	22.30	22.88	23.47

Even tons, 51 to 100 inclusive.

	51-60		61-70		71-80		81-90		91-100
T	Am't	T	Am't	T	Am't	T	Am't	T	Am't
51	599.25	61	716.75	71	834.25	81	951.75	91	1069.25
52	611.00	62	728.50	72	846.00	82	963.50	92	1081.00
53	622.75	63	740.25	73	857.75	83	975.25	93	1092.75
54	634.50	64	752.00	74	869.50	84	987.00	94	1104.50
55	646.25	65	763.75	75	881.25	85	998.75	95	1116.25
56	658.00	66	775.50	76	893.00	86	1010.50	96	1128.00
57	669.75	67	787.25	77	904.75	87	1022.25	97	1139.75
58	681.50	68	799.00	78	916.50	88	1034.00	98	1151.50
59	693.25	69	810.75	79	928.25	89	1045.75	99	1163.25
60	705.00	70	822.50	80	940.00	90	1057.50	100	1175.00

700	8225	800	9400	900	10575	1000	11750	1100	12925

9   (97)

POUNDS

Under 100	100	200	300	100		500	600	700	800	900
		AMOUNT						AMOUNT		
	.60	1.20	1.80	2.40		3.00	3.60	4.20	4.80	5.40
.03	.63	1.23	1.83	2.43	5	3.03	3.63	4.23	4.83	5.43
.06	.66	1.26	1.86	2.46	10	3.06	3.66	4.26	4.86	5.46
.09	.69	1.29	1.89	2.49	15	3.09	3.69	4.29	4.89	5.49
.12	.72	1.32	1.92	2.52	20	3.12	3.72	4.32	4.92	5.52
.15	.75	1.35	1.95	2.55	25	3.15	3.75	4.35	4.95	5.55
.18	.78	1.38	1.98	2.58	30	3.18	3.78	4.38	4.98	5.58
.21	.81	1.41	2.01	2.61	35	3.21	3.81	4.41	5.01	5.61
.24	.84·	1.44	2.04	2.64	40	3.24	3.84	4.44	5.04	5.64
.27	.87	1.47	2.07	2.67	45	3.27	3.87	4.47	5.07	5.67
.30	.90	1.50	2.10	2.70	50	3.30	3.90	4.50	5.10	5.70
.33	.93	1.53	2.13	2.73	55	3.33	3.93	4.53	5.13	5.73
.36	.96	1.56	2.16	2.76	60	3.36	3.96	4.56	5.16	5.76
.39	.99	1.59	2.19	2.79	65	3.39	3.99	4.59	5.19	5.79
.42	1.02	1.62	2.22	2.82	70	3.42	4.02	4.62	5.22	5.82
.45	1.05	1.65	2.25	2.85	75	3.45	4.05	4.65	5.25	5.85
.48	1.08	1.68	2.28	2.88	80	3.48	4.08	4.68	5.28	5.88
.51	1.11	1.71	2.31	2.91	85	3.51	4.11	4.71	5.31	5.91
.54	1.14	1.74	2.34	2.94	90	3.54	4.14	4.74	5.34	5.94
.57	1.17	1.77	2.37	2.97	95	3.57	4.17	4.77	5.37	5.97

POUNDS

1000	1100	1200	1300	1400		1500	1600	1700	1800	1900
		AMOUNT						AMOUNT		
6.00	6.60	7.20	7.80	8.40		9.00	9.60	10.20	10.80	11.40
6.03	6.63	7.23	7.83	8.43	5	9.03	9.63	10.23	10.83	11.43
6.06	6.66	7.26	7.86	8.46	10	9.06	9.66	10.26	10.86	11.46
6.09	6.69	7.29	7.89	8.49	15	9.09	9.69	10.29	10.89	11.49
6.12	6.72	7.32	7.92	8.52	20	9.12	9.72	10.32	10.92	11.52
6.15	6.75	7.35	7.95	8.55	25	9.15	9.75	10.35	10.95	11.55
6.18	6.78	7.38	7.98	8.58	30	9.18	9.78	10.38	10.98	11.58
6.21	6.81	7.41	8.01	8.61	35	9.21	9.81	10.41	11.01	11.61
6.24	6.84	7.44	8.04	8.64	40	9.24	9.84	10.44	11.04	11.64
6.27	6.87	7.47	8.07	8.67	45	9.27	9.87	10.47	11.07	11.67
6.30	6.90	7.50	8.10	8.70	50	9.30	9.90	10.50	11.10	11.70
6.33	6.93	7.53	8.13	8.73	55	9.33	9.93	10.53	11.13	11.73
6.36	6.96	7.56	8.16	8.76	60	9.36	9.96	10.56	11.16	11.76
6.39	6.99	7.59	8.19	8.79	65	9.39	9.99	10.59	11.19	11.79
6.42	7.02	7.62	8.22	8.82	70	9.42	10.02	10.62	11.22	11.82
6.45	7.05	7.65	8.25	8.85	75	9.45	10.05	10.65	11.25	11.85
6.48	7.08	7.68	8.28	8.88	80	9.48	10.08	10.68	11.28	11.88
6.51	7.11	7.71	8.31	8.91	85	9.51	10.11	10.71	11.31	11.91
6.54	7.14	7.74	8.34	8.94	90	9.54	10.14	10.74	11.34	11.94
6.57	7.17	7.77	8.37	8.97	95	9.57	10.17	10.77	11.37	11.97

Even tons, 1 to 50 inclusive.

1-10		11-20		21-30		31-40		41-50	
T	Am't	T	Am't	T	Am't	T	Am't	T	Am't
1	12.00	11	132.00	21	252.00	31	372.00	41	492.00
2	24.00	12	144.00	22	264.00	32	384.00	42	504.00
3	36.00	13	156.00	23	276.00	33	396.00	43	516.00
4	48.00	14	168.00	24	288.00	34	408.00	44	528.00
5	60.00	15	180.00	25	300.00	35	420.00	45	540.00
6	72.00	16	192.00	26	312.00	36	432.00	46	552.00
7	84.00	17	204.00	27	324.00	37	444.00	47	564.00
8	96.00	18	216.00	28	336.00	38	456.00	48	576.00
9	108.00	19	228.00	29	348.00	39	468.00	49	588.00
10	120.00	20	240.00	30	360.00	40	480.00	50	600.00

200	2400	300	3600	400	4800	500	6000	600	7200

—POUNDS—

2000	2100	2200	2300	2100		2500	2600	2700	2800	2900
		AMOUNT						AMOUNT		
12.00	12.60	13.20	13.80	14.40		15.00	15.60	16.20	16.80	17.40
12.03	12.63	13.23	13.83	14.43	5	15.03	15.63	16.23	16.83	17.43
12.06	12.66	13.26	13.86	14.46	10	15.06	15.66	16.26	16.86	17.46
12.09	12.69	13.29	13.89	14.49	15	15.09	15.69	16.29	16.89	17.49
12.12	12.72	13.32	13.92	14.52	20	15.12	15.72	16.32	16.92	17.52
12.15	12.75	13.35	13.95	14.55	25	15.15	15.75	16.35	16.95	17.55
12.18	12.78	13.38	13.98	14.58	30	15.18	15.78	16.38	16.98	17.58
12.21	12.81	13.41	14.01	14.61	35	15.21	15.81	16.41	17.01	17.61
12.24	12.84	13.44	14.04	14.64	40	15.24	15.84	16.44	17.04	17.64
12.27	12.87	13.47	14.07	14.67	45	15.27	15.87	16.47	17.07	17.67
12.30	12.90	13.50	14.10	14.70	50	15.30	15.90	16.50	17.10	17.70
12.33	12.93	13.53	14.13	14.73	55	15.33	15.93	16.53	17.13	17.73
12.36	12.96	13.56	14.16	14.76	60	15.36	15.96	16.56	17.16	17.76
12.39	12.99	13.59	14.19	14.79	65	15.39	15.99	16.59	17.19	17.79
12.42	13.02	13.62	14.22	14.82	70	15.42	16.02	16.62	17.22	17.82
12.45	13.05	13.65	14.25	14.85	75	15.45	16.05	16.65	17.25	17.85
12.48	13.08	13.68	14.28	14.88	80	15.48	16.08	16.68	17.28	17.88
12.51	13.11	13.71	14.31	14.91	85	15.51	16.11	16.71	17.31	17.91
12.54	13.14	13.74	14.34	14.94	90	15.54	16.14	16.74	17.34	17.94
12.57	13.17	13.77	14.37	14.97	95	15.57	16.17	16.77	17.37	17.97

—POUNDS—

3000	3100	3200	3300	3400		3500	3600	3700	3800	3900
		AMOUNT						AMOUNT		
18.00	18.60	19.20	19.80	20.40		21.00	21.60	22.20	22.80	23.40
18.03	18.63	19.23	19.83	20.43	5	21.03	21.63	22.23	22.83	23.43
18.06	18.66	19.26	19.86	20.46	10	21.06	21.66	22.26	22.86	23.46
18.09	18.69	19.29	19.89	20.49	15	21.09	21.69	22.29	22.89	23.49
18.12	18.72	19.32	19 92	20.52	20	21.12	21.72	22.32	22.92	23.52
18.15	18.75	19.35	19.95	20.55	25	21.15	21.75	22.35	22.95	23.55
18.18	18.78	19.38	19.98	20.58	30	21.18	21.78	22.38	22.98	23.58
18.21	18.81	19.41	20.01	20.61	35	21.21	21.81	22.41	23.01	23.61
18.24	18.84	19.44	20.04	20.64	40	21.24	21.84	22.44	23.04	23.64
18.27	18.87	19.47	20.07	20.67	45	21.27	21.87	22.47	23.07	23.67
18.30	18.90	19.50	20.10	20.70	50	21.30	21.90	22.50	23.10	23.70
18.33	18.93	19.53	20.13	20.73	55	21.33	21.93	22.53	23.13	23.73
18.36	18.96	19.56	20.16	20.76	60	21.36	21.96	22.56	23.16	23.76
18.39	18.99	19.59	20.19	20.79	65	21.39	21.99	22.59	23.19	23.79
18.42	19.02	19.62	20.22	20.82	70	21.42	22.02	22.62	23.22	23.82
18.45	19.05	19.65	20.25	20.85	75	21.45	22.05	22.65	23.25	23.85
18.48	19.08	19.68	20.28	20.88	80	21.48	22.08	22.68	23.28	23.88
18.51	19.11	19.71	20.31	20.91	85	21.51	22.11	22.71	23.31	23.91
18.54	19.14	19.74	20.34	20.94	90	21.54	22.14	22.74	23.34	23.94
18.57	19.17	19.77	20.37	20.97	95	21.57	22.17	22.77	23.37	23.97

Even tons, 51 to 100 inclusive.

51-60		61-70		71-80		81-90		91-100	
T	Am't	T	Am't	T	Am't	T	Am't	T	Am't
51	612.00	61	732.00	71	852.00	81	972.00	91	1092.00
52	624.00	62	744.00	72	864.00	82	984.00	92	1104.00
53	636.00	63	756.00	73	876.00	83	996.00	93	1116.00
54	648.00	64	768.00	74	888.00	84	1008.00	94	1128.00
55	660.00	65	780.00	75	900.00	85	1020.00	95	1140.00
56	672.00	66	792.00	76	912.00	86	1032.00	96	1152.00
57	684.00	67	804.00	77	924.00	87	1044.00	97	1164.00
58	696.00	68	816.00	78	936.00	88	1056.00	98	1176.00
59	708.00	69	828.00	79	948.00	89	1068.00	99	1188.00
60	720.00	70	840.00	80	960.00	90	1080.00	100	1200.00

700	8400	800	9600	900	10800	1000	12000	1100	13200

49c a bu.   **$12.25 a T.**   6 1¼c a 100 lbs.
————————————————————————POUNDS————————————————————————

Under 100	100	200	300	400		500	600	700	800	900
	AMOUNT							AMOUNT		
	.61	1.23	1.84	2.45		3.06	3.68	4.29	4.90	5.51
.03	.64	1.26	1.87	2.48	5	3.09	3.71	4.32	4.93	5.54
.06	.67	1.29	1.90	2.51	10	3.12	3.74	4.35	4.96	5.57
.09	.70	1.32	1.93	2.54	15	3.15	3.77	4.38	4.99	5.60
.12	.74	1.35	1.96	2.57	20	3.19	3.80	4.41	5.02	5.64
.15	.77	1.38	1.99	2.60	25	3.22	3.83	4.44	5.05	5.67
.18	.80	1.41	2.02	2.63	30	3.25	3.86	4.47	5.08	5.70
.21	.83	1.44	2.05	2.66	35	3.28	3.89	4.50	5.11	5.73
.25	.86	1.47	2.08	2.70	40	3.31	3.92	4.53	5.15	5.76
.28	.89	1.50	2.11	2.73	45	3.34	3.95	4.56	5.18	5.79
.31	.92	1.53	2.14	2.76	50	3.37	3.98	4.59	5.21	5.82
.34	.95	1.56	2.17	2.79	55	3.40	4.01	4.62	5.24	5.85
.37	.98	1.59	2.21	2.82	60	3.43	4.04	4.66	5.27	5.88
.40	1.01	1.62	2.24	2.85	65	3.46	4.07	4.69	5.30	5.91
.43	1.04	1.65	2.27	2.88	70	3.49	4.10	4.72	5.33	5.94
.46	1.07	1.68	2.30	2.91	75	3.52	4.13	4 75	5.36	5.97
.49	1.10	1.72	2.33	2.94	80	3.55	4.17	4.78	5.39	6.00
.52	1.13	1.75	2.36	2.97	85	3.58	4.20	4.81	5.42	6.03
.55	1.16	1.78	2.39	3.00	90	3.61	4.23	4.84	5.45	6.06
.58	1.19	1.81	2.42	3.03	95	3.64	4.26	4.87	5.48	6.09

————————————————————————POUNDS————————————————————————

1000	1100	1200	1300	1400		1500	1600	1700	1800	1900
	AMOUNT							AMOUNT		
6.13	6.74	7.35	7.96	8.58		9.19	9.80	10.41	11.03	11.64
6.16	6.77	7.38	7.99	8.61	5	9.22	9.83	10.44	11.06	11.67
6.19	6.80	7.41	8.02	8.64	10	9.25	9.86	10.47	11.09	11.70
6.22	6.83	7.44	8.05	8.67	15	9.28	9.89	10.50	11.12	11.73
6.25	6.86	7.47	8.09	8.70	20	9.31	9.92	10.54	11.15	11.76
6.28	6.89	7.50	8.12	8.73	25	9.34	9.95	10.57	11.18	11.79
6.31	6.92	7.53	8.15	8.76	30	9.37	9.98	10.60	11.21	11.82
6.34	6.95	7.56	8.18	8.79	35	9.40	10.01	10.63	11.24	11.85
6.37	6.98	7.60	8.21	8.82	40	9.43	10.05	10.66	11.27	11.88
6.40	7.01	7.63	8.24	8.85	45	9.46	10.08	10.69	11.30	11.91
6.43	7.04	7.66	8.27	8.88	50	9.49	10.11	10.72	11.33	11.94
6.46	7.07	7.69	8.30	8.91	55	9.52	10.14	10.75	11.36	11.97
6.49	7.11	7.72	8.33	8.94	60	9.56	10.17	10.78	11.39	12.01
6.52	7.14	7.75	8.36	8.97	65	9.59	10.20	10.81	11.42	12.04
6.55	7.17	7.78	8.39	9.00	70	9.62	10.23	10.84	11.45	12.07
6.58	7.20	7.81	8.42	9.03	75	9.65	10.26	10.87	11.48	12.10
6.62	7.23	7.84	8.45	9.07	80	9.68	10.29	10.90	11.52	12.13
6.65	7.26	7.87	8.48	9.10	85	9.71	10.32	10.93	11.55	12.16
6.68	7.29	7.90	8.51	9.13	90	9.74	10.35	10.96	11.58	12.19
6.71	7.32	7.93	8.54	9.16	95	9.77	10.38	10.99	11.61	12.22

Even tons, 1 to 50 inclusive.

1-10		11-20		21-30		31-40		41-50	
T	Am't	T	Am't	T	Am't	T	Am't	T	Am't
1	12.25	11	134.75	21	257.25	31	379.75	41	502.25
2	24.50	12	147.00	22	269.50	32	392.00	42	514.50
3	36.75	13	159.25	23	281.75	33	404.25	43	526.75
4	49.00	14	171.50	24	294.00	34	416.50	44	539.00
5	61.25	15	183.75	25	306.25	35	428.75	45	551.25
6	73.50	16	196.00	26	318.50	36	441.00	46	563.50
7	85.75	17	208.25	27	330.75	37	453.25	47	575.75
8	98.00	18	220.50	28	343.00	38	465.50	48	588.00
9	110.25	19	232.75	29	355.25	39	477.75	49	600.25
10	122.50	20	245.00	30	367.50	40	490.00	50	612.50

200	2450	300	3675	400	4900	500	6125	600	7350

——— Pounds ———

2000	2100	2200	2300	2400		2500	2600	2700	2800	2900
12.25	12.86	13.48	14.09	14.70		15.31	15.93	16.54	17.15	17.76
12.28	12.89	13.51	14.12	14.73	5	15.34	15.96	16.57	17.18	17.79
12.31	12.92	13.54	14.15	14.76	10	15.37	15.99	16.60	17.21	17.82
12.34	12.95	13.57	14.18	14.79	15	15.40	16.02	16.63	17.24	17.85
12.37	12.99	13.60	14.21	14.82	20	15.44	16.05	16.66	17.27	17.89
12.40	13.02	13.63	14.24	14.85	25	15.47	16.08	16.69	17.30	17.92
12.43	13.05	13.66	14.27	14.88	30	15.50	16.11	16.72	17.33	17.95
12.46	13.08	13.69	14.30	14.91	35	15.53	16.14	16.75	17.36	17.98
12.50	13.11	13.72	14.33	14.95	40	15.56	16.17	16.78	17.40	18.01
12.53	13.14	13.75	14.36	14.98	45	15.59	16.20	16.81	17.43	18.04
12.56	13.17	13.78	14.39	15.01	50	15.62	16.23	16.84	17.46	18.07
12.59	13.20	13.81	14.42	15.04	55	15.65	16.26	16.87	17.49	18.10
12.62	13.23	13.84	14.46	15.07	60	15.68	16.29	16.91	17.52	18.13
12.65	13.26	13.87	14.49	15.10	65	15.71	16.32	16.94	17.55	18.16
12.68	13.29	13.90	14.52	15.13	70	15.74	16.35	16.97	17.58	18.19
12.71	13.32	13.93	14.55	15.16	75	15.77	16.38	17.00	17.61	18.22
12.74	13.35	13.97	14.58	15.19	80	15.80	16.42	17.03	17.64	18.25
12.77	13.38	14.00	14.61	15.22	85	15.83	16.45	17.06	17.67	18.28
12.80	13.41	14.03	14.64	15.25	90	15.86	16.48	17.09	17.70	18.31
12.83	13.44	14.06	14.67	15.28	95	15.89	16.51	17.12	17.73	18.34

——— Pounds ———

3000	3100	3200	3300	3400		3500	3600	3700	3800	3900
18.38	18.99	19.60	20.21	20.83		21.44	22.05	22.66	23.28	23.89
18.41	19.02	19.63	20.24	20.86	5	21.47	22.08	22.69	23.31	23.91
18.44	19.05	19.66	20.27	20.89	10	21.50	22.11	22.72	23.34	23.95
18.47	19.08	19.69	20.30	20.92	15	21.53	22.14	22.75	23.37	23.98
18.50	19.11	19.72	20.34	20.95	20	21.56	22.17	22.79	23.40	24.01
18.53	19.14	19.75	20.37	20.98	25	21.59	22.20	22.82	23.43	24.04
18.56	19.17	19.78	20.40	21.01	30	21.62	22.23	22.85	23.46	24.07
18.59	19.20	19.81	20.43	21.04	35	21.65	22.26	22.88	23.49	24.10
18.62	19.23	19.85	20.46	21.07	40	21.68	22.30	22.91	23.52	24.13
18.65	19.26	19.88	20.49	21.10	45	21.71	22.33	22.94	23.55	24.16
18.68	19.29	19.91	20.52	21.13	50	21.74	22.36	22.97	23.58	24.19
18.71	19.32	19.94	20.55	21.16	55	21.77	22.39	23.00	23.61	24.22
18.74	19.36	19.97	20.58	21.19	60	21.81	22.42	23.03	23.64	24.26
18.77	19.39	20.00	20.61	21.22	65	21.84	22.45	23.06	23.67	24.29
18.80	19.42	20.03	20.64	21.25	70	21.87	22.48	23.09	23.70	24.32
18.83	19.45	20.06	20.67	21.28	75	21.90	22.51	23.12	23.73	24.35
18.87	19.48	20.09	20.70	21.32	80	21.93	22.54	23.15	23.77	24.38
18.90	19.51	20.12	20.73	21.35	85	21.96	22.57	23.18	23.80	24.41
18.93	19.54	20.15	20.76	21.38	90	21.99	22.60	23.21	23.83	24.44
18.96	19.57	20.18	20.79	21.41	95	22.02	22.63	23.24	23.86	24.47

Even tons, 51 to 100 inclusive.

\	51-60	\	61-70	\	71-80	\	81-90	\	91-100
T	Am't	T	Am't	T	Am't	T	Am't	T	Am't
51	624.75	61	747.25	71	869.75	81	992.25	91	1114.75
52	637.00	62	759.50	72	882.00	82	1004.50	92	1127.00
53	649.25	63	771.75	73	894.25	83	1016.75	93	1139.25
54	661.50	64	784.00	74	906.50	84	1029.00	94	1151.50
55	673.75	65	796.25	75	918.75	85	1041.25	95	1163.75
56	686.00	66	808.50	76	931.00	86	1053.50	96	1176.00
57	698.25	67	820.75	77	943.25	87	1065.75	97	1188.25
58	710.50	68	833.00	78	955.50	88	1078.00	98	1200.50
59	722.75	69	845.25	79	967.75	89	1090.25	99	1212.75
60	735.00	70	857.50	80	980.00	90	1102.50	100	1225.00

700	8575	800	9800	900	11025	1000	12250	1100	13475

50c a bu. **$12.50 a T.** 62½c a 100 lbs.

— POUNDS —

Under 100	100	200	300	400		500	600	700	800	900
	.63	1.25	1.88	2.50		3.13	3.75	4.38	5.00	5.63
.03	.66	1.28	1.91	2.53	5	3.16	3.78	4.41	5.03	5.66
.06	.69	1.31	1.94	2.56	10	3.19	3.81	4.44	5.06	5.69
.09	.72	1.34	1.97	2.59	15	3.22	3.84	4.47	5.09	5.72
.13	.75	1.38	2.00	2.63	20	3.25	3.88	4.50	5.13	5.75
.16	.78	1.41	2.03	2.66	25	3.28	3.91	4.53	5.16	5.78
.19	.81	1.44	2.06	2.69	30	3.31	3.94	4.56	5.19	5.81
.22	.84	1.47	2.09	2.72	35	3.34	3.97	4.59	5.22	5.84
.25	.88	1.50	2.13	2.75	40	3.38	4.00	4.63	5.25	5.88
.28	.91	1.53	2.16	2.78	45	3.41	4.03	4.66	5.28	5.91
.31	.94	1.56	2.19	2.81	50	3.44	4.06	4.69	5.31	5.94
.34	.97	1.59	2.22	2.84	55	3.47	4.09	4.72	5.34	5.97
.38	1.00	1.63	2.25	2.88	60	3.50	4.13	4.75	5.38	6.00
.41	1.03	1.66	2.28	2.91	65	3.53	4.16	4.78	5.41	6.03
.44	1.06	1.69	2.31	2.94	70	3.56	4.19	4.81	5.44	6.06
.47	1.09	1.72	2.34	2.97	75	3.59	4.22	4.84	5.47	6.09
.50	1.13	1.75	2.38	3.00	80	3.63	4.25	4.88	5.50	6.13
.53	1.16	1.78	2.41	3.03	85	3.66	4.28	4.91	5.53	6.16
.56	1.19	1.81	2.44	3.06	90	3.69	4.31	4.94	5.56	6.19
.59	1.22	1.84	2.47	3.09	95	3.72	4.34	4.97	5.59	6.22

— POUNDS —

1000	1100	1200	1300	1400		1500	1600	1700	1800	1900
6.25	6.88	7.50	8.13	8.75		9.38	10.00	10.63	11.25	11.88
6.28	6.91	7.53	8.16	8.78	5	9.41	10.03	10.66	11.28	11.91
6.31	6.94	7.56	8.19	8.81	10	9.44	10.06	10.69	11.31	11.94
6.34	6.97	7.59	8.22	8.84	15	9.47	10.09	10.72	11.34	11.97
6.38	7.00	7.63	8.25	8.88	20	9.50	10.13	10.75	11.38	12.00
6.41	7.03	7.66	8.28	8.91	25	9.53	10.16	10.78	11.41	12.03
6.44	7.06	7.69	8.31	8.94	30	9.56	10.19	10.81	11.44	12.06
6.47	7.09	7.72	8.34	8.97	35	9.59	10.22	10.84	11.47	12.09
6.50	7.13	7.75	8.38	9.00	40	9.63	10.25	10.88	11.50	12.13
6.53	7.16	7.78	8.41	9.03	45	9.66	10.28	10.91	11.53	12.16
6.56	7.19	7.81	8.44	9.06	50	9.69	10.31	10.94	11.56	12.19
6.59	7.22	7.84	8.47	9.09	55	9.72	10.34	10.97	11.59	12.22
6.63	7.25	7.88	8.50	9.13	60	9.75	10.38	11.00	11.63	12.25
6.66	7.28	7.91	8.53	9.16	65	9.78	10.41	11.03	11.66	12.28
6.69	7.31	7.94	8.56	9.19	70	9.81	10.44	11.06	11.69	12.31
6.72	7.34	7.97	8.59	9.22	75	9.84	10.47	11.09	11.72	12.34
6.75	7.38	8.00	8.63	9.25	80	9.88	10.50	11.13	11.75	12.38
6.78	7.41	8.03	8.66	9.28	85	9.91	10.53	11.16	11.78	12.41
6.81	7.44	8.06	8.69	9.31	90	9.94	10.56	11.19	11.81	12.44
6.84	7.47	8.09	8.72	9.34	95	9.97	10.59	11.22	11.84	12.47

Even tons, 1 to 50 inclusive.

1-10 T	Am't	11-20 T	Am't	21-30 T	Am't	31-40 T	Am't	41-50 T	Am't
1	12.50	11	137.50	21	262.50	31	387.50	41	512.50
2	25.00	12	150.00	22	275.00	32	400.00	42	525.00
3	37.50	13	162.50	23	287.50	33	412.50	43	537.50
4	50.00	14	175.00	24	300.00	34	425.00	44	550.00
5	.62.50	15	187.50	25	312.50	35	437.50	45	562.50
6	75.00	16	200.00	26	325.00	36	450.00	46	575.00
7	87.50	17	212.50	27	337.50	37	462.50	47	587.50
8	100.00	18	225.00	28	350.00	38	475.00	48	600.00
9	112.50	19	237.50	29	362.50	39	487.50	49	612.50
10	125.00	20	250.00	30	375.00	40	500.00	50	625.00

200	2500	300	3750	400	5000	500	6250	600	7500

---POUNDS---

2000	2100	2200	2300	2400	lbs	2500	2600	2700	2800	2900
12.50	13.13	13.75	14.38	15.00		15.63	16.25	16.88	17.50	18.13
12.53	13.16	13.78	14.41	15.03	5	15.66	16.28	16.91	17.53	18.16
12.56	13.19	13.81	14.44	15.06	10	15.69	16.31	16.94	17.56	18.19
12.59	13.22	13.84	14.47	15.09	15	15.72	16.34	16.97	17.59	18.22
12.63	13.25	13.88	14.50	15.13	20	15.75	16.38	17.00	17.63	18.25
12.66	13.28	13.91	14.53	15.16	25	15.78	16.41	17.03	17.66	18.28
12.69	13.31	13.94	14.56	15.19	30	15.81	16.44	17.06	17.69	18.31
12.72	13.34	13.97	14.59	15.22	35	15.84	16.47	17.09	17.72	18.34
12.75	13.38	14.00	14.63	15.25	40	15.88	16.50	17.13	17.75	18.38
12.78	13.41	14.03	14.66	15.28	45	15.91	16.53	17.16	17.78	18.41
12.81	13.44	14.06	14.69	15.31	50	15.94	16.56	17.19	17.81	18.44
12.84	13.47	14.09	14.72	15.34	55	15.97	16.59	17.22	17.84	18.47
12.88	13.50	14.13	14.75	15.38	60	16.00	16.63	17.25	17.88	18.50
12.91	13.53	14.16	14.78	15.41	65	16.03	16.66	17.28	17.91	18.53
12.94	13.56	14.19	14.81	15.44	70	16.06	16.69	17.31	17.94	18.56
12.97	13.59	14.22	14.84	15.47	75	16.09	16.72	17.34	17.97	18.59
13.00	13.63	14.25	14.88	15.50	80	16.13	16.75	17.38	18.00	18.63
13.03	13.66	14.28	14.91	15.53	85	16.16	16.78	17.41	18.03	18.66
13.06	13.69	14.31	14.94	15.56	90	16.19	16.81	17.44	18.06	18.69
13.09	13.72	14.34	14.97	15.59	95	16.22	16.84	17.47	18.09	18.72

---POUNDS---

3000	3100	3200	3300	3400	lbs	3500	3600	3700	3800	3900
18.75	19.38	20.00	20.63	21.25		21.88	22.50	23.13	23.75	24.38
18.78	19.41	20.03	20.66	21.28	5	21.91	22.53	23.16	23.78	24.41
18.81	19.44	20.06	20.69	21.31	10	21.94	22.56	23.19	23.81	24.44
18.84	19.47	20.09	20.72	21.34	15	21.97	22.59	23.22	23.84	24.47
18.88	19.50	20.13	20.75	21.38	20	22.00	22.63	23.25	23.88	24.50
18.91	19.53	20.16	20.78	21.41	25	22.03	22.66	23.28	23.91	24.53
18.94	19.56	20.19	20.81	21.44	30	22.06	22.69	23.31	23.94	24.56
18.97	19.59	20.22	20.84	21.47	35	22.09	22.72	23.34	23.97	24.59
19.00	19.63	20.25	20.88	21.50	40	22.13	22.75	23.38	24.00	24.63
19.03	19.66	20.28	20.91	21.53	45	22.16	22.78	23.41	24.03	24.66
19.06	19.69	20.31	20.94	21.56	50	22.19	22.81	23.44	24.06	24.69
19.09	19.72	20.34	20.97	21.59	55	22.22	22.84	23.47	24.09	24.72
19.13	19.75	20.38	21.00	21.63	60	22.25	22.88	23.50	24.13	24.75
19.16	19.78	20.41	21.03	21.66	65	22.28	22.91	23.53	24.16	24.78
19.19	19.81	20.44	21.06	21.69	70	22.31	22.94	23.56	24.19	24.81
19.22	19.84	20.47	21.09	21.72	75	22.34	22.97	23.59	24.22	24.84
19.25	19.88	20.50	21.13	21.75	80	22.38	23.00	23.63	24.25	24.88
19.28	19.91	20.53	21.16	21.78	85	22.41	23.03	23.66	24.28	24.91
19.31	19.94	20.56	21.19	21.81	90	22.44	23.06	23.69	24.31	24.94
19.34	19.97	20.59	21.22	21.84	95	22.47	23.09	23.72	24.34	24.97

Even tons, 51 to 100 inclusive.

51-60	Am't	61-70	Am't	71-80	Am't	81-90	Am't	91-100	Am't
51	637.50	61	762.50	71	887.50	81	1012.50	91	1137.50
52	650.00	62	775.00	72	900.00	82	1025.00	92	1150.00
53	662.50	63	787.50	73	912.50	83	1037.50	93	1162.50
54	675.00	64	800.00	74	925.00	84	1050.00	94	1175.00
55	687.50	65	812.50	75	937.50	85	1062.50	95	1187.50
56	700.00	66	825.00	76	950.00	86	1075.00	96	1200.00
57	712.50	67	837.50	77	962.50	87	1087.50	97	1212.50
58	725.00	68	850.00	78	975.00	88	1100.00	98	1225.00
59	737.50	69	862.50	79	987.50	89	1112.50	99	1237.50
60	750.00	70	875.00	80	1000.00	90	1125.00	100	1250.00
700	8750	800	10000	900	11250	1000	12500	1100	13750

POUNDS

Under 100	100	200	300	400		500	600	700	800	900
		AMOUNT					AMOUNT			
	.64	1.28	1.91	2.55		3.19	3.83	4.46	5.10	5.74
.03	.67	1.31	1.94	2.58	5	3.22	3.86	4.49	5.13	5.77
.06	.70	1.34	1.98	2.61	10	3.25	3.89	4.53	5.16	5.80
.10	.73	1.37	2.01	2.65	15	3.28	3.92	4.56	5.20	5.83
.13	.77	1.40	2.04	2.68	20	3.32	3.95	4.59	5.23	5.87
.16	.80	1.43	2.07	2.71	25	3.35	3.98	4.62	5.26	5.90
.19	.83	1.47	2.10	2.74	30	3.38	4.02	4.65	5.29	5.93
.22	.86	1.50	2.14	2.77	35	3.41	4.05	4.69	5.32	5.96
.26	.89	1.53	2.17	2.81	40	3.44	4.08	4.72	5.36	5.99
.29	.92	1.56	2.20	2.84	45	3.47	4.11	4.75	5.39	6.02
.32	.96	1.59	2.23	2.87	50	3.51	4.14	4.78	5.42	6.06
.35	.99	1.63	2.26	2.90	55	3.54	4.18	4.81	5.45	6.09
.38	1.02	1.66	2.30	2.93	60	3.57	4.21	4.85	5.48	6.12
.41	1.05	1.69	2.33	2.96	65	3.60	4.24	4.88	5.51	6.15
.45	1.08	1.72	2.36	3.00	70	3.63	4.27	4.91	5.55	6.18
.48	1.12	1.75	2.39	3.03	75	3.67	4.30	4.94	5.58	6.22
.51	1.15	1.79	2.42	3.06	80	3.70	4.34	4.97	5.61	6.25
.54	1.18	1.82	2.45	3.09	85	3.73	4.37	5.00	5.64	6.28
.57	1.21	1.85	2.49	3.12	90	3.76	4.40	5.04	5.67	6.31
.61	1.24	1.88	2.52	3.16	95	3.79	4.43	5.07	5.71	6.34

POUNDS

1000	1100	1200	1300	1400		1500	1600	1700	1800	1900
		AMOUNT					AMOUNT			
6.38	7.01	7.65	8.29	8.93		9.56	10.20	10.84	11.48	12.11
6.41	7.04	7.68	8.32	8.96	5	9.59	10.23	10.87	11.51	12.14
6.44	7.08	7.71	8.35	8.99	10	9.63	10.26	10.90	11.54	12.18
6.47	7.11	7.75	8.38	9.02	15	9.66	10.30	10.93	11.57	12.21
6.50	7.14	7.78	8.42	9.05	20	9.69	10.33	10.97	11.60	12.24
6.53	7.17	7.81	8.45	9.08	25	9.72	10.36	11.00	11.63	12.27
6.57	7.20	7.84	8.48	9.12	30	9.75	10.39	11.03	11.67	12.30
6.60	7.24	7.87	8.51	9.15	35	9.79	10.42	11.06	11.70	12.34
6.63	7.27	7.91	8.54	9.18	40	9.82	10.46	11.09	11.73	12.37
6.66	7.30	7.94	8.57	9.21	45	9.85	10.49	11.12	11.76	12.40
6.69	7.33	7.97	8.61	9.24	50	9.88	10.52	11.16	11.79	12.43
6.73	7.36	8.00	8.64	9.28	55	9.91	10.55	11.19	11.83	12.46
6.76	7.40	8.03	8.67	9.31	60	9.95	10.58	11.22	11.86	12.50
6.79	7.43	8.06	8.70	9.34	65	9.98	10.61	11.25	11.89	12.53
6.82	7.46	8.10	8.73	9.37	70	10.01	10.65	11.28	11.92	12.56
6.85	7.49	8.13	8.77	9.40	75	10.04	10.68	11.32	11.95	12.59
6.89	7.52	8.16	8.80	9.44	80	10.07	10.71	11.35	11.99	12.62
6.92	7.55	8.19	8.83	9.47	85	10.10	10.74	11.38	12.02	12.65
6.95	7.59	8.22	8.86	9.50	90	10.14	10.77	11.41	12.05	12.69
6.98	7.62	8.26	8.89	9.53	95	10.17	10.81	11.44	12.08	12.72

Even tons, 1 to 50 inclusive.

	1-10		11-20		21-30		31-40		41-50
T	Am't	T	Am't	T	Am't	T	Am't	T	Am't
1	12.75	11	140.25	21	267.75	31	395.25	41	522.75
2	25.50	12	153.00	22	280.50	32	408.00	42	535.50
3	38.25	13	165.75	23	293.25	33	420.75	43	548.25
4	51.00	14	178.50	24	306.00	34	433.50	44	561.00
5	63.75	15	181.75	25	318.75	35	446.25	45	573.75
6	76.50	16	204.00	26	331.50	36	459.00	46	586.50
7	89.25	17	216.75	27	344.25	37	471.75	47	599.25
8	102.00	18	229.50	28	357.00	38	484.50	48	612.00
9	114.75	19	242.25	29	369.75	39	497.25	49	624.75
10	127.50	20	255.00	30	382.50	40	510.00	50	637.50

200	2550	300	3825	400	5100	509	6375	600	7650

POUNDS

2000	2100	2200	2300	2400		2500	2600	2700	2800	2900
		AMOUNT						AMOUNT		
12.75	13.39	14.03	14.66	15.30		15.94	16.58	17.21	17.85	18.49
12.78	13.42	14.06	14.69	15.33	5	15.97	16.61	17.24	17.88	18.52
12.81	13.45	14.09	14.73	15.36	10	16.00	16.64	17.28	17.91	18.55
12.85	13.48	14.12	14.76	15.40	15	16.03	16.67	17.31	17.95	18.58
12.88	13.52	14.15	14.79	15.43	20	16.07	16.70	17.34	17.98	18.62
12.91	13.55	14.18	14.82	15.46	25	16.10	16.73	17.37	18.01	18.65
12.94	13.58	14.22	14.85	15.49	30	16.13	16.77	17.40	18.04	18.68
12.97	13.61	14.25	14.89	15.52	35	16.16	16.80	17.44	18.07	18.71
13.01	13.64	14.28	14.92	15.56	40	16.19	16.83	17.47	18.11	18.74
13.04	13.67	14.31	14.95	15.59	45	16.22	16.86	17.50	18.14	18.77
13.07	13.71	14.34	14.98	15.62	50	16.26	16.89	17.53	18.17	18.81
13.10	13.74	14.38	15.01	15.65	55	16.29	16.93	17.56	18.20	18.84
13.13	13.77	14.41	15.05	15.68	60	16.32	16.96	17.60	18.23	18.87
13.16	13.80	14.44	15.08	15.71	65	16.35	16.99	17.63	18.26	18.90
13.20	13.83	14.47	15.11	15.75	70	16.38	17.02	17.66	18.30	18.93
13.23	13.87	14.50	15.14	15.78	75	16.42	17.05	17.69	18.33	18.97
13.26	13.90	14.54	15.17	15.81	80	16.45	17.09	17.72	18.36	19.00
13.29	13.93	14.57	15.20	15.84	85	16.48	17.12	17.75	18.39	19.03
13.32	13.96	14.60	15.24	15.87	90	16.51	17.15	17.79	18.42	19.06
13.36	13.99	14.63	15.27	15.91	95	16.54	17.17	17.82	18.46	19.09

POUNDS

3000	3100	3200	3300	3400		3500	3600	3700	3800	3900
		AMOUNT						AMOUNT		
19.13	19.76	20.40	21.04	21.68		22.31	22.95	23.59	24.23	24.86
19.16	19.79	20.43	21.07	21.71	5	22.34	22.98	23.62	24.26	24.89
19.19	19.83	20.46	21.10	21.74	10	22.38	23.01	23.65	24.29	24.93
19.22	19.86	20.50	21.13	21.77	15	22.41	23.05	23.68	24.32	24.96
19.25	19.89	20.53	21.17	21.80	20	22.44	23.08	23.72	24.35	24.99
19.28	19.92	20.56	21.20	21.83	25	22.47	23.11	23.75	24.38	25.02
19.32	19.95	20.59	21.23	21.87	30	22.50	23.14	23.78	24.42	25.05
19.35	19.99	20.62	21.26	21.90	35	22.54	23.17	23.81	24.45	25.09
19.38	20.02	20.66	21.29	21.93	40	22.57	23.21	23.84	24.48	25.12
19.41	20.05	20.69	21.32	21.96	45	22.60	23.24	23.87	24.51	25.15
19.44	20.08	20.72	21.36	21.99	50	22.63	23.27	23.91	24.54	25.18
19.48	20.11	20.75	21.39	22.03	55	22.66	23.30	23.94	24.58	25.21
19.51	20.15	20.78	21.42	22.06	60	22.70	23.33	23.97	24.61	25.25
19.54	20.18	20.81	21.45	22.09	65	22.73	23.36	24.00	24.64	25.28
19.57	20.21	20.85	21.48	22.12	70	22.76	23.40	24.03	24.67	25.31
19.60	20.24	20.88	21.52	22.15	75	22.79	23.43	24.07	24.70	25.34
19.64	20.27	20.91	21.55	22.19	80	22.82	23.46	24.10	24.74	25.37
19.67	20.30	20.94	21.58	22.22	85	22.85	23.49	24.13	24.77	25.40
19.70	20.34	20.97	21.61	22.25	90	22.89	23.52	24.16	24.80	25.44
19.73	20.37	21.01	21.64	22.28	95	22.92	23.56	24.19	24.83	25.47

Even tons, 51 to 100 inclusive.

51-60		61-70		71-80		81-90		91-100	
T	Am't	T	Am't	T	Am't	T	Am't	T	Am't
51	650.25	61	777.75	71	905.25	81	1032.75	91	1160.25
52	663.00	62	790.50	72	918.00	82	1045.50	92	1173.00
53	675.75	63	803.25	73	930.75	83	1058.25	93	1185.75
54	688.50	64	816.00	74	943.50	84	1071.00	94	1198.50
55	701.25	65	828.75	75	956.25	85	1083.75	95	1211.25
56	714.00	66	841.50	76	969.00	86	1096.50	96	1224.00
57	726.75	67	854.25	77	981.75	87	1109.25	97	1236.75
58	739.50	68	867.00	78	994.50	88	1122.00	98	1249.50
59	752.25	69	879.75	79	1007.25	89	1134.75	99	1262.25
60	765.00	70	892.50	80	1020.00	90	1147.50	100	1275.00

700	8925	800	10200	900	11475	1000	12750	1100	14025

POUNDS

Under 100	100	200	300	400		500	600	700	800	900
		AMOUNT						AMOUNT		
	.65	1.30	1.95	2.60		3.25	3.90	4.55	5.20	5.85
.03	.68	1.33	1.98	2.63	5	3.28	3.93	4.58	5.23	5.88
.07	.72	1.37	2.02	2.67	10	3.32	3.97	4.62	5.27	5.92
.10	.75	1.40	2.05	2.70	15	3.35	4.00	4.65	5.30	5.95
.13	.78	1.43	2.08	2.73	20	3.38	4.03	4.68	5.33	5.98
.16	.81	1.46	2.11	2.76	25	3.41	4.06	4.71	5.36	6.01
.20	.85	1.50	2.15	2.80	30	3.45	4.10	4.75	5.40	6.05
.23	.88	1.53	2.18	2.83	35	3.48	4.13	4.78	5.43	6.08
.26	.91	1.56	2.21	2.86	40	3.51	4.16	4.81	5.46	6.11
.29	.94	1.59	2.24	2.89	45	3.54	4.19	4.84	5.49	6.14
.33	.98	1.63	2.28	2.93	50	3.58	4.23	4.88	5.53	6.18
.36	1.01	1.66	2.31	2.96	55	3.61	4.26	4.91	5.56	6.21
.39	1.04	1.69	2.34	2.99	60	3.64	4.29	4.94	5.59	6.24
.42	1.07	1.72	2.37	3.02	65	3.67	4.32	4.97	5.62	6.27
.46	1.11	1.76	2.41	3.06	70	3.71	4.36	5.01	5.66	6.31
.49	1.14	1.79	2.44	3.09	75	3.74	4.39	5.04	5.69	6.34
.52	1.17	1.82	2.47	3.12	80	3.77	4.42	5.07	5.72	6.37
.55	1.20	1.85	2.50	3.15	85	3.80	4.45	5.10	5.75	6.40
.59	1.24	1.89	2.54	3.19	90	3.84	4.49	5.14	5.79	6.44
.62	1.27	1.92	2.57	3.22	95	3.87	4.52	5.17	5.82	6.47

POUNDS

1000	1100	1200	1300	1400		1500	1600	1700	1800	1900
		AMOUNT						AMOUNT		
6.50	7.15	7.80	8.45	9.10		9.75	10.40	11.05	11.70	12.35
6.53	7.18	7.83	8.48	9.13	5	9.78	10.43	11.08	11.73	12.38
6.57	7.22	7.87	8.52	9.17	10	9.82	10.47	11.12	11.77	12.42
6.60	7.25	7.90	8.55	9.20	15	9.85	10.50	11.15	11.80	12.45
6.63	7.28	7.93	8.58	9.23	20	9.88	10.53	11.18	11.83	12.48
6.66	7.31	7.96	8.61	9.26	25	9.91	10.56	11.21	11.86	12.51
6.70	7.35	8.00	8.65	9.30	30	9.95	10.60	11.25	11.90	12.55
6.73	7.38	8.03	8.68	9.33	35	9.98	10.63	11.28	11.93	12.58
6.76	7.41	8.06	8.71	9.36	40	10.01	10.66	11.31	11.96	12.61
6.79	7.44	8.09	8.74	9.39	45	10.04	10.69	11.34	11.99	12.64
6.83	7.48	8.13	8.78	9.43	50	10.08	10.73	11.38	12.03	12.68
6.86	7.51	8.16	8.81	9.46	55	10.11	10.76	11.41	12.06	12.71
6.89	7.54	8.19	8.84	9.49	60	10.14	10.79	11.44	12.09	12.74
6.92	7.57	8.22	8.87	9.52	65	10.17	10.82	11.47	12.12	12.77
6.96	7.61	8.26	8.91	9.56	70	10.21	10.86	11.51	12.16	12.81
6.99	7.64	8.29	8.94	9.59	75	10.24	10.89	11.54	12.19	12.84
7.02	7.67	8.32	8.97	9.62	80	10.27	10.92	11.57	12.22	12.87
7.05	7.70	8.35	9.00	9.65	85	10.30	10.95	11.60	12.25	12.90
7.09	7.74	8.39	9.04	9.69	90	10.34	10.99	11.64	12.29	12.94
7.12	7.77	8.42	9.07	9.72	95	10.37	11.02	11.67	12.32	12.97

Even tons, 1 to 50 inclusive.

1-10		11-20		21-30		31-40		41-50	
T	Am't	T	Am't	T	Am't	T	Am't	T	Am't
1	13.00	11	143.00	21	273.00	31	403.00	41	533.00
2	26.00	12	156.00	22	286.00	32	416.00	42	546.00
3	39.00	13	169.00	23	299.00	33	429.00	43	559.00
4	52.00	14	182.00	24	312.00	34	442.00	44	572.00
5	65.00	15	195.00	25	325.00	35	455.00	45	585.00
6	78.00	16	208.00	26	338.00	36	468.00	46	598.00
7	91.00	17	221.00	27	351.00	37	481.00	47	611.00
8	104.00	18	234.00	28	364.00	38	494.00	48	624.00
9	117.00	19	247.00	29	377.00	39	507.00	49	637.00
10	130.00	20	260.00	30	390.00	40	520.00	50	650.00

200	2600	300	3900	400	5200	500	6500	600	7800

POUNDS

2000	2100	2200	2300	2400		2500	2600	2700	2800	2900
		AMOUNT						AMOUNT		
13.00	13.65	14.30	14.95	15.60		16.25	16.90	17.55	18.20	18.85
13.03	13.68	14.33	14.98	15.63	5	16.28	16.93	17.58	18.23	18.88
13.07	13.72	14.37	15.02	15.67	10	16.32	16.97	17.62	18.27	18.92
13.10	13.75	14.40	15.05	15.70	15	16.35	17.00	17.65	18.30	18.95
13.13	13.78	14.43	15.08	15.73	20	16.38	17.03	17.68	18.33	18.98
13.16	13.81	14.46	15.11	15.76	25	16.41	17.06	17.71	18.36	19.01
13.20	13.85	14.50	15.15	15.80	30	16.45	17.10	17.75	18.40	19.05
13.23	13.88	14.53	15.18	15.83	35	16.48	17.13	17.78	18.43	19.08
13.26	13.91	14.56	15.21	15.86	40	16.51	17.16	17.81	18.46	19.11
13.29	13.94	14.59	15.24	15.89	45	16.54	17.19	17.84	18.49	19.14
13.33	13.98	14.63	15.28	15.93	50	16.58	17.23	17.88	18.53	19.18
13.36	14.01	14.66	15.31	15.96	55	16.61	17.26	17.91	18.56	19.21
13.39	14.04	14.69	15.34	15.99	60	16.64	17.29	17.94	18.59	19.24
13.42	14.07	14.72	15.37	16.02	65	16.67	17.32	17.97	18.62	19.27
13.46	14.11	14.76	15.41	16.06	70	16.71	17.36	18.01	18.66	19.31
13.49	14.14	14.79	15.44	16.09	75	16.74	17.39	18.04	18.69	19.34
13.52	14.17	14.82	15.47	16.12	80	16.77	17.42	18.07	18.72	19.37
13.55	14.20	14.85	15.50	16.15	85	16.80	17.45	18.10	18.75	19.40
13.59	14.24	14.89	15.54	16.19	90	16.84	17.49	18.14	18.79	19.44
13.62	14.27	14.92	15.57	16.22	95	16.87	17.52	18.17	18.82	19.47

POUNDS

3000	3100	3200	3300	3400		3500	3600	3700	3800	3900
		AMOUNT						AMOUNT		
19.50	20.15	20.80	21.45	22.10		22.75	23.40	24.05	24.70	25.35
19.53	20.18	20.83	21.48	22.13	5	22.78	23.43	24.08	24.73	25.38
19.57	20.22	20.87	21.52	22.17	10	22.82	23.47	24.12	24.77	25.42
19.60	20.25	20.90	21.55	22.20	15	22.85	23.50	24.15	24.80	25.45
19.63	20.28	20.93	21.58	22.23	20	22.88	23.53	24.18	24.83	25.48
19.66	20.31	20.96	21.61	22.26	25	22.91	23.56	24.21	24.86	25.51
19.70	20.35	21.00	21.65	22.30	30	22.95	23.60	24.25	24.90	25.55
19.73	20.38	21.03	21.68	22.33	35	22.98	23.63	24.28	24.93	25.58
19.76	20.41	21.06	21.71	22.36	40	23.01	23.66	24.31	24.96	25.61
19.79	20.44	21.09	21.74	22.39	45	23.04	23.69	24.34	24.99	25.64
19.83	20.48	21.13	21.78	22.43	50	23.08	23.73	24.38	25.03	25.68
19.86	20.51	21.16	21.81	22.46	55	23.11	23.76	24.41	25.06	25.71
19.89	20.54	21.19	21.84	22.49	60	23.14	23.79	24.44	25.09	25.74
19.92	20.57	21.22	21.87	22.52	65	23.17	23.82	24.47	25.12	25.77
19.96	20.61	21.26	21.91	22.56	70	23.21	23.86	24.51	25.16	25.81
19.99	20.64	21.29	21.94	22.59	75	23.24	23.89	24.54	25.19	25.84
20.02	20.67	21.32	21.97	22.62	80	23.27	23.92	24.57	25.22	25.87
20.05	20.70	21.35	22.00	22.65	85	23.30	23.95	24.60	25.25	25.90
20.09	20.74	21.39	22.04	22.69	90	23.34	23.99	24.64	25.29	25.94
20.12	20.77	21.42	22.07	22.72	95	23.37	24.02	24.67	25.32	25.97

Even tons, 51 to 100 inclusive.

51-60		61-70		71-80		81-90		91-100	
T	Am't	T	Am't	T	Am't	T	Am't	T	Am't
51	663.00	61	793.00	71	923.00	81	1053.00	91	1183.00
52	676.00	62	806.00	72	936.00	82	1066.00	92	1196.00
53	689.00	63	819.00	73	949.00	83	1079.00	93	1209.00
54	702.00	64	832.00	74	962.00	84	1092.00	94	1222.00
55	715.00	65	845.00	75	975.00	85	1105.00	95	1235.00
56	728.00	66	858.00	76	988.00	86	1118.00	96	1248.00
57	741.00	67	871.00	77	1001.00	87	1131.00	97	1261.00
58	754.00	68	884.00	78	1014.00	88	1144.00	98	1274.00
59	767.00	69	897.00	79	1027.00	89	1157.00	99	1287.00
60	780.00	70	910.00	80	1040.00	90	1170.00	100	1300.00

700	9100	800	10400	900	11700	1000	13000	1100	14300

POUNDS

Under 100	100	200	300	400		500	600	700	800	900
	AMOUNT						AMOUNT			
	.66	1.33	1.99	2.65		3.31	3.98	4.64	5.30	5.96
.03	.70	1.36	2.02	2.68	5	3.35	4.01	4.67	5.33	6.00
.07	.73	1.39	2.05	2.72	10	3.38	4.04	4.70	5.37	6.03
.10	.76	1.42	2.09	2.75	15	3.41	4.07	4.74	5.40	6.06
.13	.80	1.46	2.12	2.78	20	3.45	4.11	4.77	5.43	6.10
.17	.83	1.49	2.15	2.82	25	3.48	4.14	4.80	5.47	6.13
.20	.86	1.52	2.19	2.85	30	3.51	4.17	4.84	5.50	6.16
.23	.89	1.56	2.22	2.88	35	3.54	4.21	4.87	5.53	6.19
.27	.93	1.59	2.25	2.92	40	3.58	4.24	4.90	5.57	6.23
.30	.96	1.62	2.29	2.95	45	3.61	4.27	4.94	5.60	6.26
.33	.99	1.66	2.32	2.98	50	3.64	4.31	4.97	5.63	6.29
.36	1.03	1.69	2.35	3.01	55	3.68	4.34	5.00	5.66	6.33
.40	1.06	1.72	2.39	3.05	60	3.71	4.37	5.04	5.70	6.36
.43	1.09	1.76	2.42	3.08	65	3.74	4.41	5.07	5.73	6.39
.46	1.13	1.79	2.45	3.11	70	3.78	4.44	5.10	5.76	6.43
.50	1.16	1.82	2.48	3.15	75	3.81	4.47	5.13	5.80	6.46
.53	1.19	1.86	2.52	3.18	80	3.84	4.51	5.17	5.83	6.49
.56	1.23	1.89	2.55	3.21	85	3.88	4.54	5.20	5.86	6.53
.60	1.26	1.92	2.58	3.25	90	3.91	4.57	5.23	5.90	6.56
.63	1.29	1.95	2.62	3.28	95	3.94	4.60	5.27	5.93	6.59

POUNDS

1000	1100	1200	1300	1400		1500	1600	1700	1800	1900
	AMOUNT						AMOUNT			
6.63	7.29	7.95	8.61	9.28		9.94	10.60	11.26	11.93	12.59
6.66	7.32	7.98	8.65	9.31	5	9.97	10.63	11.30	11.96	12.62
6.69	7.35	8.02	8.68	9.34	10	10.00	10.67	11.33	11.99	12.65
6.72	7.39	8.05	8.71	9.37	15	10.04	10.70	11.36	12.02	12.69
6.76	7.42	8.08	8.75	9.41	20	10.07	10.73	11.40	12.06	12.72
6.79	7.45	8.12	8.78	9.44	25	10.10	10.77	11.43	12.09	12.75
6.82	7.49	8.15	8.81	9.47	30	10.14	10.80	11.46	12.12	12.79
6.86	7.52	8.18	8.84	9.51	35	10.17	10.83	11.49	12.16	12.82
6.89	7.55	8.22	8.88	9.54	40	10.20	10.87	11.53	12.19	12.85
6.92	7.59	8.25	8.91	9.57	45	10.24	10.90	11.56	12.22	12.89
6.96	7.62	8.28	8.94	9.61	50	10.27	10.93	11.59	12.26	12.92
6.99	7.65	8.31	8.98	9.64	55	10.30	10.96	11.63	12.29	12.95
7.02	7.69	8.35	9.01	9.67	60	10.34	11.00	11.66	12.32	12.99
7.06	7.72	8.38	9.04	9.71	65	10.37	11.03	11.69	12.36	13.02
7.09	7.75	8.41	9.08	9.74	70	10.40	11.06	11.73	12.39	13.05
7.12	7.78	8.45	9.11	9.77	75	10.43	11.10	11.76	12.42	13.08
7.16	7.82	8.48	9.14	9.81	80	10.47	11.13	11.79	12.46	13.12
7.19	7.85	8.51	9.18	9.84	85	10.50	11.16	11.83	12.49	13.15
7.22	7.88	8.55	9.21	9.87	90	10.53	11.20	11.86	12.52	13.18
7.25	7.92	8.58	9.24	9.90	95	10.57	11.23	11.89	12.55	13.22

Even tons, 1 to 50 inclusive.

1-10		11-20		21-30		31-40		41-50	
T	Am't	T	Am't	T	Am't	T	Am't	T	Am't
1	13.25	11	145.75	21	278.25	31	410.75	41	543.25
2	26.50	12	159.00	22	291.50	32	424.00	42	556.50
3	39.75	13	172.25	23	304.75	33	437.25	43	569.75
4	53.00	14	185.50	24	318.00	34	450.50	44	583.00
5	66.25	15	198.75	25	331.25	35	463.75	45	596.25
6	79.50	16	212.00	26	344.50	36	477.00	46	609.50
7	92.75	17	225.25	27	357.75	37	490.25	47	622.75
8	106.00	18	238.50	28	371.00	38	503.50	48	636.00
9	119.25	19	251.75	29	384.25	39	516.75	49	649.25
10	132.50	20	265.00	30	397.50	40	530.00	50	662.50
200	2650	300	3975	400	5300	500	6625	600	7950

—POUNDS—

2000	2100	2200	2300	2400		2500	2600	2700	2800	2900
—AMOUNT—						—AMOUNT—				
13.25	13.91	14.58	15.24	15.90		16.56	17.23	17.89	18.55	19.21
13.28	13.95	14.61	15.27	15.93	5	16.60	17.26	17.92	18.58	19.25
13.32	13.98	14.64	15.30	15.97	10	16.63	17.29	17.95	18.62	19.28
13.35	14.01	14.67	15.34	16.00	15	16.66	17.32	17.99	18.65	19.31
13.38	14.05	14.71	15.37	16.03	20	16.70	17.36	18.02	18.68	19.35
13.42	14.08	14.74	15.40	16.07	25	16.73	17.39	18.05	18.72	19.38
13.45	14.11	14.77	15.44	16.10	30	16.76	17.42	18.09	18.75	19.41
13.48	14.14	14.81	15.47	16.13	35	16.79	17.46	18.12	18.78	19.44
13.52	14.18	14.84	15.50	16.17	40	16.83	17.49	18.15	18.82	19.48
13.55	14.21	14.87	15.54	16.20	45	16.86	17.52	18.19	18.85	19.51
13.58	14.24	14.91	15.57	16.23	50	16.89	17.56	18.22	18.88	19.54
13.61	14.28	14.94	15.60	16.26	55	16.93	17.59	18.25	18.91	19.58
13.65	14.31	14.97	15.64	16.30	60	16.96	17.62	18.29	18.95	19.61
13.68	14.34	15.01	15.67	16.33	65	16.99	17.66	18.32	18.98	19.64
13.71	14.38	15.04	15.70	16.36	70	17.03	17.69	18.35	19.01	19.68
13.75	14.41	15.07	15.73	16.40	75	17.06	17.72	18.38	19.05	19.71
13.78	14.44	15.11	15.77	16.43	80	17.09	17.76	18.42	19.08	19.74
13.81	14.48	15.14	15.80	16.46	85	17.13	17.79	18.45	19.11	19.78
13.85	14.51	15.17	15.83	16.50	90	17.16	17.82	18.48	19.15	19.81
13.88	14.54	15.20	15.87	16.53	95	17.19	17.85	18.52	19.18	19.84

—POUNDS—

3000	3100	3200	3300	3400		3500	3600	3700	3800	3900
—AMOUNT—						—AMOUNT—				
19.88	20.54	21.20	21.86	22.53		23.19	23.85	24.51	25.18	25.84
19.91	20.57	21.23	21.90	22.56	5	23.22	23.88	24.55	25.21	25.87
19.94	20.60	21.27	21.93	22.59	10	23.25	23.92	24.58	25.24	25.90
19.97	20.64	21.30	21.96	22.62	15	23.29	23.95	24.61	25.27	25.94
20.01	20.67	21.33	22.00	22.66	20	23.32	23.98	24.65	25.31	25.97
20.04	20.70	21.37	22.03	22.69	25	23.35	24.02	24.68	25.34	26.00
20.07	20.74	21.40	22.06	22.72	30	23.39	24.05	24.71	25.37	26.04
20.11	20.77	21.43	22.09	22.76	35	23.42	24.08	24.74	25.41	26.07
20.14	20.80	21.47	22.13	22.79	40	23.45	24.12	24.78	25.44	26.10
20.17	20.84	21.50	22.16	22.82	45	23.49	24.15	24.81	25.47	26.14
20.21	20.87	21.53	22.19	22.86	50	23.52	24.18	24.84	25.51	26.17
20.24	20.90	21.56	22.23	22.89	55	23.55	24.21	24.88	25.54	26.20
20.27	20.94	21.60	22.26	22.92	60	23.59	24.25	24.91	25.57	26.24
20.31	20.97	21.63	22.29	22.96	65	23.62	24.28	24.94	25.61	26.27
20.34	21.00	21.66	22.33	22.99	70	23.65	24.31	24.98	25.64	26.30
20.37	21.03	21.70	22.36	23.02	75	23.68	24.35	25.01	25.67	26.33
20.41	21.07	21.73	22.39	23.06	80	23.72	24.38	25.04	25.71	26.37
20.44	21.10	21.76	22.43	23.09	85	23.75	24.41	25.08	25.74	26.40
20.47	21.13	21.80	22.46	23.12	90	23.78	24.45	25.11	25.77	26.43
20.50	21.17	21.83	22.49	23.15	95	23.82	24.48	25.14	25.80	26.47

Even tons, 51 to 100 inclusive.

51-60		61-70		71-80		81-90		91-100	
T	Am't	T	Am't	T	Am't	T	Am't	T	Am't
51	675.75	61	808.25	71	940.75	81	1073.25	91	1205.75
52	689.00	62	821.50	72	954.00	82	1086.50	92	1219.00
53	702.25	63	834.75	73	967.25	83	1099.75	93	1232.25
54	715.50	64	848.00	74	980.50	84	1113.00	94	1245.50
55	728.75	65	861.25	75	993.75	85	1126.25	95	1258.75
56	742.00	66	874.50	76	1007.00	86	1139.50	96	1272.00
57	755.25	67	887.75	77	1020.25	87	1152.75	97	1285.25
58	768.50	68	901.00	78	1033.50	88	1166.00	98	1298.50
59	781.75	69	914.25	79	1046.75	89	1179.25	99	1311.75
60	795.00	70	927.50	80	1060.00	90	1192.50	100	1325.00

700	9275	800	10600	900	11925	1000	13250	1100	14575

POUNDS

Under 100	100	200	300	400		500	600	700	800	900
	.68	1.35	2.03	2.70		3.38	4.05	4.73	5.40	6.08
.03	.71	1.38	2.06	2.73	5	3.41	4.08	4.76	5.43	6.11
.07	.74	1.42	2.09	2.77	10	3.44	4.12	4.79	5.47	6.14
.10	.78	1.45	2.13	2.80	15	3.48	4.15	4.83	5.50	6.18
.14	.81	1.49	2.16	2.84	20	3.51	4.19	4.86	5.54	6.21
.17	.84	1.52	2.19	2.87	25	3.54	4.22	4.89	5.57	6.24
.20	.88	1.55	2.23	2.90	30	3.58	4.25	4.93	5.60	6.28
.24	.91	1.59	2.26	2.94	35	3.61	4.29	4.96	5.64	6.31
.27	.95	1.62	2.30	2.97	40	3.65	4.32	5.00	5.67	6.35
.30	.98	1.65	2.33	3.00	45	3.68	4.35	5.03	5.70	6.38
.34	1.01	1.69	2.36	3.04	50	3.71	4.39	5.06	5.74	6.41
.37	1.05	1.72	2.40	3.07	55	3.75	4.42	5.10	5.77	6.45
.41	1.08	1.76	2.43	3.11	60	3.78	4.46	5.13	5.81	6.48
.44	1.11	1.79	2.46	3.14	65	3.81	4.49	5.16	5.84	6.51
.47	1.15	1.82	2.50	3.17	70	3.85	4.52	5.20	5.87	6.55
.51	1.18	1.86	2.53	3.21	75	3.88	4.56	5.23	5.91	6.58
.54	1.22	1.89	2.57	3 24	80	3.92	4.59	5.27	5.94	6.62
.57	1.25	1.92	2.60	3.27	85	3.95	4.62	5.30	5.97	6.65
.61	1.28	1.96	2.63	3.31	90	3.98	4.66	5.33	6.01	6.68
.64	1.32	1.99	2.67	3.34	95	4.02	4.69	5.37	6.04	6.72

POUNDS

1000	1100	1200	1300	1400		1500	1600	1700	1800	1900
6.75	7.43	8.10	8.78	9.45		10.13	10.80	11.48	12.15	12.83
6.78	7.46	8.13	8.81	9.48	5	10.16	10.83	11.51	12.18	12.86
6.82	7.49	8.17	8.84	9.52	10	10.19	10.87	11.54	12.22	12.89
6.85	7.53	8.20	8.88	9.55	15	10.23	10 90	11.58	12.25	12.93
6.89	7.56	8.24	8.91	9.50	20	10.26	10.94	11.61	12.29	12.96
6.92	7.59	8.27	8.94	9.62	25	10.29	10.97	11.64	12.32	12.99
6.95	7.63	8.30	8.98	9.65	30	10.33	11.00	11.68	12.35	13.03
6.99	7.66	8.34	9.01	9.69	35	10.36	11.04	11.71	12.39	13.06
7.02	7.70	8.37	9.05	9.72	40	10.40	11.07	11.75	12.42	13.10
7.05	7.73	8.40	9.08	9.75	45	10.43	11.10	11.78	12.45	13.13
7.09	7.76	8.44	9.11	9.79	50	10.46	11.14	11.81	12.49	13.16
7.12	7.80	8.47	9.15	9.82	55	10.50	11.17	11.85	12.52	13.20
7.16	7.83	8.51	9.18	9.86	60	10.53	11.21	11.88	12.56	13.23
7.19	7.86	8.54	9.21	9.89	65	10.56	11.24	11.91	12.59	13.26
7.22	7.90	8.57	9.25	9.92	70	10.60	11.27	11.95	12.62	13.30
7.26	7.93	8.61	9.28	9.96	75	10.63	11.31	11.98	12.66	13.33
7.29	7.97	8.64	9.32	9.99	80	10.67	11.34	12.02	12.69	13.37
7.32	8.00	8.67	9.35	10.02	85	10.70	11.37	12.05	12.72	13.40
7.36	8.03	8.71	9.38	10.06	90	10.73	11.41	12.08	12.76	13.43
7.39	8.07	8.74	9.42	10.09	95	10.77	11.44	12.12	12.79	13.47

Even tons, 1 to 50 inclusive.

1-10		11-20		21-30		31-40		41-50	
T	Am't	T	Am't	T	Am't	T	Am't	T	Am't
1	13.50	11	148.50	21	283.50	31	418.50	41	553.50
2	27.00	12	162.00	22	297.00	32	432.00	42	567.00
3	40.50	13	175.50	23	310.50	33	445.50	43	580.50
4	54.00	14	189.00	24	324.00	34	459.00	44	594.00
5	67.50	15	202.50	25	337.50	35	472.50	45	607.50
6	81.00	16	216.00	26	351.00	36	486.00	46	621.00
7	94.50	17	229.50	27	364.50	37	499.50	47	634.50
8	108.00	18	243.00	28	378.00	38	513.00	48	648.00
9	121.50	19	256.50	29	391.50	39	526.50	49	661.50
10	135.00	20	270.00	30	405.00	40	540.00	50	675.00

200	2700	300	4050	400	5400	500	6750	600	8100

— POUNDS —

2000	2100	2200	2300	2400		2500	2600	2700	2800	2900
		AMOUNT						AMOUNT		
13.50	14.18	14.85	15.53	16.20		16.88	17.55	18.23	18.90	19.58
13.53	14.21	14.88	15.56	16.23	5	16.91	17.58	18.26	18.93	19.61
13.57	14.24	14.92	15.59	16.27	10	16.94	17.62	18.29	18.97	19.64
13.60	14.28	14.95	15.63	16.30	15	16.98	17.65	18.33	19.00	19.68
13.64	14.31	14.99	15.66	16.34	20	17.01	17.69	18.36	19.04	19.71
13.67	14.34	15.02	15.69	16.37	25	17.04	17.72	18.39	19.07	19.74
13.70	14.38	15.05	15.73	16.40	30	17.08	17.75	18.43	19.10	19.78
13.74	14.41	15.09	15.76	16.44	35	17.11	17.79	18.46	19.14	19.81
13.77	14.45	15.12	15.80	16.47	40	17.15	17.82	18.50	19.17	19.85
13.80	14.48	15.15	15.83	16.50	45	17.18	17.85	18.53	19.20	19.88
13.84	14.51	15.19	15.86	16.54	50	17.21	17.89	18.56	19.24	19.91
13.87	14.55	15.22	15.90	16.57	55	17.25	17.92	18.60	19.27	19.95
13.91	14.58	15.26	15.93	16.61	60	17.28	17.96	18.63	19.31	19.98
13.94	14.61	15.29	15.96	16.64	65	17.31	17.99	18.66	19.34	20.01
13.97	14.65	15.32	16.00	16.67	70	17.35	18.02	18.70	19.37	20.05
14.01	14.68	15.36	16.03	16.71	75	17.38	18.06	18.73	19.41	20.08
14.04	14.72	15.39	16.07	16.74	80	17.42	18.09	18.77	19.44	20.12
14.07	14.75	15.42	16.10	16.77	85	17.45	18.12	18.80	19.47	20.15
14.11	14.78	15.46	16.13	16.81	90	17.48	18.16	18.83	19.51	20.18
14.14	14.82	15.49	16.17	16.84	95	17.52	18.19	18.87	19.54	20.22

— POUNDS —

3000	3100	3200	3300	3400		3500	3600	3700	3800	3900
		AMOUNT						AMOUNT		
20.25	20.93	21.60	22.28	22.95		23.63	24.30	24.98	25.65	26.33
20.28	20.96	21.63	22.31	22.98	5	23.66	24.33	25.01	25.68	26.36
20.32	20.99	21.67	22.34	23.02	10	23.69	24.37	25.04	25.72	26.39
20.35	21.03	21.70	22.38	23.05	15	23.73	24.40	25.08	25.75	26.43
20.39	21.06	21.74	22.41	23.09	20	23.76	24.44	25.11	25.79	26 46
20.42	21.09	21.77	22.44	23.12	25	23.79	24.47	25.14	25.82	26.49
20.45	21.13	21.80	22.48	23.15	30	23.83	24.50	25.18	25.85	26.53
20.49	21.16	21.84	22.51	23.19	35	23.86	24.54	25.21	25.89	26.56
20.52	21.20	21.87	22.55	23.22	40	23.90	24.57	25.25	25.92	26.60
20.55	21.23	21.90	22.58	23.25	45	23.93	24.60	25.28	25.95	26.63
20.59	21.26	21.94	22.61	23.29	50	23.96	24.64	25.31	25.99	26.66
20.62	21.30	21.97	22.65	23.32	55	24.00	24.67	25.35	26.02	26.70
29.66	21.33	22.01	22.68	23.36	60	24.03	24.71	25.38	26.06	26.73
20.69	21.36	22.04	22.71	23.39	65	24.06	24.74	25.41	26.09	26.76
20.72	21.40	22.07	22.75	23.42	70	24.10	24.77	25.45	26.12	26.80
20.76	21.43	22.11	22.78	23.46	75	24.13	24.81	25.48	26.16	26.83
20.79	21.47	22.14	22.82	23.49	80	24.17	24.84	25.52	26.19	26.87
20.82	21.50	22.17	22.85	23.52	85	24.20	24.87	25.55	26.22	26.90
20.86	21.53	22.21	22.88	23.56	90	24.23	24.91	25.58	26.26	26.93
20.89	21.57	22.24	22.92	23.59	95	24.27	24.94	25.62	26.29	26.97

Even tons, 51 to 100 inclusive.

51-60		61-70		71-80		81-90		91-100	
T	Am't	T	Am't	T	Am't	T	Am't	T	Am't
51	688.50	61	823.50	71	958.50	81	1093.50	91	1228.50
52	702.00	62	837.00	72	972.00	82	1107.00	92	1242.00
53	715.50	63	850.50	73	985.50	83	1120.50	93	1255.50
54	729.00	64	864.00	74	999.00	84	1134.00	94	1269.00
55	742.50	65	877.50	75	1012.50	85	1147.50	95	1282.50
56	756.00	66	891.00	76	1026.00	86	1161.00	96	1296.00
57	769.50	67	904.50	77	1039.50	87	1174.50	97	1309.50
58	783.00	68	918.00	78	1053.00	88	1188.00	98	1323.00
59	796.50	69	931.50	79	1066.50	89	1201.50	99	1336.50
60	810.00	70	945.00	80	1080.00	90	1215.00	100	1350.00

700	9450	800	10800	900	12150	1000	13500	1100	14850

— POUNDS —

Under 100	100	200	300	400		500	600	700	800	900
	.69	1.38	2.06	2.75		3.44	4.13	4.81	5.50	6.19
.03	.72	1.41	2.10	2.78	5	3.47	4.16	4.85	5.53	6.22
.07	.75	1.44	2.13	2.82	10	3.51	4.19	4.88	5.57	6.25
.10	.79	1.48	2.17	2.85	15	3.54	4.23	4.92	5.60	6.29
.14	.83	1.51	2.20	2.89	20	3.58	4.26	4.95	5.64	6.33
.17	.86	1.55	2.23	2.92	25	3.61	4.30	4.98	5.67	6.36
.20	.89	1.58	2.27	2.96	30	3.64	4.33	5.02	5.70	6.39
.24	.93	1.62	2.30	2.99	35	3.68	4.37	5.05	5.74	6.43
.28	.96	1.65	2.34	3.03	40	3.71	4.40	5.09	5.78	6.46
.31	1.00	1.68	2.37	3.06	45	3.75	4.43	5.12	5.81	6.50
.34	1.03	1.72	2.41	3.09	50	3.78	4.47	5.15	5.84	6.53
.38	1.07	1.75	2.44	3.13	55	3.82	4.50	5.19	5.88	6.57
.41	1.10	1.79	2.48	3.16	60	3.85	4.54	5.23	5.91	6.60
.45	1.13	1.82	2.51	3.20	65	3.88	4.57	5.26	5.95	6.63
.48	1.17	1.86	2.54	3.23	70	3.92	4.60	5.29	5.98	6.67
.52	1.20	1.89	2.58	3.27	75	3.95	4.64	5.33	6.02	6.70
.55	1.24	1.93	2.61	3.30	80	3.99	4.68	5.36	6.05	6.74
.58	1.27	1.96	2.65	3.33	85	4.02	4.71	5.40	6.08	6.77
.62	1.30	1.99	2.68	3.37	90	4.05	4.74	5.43	6.12	6.80
.65	1.34	2.03	2.72	3.40	95	4.09	4.78	5.47	6.15	6.84

— POUNDS —

1000	1100	1200	1300	1400		1500	1600	1700	1800	1900
6.88	7.56	8.25	8.94	9.63		10.31	11.00	11.69	12.38	13.06
6.91	7.60	8.28	8.97	9.66	5	10.35	11.03	11.72	12.41	13.10
6.94	7.63	8.32	9.01	9.69	10	10.38	11.07	11.75	12.44	13.13
6.98	7.67	8.35	9.04	9.73	15	10.42	11.10	11.79	12.48	13.17
7.01	7.70	8.39	9.08	9.76	20	10.45	11.14	11.83	12.51	13.20
7.05	7.73	8.42	9.11	9.80	25	10.48	11.17	11.86	12.55	13.23
7.08	7.77	8.46	9.14	9.83	30	10.52	11.20	11.89	12.58	13.27
7.12	7.80	8.49	9.18	9.87	35	10.55	11.24	11.93	12.62	13.30
7.15	7.84	8.53	9.21	9.90	40	10.59	11.28	11.96	12.65	13.34
7.18	7.87	8.56	9.25	9.93	45	10.62	11.31	12.00	12.68	13.37
7.22	7.91	8.59	9.28	9.97	50	10.65	11.34	12.03	12.72	13.41
7.25	7.94	8.63	9.32	10.00	55	10.69	11.38	12.07	12.75	13.44
7.29	7.98	8.66	9.35	10.04	60	10.73	11.41	12.10	12.79	13.48
7.32	8.01	8.70	9.38	10.07	65	10.76	11.45	12.13	12.82	13.51
7.36	8.04	8.73	9.42	10.10	70	10.79	11.48	12.17	12.86	13.54
7.39	8.08	8.77	9.45	10.14	75	10.83	11.52	12.20	12.89	13.58
7.43	8.11	8.80	9.49	10.18	80	10.86	11.55	12.24	12.93	13.61
7.46	8.15	8.83	9.52	10.21	85	10.90	11.58	12.27	12.96	13.65
7.49	8.18	8.87	9.55	10.24	90	10.93	11.62	12.30	12.99	13.68
7.53	8.22	8.90	9.59	10.28	95	10.97	11.65	12.34	13.03	13.72

Even tons, 1 to 50 inclusive.

1-10		11-20		21-30		31-40		41-50	
T	Am't	T	Am't	T	Am't	T	Am't	T	Am't
1	13.75	11	151.25	21	288.75	31	426.25	41	563.75
2	27.50	12	165.00	22	302.50	32	440.00	42	577.50
3	41.25	13	178.75	23	316.25	33	453.75	43	591.25
4	55.00	14	192.50	24	330.00	34	467.50	44	605.00
5	68.75	15	206.25	25	343.75	35	481.25	45	618.75
6	82.50	16	220.00	26	357.50	36	495.00	46	632.50
7	96.25	17	233.75	27	371.25	37	508.75	47	646.25
8	110.00	18	247.50	28	385.00	38	522.50	48	660.00
9	123.75	19	261.25	29	398.75	39	536.25	49	673.75
10	137.50	20	275.00	30	412.50	40	550.00	50	687.50

200	2750	300	4125	400	5500	500	6875	600	8250

— POUNDS —

2000	2100	2200	2300	2400		2500	2600	2700	2800	2900
		—AMOUNT—					—AMOUNT—			
13.75	14.44	15.13	15.81	16.50		17.19	17.88	18.56	19.25	19.94
13.78	14.47	15.16	15.85	16.53	.5	17.22	17.91	18.60	19.28	19.97
13.82	14.50	15.19	15.88	16.57	10	17.26	17.94	18.63	19.32	20.00
13.85	14.54	15.23	15.92	16.60	15	17.29	17.98	18.67	19.35	20.04
13.89	14.58	15.26	15.95	16.64	20	17.33	18.01	18.70	19.39	20.08
13.92	14.61	15.30	15.98	16.67	25	17.36	18.05	18.73	19.42	20.11
13.95	14.64	15.33	16.02	16.71	30	17.39	18.08	18.77	19.45	20.14
13.99	14.68	15.37	16.05	16.74	35	17.43	18.12	18.80	19.49	20.18
14.03	14.71	15.40	16.09	16.78	40	17.46	18.15	18.84	19.53	20.21
14.06	14.75	15.43	16.12	16.81	45	17.50	18.18	18.87	19.56	20.25
14.09	14.78	15.47	16.16	16.84	50	17.53	18.22	18.90	19.59	20.28
14.13	14.82	15.50	16.19	16.88	55	17.57	18.25	18.94	19.63	20.32
14.16	14.85	15.54	16.23	16.91	60	17.60	18.29	18.98	19.66	20.35
14.20	14.88	15.57	16.26	16.95	65	17.63	18.32	19.01	19.70	20.38
14.23	14.92	15.61	16.29	16.98	70	17.67	18.35	19.04	19.73	20.42
14.27	14.95	15.64	16.33	17.02	75	17.70	18.39	19.08	19.77	20.45
14.30	14.99	15.68	16.36	17.05	80	17.74	18.43	19.11	19.80	20.49
14.33	15.02	15.71	16.40	17.08	85	17.77	18.46	19.15	19.83	20.52
14.37	15.05	15.74	16.43	17.12	90	17.80	18.49	19.18	19.87	20.55
14.40	15.09	15.78	16.47	17.15	95	17.84	18.53	19.22	19.90	20.59

— POUNDS —

3000	3100	3200	3300	3400		3500	3600	3700	3800	3900
		—AMOUNT—					—AMOUNT—			
20.63	21.31	22.00	22.69	23.38		24.06	24.75	25.44	26.13	26.81
20.66	21.35	22.03	22.72	23.41	5	24.10	24.78	25.47	26.16	26.85
20.69	21.38	22.07	22.76	23.44	10	24.13	24.82	25.50	26.19	26.88
20.73	21.42	22.10	22.79	23.48	15	24.17	24.85	25.54	26.23	26.92
20.76	21.45	22.14	22.83	23.51	20	24.20	24.89	25.58	26.26	26.95
20.80	21.48	22.17	22.86	23.55	25	24.23	24.92	25.61	26.30	26.98
20.83	21.52	22.21	22.89	23.62	30	24.27	24.95	25.64	26.33	27.02
20.87	21.55	22.24	22.93	23.62	35	24.30	24.99	25.68	26.37	27.05
20.90	21.59	22.28	22.96	23.65	40	24.34	25.03	25.71	26.40	27.09
20.93	21.62	22.31	23.00	23.68	45	24.37	25.06	25.75	26.43	27.12
20.97	21.66	22.34	23.03	23.72	50	24.40	25.09	25.78	26.47	27.16
21.00	21.69	22.38	23.07	23.75	55	24.44	25.13	25.82	26.50	27.19
21.04	21.73	22.41	23.10	23.79	60	24.48	25.16	25.85	26.54	27.23
21.07	21.76	22.45	23.13	23.82	65	24.51	25.20	25.88	26.57	27.26
21.11	21.79	22.48	23.17	23.85	70	24.54	25.23	25.92	26.61	27.29
21.14	21.83	22.52	23.20	23.89	75	24.58	25.27	25.95	26.64	27.33
21.18	21.86	22.55	23.24	23.93	80	24.61	25.30	25.99	26.68	27.36
21.21	21.90	22.58	23.27	23.96	85	24.65	25.33	26.02	26.71	27.40
21.24	21.93	22.62	23.30	23.99	90	24.68	25.37	26.05	26.74	27.43
21.28	21.97	22.65	23.34	24.03	95	24.72	25.40	26.09	26.78	27.47

Even tons, 51 to 100 inclusive.

51-60		61-70		71-80		81-90		91-100	
T	Am't	T	Am't	T	Am't	T	Am't	T	Am't
51	701.25	61	838.75	71	976.25	81	1113.75	91	1251.25
52	715.00	62	852.50	72	990.00	82	1127.50	92	1265.00
53	728.75	63	866.25	73	1003.75	83	1141.25	93	1278.75
54	742.50	64	880.00	74	1017.50	84	1155.00	94	1292.50
55	756.25	65	893.75	75	1031.25	85	1168.75	95	1306.25
56	770.00	66	907.50	76	1045.00	86	1182.50	96	1320.00
57	783.75	67	921 25	77	1058.75	87	1196.25	97	1333.75
58	807.50	68	935 00	78	1072.50	88	1210.00	98	1347.50
59	811.25	69	948.75	79	1086.25	89	1223.75	99	1361.25
60	825.00	70	962.50	80	1100.00	90	1237.50	100	1375.00

700	9625	800	11000	900	12375	1000	13750	1100	15125

POUNDS

Under 100	100	200	300	400		500	600	700	800	900
	.70	1.40	2.10	2.80		3.50	4.20	4.90	5.60	6.30
.04	.74	1.44	2.14	2.84	5	3.54	4.24	4.94	5.64	6.34
.07	.77	1.47	2.17	2.87	10	3.57	4.27	4.97	5.67	6.37
.11	.81	1.51	2.21	2.91	15	3.61	4.31	5.01	5.71	6.41
.14	.84	1.54	2.24	2.94	20	3.64	4.34	5.04	5.74	6.44
.18	.88	1.58	2.28	2.98	25	3.68	4.38	5.08	5.78	6.48
.21	.91	1.61	2.31	3.01	30	3.71	4.41	5.11	5.81	6.51
.25	.95	1.65	2.35	3.05	35	3.75	4.45	5.15	5.85	6.55
.28	.98	1.68	2.38	3.08	40	3.78	4.48	5.18	5.88	6.58
.32	1.02	1.72	2.42	3.12	45	3.82	4.52	5.22	5.92	6.62
.35	1.05	1.75	2.45	3.15	50	3.85	4.55	5.25	5.95	6.65
.39	1.09	1.79	2.49	3.19	55	3.89	4.59	5.29	5.99	6.69
.42	1.12	1.82	2.52	3.22	60	3.92	4.62	5.32	6.02	6.72
.46	1.16	1.86	2.56	3.26	65	3.96	4.66	5.36	6.06	6.76
.49	1.19	1.89	2.59	3.29	70	3.99	4.69	5.39	6.09	6.79
.53	1.23	1.93	2.63	3.33	75	4.03	4.73	5.43	6.13	6.83
.56	1.26	1.96	2.66	3.36	80	4.06	4.76	5.46	6.16	6.86
.60	1.30	2.00	2.70	3.40	85	4.10	4.80	5.50	6.20	6.90
.63	1.33	2.03	2.73	3.43	90	4.13	4.83	5.53	6.23	6.93
.67	1.37	2.07	2.77	3.47	95	4.17	4.87	5.57	6.27	6.97

POUNDS

1000	1100	1200	1300	1400		1500	1600	1700	1800	1900
7.00	7.70	8.40	9.10	9.80		10.50	11.20	11.90	12.60	13.30
7.04	7.74	8.44	9.14	9.84	5	10.54	11.24	11.94	12.64	13.34
7.07	7.77	8.47	9.17	9.87	10	10.57	11.27	11.97	12.67	13.37
7.11	7.81	8.51	9.21	9.91	15	10.61	11.31	12.01	12.71	13.41
7.14	7.84	8.54	9.24	9.94	20	10.64	11.34	12.04	12.74	13.44
7.18	7.88	8.58	9.28	9.98	25	10.68	11.38	12.08	12.78	13.48
7.21	7.91	8.61	9.31	10.01	30	10.71	11.41	12.11	12.81	13.51
7.25	7.95	8.65	9.35	10.05	35	10.75	11.45	12.15	12.85	13.55
7.28	7.98	8.68	9.38	10.08	40	10.78	11.48	12.18	12.88	13.58
7.32	8.02	8.72	9.42	10.12	45	10.82	11.52	12.22	12.92	13.62
7.35	8.05	8.75	9.45	10.15	50	10.85	11.55	12.25	12.95	13.65
7.39	8.09	8.79	9.49	10.19	55	10.89	11.59	12.29	12.99	13.69
7.42	8.12	8.82	9.52	10.22	60	10.92	11.62	12.32	13.02	13.72
7.46	8.16	8.86	9.56	10.26	65	10.96	11.66	12.36	13.06	13.76
7.49	8.19	8.89	9.59	10.29	70	10.99	11.69	12.39	13.09	13.79
7.53	8.23	8.93	9.63	10.33	75	11.03	11.73	12.43	13.13	13.83
7.56	8.26	8.96	9.66	10.36	80	11.06	11.76	12.46	13.16	13.86
7.60	8.30	9.00	9.70	10.40	85	11.10	11.80	12.50	13.20	13.90
7.63	8.33	9.03	9.73	10.43	90	11.13	11.83	12.53	13.23	13.93
7.67	8.37	9.07	9.77	10.47	95	11.17	11.87	12.57	13.27	13.97

Even tons, 1 to 50 inclusive.

1-10		11-20		21-30		31-40		41-50	
T	Am't	T	Am't	T	Am't	T	Am't	T	Am't
1	14.00	11	154.00	21	294.00	31	434.00	41	574.00
2	28.00	12	168.00	22	308.00	32	448.00	42	588.00
3	42.00	13	182.00	23	322.00	33	462.00	43	602.00
4	56.00	14	196.00	24	336.00	34	476.00	44	616.00
5	70.00	15	210.00	25	350.00	35	490.00	45	630.00
6	84.00	16	224.00	26	364.00	36	504.00	46	644.00
7	98.00	17	238.00	27	378.00	37	518.00	47	658.00
8	112.00	18	252.00	28	392.00	38	532.00	48	672.00
9	126.00	19	266.00	29	406.00	39	546.00	49	686.00
10	140.00	20	280.00	30	420.00	40	560.00	50	700.00

200	2800	300	4200	400	5600	500	7000	600	8400

—POUNDS—

2000	2100	2200	2300	2400		2500	2600	2700	2800	2900
		AMOUNT						AMOUNT		
14.00	14.70	15.40	16.10	16.80		17.50	18.20	18.90	19.60	20.30
14.04	14.74	15.44	16.14	16.84	5	17.54	18.24	18.94	19.64	20.34
14.07	14.77	15.47	16.17	16.87	10	17.57	18.27	18.97	19.67	20.37
14.11	14.81	15.51	16.21	16.91	15	17.61	18.31	19.01	19.71	20.41
14.14	14.84	15.54	16.24	16.94	20	17.64	18.34	19.04	19.74	20.44
14.18	14.88	15.58	16.28	16.98	25	17.68	18.38	19.08	19.78	20.48
14.21	14.91	15.61	16.31	17.01	30	17.71	18.41	19.11	19.81	20.51
14.25	14.95	15.65	16.35	17.05	35	17.75	18.45	19.15	19.85	20.55
14.28	14.98	15.68	16.38	17.08	40	17.78	18.48	19.18	19.88	20.58
14.32	15.02	15.72	16.42	17.12	45	17.82	18.52	19.22	19.92	20.62
14.35	15.05	15.75	16.45	17.15	50	17.85	18.55	19.25	19.95	20.65
14.39	15.09	15.79	16.49	17.19	55	17.89	18.59	19.29	19.99	20.69
14.42	15.12	15.82	16.52	17.22	60	17.92	18.62	19.32	20.02	20.72
14.46	15.16	15.86	16.56	17.26	65	17.96	18.66	19.36	20.06	20.76
14.49	15.19	15.89	16.59	17.29	70	17.99	18.69	19.39	20.09	20.79
14.53	15.23	15.93	16.63	17.33	75	18.03	18.73	19.43	20.13	20.83
14.56	15.26	15.96	16.66	17.36	80	18.06	18.76	19.46	20.16	20.86
14.60	15.30	16.00	16.70	17.40	85	18.10	18.80	19.50	20.20	20.90
14.63	15.33	16.03	16.73	17.43	90	18.13	18.83	19.53	20.23	20.93
14.67	15.37	16.07	16.77	17.47	95	18.17	18.87	19.57	20.27	20.97

—POUNDS—

3000	3100	3200	3300	3400		3500	3600	3700	3800	3900
		AMOUNT						AMOUNT		
21.00	21.70	22.40	23.10	23.80		24.50	25.20	25.90	26.60	27.30
21.04	21.74	22.44	23.14	23.84	5	24.54	25.24	25.94	26.64	27.34
21.07	21.77	22.47	23.17	23.87	10	24.57	25.27	25.97	26.67	27.37
21.11	21.81	22.51	23.21	23.91	15	24.61	25.31	26.01	26.71	27.41
21.14	21.84	22.54	23.24	23.94	20	24.64	25.34	26.04	26.74	27.44
21.18	21.88	22.58	23.28	23.98	25	24.68	25.38	26 08	26.78	27.48
21.21	21.91	22.61	23.31	24.01	30	24.71	25.41	26.11	26.81	27.51
21.25	21.95	22.65	23.35	24.05	35	24.75	25.45	26.15	26.85	27.55
21.28	21.98	22.68	23.38	24.08	40	24.78	25.48	26.18	26.88	27.58
21.32	22.02	22.72	23.42	24.12	45	24.82	25.52	26.22	26.92	27.62
21.35	22.05	22.75	23.45	24.15	50	24.85	25.55	26.25	26.95	27.65
21.39	22.09	22.79	23.49	24.19	55	24.89	25.59	26.29	26.99	27.69
21.42	22.12	22.82	23.52	24.22	60	24.92	25.62	26.32	27.02	27.72
21.46	22.16	22.86	23.56	24.26	65	24.96	25.66	26.36	27.06	27.76
21.49	22.19	22.89	23.59	24.29	70	24.99	25.69	26.39	27.09	27.79
21.53	22.23	22.93	23.63	24.33	75	25.03	25.73	26.43	27.13	27.83
21.56	22.26	22.96	23.66	24.36	80	25.06	25.76	26.46	27.16	27.86
21.60	22.30	23.00	23.70	24.40	85	25.10	25.80	26.50	27.20	27.90
21.63	22.33	23.03	23.73	24.43	90	25.13	25.83	26.53	27.23	27.93
21.67	22.37	23.07	23.77	24.47	95	25.17	25.87	26.57	27.27	27.97

Even tons, 51 to 100 inclusive.

	51-60		61-70		71-80		81-90		91-100
T	Am't	T	Am't	T	Am't	T	Am't	T	Am't
51	714.00	61	854.00	71	994.00	81	1134.00	91	1274.00
52	728.00	62	868.00	72	1008.00	82	1148.00	92	1288.00
53	742.00	63	882.00	73	1022.00	83	1162.00	93	1302.00
54	756.00	64	896.00	74	1036.00	84	1176.00	94	1316.00
55	770.00	65	910.00	75	1050.00	85	1190.00	95	1330.00
56	784.00	66	924.00	76	1064.00	86	1204.00	96	1344.00
57	798.00	67	938.00	77	1078.00	87	1218.00	97	1358.00
58	812.00	68	952.00	78	1092.00	88	1232.00	98	1372.00
59	826.00	69	966.00	79	1106.00	89	1246 00	99	1386.00
60	840.00	70	980.00	80	1120.00	90	1260.00	100	1400.00

700	9800	800	11200	900	12600	1000	14000	1100	15400

POUNDS

Under 100	100	200	300	400		500	600	700	800	900
	—AMOUNT—						—AMOUNT—			
	.71	1.43	2.14	2.85		3.56	4.28	4.99	5.70	6.41
.04	.75	1.46	2.17	2.89	5	3.60	4.31	5.02	5.74	6.45
.07	.78	1.50	2.21	2.92	10	3.63	4.35	5.06	5.77	6.48
.11	.82	1.53	2.24	2.96	15	3.67	4.38	5.09	5.81	6.52
.14	.86	1.57	2.28	2.99	20	3.71	4.42	5 13	5.84	6.56
.18	.89	1.60	2.32	3.03	25	3.74	4.45	5.17	5.88	6.59
.21	.93	1.64	2.35	3.06	30	3.78	4.49	5.20	5.91	6.63
.25	.96	1.67	2.39	3.10	35	3.81	4.52	5.24	5.95	6.66
.28	1.00	1.71	2.42	.3.14	40	3.85	4.56	5.27	5.98	6.70
.32	1.03	1.75	2.46	3.17	45	3.88	4.60	5.31	6.02	6.73
.36	1.07	1.78	2.49	3.21	50	3.92	4.63	5.34	6.06	6.77
.39	1.10	1.82	2.53	3.24	55	3.95	4.67	5.38	6.09	6.80
.43	1.14	1.85	2.57	3.28	60	3.99	4.70	5.42	6.13	6.84
.46	1.18	1.89	2.60	3.31	65	4.03	4.74	5.45	6.16	6.88
50	1.21	1.92	2.64	3.35	70	4.06	4.77	5.48	6.20	6.91
.53	1.25	1.96	2.67	3.38	75	4.10	4.81	5 52	6.23	6.95
.57	1.28	2.00	2.71	3.42	80	4.13	4.85	5.55	6.27	6.98
.60	1.32	2.03	2.74	3.46	85	4.17	4.88	5.59	6.30	7.02
.64	1.35	2.07	2.78	3.49	90	4.20	4.92	5.62	6.34	7.05
.68	1.39	2.10	2.81	3.53	95	4.24	4.95	5.66	6.38	7.09

POUNDS

1000	1100	1200	1300	1400		1500	1600	1700	1800	1900
	—AMOUNT—						—AMOUNT—			
7.13	7.84	8.55	9.26	9.98		10.69	11.40	12.11	12.83	13.54
7.16	7.87	8.59	9.30	10.01	5	10.72	11.44	12.15	12.86	13.57
7.20	7.91	8.62	9.33	10.05	10	10.76	11.47	12.18	12.90	13.61
7.23	7.94	8.66	9.37	10.08	15	10.79	11.51	12.22	12.93	13.64
7.27	7.98	8.69	9.41	10.12	20	10.83	11.54	12.26	12.97	13.68
7.30	8.02	8.73	9.44	10.15	25	10.87	11.58	12.29	13.00	13.72
7 34	8.05	8.76	9.48	10.19	30	10.90	11.61	12.33	13.04	13.75
7.37	8.09	8.80	9.51	10.22	35	10.94	11.65	12.36	13.07	13.79
7.41	8.12	8.84	9.55	10.26	40	10.97	11.68	12.40	13.11	13.82
7.45	8.16	8.87	9.58	10.30	45	11.01	11.72	12.43	13.15	13.86
7 48	8.19	8.91	9.62	10.33	50	11.04	11.76	12.47	13.18	13.89
7.52	8.23	8.94	9.65	10.37	55	11.08	11.79	12.50	13.22	13.93
7 55	8.27	8.98	9.69	10.40	60	11.12	11.83	12.54	13.25	13.97
7.59	8.30	9.01	9.73	10.44	65	11.15	11.86	12.58	13.29	14.01
7.62	8.34	9.05	9.76	10.47	70	11.18	11.90	12.61	13.32	14 04
7 66	8.37	9.08	9.80	10.51	75	11.22	11.93	12.65	13.36	14.07
7.70	8.41	9.12	9.83	10.55	80	11.25	11.97	12.68	13.40	14.11
7.73	8.44	9.16	9.87	10.58	85	11.29	12.00	12.72	13.43	14.14
7.77	8.48	9.19	9.90	10.62	90	11.32	12.04	12.75	13.47	14.18
7.80	8.51	9.23	9.94	10.65	95	11.36	12.08	12.79	13.50	14.21

Even tons, 1 to 50 inclusive.

1-10		11-20		21-30		31-40		41-50	
T	Am't	T	Am't	T	Am't	T	Am't	T	Am't
1	14.25	11	156.75	21	299.25	31	441.75	41	584.25
2	28.50	12	171.00	22	313.50	32	456.00	42	598.50
3	42.75	13	185.25	23	327.75	33	470.25	43	612.75
4	57.00	14	199.50	24	342.00	34	484.50	44	627.00
5	71.25	15	213.75	25	356.25	35	498.75	45	641.25
6	85.50	16	228.00	26	370.50	36	513.00	46	655.50
7	99.75	17	242.25	27	384.75	37	527.25	47	669.75
8	114.00	18	256.50	28	399.00	38	541.50	48	684.00
9	128.25	19	270.75	29	413.25	39	555.75	49	698.25
10	142.50	20	285.00	30	427.50	40	570.00	50	712.50

200	2850	300	4275	400	5700	500	7125	600	8550

-POUNDS-

2000	2100	2200	2300	2400		2500	2600	2700	2800	2900
		AMOUNT						AMOUNT		
14.25	14.96	15.68	16.39	17.10		17.81	18.53	19.24	19.95	20.66
14.29	15.00	15.71	16.42	17.14	5	17.85	18.56	19.27	19.99	20.70
14.32	15.03	15.75	16.46	17.17	10	17.88	18.60	19.31	20.02	20.73
14.36	15.07	15.78	16.49	17.21	15	17.92	18.63	19.34	20.06	20.77
14.39	15.11	15.82	16.53	17.24	20	17.96	18.67	19.38	20.09	20.81
14.43	15.14	15.85	16.57	17.28	25	17.99	18.70	19.42	20.13	20.84
14.46	15.18	15.89	16.60	17.31	30	18.03	18.74	19.45	20.16	20.88
14.50	15.21	15 92	16.64	17.35	35	18.06	18.77	19.49	20.20	20.91
14.53	15.25	15.96	16.67	17.39	40	18.10	18.81	19.52	20.23	20.95
14.57	15.28	16.00	16.71	17.42	45	18.13	18.85	19.56	20.27	20.98
14.61	15.32	16.03	16.74	17.46	50	18.17	18.88	19.59	20.31	21.02
14.64	15.35	16.07	16.78	17.49	55	18.20	18.92	19.63	20.34	21.05
14.68	15.39	16.10	16.82	17.53	60	18.24	18.95	19.67	20.38	21.09
14.71	15.43	16.14	16.85	17.56	65	18.28	18.99	19.70	20.41	21.13
14.75	15.46	16.17	16.89	17.60	70	18.31	19.02	19.73	20.45	21.16
14.78	15.50	16.21	16.92	17.63	75	18.35	19.06	19.77	20.48	21.20
14.82	15.53	16.25	16.96	17.67	80	18.38	19.10	19.80	20.52	21.23
14.85	15.57	16.28	16.99	17.71	85	18.42	19.13	19.84	20.55	21.27
14.89	15.60	16.32	17.03	17.74	90	18.45	19.17	19.87	20.59	21.30
14.93	15.64	16.35	17.06	17.78	95	18.49	19.20	19.91	20.63	21.34

-POUNDS-

3000	3100	3200	3300	3400		3500	3600	3700	3800	3900
		AMOUNT						AMOUNT		
21.38	22.09	22.80	23.51	24.23		24.94	25.65	26.36	27.08	27.79
21.41	22.12	22.84	23.55	24.26	5	24.97	25.69	26.40	27.11	27.82
21.45	22.16	22.87	23.58	24.30	10	25.01	25.72	26.43	27.15	27.86
21.48	22.19	22.91	23.62	24.33	15	25.04	25.76	26.47	27.18	27.89
21.52	22.23	22.94	23.66	24.37	20	25.08	25.79	26.51	27.22	27 93
21.55	22.27	22.98	23.69	24.40	25	25.12	25.83	26.54	27.25	27.97
21.59	22.30	23.01	23.73	24.44	30	25.15	25.86	26.58	27.29	28.00
21.62	22.34	23.05	23.76	24.47	35	25.19	25.90	26.61	27.32	28.04
21.66	22.37	23.09	23.80	24.51	40	25.22	25.93	26.65	27.36	28.07
21.70	22.41	23.12	23.83	24.55	45	25.26	25.97	26.68	27.40	28.11
21.73	22.44	23.16	23.87	24.58	50	25.29	26.01	26.72	27.43	28.14
21.77	22.48	23.19	23.90	24.62	55	25.33	26.04	26.75	27.47	28.18
21.80	22.52	23.23	23.94	24.65	60	25.37	26.08	26.79	27.50	28.22
21.84	22.55	23.26	23.98	24.69	65	25.40	26.11	26.83	27.54	28.26
21.87	22.59	23.30	24.01	24.72	70	25.43	26.15	26.86	27.57	28.29
21.91	22.62	23.33	24.05	24.76	75	25.47	26.18	26.90	27.61	28.32
21.95	22.66	23.37	24.08	24.80	80	25.50	26.22	26.93	27.65	28.36
21.98	22.69	23.41	24.12	24.83	85	25.54	26.25	26.97	27.68	28.39
22.02	22.73	23.44	24.15	24.87	90	25.57	26.29	27.00	27.72	28.43
22.05	22.76	23.48	24.19	24.90	95	25.61	26.33	27.04	27.75	28.46

Even tons, 51 to 100 inclusive.

51-60		61-70		71-80		81-90		91-100	
T	Am't	T	Am't	T	Am't	T	Am't	T	Am't
51	726.75	61	869.25	71	1011.75	81	1154.25	91	1296.75
52	741.00	62	883.50	72	1026.00	82	1168.50	92	1311.00
53	755.25	63	897.75	73	1040.25	83	1182.75	93	1325.25
54	769.50	64	912.00	74	1054.50	84	1197.00	94	1339.50
55	783.75	65	926.25	75	1068.75	85	1211.25	95	1353.75
56	798.00	66	940.50	76	1083.00	86	1225.50	96	1368.00
57	812.25	67	954.75	77	1097.25	87	1239.75	97	1382.25
58	826.50	68	969.00	78	1111.50	88	1254.00	98	1396.50
59	840.75	69	983.25	79	1125.75	89	1268.25	99	1410.75
60	855.00	70	997.50	80	1140.00	90	1282.50	100	1425.00

700	9975	800	11400	900	12825	1000	14250	1100	15675

POUNDS

Under 100	100	200	300	400		500	600	700	800	900
	.73	1.45	2.18	2.90		3.63	4.35	5.08	5.80	6 53
.04	.76	1.49	2.21	2.94	5	3.66	4.39	5.11	5.84	6.56
.07	.80	1.52	2.25	2.97	10	3.70	4.42	5.15	5.87	6.60
.11	.83	1.56	2.28	3.01	15	3.73	4.46	5.18	5.91	6.63
.15	.87	1.60	2.32	3.05	20	3.77	4.50	5.22	5.95	6.67
.18	.91	1.63	2.36	3.08	25	3.81	4.53	5.26	5.98	6.71
.22	.94	1.67	2.39	3.12	30	3.84	4.57	5.29	6.02	6.74
.25	.98	1.70	2.43	3.15	35	3.88	4.60	5.33	6.05	6.78
.29	1.02	1.74	2.47	3.19	40	3.92	4.64	5.37	6.09	6.82
.33	1.05	1.78	2.50	3.23	45	3.95	4.68	5.40	6.13	6.85
·36	1.09	1.81	2.54	3.26	50	3.99	4.71	5.44	6.16	6.89
.40	1.12	1.85	2.57	3.30	55	4.02	4.75	5.47	6.20	6.92
.44	1.16	1.89	2.61	3.34	60	4.06	4.79	5.51	6.24	6.96
.47	1.20	1.92	2.65	3.37	65	4.10	4.82	5.55	6.27	7.00
.51	1.23	1.96	2.68	3.41	70	4.13	4.86	5.58	6.31	7.03
.54	1.27	1.99	2.72	3.44	75	4.17	4.89	5.62	6.34	7.07
.58	1.31	2.03	2.76	3.48	80	4.21	4.93	5.66	6.38	7.11
.62	1.34	2.07	2.79	3.52	85	4.24	4.97	5.69	6.42	7.14
.65	1.38	2.10	2.83	3.55	90	4.28	5.00	5.73	6.45	7.18
.69	1.41	2.14	2.86	3.59	95	4.31	5.04	5.76	6.49	7.21

POUNDS

1000	1100	1200	1300	1400		1500	1600	1700	1800	1900
7.25	7.98	8.70	9.43	10.15		10.88	11.60	12.33	13.05	13.78
7.29	8.01	8.74	9.46	10.19	5	10.91	11.64	12.36	13.09	13.81
7.32	8.05	8.77	9.50	10.22	10	10.95	11.67	12.40	13.12	13.85
7.36	8.08	8.81	9.53	10.26	15	10.98	11.71	12.43	13.16	13.88
7.40	8.12	8.85	9.57	10.30	20	11.02	11.75	12.47	13.20	13.92
7.43	8.16	8.88	9.61	10.33	25	11.06	11.78	12.51	13.23	13.96
7.47	8.19	8.92	9.64	10.37	30	11.09	11.82	12.54	13.27	13.99
7.50	8.23	8.95	9.68	10.40	35	11.13	11.85	12.58	13.30	14.03
7.54	8.27	8.99	9.72	10.44	40	11.17	11.89	12.62	13.34	14.07
7.58	8.30	9.03	9.75	10.48	45	11.20	11.93	12.65	13.38	14.10
7.61	8.34	9.06	9.79	10.51	50	11.24	11.96	12.69	13.41	14.14
7.65	8.37	9.10	9.82	10.55	55	11.27	12.00	12.72	13.45	14.17
7.69	8.41	9.14	9.86	10.59	60	11.31	12.04	12.76	13.49	14.21
7.72	8.45	9.17	9.90	10.62	65	11.35	12.07	12.80	13.52	14.25
7.76	8.48	9.21	9.93	10.66	70	11.38	12.11	12.83	13.56	14.28
7.79	8.52	9.24	9.97	10.69	75	11.42	12.14	12.87	13.59	14.32
7.83	8.56	9.28	10.01	10.73	80	11.46	12.18	12.91	13.63	14.36
7.87	8.59	9.32	10.04	10.77	85	11.49	12.22	12.94	13.67	14.39
7.90	8.63	9.35	10.08	10.80	90	11.53	12.25	12.98	13.70	14.43
7.94	8.66	9.39	10.11	10.84	95	11.56	12.29	13.01	13.74	14.46

Even tons, 1 to 50 inclusive.

1-10		11-20		21-30		31-40		41-50	
T	Am't	T	Am't	T	Am't	T	Am't	T	Am't
1	14.50	11	159.50	21	304.50	31	449.50	41	594.50
2	29.00	12	174.00	22	319.00	32	464.00	42	609.00
3	43.50	13	188.50	23	333.50	33	478.50	43	623.50
4	58.00	14	203.00	24	348.00	34	493.00	44	638.00
5	72.50	15	217.50	25	362.50	35	507 50	45	652.50
6	87.00	16	232.00	26	377.00	36	522.00	46	667.00
7	101.50	17	246.50	27	391.50	37	536.50	47	681.50
8	116.00	18	261.00	28	406.00	38	551.00	48	696.00
9	130.50	19	275.50	29	420.50	39	565.50	49	710.50
10	145.00	20	290.00	30	435.00	40	580.00	50	725.00

200	2900	300	4350	400	5800	500	7250	600	8700

——Pounds——

2000	2100	2200	2300	2400		2500	2600	2700	2800	2900
		—Amount—						—Amount—		
14.50	15.23	15.95	16.68	17.40		18.13	18.85	19.58	20.30	21.03
14.54	15.26	15.99	16.71	17.44	5	18.16	18.89	19.61	20.34	21.06
14.57	15.30	16.02	16.75	17.47	10	18.20	18.92	19.65	20.37	21.10
14.61	15.33	16.06	16.78	17.51	15	18.23	18.96	19.68	20.41	21.13
14.65	15.37	16.10	16.82	17.55	20	18.27	19.00	19.72	20.45	21.17
14.68	15.41	16.13	16.86	17.58	25	18.31	19.03	19.76	20.48	21.21
14.72	15.44	16.17	16.89	17.62	30	18.34	19.07	19.79	20.52	21.24
14.75	15.48	16.20	16.93	17.65	35	18.38	19.10	19.83	20.55	21.28
14.79	15.52	16.24	16.97	17.69	40	18.42	19.14	19.87	20.59	21.32
14.83	15.55	16.28	17.00	17.73	45	18.45	19.18	19.90	20.63	21.35
14.86	15.59	16.31	17.04	17.76	50	18.49	19.21	19.94	20.66	21.39
14.90	15.62	16.35	17.07	17.80	55	18.52	19.25	19.97	20.70	21.42
14.94	15.66	16.39	17.11	17.84	60	18.56	19.29	20.01	20.74	21.46
14.97	15.70	16.42	17.15	17.87	65	18.60	19.32	20.05	20.77	21.50
15.01	15.73	16.46	17.18	17.91	70	18.63	19.36	20.08	20.81	21.53
15.04	15.77	16.49	17.22	17.94	75	18.67	19.39	20.12	20.84	21.57
15.08	15.81	16.53	17.26	17.98	80	18.71	19.43	20.16	20.88	21.61
15.12	15.84	16.57	17.29	18.02	85	18.74	19.47	20.19	20.92	21.64
15.15	15.88	16.60	17.33	18.05	90	18.78	19.50	20.23	20.95	21.68
15.19	15.91	16.64	17.36	18.09	95	18.81	19.54	20.26	20.99	21.71

——Pounds——

3000	3100	3200	3300	3400		3500	3600	3700	3800	3900
		—Amount—						—Amount—		
21.75	22.48	23.20	23.93	24.65		25.38	26.10	26.83	27.55	28.28
21.79	22.51	23.24	23.96	24.69	5	25.41	26.14	26.86	27.59	28.31
21.82	22.55	23.27	24.00	24.72	10	25.45	26.17	26.90	27.62	28.35
21.86	22.58	23.31	24.03	24.76	15	25.48	26.21	26.93	27.66	28.38
21.90	22.62	23.35	24.07	24.80	20	25.52	26.25	26.97	27.70	28.42
21.93	22.66	23.38	24.11	24.83	25	25.56	26.28	27.01	27.73	28.46
21.97	22.69	23.42	24.14	24.87	30	25.59	26.32	27.04	27.77	28.49
22.00	22.73	23.45	24.18	24.90	35	25.63	26.35	27.08	27.80	28.53
22.04	22.77	23.49	24.22	24.94	40	25.67	26.39	27.12	27.84	28.57
22.08	22.80	23.53	24.25	24.98	45	25.70	26.43	27.15	27.88	28.60
22.11	22.84	23.56	24.29	25.01	50	25.74	26.46	27.19	27.91	28.64
22.15	22.87	23.60	24.32	25.05	55	25.77	26.50	27.22	27.95	28.67
22.19	22.91	23.64	24.36	25.09	60	25.81	26.54	27.26	27.99	28.71
22.22	22.95	23.67	24.40	25.12	65	25.85	26.57	27.30	28.02	28.75
22.26	22.98	23.71	24.43	25.16	70	25.88	26.61	27.33	28.06	28.78
22.29	23.02	23.74	24.47	25.19	75	25.92	26.64	27.37	28.09	28.82
22.33	23.06	23.78	24.51	25.23	80	25.96	26.68	27.41	28.13	28.86
22.37	23.09	23.82	24.54	25.27	85	25.99	26.72	27.44	28.17	28.89
22.40	23.13	23.85	24.58	25.30	90	26.03	26.75	27.48	28.20	28.93
22.44	23.16	23.89	24.61	25.34	95	26.06	26.79	27.51	28.24	28.96

Even tons, 51 to 100 inclusive.

51-60		61-70		71-80		81-90		91-100	
T	Am't	T	Am't	T	Am't	T	Am't	T	Am't
51	739.50	61	884.50	71	1029.50	81	1174.50	91	1319.50
52	754.00	62	899.00	72	1044.00	82	1189.00	92	1334.00
53	768.50	63	913.50	73	1058.50	83	1203.50	93	1348.50
54	783.00	64	928.00	74	1073.00	84	1218.00	94	1363.00
55	797.50	65	942.50	75	1087.50	85	1232.50	95	1377.50
56	812.00	66	957.00	76	1102.00	86	1247.00	96	1392.00
57	826.50	67	971.50	77	1116.50	87	1261.50	97	1406.50
58	841.00	68	986.00	78	1131.00	88	1276.00	98	1421.00
59	855.50	69	1000.50	79	1145.50	89	1290.50	99	1435.50
60	870.00	70	1015.00	80	1160.00	90	1305.00	100	1450.00

700	10150	800	11600	900	13050	1000	14500	1100	15950

POUNDS

Under 100	100	200	300	400		500	600	700	800	900
	AMOUNT							AMOUNT		
	.74	1.48	2.21	2.95		3.69	4.43	5.16	5.90	6.64
.04	.77	1.51	2.25	2.99	5	3.72	4.46	5.20	5.94	6.67
.07	.81	1.55	2.29	3.02	10	3.76	4.50	5.24	5.97	6.71
.11	.85	1.59	2.32	3.06	15	3.80	4.54	5.27	6.01	6.75
.15	.89	1.62	2.36	3.10	20	3.84	4.57	5.31	6.05	6.79
.18	.92	1.66	2.40	3.13	25	3.87	4.61	5.35	6.08	6.82
.22	.96	1.70	2.43	3.17	30	3.91	4.65	5.38	6.12	6.86
.26	1.00	1.73	2.47	3.21	35	3.95	4.68	5.42	6.16	6.90
.30	1.03	1.77	2.51	3.25	40	3.98	4.72	5.46	6.20	6.93
.33	1.07	1.81	2.54	3.28	45	4.02	4.76	5.49	6.23	6.97
.37	1.11	1.84	2.58	3.32	50	4.06	4.79	5.53	6.27	7.01
.41	1.14	1.88	2.62	3.36	55	4.09	4.83	5.57	6.31	7.04
.44	1.18	1.92	2.66	3.39	60	4.13	4.87	5.61	6.34	7.08
.48	1.22	1.95	2.69	3.43	65	4.17	4.90	5.64	6.38	7.12
.52	1.25	1.99	2.73	3.47	70	4.20	4.94	5.68	6.42	7.15
.55	1.29	2.03	2.77	3.50	75	4.24	4.98	5.72	6.45	7.19
.59	1.33	2.07	2.80	3.54	80	4.28	5.02	5.75	6.49	7.23
.63	1.36	2.10	2.84	3.58	85	4.31	5.05	5.79	6.53	7.26
.66	1.40	2.14	2.88	3.61	90	4.35	5.09	5.83	6.56	7.30
.70	1.44	2.18	2.91	3.65	95	4.39	5.13	5.86	6.60	7.34

POUNDS

1000	1100	1200	1300	1400		1500	1600	1700	1800	1900
	AMOUNT							AMOUNT		
7.38	8.11	8.85	9.59	10.33		11.06	11.80	12.54	13.28	14.01
7.41	8.15	8.89	9.62	10.36	5	11.10	11.84	12.57	13.31	14.05
7.45	8.19	8.92	9.66	10.40	10	11.14	11.87	12.61	13.35	14.09
7.49	8.22	8.96	9.70	10.44	15	11.17	11.91	12.65	13.39	14.12
7.52	8.26	9.00	9.74	10.47	20	11.21	11.95	12.69	13.42	14.16
7.56	8.30	9.03	9.77	10.51	25	11.25	11.98	12.72	13.46	14.20
7.60	8.33	9.07	9.81	10.55	30	11.28	12.02	12.76	13.50	14.23
7.63	8.37	9.11	9.85	10.58	35	11.32	12.06	12.80	13.53	14.27
7.67	8.41	9.15	9.88	10.62	40	11.36	12.10	12.83	13.57	14.31
7.71	8.44	9.18	9.92	10.66	45	11.39	12.13	12.87	13.61	14.34
7.74	8.48	9.22	9.96	10.69	50	11.43	12.17	12.91	13.64	14.38
7.78	8.52	9.26	9.99	10.73	55	11.47	12.21	12.94	13.68	14.42
7.82	8.56	9.29	10.03	10.77	60	11.51	12.24	12.98	13.72	14.46
7.85	8.59	9.33	10.07	10.80	65	11.54	12.28	13.02	13.75	14.49
7.89	8.63	9.37	10.10	10.84	70	11.58	12.32	13.05	13.79	14.53
7.93	8.67	9.40	10.14	10.88	75	11.62	12.35	13.09	13.83	14.57
7.97	8.70	9.44	10.18	10.92	80	11.65	12.39	13.12	13.86	14.60
8.00	8.74	9.48	10.21	10.95	85	11.69	12.43	13.16	13.90	14.64
8.04	8.78	9.51	10.25	10.99	90	11.73	12.46	13.20	13.94	14.68
8.08	8.81	9.55	10.29	11.03	95	11.76	12.50	13.24	13.98	14.71

Even tons, 1 to 50 inclusive.

T	Am't	T	Am't	T	Am't	T	Am't	T	Am't
1	14.75	11	162.25	21	309.75	31	457.25	41	604.75
2	29.50	12	177.00	22	324.50	32	472.00	42	619.50
3	44.25	13	191.75	23	339.25	33	486.75	43	634.25
4	59.00	14	206.50	24	354.00	34	501.50	44	649.00
5	73.75	15	221.25	25	368.75	35	516.25	45	663.75
6	88.50	16	236.00	26	383.50	36	531.00	46	678.50
7	103.25	17	250.75	27	398.25	37	545.75	47	693.25
8	118.00	18	265.50	28	413.00	38	560.50	48	708.00
9	132.75	19	280.25	29	427.75	39	575.25	49	722.75
10	147.50	20	295.00	30	442.50	40	590.00	50	737.50

200	2950	300	4425	400	5900	500	7375	600	8850

POUNDS

2000	2100	2200	2300	2400		2500	2600	2700	2800	2900
14.75	15.49	16.23	16.96	17.70		18.44	19.18	19.91	20.65	21.39
14.79	15.52	16.26	17.00	17.74	5	18.47	19.21	19.95	20.69	21.42
14.82	15.56	16.30	17.04	17.77	10	18.51	19.25	19.99	20.72	21.46
14.86	15.60	16.34	17.07	17.81	15	18.55	19.29	20.02	20.76	21.50
14.90	15.64	16.37	17.11	17.85	20	18.59	19.32	20.06	20.80	21.54
14.93	15.67	16.41	17.15	17.88	25	18.62	19.36	20.10	20.83	21.57
14.97	15.71	16.45	17.18	17.92	30	18.66	19.40	20.13	20.87	21.61
15.01	15.75	16.48	17.22	17.96	35	18.70	19.43	20.17	20.91	21.65
15.05	15.78	16.52	17.26	18.00	40	18.73	19.47	20.21	20.95	21.68
15.08	15.82	16.56	17.29	18.03	45	18.77	19.51	20.24	20.98	21.72
15.12	15.86	16.59	17.33	18.07	50	18.81	19.54	20.28	21.02	21.76
15.16	15.89	16.63	17.37	18.11	55	18.84	19.58	20.32	21.06	21.79
15.19	15.93	16.67	17.41	18.14	60	18.88	19.62	20.36	21.09	21.83
15.23	15.97	16.70	17.44	18.18	65	18.92	19.65	20.39	21.13	21.87
15.27	16.00	16.74	17.48	18.22	70	18.95	19.69	20.43	21.17	21.90
15.30	16.04	16.78	17.52	18.25	75	18.99	19.73	20.47	21.20	21.94
15.34	16.08	16.82	17.55	18.29	80	19.03	19.77	20.50	21.24	21.98
15.38	16.11	16.85	17.59	18.33	85	19.06	19.80	20.54	21.28	22.01
15.41	16.15	16.89	17.63	18.36	90	19.10	19.84	20.58	21.31	22.05
15.45	16.19	16.93	17.66	18.40	95	19.14	19.88	20.61	21.35	22.09

POUNDS

3000	3100	3200	3300	3400		3500	3600	3700	3800	3900
22.13	22.86	23.60	24.34	25.08		25.81	26.55	27.29	28.03	28.76
22.16	22.90	23.64	24.37	25.11	5	25.85	26.59	27.32	28.06	28.80
22.20	22.94	23.67	24.41	25.15	10	25.89	26.62	27.36	28.10	28.84
22.24	22.97	23.71	24.45	25.19	15	25.92	26.66	27.40	28.14	28.87
22.27	23.01	23.75	24.49	25.22	20	25.96	26.70	27.44	28.17	28.91
22.31	23.05	23.78	24.52	25.26	25	26.00	26.73	27.47	28.21	28.95
22.35	23.08	23.82	24.56	25.30	30	26.03	26.77	27.51	28.25	28.98
22.38	23.12	23.86	24.60	25.33	35	26.07	26.81	27.55	28.28	29.02
22.42	23.16	23.90	24.63	25.37	40	26.11	26.85	27.58	28.32	29.06
22.46	23.19	23.93	24.67	25.41	45	26.14	26.88	27.62	28.36	29.09
22.49	23.23	23.97	24.71	25.44	50	26.18	26.92	27.66	28.39	29.13
22.53	23.27	24.01	24.74	25.48	55	26.22	26.96	27.69	28.43	29.17
22.57	23.31	24.04	24.78	25.52	60	26.26	26.99	27.73	28.47	29.21
22.60	23.34	24.08	24.82	25.55	65	26.29	27.03	27.77	28.50	29.24
22.64	23.38	24.12	24.85	25.59	70	26.33	27.07	27.80	28.54	29.28
22.68	23.42	24.15	24.89	25.63	75	26.37	27.10	27.84	28.58	28.76
22.72	23.45	24.19	24.93	25.67	80	26.40	27.14	27.88	28.62	29.35
22.75	23.49	24.23	24.96	25.70	85	26.44	27.18	27.91	28.65	29.39
22.79	23.53	24.26	25.00	25.74	90	26.48	27.21	27.95	28.69	29.43
22.83	23.56	24.30	25.04	25.78	95	26.51	27.25	27.99	28.73	29.46

Even tons, 51 to 100 inclusive.

51-60		61-70		71-80		81-90		91-100	
T	Am't	T	Am't	T	Am't	T	Am't	T	Am't
51	752.25	61	899.75	71	1047.25	81	1194.75	91	1342.25
52	767.00	62	914.50	72	1062.00	82	1209.50	92	1357.00
53	781.75	63	929.75	73	1076.75	83	1224.25	93	1371.75
54	796.50	64	944.00	74	1091.50	84	1239.00	94	1386.50
55	811.25	65	958.75	75	1106.25	85	1253.75	95	1401.25
56	826.00	66	973.50	76	1121.00	86	1268.50	96	1416.00
57	840.75	67	988.25	77	1135.75	87	1283.25	97	1430.75
58	855.50	68	1003.00	78	1150.50	88	1298.00	98	1445.50
59	870.75	69	1017.75	79	1165.25	89	1312.75	99	1460.25
60	885.00	70	1032.50	80	1180.00	90	1327.50	100	1475.00
700	10325	800	11800	900	13275	1000	14750	1100	16225

POUNDS

Under 100	100	200	300	400		500	600	700	800	900
		AMOUNT						AMOUNT		
	.75	1.50	2.25	3.00		3.75	4.50	5.25	6.00	6.75
.04	.79	1.54	2.29	3.04	5	3.79	4.54	5.29	6.04	6.79
.08	.83	1.58	2.33	3.08	10	3.83	4.58	5.33	6.08	6.83
.11	.86	1.61	2.36	3.11	15	3.86	4.61	5.36	6.11	6.86
.15	.90	1.65	2.40	3.15	20	3.90	4.65	5.40	6.15	6.90
.19	.94	1.69	2.44	3.19	25	3.94	4.69	5.44	6.19	6.94
.23	.98	1.73	2.48	3.23	30	3.98	4.73	5.48	6.23	6.98
.26	1.01	1.76	2.51	3.26	35	4.01	4.76	5.51	6.26	7.01
.30	1.05	1.80	2.55	3.30	40	4.05	4.80	5.55	6.30	7.05
.34	1.09	1.84	2.59	3.34	45	4.09	4.84	5.59	6.34	7.09
.38	1.13	1.88	2.63	3.38	50	4.13	4.88	5.63	6.38	7.13
.41	1.16	1.91	2.66	3.41	55	4.16	4.91	5.66	6.41	7.16
.45	1.20	1.95	2.70	3.45	60	4.20	4.95	5.70	6.45	7.20
.49	1.24	1.99	2.74	3.49	65	4.24	4.99	5.74	6.49	7.24
.53	1.28	2.03	2.78	3.53	70	4.28	5.03	5.78	6.53	7.28
.56	1.31	2.06	2.81	3.56	75	4.31	5.06	5.81	6.56	7.31
.60	1.35	2.10	2.85	3.60	80	4.35	5.10	5.85	6.60	7.35
.64	1.39	2.14	2.89	3.64	85	4.39	5.14	5.89	6.64	7.39
.68	1.43	2.18	2.93	3.68	90	4.43	5.18	5.93	6.68	7.43
.71	1.46	2.21	2.96	3.71	95	4.46	5.21	5.96	6.71	7.46

POUNDS

1000	1100	1200	1300	1400		1500	1600	1700	1800	1900
		AMOUNT						AMOUNT		
7.50	8.25	9.00	9.75	10.50		11.25	12.00	12.75	13.50	14.25
7.54	8.29	9.04	9.79	10.54	5	11.29	12.04	12.79	13.54	14.29
7.58	8.33	9.08	9.83	10.58	10	11.33	12.08	12.83	13.58	14.33
7.61	8.36	9.11	9.86	10.61	15	11.36	12.11	12.86	13.61	14.36
7.65	8.40	9.15	9.90	10.65	20	11.40	12.15	12.90	13.65	14.40
7.69	8.44	9.19	9.94	10.69	25	11.44	12.19	12.94	13.69	14.44
7.73	8.48	9.23	9.98	10.73	30	11.48	12.23	12.98	13.73	14.48
7.76	8.51	9.26	10.01	10.76	35	11.51	12.26	13.01	13.76	14.51
7.80	8.55	9.30	10.05	10.80	40	11.55	12.30	13.05	13.80	14.55
7.84	8.59	9.34	10.09	10.84	45	11.59	12.34	13.09	13.84	14.59
7.88	8.63	9.38	10.13	10.88	50	11.63	12.38	13.13	13.88	14.63
7.91	8.66	9.41	10.16	10.91	55	11.66	12.41	13.16	13.91	14.66
7.95	8.70	9.45	10.20	10.95	60	11.70	12.45	13.20	13.95	14.70
7.99	8.74	9.49	10.24	10.99	65	11.74	12.49	13.24	13.99	14.74
8.03	8.78	9.53	10.28	11.03	70	11.78	12.53	13.28	14.03	14.78
8.06	8.81	9.56	10.31	11.06	75	11.81	12.56	13.31	14.06	14.81
8.10	8.85	9.60	10.35	11.10	80	11.85	12.60	13.35	14.10	14.85
8.14	8.89	9.64	10.39	11.14	85	11.89	12.64	13.39	14.14	14.89
8.17	8.93	9.67	10.43	11.17	90	11.93	12.67	13.43	14.17	14.93
8.21	8.96	9.71	10.46	11.21	95	11.96	12.71	13.46	14.21	14.96

Even tons, 1 to 50 inclusive.

1-10		11-20		21-30		31-40		41-50	
T	Am't	T	Am't	T	Am't	T	Am't	T	Am't
1	15.00	11	165.00	21	315.00	31	465.00	41	615.00
2	30.00	12	180.00	22	330.00	32	480.00	42	630.00
3	45.00	13	195.00	23	345.00	33	495.00	43	645.00
4	60.00	14	210.00	24	360.00	34	510.00	44	660.00
5	75.00	15	225.00	25	375.00	35	525.00	45	675.00
6	90.00	16	240.00	26	390.00	36	540.00	46	690.00
7	105.00	17	255.00	27	405.00	37	555.00	47	705.00
8	120.00	18	270.00	28	420.00	38	570.00	48	720.00
9	135.00	19	285.00	29	435.00	39	585.00	49	735.00
10	150.00	20	300.00	30	450.00	40	600.00	50	750.00

200	3000	300	4500	400	6000	500	7500	600	9000

POUNDS

2000	2100	2200	2300	2400		2500	2600	2700	2800	2900
		AMOUNT						AMOUNT		
15.00	15.75	16.50	17.25	18.00		18.75	19.50	20.25	21.00	21.75
15.04	15.79	16.54	17.29	18.04	5	18.79	19.51	20.29	21.04	21.79
15.08	15.83	16.58	17.33	18.08	10	18.83	19.58	20.33	21.08	21.83
15.11	15.86	16.61	17.36	18.11	15	18.86	19.61	20.36	21.11	21.86
15.15	15.90	16.65	17.40	18.15	20	18.90	19.65	20.40	21.15	21.90
15.19	15.94	16.69	17.44	18.19	25	18.94	19.69	20.44	21.19	21.94
15.23	15.98	16.73	17.48	18.23	30	18.98	19.73	20.48	21.23	21.98
15.26	16.01	16.76	17.51	18.26	35	19.01	19.76	20.51	21.26	22.01
15.30	16.05	16.80	17.55	18.30	40	19.05	19.80	20.55	21.30	22.05
15.34	16.09	16.84	17.59	18.34	45	19.09	19.84	20.59	21.34	22.09
15.38	16.13	16.88	17.63	18.38	50	19.13	19.88	20.63	21.38	22.13
15.41	16.16	16.91	17.66	18.41	55	19.16	19.91	20.66	21.41	22.16
15.45	16.20	16.95	17.70	18.45	60	19.20	19.95	20.70	21.45	22.20
15.49	16.24	16.99	17.74	18.49	65	19.24	19.99	20.74	21.49	22.24
15.53	16.28	17.03	17.78	18.53	70	19.28	20.03	20.78	21.53	22.28
15.56	16.31	17.06	17.81	18.56	75	19.31	20.06	20.81	21.56	22.31
15.60	16.35	17.10	17.85	18.60	80	19.35	20.10	20.85	21.60	22.35
15.64	16.39	17.14	17.89	18.64	85	19.39	20.14	20.89	21.64	22.39
15.68	16.43	17.18	17.93	18.68	90	19.43	20.18	20.93	21.68	22.43
15.71	16.46	17.21	17.96	18.71	95	19.46	20.21	20.96	21.71	22.46

POUNDS

3000	3100	3200	3300	3400		3500	3600	3700	3800	3900
		AMOUNT						AMOUNT		
22.50	23.25	24.00	24.75	25.50		26.25	27.00	27.75	28.50	29.25
22.54	23.29	24.04	24.79	25.54	5	26.29	27.04	27.79	28.54	29.29
22.58	23.33	24.08	24.83	25.58	10	26.33	27.08	27.83	28.58	29.33
22.61	23.36	24.11	24.86	25.61	15	26.36	27.11	27.86	28.61	29.36
22.65	23.40	24.15	24.90	25.65	20	26.40	27.15	27.90	28.65	29.40
22.69	23.44	24.19	24.94	25.69	25	26.44	27.19	27.94	28.69	29.44
22.73	23.48	24.23	24.98	25.73	30	26.48	27.23	27.98	28.73	29.48
22.76	23.51	24.26	25.01	25.76	35	26.51	27.26	28.01	28.76	29.51
22.80	23.55	24.30	25.05	25.80	40	26.55	27.30	28.05	28.80	29.55
22.84	23.59	24.34	25.09	25.84	45	26.59	27.34	28.09	28.84	29.59
22.88	23.63	24.38	25.13	25.88	50	26.63	27.38	28.13	28.88	29.63
22.91	23.66	24.41	25.16	25.91	55	26.66	27.41	28.16	28.91	29.66
22.95	23.70	24.45	25.20	25.95	60	26.70	27.45	28.20	28.95	29.70
22.99	23.74	24.49	25.24	25.99	65	26.74	27.49	28.24	28.99	29.74
23.03	23.78	24.53	25.28	26.03	70	26.78	27.53	28.28	29.03	29.78
23.06	23.81	24.56	25.31	26.06	75	26.81	27.56	28.31	29.06	29.81
23.10	23.85	24.60	25.35	26.10	80	26.85	27.60	28.35	29.10	29.85
23.14	23.89	24.64	25.39	26.14	85	26.89	27.64	28.39	29.14	29.89
23.17	23.93	24.67	25.43	26.17	90	26.93	27.67	28.43	29.17	29.93
23.21	23.96	24.71	25.46	26.21	95	26.96	27.71	28.46	29.21	29.96

Even tons, 51 to 100 inclusive.

51-60		61-70		71-80		81-90		91-100	
T	Am't	T	Am't	T	Am't	T	Am't	T	Am't
51	765.00	61	915.00	71	1065.00	81	1215.00	91	1365.00
52	780.00	62	930.00	72	1080.00	82	1230.00	92	1380.00
53	795.00	63	945.00	73	1095.00	83	1245.00	93	1395.00
54	810.00	64	960.00	74	1110.00	84	1260.00	94	1410.00
55	825.00	65	975.00	75	1125.00	85	1275.00	95	1425.00
56	840.00	66	990.00	76	1140.00	86	1290.00	96	1440.00
57	855.00	67	1005.00	77	1155.00	87	1305.00	97	1455.00
58	870.00	68	1020.00	78	1170.00	88	1320.00	98	1470.00
59	885.00	69	1035.00	79	1185.00	89	1335.00	99	1485.00
60	900.00	70	1050.00	80	1200.00	90	1350.00	100	1500.00

700	10500	800	12000	900	13500	1000	15000	1100	16500

POUNDS

Under 100	100	200	300	400		500	600	700	800	900
		BUSHELS						BUSHELS		
	1.25	2.50	3.75	5.00		6.25	7.50	8.75	10.00	11.25
.13	1.38	2.63	3.88	5.13	10	6.38	7.63	8.88	10.13	11.38
.25	1.50	2.75	4.00	5.25	20	6.50	7.75	9.00	10.25	11.50
.38	1.63	2.88	4.13	5.38	30	6.63	7.88	9.13	10.38	11.63
.50	1.75	3.00	4.25	5.50	40	6.75	8.00	9.25	10.50	11.75
.63	1.88	3.13	4.38	5.63	50	6.88	8.13	9.38	10.63	11.88
.75	2.00	3.25	4.50	5.75	60	7.00	8.25	9.50	10.75	12.00
.88	2.13	3.38	4.63	5.88	70	7.13	8.38	9.63	10.88	12.13
1.00	2.25	3.50	4.75	6.00	80	7.25	8.50	9.75	11.00	12.25
1.13	2.38	3.63	4.88	6.13	90	7.38	8.63	9.88	11.13	12.38

POUNDS

1000	1100	1200	1300	1400		1500	1600	1700	1800	1900
		BUSHELS						BUSHELS		
12.50	13.75	15.00	16.25	17.50		18.75	20.00	21.25	22.50	23.75
12.63	13.88	15.13	16.38	17.63	10	18.88	20.13	21.38	22.63	23.88
12.75	14.00	15.25	16.50	17.75	20	19.00	20.25	21.50	22.75	24.00
12.88	14.13	15.38	16.63	17.88	30	19.13	20.38	21.63	22.88	24.13
13.00	14.25	15.50	16.75	18.00	40	19.25	20.50	21.75	23.00	24.25
13.13	14.38	15.63	16.88	18.13	50	19.38	20.63	21.88	23.13	24.38
13.25	14.50	15.75	17.00	18.25	60	19.50	20.75	22.00	23.25	24.50
13.38	14.63	15.88	17.13	18.38	70	19.63	20.88	22.13	23.38	24.63
13.50	14.75	16.00	17.25	18.50	80	19.75	21.00	22.25	23.50	24.75
13.63	14.88	16.13	17.38	18.63	90	19.88	21.13	22.38	23.63	24.88

POUNDS

2000	2100	2200	2300	2400		2500	2600	2700	2800	2900
		BUSHELS						BUSHELS		
25.00	26.25	27.50	28.75	30.00		31.25	32.50	33.75	35.00	36.25
25.13	26.38	27.63	28.88	30.13	10	31.38	32.63	33.88	35.13	36.38
25.25	26.50	27.75	29.00	30.25	20	31.50	32.75	34.00	35.25	36.50
25.38	26.63	27.88	29.13	30.38	30	31.63	32.88	34.13	35.38	36.63
25.50	26.75	28.00	29.25	30.50	40	31.75	33.00	34.25	35.50	36.75
25.63	26.88	28.13	29.38	30.63	50	31.88	33.13	34.38	35.63	36.88
25.75	27.00	28.25	29.50	30.75	60	32.00	33.25	34.50	35.75	37.00
25.88	27.13	28.38	29.63	30.88	70	32.13	33.38	34.63	35.88	37.13
26.00	27.25	28.50	29.75	31.00	80	32.25	33.50	34.75	36.00	37.25
26.13	27.38	28.63	29.88	31.13	90	32.38	33.63	34.88	36.13	37.38

POUNDS

3000	3100	3200	3300	3400		3500	3600	3700	3800	3900
		BUSHELS						BUSHELS		
37.50	38.75	40.00	41.25	42.50		43.75	45.00	46.25	47.50	48.75
37.63	38.88	40.13	41.38	42.63	10	43.88	45.13	46.38	47.63	48.88
37.75	39.00	40.25	41.50	42.75	20	44.00	45.25	46.50	47.75	49.00
37.88	39.13	40.38	41.63	42.88	30	44.13	45.38	46.63	47.88	49.13
38.00	39.25	40.50	41.75	43.00	40	44.25	45.50	46.75	48.00	49.25
38.13	39.38	40.63	41.88	43.13	50	44.38	45.63	46.88	48.13	49.38
38.25	39.50	40.75	42.00	43.25	60	44.50	45.75	47.00	48.25	49.50
38.38	39.63	40.88	42.13	43.38	70	44.63	45.88	47.13	48.38	49.63
38.50	39.75	41.00	42.25	43.50	80	44.75	46.00	47.25	48.50	49.75
38.63	39.88	41.13	42.38	43.63	90	44.88	46.13	47.38	48.63	49.88

Lbs.	4m	5m	6m	7m	8m	9m	10m	11m	12m	13m	14m
Bu.	50.00	62.50	75.00	87.50	100.00	112.50	125.00	137.50	150.00	162.50	175.00

Lbs.	15m	16m	17m	18m	19m	20m	21m	22m	23m	24m	25m
Bu.	187.50	200.00	212.50	225.00	237.50	250.00	262.50	275.00	287.50	300.00	312.50

Pounds over the even bushel................ 10   20   30   40   50   60   70
Expressed as hundredths of a bushel... .13   .25   .38   .50   .63   .75   .88

Potatoes, White Beans. **Wheat—60.** Peas, Clover Seed.

POUNDS

Under 100	100	200	300	400		500	600	700	800	900
								BUSHELS		
	1.67	3.33	5.00	6.67		8.33	10.00	11.67	13.33	15.00
.17	1.83	3.50	5.17	6.83	10	8.50	10.17	11.83	13.50	15.17
.33	2.00	3.67	5.33	7.00	20	8.67	10.33	12.00	13.67	15.33
.50	2.17	3.83	5.50	7.17	30	8.83	10.50	12.17	13.83	15.50
.67	2.33	4.00	5.67	7.33	40	9.00	10.67	12.33	14.00	15.67
.83	2.50	4.17	5.83	7.50	50	9.17	10.83	12.50	14.17	15.83
1.00	2.67	4.33	6.00	7.67	60	9.33	11.00	12.67	14.33	16.00
1.17	2.83	4.50	6.17	7.83	70	9.50	11.17	12.83	14.50	16.17
1.33	3.00	4.67	6.33	8.00	80	9.67	11.33	13.00	14.67	16.33
1.50	3.17	4.83	6.50	8.17	90	9.83	11.50	13.17	14.83	16.50

POUNDS

1000	1100	1200	1300	1400		1500	1600	1700	1800	1900
		BUSHELS						BUSHELS		
16.67	18.33	20.00	21.67	23.33		25.00	26.67	28.33	30.00	31.67
16.83	18.50	20.17	21.83	23.50	10	25.17	26.83	28.50	30.17	31.83
17.00	18.67	20.33	22.00	23.67	20	25.33	27.00	28.67	30.33	32.00
17.17	18.83	20.50	22.17	23.83	30	25.50	27.17	28.83	30.50	32.17
17.33	19.00	20.67	22.33	24.00	40	25.67	27.33	29.00	30.67	32.33
17.50	19.17	20.83	22.50	24.17	50	25.83	27.50	29.17	30.83	32.50
17.67	19.33	21.00	22.67	24.33	60	26.00	27.67	29.33	31.00	32.67
17.83	19.50	21.17	22.83	24.50	70	26.17	27.83	29.50	31.17	32.83
18.00	19.67	21.33	23.00	24.67	80	26.33	28.00	29.67	31.33	33.00
18.17	19.83	21.50	23.17	24.83	90	26.50	28.17	29.83	31.50	33.17

POUNDS

2000	2100	2200	2300	2400		2500	2600	2700	2800	2900
		BUSHELS						BUSHELS		
33.33	35.00	36.67	38.33	40.00		41.67	43.33	45.00	46.67	48.33
33.50	35.17	36.83	38.50	40.17	10	41.83	43.50	45.17	46.83	48.50
33.67	35.33	37.00	38.67	40.33	20	42.00	43.67	45.33	47.00	48.67
33.83	35.50	37.17	38.83	40.50	30	42.17	43.83	45.50	47.17	48.83
34.00	35.63	37.33	39.00	40.67	40	42.33	44.00	45.67	47.33	49.00
34.17	35.83	37.50	39.17	40.83	50	42.50	44.17	45.83	47.50	49.17
34.33	36.00	37.67	39.33	41.00	60	42.67	44.33	46.00	47.67	49.33
34.50	36.17	37.83	39.50	41.17	70	42.83	44.50	46.17	47.83	49.50
34.67	36.33	38.00	39.67	41.33	80	43.00	44.67	46.33	48.00	49.67
34.83	36.50	38.17	39.83	41.50	90	43.17	44.83	46.50	48.17	49.83

POUNDS

3000	3100	3200	3300	3400		3500	3600	3700	3800	3900
		BUSHELS						BUSHELS		
50.00	51.67	53.33	55.00	56.67		58.33	60.00	61.67	63.33	65.00
50.17	51.83	53.50	55.17	56.83	10	58.50	60.17	61.83	63.50	65.17
50.33	52.00	53.67	55.33	57.00	20	58.67	60.33	62.00	63.67	65.33
50.50	52.17	53.83	55.50	57.17	30	58.83	60.50	62.17	63.83	65.50
50.67	52.33	54.00	55.67	57.33	40	59.00	60.67	62.33	64.00	65.67
50.83	52.50	54.17	55.83	57.50	50	59.17	60.83	62.50	64.17	65.83
51.00	52.67	54.33	56.00	57.67	60	59.33	61.00	62.67	64.33	66.00
51.17	52.83	54.50	56.17	57.83	70	59.50	61.17	62.83	64.50	66.17
51.33	53.00	54.67	56.33	58.00	80	59.67	61.33	63.00	64.67	66.33
51.50	53.17	54.83	56.50	58.17	90	59.83	61.50	63.17	64.83	66.50

Lbs.	4m	5m	6m	7m	8m	9m	10m	11m	12m	13m	14m
Bu.	66 67	83.33	100 00	116.67	133.33	150.00	166.67	183.33	200.00	216.67	233.33

Lbs.	15m	16m	17m	18m	19m	20m	21m	22m	23m	24m	25m
Bu.	250.00	266.67	283.33	300.00	316.67	333.33	350.00	366.67	383.33	400.00	416.67

		10	20	30	40	50
Pounds over the even bushel..................		10	20	30	40	50
Expressed as hundredths of a bushel.....		.17	.33	.50	.67	.83

Ear Corn—70.

Under 100	100	200	300	400		500	600	700	800	900
	BUSHELS						BUSHELS			
·	1.43	2.86	4.29	5.71		7.14	8.57	10.00	11.43	12.86
.14	1.57	3.00	4.43	5.86	10	7.29	8.71	10.14	11.57	13.00
.29	1.71	3.14	4.57	6.00	20	7.43	8.86	10.29	11.71	13.14
.43	1.86	3.29	4.71	6.14	30	7.57	9.00	10.43	11.86	13.29
.57	2.00	3.43	4.86	6.29	40	7.71	9.14	10.57	12.00	13.43
.71	2.14	3.57	5.00	6.43	50	7.86	9.29	10.71	12.14	13.57
.86	2.29	3.71	5.14	6.57	60	8.00	9.43	10.86	12.29	13.71
1.00	2.43	3.86	5.29	6.71	70	8.14	9.57	11.00	12.43	13.86
1.14	2.57	4.00	5.43	6.86	80	8.29	9.71	11.14	12.57	14.00
1.29	2.71	4.14	5.57	7.00	90	8.43	9.86	11.29	12.71	14.14

POUNDS

1000	1100	1200	1300	1400		1500	1600	1700	1800	1900
	BUSHELS						BUSHELS			
14.29	15.71	17.14	18.57	20.00		21.43	22.86	24.29	25.71	27.14
14.43	15.86	17.29	18.71	20.14	10	21.57	23.00	24.43	25.86	27.29
14.57	16.00	17.43	18.86	20.29	20	21.71	23.14	24.57	26.00	27.43
14.71	16.14	17.57	19.00	20.43	30	21.86	23.29	24.71	26.14	27.57
14.86	16.29	17.71	19.14	20.57	40	22.00	23.43	24.86	26.29	27.71
15.00	16.43	17.86	19.29	20.71	50	22.14	23.57	25.00	26.43	27.86
15.14	16.57	18.00	19.43	20.86	60	22.29	23.71	25.14	26.57	28.00
15.29	16.71	18.14	19.57	21.00	70	22.43	23.86	25.29	26.71	28.14
15.43	16.86	18.29	19.71	21.14	80	22.57	24.00	25.43	26.86	28.29
15.57	17.00	18.43	19.86	21.29	90	22.71	24.14	25.57	27.00	28.43

POUNDS

2000	2100	2200	2300	2400		2500	2600	2700	2800	2900
	BUSHELS						BUSHELS			
28.57	30.00	31.43	32.86	34.29		35.71	37.14	38.57	40.00	41.43
28.71	30.14	31.57	33.00	34.43	10	35.86	37.29	38.71	40.14	41.57
28.86	30.29	31.71	33.14	34.57	20	36.00	37.43	38.86	40.29	41.71
29.00	30.43	31.86	33.29	34.71	30	36.14	37.57	39.00	40.43	41.86
29.14	30.57	32.00	33.43	34.86	40	36.29	37.71	39.14	40.57	42.00
29.29	30.71	32.14	33.57	35.00	50	36.43	37.86	39.29	40.71	42.14
29.43	30.86	32.29	32.71	35.14	60	36.57	38.00	39.43	40.86	42.29
29.57	31.00	32.43	33.86	35.29	70	36.71	38.14	39.57	41.00	42.43
29.71	31.14	32.57	34.00	35.43	80	36.86	38.29	39.71	41.14	42.57
29.86	31.29	32.71	34.14	35.57	90	37.00	38.43	39.86	41.29	42.71

POUNDS

3000	3100	3200	3300	3400		3500	3600	3700	3800	3900
	BUSHELS						BUSHELS			
42.86	44.29	45.71	47.14	48.57		50.00	51.43	52.86	54.29	55.71
43.00	44.43	45.86	47.29	48.71	10	50.14	51.57	53.00	54.43	55.86
43.14	44.57	46.00	47.43	48.86	20	50.29	51.71	53.14	54.57	56.00
43.29	44.71	46.14	47.57	49.00	30	50.43	51.86	53.29	54.71	56.14
43.43	44.86	46.29	47.71	49.14	40	50.57	52.00	53.43	54.86	56.29
43.57	45.00	46.43	47.86	49.29	50	50.71	52.14	53.57	55.00	56.43
43.71	45.14	46.57	48.00	49.43	60	50.86	52.29	53.71	55.14	56.57
43.86	45.29	46.71	48.14	49.57	70	51.00	52.43	53.86	55.29	56.71
44.00	45.43	46.86	48.29	49.71	80	51.14	52.57	54.00	55.43	56.86
44.14	45.57	47.00	48.43	49.86	90	51.29	52.71	54.14	55.57	57.00

Lbs.	4m	5m	6m	7m	8m	9m	10m	11m	12m	13m	14m
Bu.	57.14	71.43	85.71	100.00	114.29	128.57	142.86	157.14	171.43	185.71	200.00

Lbs.	15m	16m	17m	18m	19m	20m	21m	22m	23m	24m	25m
Bu.	214.29	228.57	242.86	257.14	271.43	285.71	300.00	314.29	328.57	342.86	357.14

Pounds over the even bushel..............	10	20	30	40	50	60
Expressed as hundredths of a bushel.....	.14	.29	.43	.57	.71	.86

Ear Corn—75.

POUNDS

Under 100	100	200	300	400		500	600	700	800	900
	1.33	2.67	4.00	5.33		6.67	8.00	9.33	10.67	12.00
.13	1.47	2.80	4.13	5.47	10	6.80	8.13	9.47	10.80	12.13
.27	1.60	2.93	4.27	5.60	20	6.93	8.27	9.60	10.93	12.27
.40	1.73	3.07	4.40	5.73	30	7.07	8.40	9.73	11.07	12.40
.53	1.87	3.20	4.53	5.87	40	7.20	8.53	9.87	11.20	12.53
.67	2.00	3.33	4.67	6.00	50	7.33	8.67	10.00	11.33	12.67
.80	2.13	3.47	4.80	6.13	60	7.47	8.80	10.13	11.47	12.80
.93	2.27	3.60	4.93	6.27	70	7.60	8.93	10.27	11.60	12.93
1.07	2.40	3.73	5.07	6.40	80	7.73	9.07	10.40	11.73	13.07
1.20	2.53	3.87	5.20	6.53	90	7.87	9.20	10.53	11.87	13.20

POUNDS

1000	1100	1200	1300	1400		1500	1600	1700	1800	1900
13.33	14.67	16.00	17.33	18.67		20.00	21.33	22.67	24.00	25.33
13.47	14.80	16.13	17.47	18.80	10	20.13	21.47	22.80	24.13	25.47
13.60	14.93	16.27	17.60	18.93	20	20.27	21.60	22.93	24.27	25.60
13.73	15.07	16.40	17.73	19.07	30	20.40	21.73	23.07	24.40	25.73
13.87	15.20	16.53	17.87	19.20	40	20.53	21.87	23.20	24.53	25.87
14.00	15.33	16.67	18.00	19.33	50	20.67	22.00	23.33	24.67	26.00
14.13	15.47	16.80	18.13	19.47	60	20.80	22.13	23.47	24.80	26.13
14.27	15.60	16.93	18.27	19.60	70	20.93	22.27	23.60	24.93	26.27
14.40	15.73	17.07	18.40	19.73	80	21.07	22.40	23.73	25.07	26.40
14.53	15.87	17.20	18.53	19.87	90	21.20	22.53	23.87	25.20	26.53

POUNDS

2000	2100	2200	2300	2400		2500	2600	2700	2800	2900
26.67	28.00	29.33	30.67	32.00		33.33	34.67	36.00	37.33	38.67
26.80	28.13	29.47	30.80	32.13	10	33.47	34.80	36.13	37.47	38.80
26.93	28.27	29.60	30.93	32.27	20	33.60	34.93	36.27	37.60	38.93
27.07	28.40	29.73	31.07	32.40	30	33.73	35.07	36.40	37.73	39.07
27.20	28.53	29.87	31.20	32.53	40	33.87	35.20	36.53	37.87	39.20
27.33	28.67	30.00	31.33	32.67	50	34.00	35.33	36.67	38.00	39.33
27.47	28.80	30.13	31.47	32.80	60	34.13	35.47	36.80	38.13	39.47
27.60	28.93	30.27	31.60	32.93	70	34.27	35.60	36.93	38.27	39.60
27.73	29.07	30.40	31.73	33.07	80	34.40	35.73	37.07	38.40	39.73
27.87	29.20	30.53	31.87	33.20	90	34.53	35.87	37.20	38.53	39.87

POUNDS

3000	3100	3200	3300	3400		3500	3600	3700	3800	3900
40.00	41.33	42.67	44.00	45.33		46.67	48.00	49.33	50.67	52.00
40.13	41.47	42.80	44.13	45.47	10	46.80	48.13	49.47	50.80	52.13
40.27	41.60	42.93	44.27	45.60	20	46.93	48.27	49.60	50.93	52.27
40.40	41.73	43.07	44.40	45.73	30	47.07	48.40	49.73	51.07	52.40
40.53	41.87	43.20	44.53	45.87	40	47.20	48.53	49.87	51.20	52.53
40.67	42.00	43.33	44.67	46.00	50	47.33	48.67	50.00	51.33	52.67
40.80	42.13	43.47	44.80	46.13	60	47.47	48.80	50.13	51.47	52.80
40.93	42.27	43.60	44.93	46.27	70	47.60	48.93	50.27	51.60	52.93
41.07	42.40	43.73	45.07	46.40	80	47.73	49.07	50.40	51.73	53.07
41.20	42.53	43.87	45.20	46.53	90	47.87	49.20	50.53	51.87	53.20

Lbs.	4m	5m	6m	7m	8m	9m	10m	11m	12m	13m	14m
Bu.	53.33	66.67	80.00	93.33	106.67	120.00	133.33	146.67	160.00	173.33	186.67

Lbs.	15m	16m	17m	18m	19m	20m	21m	22m	23m	24m	25m
Bu.	200.00	213.33	226.67	240.00	253.33	266.67	280.00	293.33	306.67	320.00	333.33

Pounds over the even bushel..............		5	10	15	20	25	30	35
Expressed as hundredths of a bushel...	.07	.13	.20	.27	.33	.40	.47

40	45	50	55	60	65	70
.53	.60	.67	.73	.80	.87	.93

(127)

Oats—32.

-POUNDS-

Under 100	100	200	300	400			500	600	700	800	900
		-BUSHELS-							-BUSHELS-		
	3.13	6.25	9.38	12.50			15.63	18.75	21.88	25.00	28.13
.31	.3.44	6.56	9.69	12.81	10		15.94	19.06	22.19	25.31	28.44
.63	3.75	6.88	10.00	13.13	20		16.25	19.38	22.50	25.63	28.75
.94	4.06	7.19	10.31	13.44	30		16.56	19.69	22.81	25.94	29.06
1.25	4.38	7.50	10.63	13.75	40		16.88	20.00	23.13	26.25	29.38
1.56	4.69	7.81	10.94	14.06	50		17.19	20.31	23.44	26.56	29.69
1.88	5.00	8.13	11.25	14.38	60		17.50	20.63	23.75	26.88	30.00
2.19	5.31	8.44	11.56	14.69	70		17.81	20.94	24.06	27.19	30.31
2.50	5.63	8.75	11.88	15.00	80		18.13	21.25	24.38	27.50	30.63
2.81	5.94	9.06	12.19	15.31	90		18.44	21.56	24.69	27.81	30.94

-POUNDS-

1000	1100	1200	1300	1400			1500	1600	1700	1800	1900
		-BUSHELS-							-BUSHELS-		
31.25	34.38	37.50	40.63	43.75			46.88	50.00	53.13	56.25	59.38
31.56	34.69	37.81	40.94	44.06	10		47.19	50.31	53.44	56.56	59.69
31.88	35.00	38.13	41.25	44.38	20		47.50	50.63	53.75	56.88	60.00
32.19	35.31	38.44	41.56	44.69	30		47.81	50.94	54.06	57.19	60.31
32.50	35.63	38.75	41.88	45.00	40		48.13	51.25	54.38	57.50	60.63
32.81	35.94	39.06	42.19	45.31	50		48.44	51.56	54.69	57.81	60.94
33.13	36.25	39.38	42.50	45.63	60		48.75	51.88	55.00	58.13	61.25
33.44	36.56	39.69	42.81	45.94	70		49.06	52.19	55.31	58.44	61.56
33.75	36.88	40.00	43.13	46.25	80		49.38	52.50	55.63	58.75	61.88
34.06	37.19	40.31	43.44	46.56	90		49.69	52.81	55.94	59.06	62.19

-POUNDS-

2000	2100	2200	2300	2400			2500	2600	2700	2800	2900
		-BUSHELS-							-BUSHELS-		
62.50	65.63	68.75	71.88	75.00			78.13	81.25	84.38	87.50	90.63
62.81	65.94	69.06	72.19	75.31	10		78.44	81.56	84.69	87.81	90.94
63.13	66.25	69.38	72.50	75.63	20		78.75	81.88	85.00	88.13	91.25
63.44	66.56	69.69	72.81	75.94	30		79.06	82.19	85.31	88.44	91.56
63.75	66.88	70.00	73.13	76.25	40		79.38	82.50	85.63	88.75	91.88
64.06	67.19	70.31	73.44	76.56	50		79.69	82.81	85.94	89.06	92.19
64.38	67.50	70.63	73.75	76.88	60		80.00	83.13	86.25	89.38	92.50
64.69	67.81	70.94	74.06	77.19	70		80.31	83.44	86.56	89.69	92.81
65.00	68.13	71.25	74.38	77.50	80		80.63	83.75	86.88	90.00	93.13
65.31	68.44	71.56	74.69	77.81	90		80.94	84.06	87.19	90.31	93.44

-POUNDS-

3000	3100	3200	3300	3400			3500	3600	3700	3800	3900
		-BUSHELS-							-BUSHELS-		
93.75	96.88	100.00	103.13	106.25			109.38	112.50	115.63	118.75	121.88
94.06	97.19	100.31	103.44	106.56	10		109.69	112.81	115.94	119.06	122.19
94.38	97.50	100.63	103.75	106.88	20		110.00	113.13	116.25	119.38	122.50
94.69	97.81	100.94	104.06	107.19	30		110.31	113.44	116.56	119.69	122.81
95.00	98.13	101.25	104.38	107.50	40		110.63	113.75	116.88	120.00	123.13
95.31	98.44	101.56	104.69	107.81	50		110.94	114.06	117.19	120.31	123.44
95.63	98.75	101.88	105.00	108.13	60		111.25	114.38	117.50	120.63	123.75
95.94	99.06	102.19	105.31	108.44	70		111.56	114.69	117.81	120.94	124.06
96.25	99.38	102.50	105.63	108.75	80		111.88	115.00	118.13	121.25	124.38
96.56	99.69	102.81	105.94	109.06	90		112.19	115.31	118.44	121.56	124.69

Lbs.	4m	5m	6m	7m	8m	9m	10m	11m	12m	13m	14m	15m
Bu.	125.00	156.25	187.50	218.75	250.00	281.25	312.50	343.75	375.00	406.25	437.50	468.75

Lbs.	16m	17m	18m	19m	20m	21m	22m	23m	24m	25m
Bu.	500.00	531.25	562.50	593.75	625.00	656.25	687.50	718.75	750.00	781.25

Pounds over the even bushel	2	4	6	8	10	12	14	16
Expressed as hundredths of a bushel	.06	.13	.19	.25	.31	.38	.44	.50

	18	20	22	24	26	28	30
	.56	.63	.69	.75	.81	.88	.94

POUNDS

Under 100	100	200	300	400		500	600	700	800	900
	BUSHELS						BUSHELS			
	1.79	3.57	5.36	7.14		8.93	10.71	12.50	14.29	16.07
.18	1.96	3.75	5.54	7.32	10	9.11	10.89	12.68	14.46	16.25
.36	2.14	3.93	5.71	7.50	20	9.29	11.07	12.86	14.64	16.43
.54	2.32	4.11	5.89	7.68	30	9.46	11.25	13.04	14.82	16.61
.71	2.50	4.29	6.07	7.86	40	9.64	11.43	13.21	15.00	16.79
.89	2.68	4.46	6.25	8.04	50	9.82	11.61	13.39	15.18	16.96
1.07	2.86	4.64	6.43	8.21	60	10.00	11.79	13.57	15.36	17.14
1.25	3.04	4.82	6.61	8.39	70	10.18	11.96	13.75	15.54	17.32
1.43	3.21	5.00	6.79	8.57	80	10.36	12.14	13.93	15.71	17.50
1.61	3.39	5.18	6.96	8.75	90	10.54	12.32	14.11	15.89	17.68

POUNDS

1000	1100	1200	1300	1400		1500	1600	1700	1800	1900
	BUSHELS						BUSHELS			
17.86	19.64	21.43	23.21	25.00		26.79	28.57	30.36	32.14	33.93
18.04	19.82	21.61	23.39	25.18	10	26.96	28.75	30.54	32.32	34.11
18.21	20.00	21.79	23.57	25.36	20	27.14	28.93	30.71	32.50	34.29
18.39	20.18	21.96	23.75	25.54	30	27.32	29.11	30.89	32.68	34.46
18.57	20.36	22.14	23.93	25.71	40	27.50	29.29	31.07	32.86	34.64
18.75	20.54	22.32	24.11	25.89	50	27.68	29.46	31.25	33.04	34.82
18.93	20.71	22.50	24.29	26.07	60	27.86	29.64	31.43	33.21	35.00
19.11	20.89	22.68	24.46	26.25	70	28.04	29.82	31.61	33.39	35.18
19.29	21.07	22.86	24.64	26.43	80	28.21	30.00	31.79	33.57	35.36
19.46	21.25	23.04	24.82	26.61	90	28.39	30.18	31.96	33.75	35.54

POUNDS

2000	2100	2200	2300	2400		2500	2600	2700	2800	2900
	BUSHELS						BUSHELS			
35.71	37.50	39.29	41.07	42.86		44.64	46.43	48.21	50.00	51.79
35.89	37.68	39.46	41.25	43.04	10	44.82	46.61	48.39	50.18	51.96
36.07	37.86	39.64	41.43	43.21	20	45.00	46.79	48.57	50.36	52.14
36.25	38.04	39.82	41.61	43.39	30	45.18	46.96	48.75	50.54	52.32
36.43	38.21	40.00	41.79	43.57	40	45.36	47.14	48.93	50.71	52.50
36.61	38.39	40.18	41.96	43.75	50	45.54	47.32	49.11	50.89	52.68
36.79	38.57	40.36	42.14	43.93	60	45.71	47.50	49.29	51.07	52.86
36.96	38.75	40.54	42.32	44.11	70	45.89	47.68	49.46	51.25	53.04
37.14	38.93	40.71	42.50	44.29	80	46.07	47.86	49.64	51.43	53.21
37.32	39.11	40.89	42.68	44.46	90	46.25	48.04	49.82	51.61	53.29

POUNDS

3000	3100	3200	3300	3400		3500	3600	3700	3800	3900
	BUSHELS						BUSHELS			
53.57	55.36	57.14	58.93	60.71		62.50	64.29	66.07	67.86	69.64
53.75	55.54	57.32	59.11	60.89	10	62.68	64.46	66.25	68.04	69.82
53.93	55.71	57.50	59.29	61.07	20	62.86	64.64	66.43	68.21	70.00
54.11	55.89	57.68	59.46	61.25	30	63.04	64.82	66.61	68.39	70.18
54.29	56.07	57.86	59.64	61.43	40	63.21	65.00	66.79	68.57	70.36
54.46	56.25	58.04	59.82	61.61	50	63.39	65.18	66.96	68.75	70.54
54.64	56.43	58.21	60.00	61.79	60	63.57	65.36	67.14	68.93	70.71
54.82	56.61	58.39	60.18	61.96	70	63.75	65.54	67.32	69.11	70.89
55.00	56.79	58.57	60.36	62.14	80	63.93	65.71	67.50	69.29	71.07
55.18	56.96	58.75	60.54	62.32	90	64.11	65.89	67.68	69.46	71.25

Lbs.	4m	5m	6m	7m	8m	9m	10m	11m	12m	13m	14m
Bu.	71.43	89.29	107.14	125.00	142.82	160.71	178.57	196.43	214.29	232.14	250.00

Lbs.	15m	16m	17m	18m	19m	20m	21m	22m	23m	24m	25m
Bu.	267.82	285.71	303.57	321.43	339.29	357.14	375.00	392.82	410.71	428.57	446.43

Pounds over the even bushel.............	2	4	6	8	10	12	14	16	18	20	22
Expressed as hundredths of a bushel.	.04	.07	.11	.14	.18	.21	.25	.29	.32	.36	.39

	24	26	28	30	32	34	36	38	40	42	44	46	48	50	52	54
	.43	.46	.50	.54	.57	.61	.64	.68	.71	.75	.79	.82	.86	.89	.93	.96

(129)

POUNDS

Under 100	100	200	300	400		500	600	700	800	900
	2.08	4.17	6.25	8.33		10.42	12.50	14.58	16.67	18.75
.21	2.29	4.38	6.46	8.54	10	10.63	12.71	14.79	16.88	18.96
.42	2.50	4.58	6.67	8.75	20	10.83	12.92	15.00	17.08	19.17
.63	2.71	4.79	6.88	8.96	30	11.04	13.13	15.21	17.29	19.38
.83	2.92	5.00	7.08	9.17	40	11.25	13.33	15.42	17.50	19.58
1.04	3.13	5.21	7.29	9.38	50	11.46	13.54	15.63	17.71	19.79
1.25	3.33	5.42	7.50	9.58	60	11.67	13.75	15.83	17.92	20.00
1.46	3.54	5.63	7.71	9.79	70	11.88	13.96	16.04	18.13	20.21
1.67	3.75	5.83	7.92	10.00	80	12.08	14.17	16.25	18.33	20.42
1.88	3.96	6.04	8.13	10.21	90	12.29	14.38	16.46	18.54	20.63

POUNDS

1000	1100	1200	1300	1400		1500	1600	1700	1800	1900
20.83	22.92	25.00	27.08	29.17		31.25	33.33	35.42	37.50	39.58
21.04	23.13	25.21	27.29	29.38	10	31.46	33.54	35.63	37.71	39.79
21.25	23.33	25.42	27.50	29.58	20	31.67	33.75	35.83	37.92	40.00
21.46	23.54	25.63	27.71	29.79	30	31.88	33.96	36.04	38.13	40.21
21.67	23.75	25.83	27.92	30.00	40	32.08	34.17	36.25	38.33	40.42
21.88	23.96	26.04	28.13	30.21	50	32.29	34.38	36.46	38.54	40.63
22.08	24.17	26.25	28.33	30.42	60	32.50	34.58	36.67	38.75	40.83
22.29	24.38	26.46	28.54	30.63	70	32.71	34.79	36.88	38.96	41.04
22.50	24.58	26.67	28.75	30.83	80	32.92	35.00	37.08	39.17	41.25
22.71	24.79	26.88	28.96	31.04	90	33.13	35.21	37.29	39.38	41.46

POUNDS

2000	2100	2200	2300	2400		2500	2600	2700	2800	2900
41.67	43.75	45.83	47.92	50.00		52.08	54.17	56.25	58.33	60.42
41.88	43.96	46.04	48.13	50.21	10	52.29	54.38	56.46	58.54	60.63
42.08	44.17	46.25	48.33	50.42	20	52.50	54.58	56.67	58.75	60.83
42.29	44.38	46.46	48.54	50.63	30	52.71	54.79	56.88	58.96	61.04
42.50	44.58	46.67	48.75	50.83	40	52.92	55.00	57.08	59.17	61.25
42.71	44.79	46.88	48.96	51.04	50	53.13	55.21	57.29	59.38	61.46
42.92	45.00	47.08	49.17	51.25	60	53.33	55.42	57.50	59.58	61.67
43.13	45.21	47.29	49.38	51.46	70	53.54	55.63	57.71	59.79	61.88
43.33	45.42	47.50	49.58	51.67	80	53.75	55.83	57.92	60.00	62.08
43.54	45.63	47.71	49.79	51.88	90	53.96	56.04	58.13	60.21	62.29

POUNDS

3000	3100	3200	3300	3400		3500	3600	3700	3800	3900
62.50	64.58	66.67	68.75	70.83		72.92	75.00	77.08	79.17	81.25
62.71	64.79	66.88	68.96	71.04	10	73.13	75.21	77.29	79.38	81.46
62.92	65.00	67.08	69.17	71.25	20	73.33	75.42	77.50	79.58	81.67
63.13	65.21	67.29	69.38	71.46	30	73.54	75.63	77.71	79.79	81.88
63.33	65.42	67.50	69.58	71.67	40	73.75	75.83	77.92	80.00	82.08
63.54	65.63	67.71	69.79	71.88	50	73.96	76.04	78.13	80.21	82.29
63.75	65.83	67.92	70.00	72.08	60	74.17	76.25	78.33	80.42	82.50
63.96	66.04	68.13	70.21	72.29	70	74.38	76.46	78.54	80.63	82.71
64.17	66.25	68.33	70.42	72.50	80	74.58	76.67	78.75	80.83	82.92
64.33	66.46	68.54	70.63	72.71	90	74.79	76.88	78.96	81.04	83.13

Lbs.	4m	5m	6m	7m	8m	9m	10m	11m	12m	13m	14m
Bu.	83.33	104.17	125.00	145.83	166.67	187.50	208.33	229.17	250.00	270.83	291.67

Lbs.	15m	16m	17m	18m	19m	20m	21m	22m	23m	24m	25m
Bu.	312.50	333.33	354.17	375.00	395.83	416.67	437.50	458.33	479.17	500.00	520.83

Pounds over the even bushel	2	4	6	8	10	12	14	16	18	20
Expressed as hundredths of a bushel	.04	.08	.13	.17	.21	.25	.29	.33	.38	.42

22	24	26	28	30	32	34	36	38	40	42	44	46
.46	.50	.54	.58	.63	.67	.71	.75	.79	.83	.88	.92	.96

Equivalent Prices, Long Ton (2240 lbs.) and Short Ton (2000 lbs.).

Long	Short	Long	Short	Long	Short	Long	Short
$2.00	$1.79	$3.25	$2.90	$4.50	$4.02	$5.75	$5.13
2.05	1.84	3.30	2.95	4.55	4.06	5.80	5.18
2.10	1.88	3.35	3.00	4.60	4.10	5.85	5.22
2.15	1.93	3.40	3.04	4.65	4.15	5.90	5.27
2.20	1.97	3.45	3.08	4.70	4.20	5.95	5.32
2.25	2.02	3.50	3.13	4.75	4.24	6.00	5.36
2.30	2.05	3.55	3.18	4.80	4.29	6.05	5.40
2.35	2.10	3.60	3.22	4.85	4.33	6.10	5.45
2.40	2.15	3.65	3.27	4.90	4.38	6.15	5.49
2.45	2.19	3.70	3.30	4.95	4.42	6.20	5.53
2.50	2.24	3.75	3.35	5.00	4.46	6.25	5.58
2.55	2.28	3.80	3.40	5.05	4.51	6.30	5.62
2.60	2.33	3.85	3.43	5.10	4.55	6.35	5.67
2.65	2.37	3.90	3.48	5.15	4.60	6.40	5.71
2.70	2.42	3.95	3.53	5.20	4.64	6.45	5.76
2.75	2.46	4.00	3.57	5.25	4.69	6.50	5.80
2.80	2.50	4.05	3.62	5.30	4.73	6.55	5.85
2.85	2.55	4.10	3.66	5.35	4.78	6.60	5.89
2.90	2.60	4.15	3.70	5.40	4.82	6.65	5.94
2.95	2.63	4.20	3.75	5.45	4.87	6.70	5.98
3.00	2.68	4.25	3.80	5.50	4.91	6.75	6.03
3.05	2.73	4.30	3.84	5.55	4.95	6.80	6.07
3.10	2.77	4.35	3.88	5.60	5.00	6.85	6.12
3.15	2.82	4.40	3.93	5.65	5.04	6.90	6.16
3.20	2.86	4.45	3.98	5.70	5.09	6.95	6.20

To change from short to equivalent price per long ton add 12% to the short, thus: short 5.80 $\times$ .12 = .696. 5.80 + .696 = 6.50 long.

To change from long to short, approximate rule: Deduct the first two figures at the left, plus the first, minus one, thus: long 6.40 — (64 ÷ 6 - - 1) = 5.71 short.

Storage—to arrive at space required, or in invoicing to arrive at quantity in bin or pile:

	Cubic feet to the net ton.	Weight per cubic foot, pounds.
Anthracite, egg	34.00	57.74
stove	34.40	58.15
nut	34.62	58.26
Soft coal, Pittsburgh district	43.03	46.48
Illinois	42.35	47.22
Hocking	40.56	49.30
Indiana Block	45.61	43.85
Erie	41.61	48.07
Missouri........... estimated	42.00	
Iowa............ "	43.00	
Colorado......... "	40.00	
Wyoming......... "	47.00	

COAL DEALERS' SUPPLIES

WE MANUFACTURE and
CARRY IN STOCK

Coal Screens, Wire Cloth, Pocket Screens,
Car Screens, Coal Shutes, Coal Baskets,
Coal Barrows, Coal Scoops, Coal and
Coke Forks, Wire Office Railings, and
General Line of Wire Goods.

DESCRIPTIVE CATALOGUE FREE.

THE GILBERT & BENNETT MFG. CO.

153 Lake Street,

CHICAGO.

www.ingramcontent.com/pod-product-compliance
Lightning Source LLC
Chambersburg PA
CBHW030612270326
41927CB00007B/1142